Taming the Rascal Multitude

The Chomsky Z Collection

Z
BOOKS

Published by Z BOOKS, a project of
the Institute for Social and
Cultural Communications, Inc.
www.zcommunications.org;
zmag@zmag.org

ISBN: 978-1-938824-05-0

Preface

Noam Chomsky is an American linguist, philosopher, cognitive scientist, logician, political commentator and activist. Sometimes described as the "father of modern linguistics," Chomsky is also a major figure in analytic philosophy. He has spent most of his career at the Massachusetts Institute of Technology where he is currently Professor Emeritus, and has authored over 100 books. He has been described as a prominent cultural figure and was voted the "world's top public intellectual" in a 2005 poll.

The articles, interviews, and transciptions of talks in this Chomsky Z Collection represent a portion of the numerous Chomsky articles that have been published in *Z Magazine* from 1997-2014. Others appear in the recently published *Z Reader on Empire: We Own the World.*

Chomsky on Imperialism:

"The U.S., the most powerful state in history has proclaimed, loud and clear, that it intends to rule the world by force, the dimension in which it reigns supreme.... They have also declared that they will tolerate no competitors, now or in the future. They evidently believe that the means of violence in their hands are so extraordinary that they can dismiss with contempt anyone who stands in their way.... The doctrine is not entirely new or unique to the U.S., but it has never before been proclaimed with such brazen arrogance—at least not by anyone we would care to remember."

Chomsky on Corporate America's attack on democracy:

"The 'corporatization of America' during the past century was an attack on democracy—and on markets, part of the shift from something resembling 'capitalism' to the highly administered markets of the modern state/corporate era. A current variant is called 'minimizing the state,' that is, transferring decision-making power from the public arena to somewhere else.... All such measures are designed to limit democracy and to tame the 'rascal multitude,' as the population was called by the self-designated 'men of best quality' during the first upsurge of democracy in the modern period, in 17th century England; the 'responsible men,' as they call themselves today."

Chomsky on American exceptionalism and dangerous beliefs:

"Actually, one of the most dangerous religious beliefs, maybe the most dangerous belief, is the secular faith in the sanctity and power of the state.... Take what is called 'American exceptionalism,' the notion that we are unique in history; there is the fundamental benevolence of our leaders; they may make mistakes, but always with good intentions. That is one of the most dangerous beliefs. It is a religious belief and has no foundation in fact."

The 30 articles presented here not only expose imperial policies/institutions, they indicate important areas for organizing such as: (1) challenging institutions like capitalism, which demand hierarchical structures of class, race, and gender; (2) challenging all attempts by the U.S. Empire and its satellite/client states to ignore the will of the population; that is, to fight for, reclaim, and develop new truly democratic structures and institutions, which are counter to the current savage imperialism, oppressive heirarchies, and the democracy deficit.

- Lydia Sargent, Editor

TABLE OF CONTENTS

Part One: 1997-2004

Part Two: 2007-2014

Part One: 1997-2004

1.

Hordes of Vigilantes

The rules of global order continue to be
"written by lawyers and businesspeople"

The Multilateral Agreement on Investment (MAI) was due to be signed by the OCED countries on April 27. At the time, it was fairly clear that the MAI agreement would not be reached and that it was not an important event worth considering carefully. In part, the failure resulted from internal disputes —European objections to the U.S. federal system and the extraterritorial reach of U.S. laws, concerns about maintaining some degree of cultural autonomy, and so on. But a much more significant problem was looming. It was becoming difficult to ensure that the rules of global order would continue to be "written by the lawyers and businessmen who plan to benefit" and "by governments taking advice and guidance from these lawyers and businessmen," while "invariably, the thing missing is the public voice"—the *Chicago Tribune*'s accurate description of the negotiations for the MAI, as well as ongoing efforts to "craft rules" for "global activity" in other domains without public interference. It was, in short, becoming more difficult to restrict awareness and engagement to sectors identified by the Clinton administration as its "domestic constituencies": the U.S. Council for International Business, which "advances the global interests of American business both at home and abroad," and concentrations of private power generally—but crucially not Congress (which had not been informed, in violation of Constitutional requirements) and the general public, its voice stilled by a "veil of secrecy" that was maintained with impressive discipline during three years of intensive negotiations.

The problem had been pointed out a month earlier by the *London Economist*. Information was leaking through public interest groups and grassroots organizations, and it was becoming harder to ignore those who "want high standards written in for how foreign investors treat workers and protect the environment," issues that "barely featured" as long as deliberations were restricted to the "domestic constituencies" of the democratic states.

As expected, the OECD countries did not reach agreement on April 27, and we move to the next phase. One useful consequence was that the national press departed from its (virtual) silence. In the business pages of the *New York Times,* economic affairs correspondent Louis Uchitelle reported that the target date for the MAI had been delayed six months, under popular pressure. Treaties concerning trade and investment usually "draw little public attention" (why?); and while "labor and the environment are not excluded," the director

From Z Magazine, April and June 1997

of international trade at the National Association of Manufacturers explained, "they are not at the center" of the concerns of trade diplomats and the World Trade Organization.

But "these outsiders are clamoring to make their views known in the negotiations for a treaty that is to be called the Multilateral Agreement on Investment," Uchitelle commented (with intended irony, I presume), and the clamor sufficed to compel the delay.

The Clinton administration, "acknowledging the pressure," strove to present the matter in the proper light. Its representative at the MAI negotiations said: "There is strong support for measures in the treaty that would advance this country's environmental goals and our agenda on international labor standards." So the clamoring outsiders are pushing an open door and Washington has been the most passionate advocate of their cause, they should be relieved to discover.

The *Washington Post* also reported the delay, in its financial section, blaming primarily "the French intelligentsia," who had "seized on the idea" that the rules of the MAI "posed a threat to French culture," joined by Canadians as well. "And the Clinton administration showed little interest in fighting for the accord, especially given fervent opposition from many of the same American environmental and labor groups that battled against [NAFTA]," and that somehow fail to comprehend that their battle is misdirected since it is the Clinton administration that has been insisting upon "environmental goals" and "international labor standards" all along —not an outright falsehood, since the goals and standards are left suitably vague.

That labor "battled against NAFTA" is the characteristic way of presenting the fact that the labor movement called for a version of NAFTA that would serve the interests of the people of the three countries, not just investors; and that their detailed critique and proposals were barred from the media (as were the similar analyses and proposals of Congress's Office of Technology Assessment). *Time* reported that the deadline was missed "in no small part because of the kind of activism on display in San Jose," California, referring to a demonstration by environmentalists and others. "The charge that the MAI would eviscerate national environmental protections has turned a technical economic agreement into a cause celebre." The observation was amplified in the Canadian press, which alone in the Western world began to cover the topic seriously after only two years of silence (under intense pressure by popular organizations and activists). The *Toronto Globe and Mail* observed that the OECD governments "were no match...for a global band of grassroots organizations, which, with little more than computers and access to the Internet, helped derail a deal."

The same theme was voiced with a note of despair, if not terror, by the world's leading business daily, the *Financial Times* of London. In an article headlined "Network guerrillas," it reported that "fear and bewilderment have seized governments of industrialised countries" as, "to their consternation," their efforts to impose the MAI in secret "have been ambushed by a horde of vigilantes whose motives and methods are only dimly understood in most national capitals"— naturally enough; they are not among the "domestic constituencies," so how can governments be expected to understand them? "This week the horde claimed its first success" by blocking the agreement on the MAI, the journal continued, "and some think it could fundamentally alter the way international economic agreements are negotiated."

The hordes are a terrifying sight: "they included trade unions, environmental and human rights lobbyists and pressure groups opposed to globalization"—meaning, globalization in the particular form demanded by the domestic constituencies. The rampaging horde overwhelmed the pathetic and helpless power structures of the rich industrial societies. They are led by "fringe movements that espouse extreme positions" and have "good organization and strong finances" that enable them "to wield much influence with the media and members of national parliaments." In the United States, the "much influence" with the media was effectively zero, and in Britain, which hardly differed, it reached such heights that Home Secretary Jack Straw of the Labor government conceded over BBC that he had never heard of the MAI. But it must be understood that even the slightest breach in conformity is a terrible danger.

The journal goes on to urge that it will be necessary "to drum up business support" so as to beat back the hordes. Until now, business hasn't recognized the severity of the threat. And it is severe indeed. "Veteran trade diplomats" warn that with "growing demands for greater openness and accountability," it is becoming "harder for negotiators to do deals behind closed doors and submit them for rubber-stamping by parliaments."

"Instead, they face pressure to gain wider popular legitimacy for their actions by explaining and defending them in public," no easy task when the hordes are concerned about "social and economic security," and when the impact of trade agreements "on ordinary people's lives... risks stirring up popular resentment" and "sensitivities over issues such as environmental and food safety standards." It might even become impossible "to resist demands for direct participation by lobby groups in WTO decisions, which would violate one of the body's central principles": "'This is the place where governments collude in private against their domestic pressure groups,' says a former WTO official." If the walls are breached, the WTO and similar secret organizations of the rich and powerful might be turned into "a happy hunting ground for special interests": workers, farmers, people concerned about social and economic security and food safety and the fate of future generations, and other extremist fringe elements who do not understand that resources are efficiently used when they are directed to short-term profit for private power, served by the governments that "collude in private" to protect and enhance their power. It is superfluous to add that the lobbies and pressure groups that are causing such fear and consternation are not the U.S. Council for Interna-

tional Business, the "lawyers and businessmen" who are "writing the rules of global order," and the like, but the "public voice" that is "invariably missing."

The "collusion in private" goes well beyond trade agreements, of course. The responsibility of the public to assume cost and risk is, or should be, well known to observers of what its acolytes like to call the "free enterprise capitalist economy." In the same article, Uchitelle reports that Caterpillar, which recently relied on excess production capacity abroad to break a major strike, has moved 25 percent of its production abroad and aims to increase sales from abroad by 50 percent by 2010, with the assistance of U.S. taxpayers: "the Export-Import Bank plays a significant role in [Caterpillar's] strategy," with "low-interest credits" to facilitate the operation. Ex-Im credits already provide close to 2 percent of Caterpillar's $19 billion annual revenue and will rise with new projects planned in China. That is standard operating procedure: multinational corporations typically rely on the home state for crucial services. "In really tough, high-risk, high-opportunity markets," a Caterpillar executive explains, "you really have to have someone in your corner," and governments—especially powerful ones—"will always have greater leverage" than banks and greater willingness to offer low-interest loans, thanks to the largesse of the unwitting taxpayer.

Management is to remain in the U.S., so the people who count will be close to the protector in their corner and will enjoy a proper lifestyle, with the landscape improved as well: the hovels of the foreign work-force will not mar the view. Profits aside, the operation provides a useful weapon against workers who dare to raise their heads (as the recent strike illustrates), and who help out by paying for the loss of their jobs and for the improved weapons of class war. In the conflict over the MAI, the lines could not have been more starkly drawn. On one side are the industrial democracies and their "domestic constituencies." On the other, the "hordes of vigilantes," "special interests," and "fringe extremists" who call for openness and accountability and are displeased when parliaments rubber-stamp the secret deals of the state-private power nexus. The hordes were confronting the major concentration of power in the world, arguably in world history—the governments of the rich and powerful states, the International Financial Institutions, and the concentrated financial and manufacturing sectors, including the corporate media. And popular elements won—despite resources so minuscule and organization so limited that only the paranoia of those who demand absolute power could perceive the outcome in the terms just reviewed.

It's not the only such victory in recent months. Another was achieved last fall, when the Administration was compelled to withdraw its proposed "Fast Track" legislation. Recall that the issue was not "free trade," as commonly alleged, but democracy—the demand of the hordes "for greater openness and accountability." The Clinton administration had argued, correctly, that it was asking for nothing new, just the same authority its predecessors had enjoyed to conduct "deals behind closed doors" that are submitted "for rubber-stamping by parliaments." But times are changing. As the business press recognized when "Fast Track" faced an unexpected public challenge, opponents of the old regime had an "ultimate weapon," the general population, which was no longer satisfied to keep to the spectator role as their betters do the important work. The complaints of the business press echo those of the liberal internationalists of the Trilateral Commission 25 years ago, lamenting the efforts of the "special interests" to organize and enter the political arena. Their vulgar antics disrupted the civilized arrangements before the "crisis of democracy" erupted, when "Truman had been able to govern the country with the cooperation of a relatively small number of Wall Street lawyers and bankers" as explained by Harvard's Samuel Huntington. And now they are intruding in even more sacred chambers. These are impor-

tant developments. The OECD powers and their domestic constituencies are, of course, not going to accept defeat. They will undertake more efficient public relations to explain to the hordes that they are better off keeping to their private pursuits while the business of the world is conducted in secret and they will seek ways to implement the MAI in the OECD or some other framework. Efforts are already underway to change the IMF Charter to impose MAI-style provisions as conditions on credits, thus enforcing the rules for the weak, ultimately others. The powerful will follow their own rules, as when the Clinton administration demonstrated its devotion to free trade by slapping prohibitive tariffs on Japanese supercomputers that were undercutting U.S. manufacturers (called "private," despite their massive dependency on public subsidy and protection) or by banning Mexican tomatoes because they were preferred by American consumers, as frankly conceded.

Though power and privilege surely will not rest, nonetheless, the popular victories should be heartening. They teach lessons about what can be achieved even when opposing forces are so outlandishly unbalanced as in the MAI confrontation. It is true that recent victories are defensive. They prevent, or at least delay, steps to undermine democracy even further and to transfer even more power into the hands of the rapidly concentrating private tyrannies that seek to administer markets and to constitute a "virtual Senate" that has many ways to block popular efforts to use democratic forms for the public interest—threat of capital flight, transfer of production, and other means. But the defensive victories are real. One should attend carefully to the fear and desperation of the powerful. They understand very well the potential reach of the "ultimate weapon" and only hope is that those who seek a freer and just world will not gain the same understanding and put it effectively to use.

2.

Expanding the Floor
of the Cage, Parts 1 and 2

Welfare capitalism and democracy

BARSAMIAN: The American people have spoken once again in the 1996 elections. Clinton says it's a vindication of "the vital center," which he locates somewhere between "overheated liberalism and chilly conservatism." What was your reading of the elections?

CHOMSKY: Was there any choice other than the vital center? As far as I know, Clinton and Dole are moderate Republicans, more or less interchangeable representatives of the business community, old-time government insiders. Maybe there were personality differences. They have somewhat different constituencies. They behave slightly differently. I think the election was not a vote for the vital center, it was just a vote against. Both candidates were unpopular. Very few people expected anything from either of them. Voting was at a historic low. I think it reflected the general sense that the political system isn't functioning.

In Lewis Carroll's Through the Looking Glass, *there are characters called Tweedledum and Tweedledee. They seem to be quite different, but there was no difference between them. Ralph Nader has been talking about the Republicans and the Democrats as Tweedledum and Tweedledee.*

There's never much of a difference between the parties. After all, they are two business parties. But over the years it's probably been narrowing. In my view, the last liberal president was Richard Nixon. After that it's been straight, what they call here, conservatives, starting with Carter, running through to the present. I think it's a reflection of things happening in the economy, in social life, it's a reflection of more general things. The kind of gesture to liberalism that was required from the New Deal through, say, Nixon, became less necessary with new

David Barsamian interviews Chomsky. Parts 1 and 2 published in Z Magazine April and June 1997.

weapons of class war developing in the early 1970s and proceeding on to what the business press, in one of my favorite phrases, calls "capital's subjugation of labor" for 15 years. Actually, I'd say 20 years. Under those circumstances you can drop the window dressing. That's the standard story about welfare capitalism. Welfare capitalism is introduced in order to undercut democracy.

A classic example was in Flint, Michigan, early in this century. Flint was the center of General Motors, at the heart of the automobile revolution. Around 1910 there was a good deal of popular, socialist, and labor organizing. There were plans to really take things over, run things themselves, support unions, have public services done democratically. Flint was a GM town at that time. The wealthy business community was very upset by that, naturally. It meant that it was no longer going to be a company town.

They finally decided to come along with the progressive line, say everything you're doing is right. We'll run a candidate who will support and do all those things. We can do it a lot better because we have all these resources. So we'll take it over. You want a park? Fine. Vote for the business candidate. He'll put in a park. Look at the resources we have and the business acumen. And that won. The array of resources was such that it undermined and eliminated the incipient democratic and popular structures and indeed there was welfare capitalism until such time as they didn't need it any more. When they didn't need that weapon, then it was dropped.

During the Depression, there was a lot of popular struggle. Rights were won. They were extended. There was a union movement. There were other pressures. After World War II, attacks started on this right away. But it took time. It was getting somewhere in the 1950s, but in the 1960s there was a lot more ferment, so you get new programs, the War on Poverty, things coming out of the civil rights movement. By the early 1970s, the business attack was reaching new heights and had new weapons. You can forget the social contract. Forget welfare capitalism.

Since we've been running it, we're going to throw it out. That's pretty much what's been going on since. The population knows the political parties don't recognize them. By now, it's reached enormous disaffection. There are interesting things about the disaffection. It's mostly directed against government. We don't really know if it's directed against business because that's not the kind of question that's asked in the polls. Remember, business propaganda is designed to direct your attention to the government, not to business.

The typical picture in business propaganda since World War II has been, there's all of us together. We live in harmony. Joe Six-Pack, his loyal wife, the hard-working executive, the friendly banker, we're all one big happy family. Then there are those bad guys out there who are trying to disrupt our harmony, like union organizers and big government. But we're all going to try to get together and defend ourselves against them. That's the picture presented everywhere. And it's understandable. You want to pretend that there's class harmony between the person with the hammer and the person he is beating over the head.

Actually, the attitude is ambivalent. The popular aspects of government, the kinds of government that allow participation, they have to be beaten down. But the so-called conservatives want a very powerful state, one that works for them and is removed from public control.

You have to talk about minimizing the state and increasing the Pentagon because the Pentagon is the funnel for subsidizing high-tech industries. That's a tricky line to follow. But as long as there isn't much public debate you can get away with it. So people hate the government. What they feel about business power is unclear.

There is a recent poll which showed that 71 percent of Americans feel that corporations have too much influence in the political system.

If you look at those polls, some of them are outlandish: 95 percent of people think that "Corporations should sometimes sacrifice some profit for workers and the community." That was the way the question was asked. That shows overwhelming feeling. You never get numbers like that in polls unless something is seriously wrong. On the other hand, notice that that's still a call for welfare capitalism. It falls way short of what working people were asking for, say, 150 years ago right in Boston. I wrote up some of this stuff in Z a couple of months ago. At that time, the question wasn't being more benevolent, it was give us a little bit of your profits. It was, you have no right to rule. We should own the factories.

A benevolent autocrat is always going to try to make it appear as if autocracy is necessary. The only choice is, will I be a harsh autocrat or will I be a benevolent autocrat? The propaganda system obviously wants to have the same attitude with regard to the contemporary autocrats. So business can be a little nicer and maybe you don't have quite as much corporate welfare, but you have more welfare capitalism and the autocratic structure remains. That you're not allowed to challenge. That's distinct from the past where it was challenged, and rightly.

Voter turnout in the 1996 election was 49 percent, the lowest since 1924.

It's the lowest ever—1924 is misleading because it was the first year in which women were allowed to vote. So a smaller percentage of the electorate voted because a lot of women didn't vote the first time around. But this is the lowest percentage ever.

The other figure is that more money than ever before was spent on the campaign—$1.6 billion that we know about.

As a television commentator pointed out, these weren't conventions, they were coronations. It's another step towards eliminating whatever functioning elements there are in formal democracy. We shouldn't suggest that it was ever all that different, but yes, it's narrowing, and it's narrowing

as part of these general tendencies. On the other hand, if you find union organizing building up and the grassroots organizations developing and people pressuring, it will change.

There's some clamoring now for "campaign finance reform." What's your take on that?

It's not a bad thing, but it's not going to have much effect. There are too many ways to cheat. It's like trying to pretend to stop drugs. There are so many ways to bring drugs in that it will always happen. I don't think the real problem is campaign financing. The real problem is the overwhelming power of corporate tyrannies in running society, and campaign finance reform is not going to change that.

In August 1996, the president signed the Personal Responsibility and Work Opportunity Act, which eliminated a 61-year-old federal government commitment to the poor. You've commented that that commitment has always been very limited and declined sharply since around 1970.

Since the assault began.

You've got to like the wording.

The wording's fine. It says 7-year-old children have to have personal responsibility and now they have an opportunity which was deprived to them before, the opportunity to starve. It's just another assault against defenseless people. It's now felt, well, okay, we can kick them in the face. This, too, is based on a very effective propaganda campaign to make much of the population hate and fear the poor. That's smart. You don't want to get them to look at the rich guys. Don't let them take a look at the pages of *Fortune* and *Business Week* talking about the "dazzling" and "stupendous" profit growth. Don't let them look at the way the military system is pouring funds into advanced technology. You're not supposed to look at that. What you're supposed to look at is the black mother driving a Cadillac and picking up her welfare check so she can have more babies. Why should I pay for that? That's been done very effectively. It's striking, again, when you look at attitudes. Most people think the government has a responsibility to ensure reasonable standards, minimal standards for poor people. On the other hand, most people are against welfare, which does exactly that. That's a propaganda achievement that you have to admire.

Incidentally, there's another aspect of this which is being much less discussed, but is quite crucial. One of the purposes of driving people into work away from welfare is to lower wages. Remember there's supposed to be a natural unemployment rate. We're not allowed to get below that unemployment rate or all sorts of terrible things happen. We can talk about that.

But assuming that that's true, we ought to be paying these people to be on welfare. They're keeping the unemployment rate high. Suppose you put them in the labor market. What's going to happen? Presumably, they're going to take jobs. If they get jobs it's going to lower unemployment. Terrible thing. If they don't get jobs, they're going to drive down the wages. In fact, even if they do get jobs, it will drive down wages. It's already happening.

In New York, city services are now using partially subsidized workfare, which simply eliminates union labor. That's a good way of making everybody suffer. So put a lot of unskilled, hopeless labor into the workplace, make conditions so awful that people will take virtually anything, maybe have some public subsidy to keep them doing it, and you can drive down wages that way.

There is a campaign to undermine public confidence in Social Security.

Most of the talk about Social Security is pretty fraudulent. Take the question about privatizing it. That's a non-issue. If people believe that it would be better for Social Security to be invested in the stock market, rather than in, say, Treasury bonds, that can be done whether it's public or private. I think the main goal is really to privatize it, that is, to make people in charge of their individual assets and not to have the solidarity that comes from doing something together. It's extremely important to break down the sense that I have any responsibility for the next person. The ideal is a society based on a social unit which consists of you and your television set and nothing to do with any other people. If a person next door has invested her assets badly and is now starving in her old age, well, it isn't your responsibility.

Social Security was something that brought people together. They said we're going to have a common responsibility to ensure that all of us have a minimal standard of living. That's dangerous because it implies that people can work together.

If you can work together, for example, you can replace corporate tyranny by worker control. You can get involved in the democratic process and make your own decisions. Much better to create a mentality in which each person behaves individually. The powerful will win. The poor will get smashed. There won't be any solidarity or communication or mutual support or information sharing or any of these things that might lead to democracy and justice. I think that's what lies behind the Social Security propaganda. The other issues are technical and of whatever significance they are, but probably not much. So a slightly more progressive taxation could keep Social Security functioning the way it is functioning for the indefinite future.

The CEO of Archer Daniels Midland, the Decatur, Illinois-based grain giant says: "The only place you see a free market is in the speeches of politicians." Usually managers are careful about what they say.

Who was he talking to?

I don't know. Internal?

I imagine. That's not the kind of thing that you tell the public. But, of course, it's true. Take what's called "trade." That's the most dramatic example. About 50 percent of U.S. trade actually is internal to a single corporation. For example, if Ford Motor Co. ships a part from Indiana to Illinois, it's not called trade. If it ships it from Illinois to northern Mexico, it is called trade. It's called an export when it goes and an import when it comes back.

But all of this is centrally managed in ways which undercut markets, designed for the obvious purpose of exploiting cheaper labor and avoiding environmental regulations and playing games with where you pay your taxes. That's about 50 percent of U.S. trade. Japan is about the same. England is even higher.

When people talk about the growth in world trade, what they're talking about is largely a joke. What's growing are complicated interactions among centrally-managed institutions which are on the scale of command economies. Within them there's no free trade, and among them there are various oligopolistic relationships. But I disagree with this person when he says there's no free trade. There is free trade for 7-year-old kids and for poor people in the Third World. They have to meet responsibility.

There was an interesting study recently in England by 2 technical economists studying the top 100 transnational corporations on the *Fortune* list. One thing they discovered was that of the top 100, every single one had benefited from the industrial policy of its home country.

They say at least 20 of the 100 would not have survived if it hadn't been for either state take-over or large -scale state subsidy at points when they were facing losses. Also most of them depend heavily on the domestic market. One of them is Lockheed, Newt Gingrich's favorite, which was saved from destruction by a $2 billion government-subsidized loan when it was facing disaster back in the early 1970s.

Okay, that tells you what free trade is. Big multinationals are invariably, if this is correct, dependent on the state, meaning the public, to keep them going. They're not going to face market risks.

There's a cover story in the Nation *entitled "Eurobattle: Attacking the Welfare State" by Daniel Singer. He says, "What's at stake is the unmistakable attempt by the international financial establishment and continental governments to use this whole operation as a cover for adapting the U.S. model of Reaganomics.*

I'd be careful about using phrases like "Reaganomics," because it's a fraud. Reagan didn't know what was going on, but the people around him were the most protectionist in post-war American history. They virtually doubled various import restrictions. They poured money into advanced technology. If it hadn't been for their market interference, there probably would be no automobile or steel or semiconductor industries in the U.S. today. That's Reaganomics. So they were preaching free markets to the poor. On the other hand, James Baker, when he was Secretary of Treasury, was boasting to the business world that they had raised protection higher than any preceding government.

In France, there are fewer workers in unions than in the U.S., which is already very low. Yet, the support for French general strikes which shut down cities and at one point the whole country in December 1995 was very high. What accounts for that?

There are a lot of differences. One factor is the power of business propaganda in the U.S. This is the country where the public relations industry was developed, where it was most sophisticated. It's the home of the international entertainment industry, which is mainly propaganda. Huge funds are put into controlling the "public mind," as they put it. Although there isn't a capitalist society—and such a society wouldn't survive—this is toward the capitalist end and tends to be more business-run than others, meaning there's a huge amount of expenditure on marketing, which is a form of manipulation and deceit. The most recent estimate is that something like one-sixth of the gross domestic product goes to marketing. A large part of that is advertising. Advertising is tax-deductible, so you pay for the privilege of being manipulated and controlled. This is unusually developed here. The social democracies of, say, Sweden, have big multinationals. Sweden's economy rests heavily on some of them.

They depend, like most of the big exporters, on public subsidies and in Sweden, in particular, the military industry. The military industry seems to have provided much of the technology which allowed Ericsson to dominate a good part of the mobile phone market. Meanwhile the Swedish welfare state is being cut back. It's still way beyond us, but cut back while profits increase for the multinationals, which are being publicly subsidized. That's Sweden. This is the U.S. They're different societies and different understandings. But the same processes are at work globally.

Have you been following the new domestic political formations? The Labor Party had its founding convention in Cleveland in June 1996. The Alliance had its founding convention in Texas in November 1996. The New Party is already established and running candidates. Ralph Nader ran for president on the Green Party ticket.

There are certainly new formations developing. They ought to get together. Scattering limited energies and resources is not a good idea. But allowing new options to enter the political system is, in general, a good idea. I think probably the right way to do it might be the way that the New Party has developed, with fusion candidates, concentrating on winnable elections. But a labor-based Party is a very good idea as well. They ought to be the same party. They have the same interests. If something can be created which is like the NDP in Canada or like the Workers Party in Brazil, big umbrella organizations which foster and support grassroots activities, provide resources, bring people together, provide an umbrella under which often parallel activities can be carried out, take some part, as much as possible, in the political system, that's going to be to the good. And it can be progress toward something else. It's not going to overcome the fact that we

have one business party and they're going to run things because that's rooted in the structure of the institutions. Until we democratize the basic institutions, we won't break out of that.

When we do something, do we have to have a clear idea about the long-term goal in order to devise a strategy?

You learn by trying. New ways of thinking about the next step. You can't start now, with current understandings, and say, "Okay, let's design a libertarian society." You have to create the understanding and gain the insight that allows you to move step by step toward that end. Just like in any other aspect of life, or science, for that matter, the strategy is to do more and learn more and find out the answers and find out ways of associating with other people and create the institutions. Out of them come new problems, new methods, new strategies. If somebody can come up with a general all-purpose strategy, everybody will be delighted. It hasn't happened in the last couple thousand years. So if you look at Marxist literature, it doesn't offer any such strategies.

If, say, Marx had been asked, what's the strategy for overthrowing capitalism?, he would have laughed. Even somebody who is overwhelmingly a tactician, like Lenin, didn't have such comprehensive strategies. His general strategy was, follow me. That's a kind of strategy, I suppose. But Lenin, Trotsky, and others just adapted strategies to particular situations, circumstances, looking for their own goal—taking state power. I don't think that should be our goal. But a general strategy for overcoming authoritarian institutions, how could there be an answer to that question? There isn't any. In fact, I think those questions are mostly asked by people who don't want to become engaged. If you want to become engaged and do it, there are plenty of problems around that you can work on, whether it's what you started with, hungry children, or the destruction of the environment, the breakdown of security in the workplace, public subsidy to huge transnationals, we can go on and on.

But it's not going to happen by pushing a button. It's going to happen by dedicated, concentrated work which will slowly build up the understanding, the relationships among people, the perceptions, the support systems, the alternative institutions and so on. Then something can happen. But there's no general all-purpose strategy for that.

Urvashi Vaid, author of Virtual Equality, *castigates what she calls the "purist left" for waiting for the perfect vision, the one and only answer, and a charismatic leader. Something which I hear when I travel around the country is the one great solution—the Internet.*

I agree with that criticism. Waiting for a charismatic leader is demanding disaster. As far as the Internet is concerned, like other technology, it should be taken seriously. It has lots of opportunities, lots of dangers. Right now it's in a crucial phase, I think. Bob McChesney has pointed out that the effect of last year's telecommunications act is part of the biggest giveaway of public assets in history. As an act of privatization, meaning handing over public resources to private power, it has no counterpart. There aren't even token payments for it, as there were in, say, privatization in Mexico.

He also makes the important point that this issue was not treated as a social and political issue. It was treated as a business issue. So you read about it in the business pages. The issue, shall we give away these public resources to private power was not discussed. All that was discussed was how shall we give them away? Shall we give them away to 5 mega-corporations or 12 mega-corporations? But not, Shall we give it away? That is a tremendous propaganda victory.

Here's this enormous resource built at public expense being handed over to private power, which has its obvious interests, namely to create a society based on social units consisting of you and maybe your Internet connection. Sure, they have very good reasons for wanting that. But do we want that? The Internet could be used for all

sorts of other things if it remains under public control. So, of course, the Internet is not the answer. It's important. Modes of communication and interaction are, of course, important. Print is important. Radio is important. Television is important. This mode of communication and interaction is important and can be used very efficiently and for very good purpose and has been, in fact. But it can also be used very destructively. Technology is usually like that. You can't ask, is a hammer good or bad? Put it in the hands of a torturer, it can be bad. Put it in the hands of somebody who's trying to build a house, it can be good. The Internet is the same.

On the other hand, the comment you quoted earlier, don't sit around waiting for a charismatic leader or, for that matter, for a grand strategy, is good advice. If that comes, it will be a disaster, like it always has been. If something grows out of popular action and participation it can be healthy. Maybe it won't, but at least it can be. There's no other way.

But you've traditionally seen top-down strategies and movements as always inherently doomed.

They can succeed in doing exactly what they're designed to do, namely, maintain top-down leadership, control, and authority. It shouldn't have come as a tremendous surprise to anyone that a vanguard party would end up being a totalitarian state. In fact, Trotsky had predicted that years before he decided to play the game.

I was talking to Howard Zinn about how social change happens. He suggests that we need to reconceptualize time in terms of social change, comparing it to a sprinter versus the long-distance runner. What do you think of that?

He's right. I don't know if he was thinking of this, but it was very striking in the 1960s in parts of the student movement. It was in a way coming out of nowhere. There wasn't an organized, well-established popular-based left that it could join. So the leadership was sometimes in the hands of very young people, often very nice, decent people who were then going to do something. It was striking what they wanted to do. I don't know how much of this you were a part of.

The perception was often quite short-range. I remember at the time of the Columbia University strike their conception was, for many of them, not all of them, "We'll strike at Columbia, close down the buildings for a couple of weeks. After that we'll have a revolution." A lot of the spirit of 1968 was like that. That's not the way things work. It was a disaster for the people involved. It left a sad legacy. You have to build slowly and ensure that the next step comes out of a basis that's already established in people's understanding and their perceptions and their attitudes towards one another, their conception of what they want to attain and the circumstances in which you can attain it. For example, it makes absolutely no sense to expose yourself and others to destruction when you don't have a social base in which you can protect the gains that you've made. That has been found over and over again in guerrilla movements, in popular movements, and elsewhere. You get cut off by the powerful.

You've been spending time in South America, where you've observed popular grassroots movements. Do you see any lessons that people in the U.S. can learn from these situations?

First of all, these are very vibrant and dynamic societies with huge problems. One thing I was immediately struck by was that no one ever asked about the grand strategy for overthrowing this and that. People don't say, "What should I do? They say, here's what I'm doing." What do you think about it? There are lots of things going on. They are impressive. The circumstances are extremely difficult, much harder than anything we face. Brazil, for example, has the largest labor-based party in the world which would have won any fair election. By that I don't mean that the votes were stolen. I mean that the resources and the media were so overwhelmingly on the other side that there wasn't a serious election,

otherwise they would have won. It has its problems, but it's an impressive organization with a radical democratic and socialist thrust, a lot of popular support, lots of potential. The landless workers movement is struggling under very hard circumstances to deal with a core problem of Brazilian society, the incredible inequality of land ownership and control and inequality generally. There's organizing in shantytowns.

Is it enough to change things? I think they're trapped by many delusions. You have to free your mind. The weapon that is being used—to carry out the analogy to Reaganomics—in Brazil, is the debt. The same with most of Latin America. We've got this terrible debt, we've got to minimize the state. They don't have any debt. They have to understand that. Just as we have to understand that private tyrannies have no legitimacy.

People don't liberate themselves alone. You liberate yourself through participation with others. Just like you learn things in science by interacting with others. The complicated network of popular organizations and umbrella groups like the Workers Party help create a basis for this.

We have all sorts of advantages that they don't have, like for example, enormous wealth. Also, we have the unique advantage that we don't have a superpower standing over us. We are the superpower. That makes a huge difference. So the opportunities here are greater. It's kind of striking to see. You feel how stultifying it is, in many ways, when you come from there back here. For one thing, the doctrinal rigidity here is startling. Anybody who comes back from the Third World to the West in general, but here in particular, is struck by the narrowing of thought and understanding, the limited nature of legitimate discussion, the separation of people from one another.

I wasn't in Chile long enough to get much of an impression, but I think it's probably true there too. That's a country which is clearly under military rule. We call it a democracy, but it's a democracy with the military setting very narrow bounds as to what can happen. And it's in people's attitudes. You can see it. They know there are limits you don't transcend.

Do you have any ideas on getting your ideas, to the larger public? This seems to be a problem.

It's the usual problem. First of all, I think almost everybody agrees with these ideas. For example, 95 percent of the population thinks that corporations ought to sacrifice profits for the benefit of workers and the community. I don't think that's enough, but I certainly agree with that. Over 80 percent of the population thinks that the economic situation is inherently unfair and ought to be changed. I agree with that. How do you get out? By doing it. Everywhere you go or I go or anybody else goes, it's because some organized group has set something up. I can't go to Kansas City and say I'm going to give a talk. I won't have one person showing up. Why should they? On the other hand, if some group there which is organizing and active says, Let's put together a meeting and bring people in, then I can go and give a talk and people come from all over the place to hear it. All this goes back to the same thing. If people are going to dedicate themselves to organizing and activism, whether it's in unions or community organizations or working on health programs or on and on, yes, then you can have access to broader and broader audiences. How broad? It depends on the movement.

> I wasn't in Chile long enough to get much of an impression, but I think it's probably true there too. That's a country which is under military rule. We call it a democracy, but it's a democracy with the military setting very narrow bounds as to what can happen.

Michael Moore is a filmmaker who made Roger and Me. *He has a book called* Downsize This! *He says the problem with the left is that it whines too much and is very negative.*

That may be. If it is, it's making a mistake. For example, I don't think Howard Zinn whines too much and turns people off. Probably plenty of people do. Take the example I gave you of that media group in Brazil, which, after very careful planning and working with leadership in the community, presented television skits in public which turned people off because they were boring and full of jargon and intellectual talk. On the other hand, when they let the people do it themselves and gave them the technical assistance, it turned out not to be boring and not to turn people off. This is for people who like to write articles about the responsibility of intellectuals. That's their responsibility. Go out and do things like that. And make sure it's the people themselves who are doing it. You give them what help you can. Learn from them. That's the responsibility of intellectuals.

I produce Alternative Radio, a one-hour program. It is pretty effectively locked out of the Boston-to-Miami corridor. In contrast, in Montana, Colorado, New Mexico, places like that, it's much easier to get on the air.

The institutional reasons are pretty obvious, the same reason why discussion is narrower and more stultifying here than in other countries. This is the part of the country where the decisions are being made, so you've got to keep it under tight doctrinal control and make sure that nothing gets out of hand. It doesn't matter what people are talking about in Laramie, Wyoming. Still less in the slums of Rio. So there are institutional reasons.

On the other hand, don't just blame them. People here are not making use of the possibilities they have. So take, say, Cambridge, Massachusetts. Cambridge, like other towns, has a community cable television station. That was part of the communications act. The companies had to provide facilities. I've been there. I'm not a big techie, but even I can see that it has pretty good equipment. They claim to have outreach to the Cambridge area. It's available to the public. The one time I was there, the program was so crazy I almost walked off. Is it being used? No.

In the slums of Rio do they have cable television stations which the people can use? They'd be delighted if they had them.

Criticisms are made of what's happening to the content of the news. The program directors are saying, we're giving the public what it wants. No one's forcing them to turn on the TV and watch crime stories and sports. What do you think about that?

There are studies of what people want. What they want overwhelmingly is commercial-free television. Do you see commercial-free television? The television system here is a business where big corporations sell audiences to other businesses and they're going to keep it within a narrow framework. What people want is socially created. For example, take again that working-class slum in Brazil that I mentioned. I was there in prime television time. They had all the soap operas and all the junk.

But what people wanted was things they themselves were producing about racism and debt and internal problems and so on. What you want depends on who you are. Who you are depends on what options you've had, what kind of training you've had, what experiences you've had. The kinds of wants that come out of interactions with other people to solve a problem, those wants aren't going to be there unless there is interaction with other people to solve the problem. You can't just say, that's what people want. Sure, under that structured arrangement that's what people will choose. Change the structure, they'll choose different things.

In 1996, Gary Webb, a reporter for the San José Mercury News, *wrote a three-part article entitled "Dark Alliance," purporting to show that there was a connection between the explosion of crack cocaine in the black ghetto in LA and the CIA. You've often stayed away from such stories.*

That's not quite true. I just put it differently. For example, the relation between the CIA and drugs is certain. That's been well studied, since Al McCoy's work 25 years ago. The trail of clandestine activities is followed very closely by drug activities. There are pretty good reasons for that. Clandestine activities require untraceable money. They require lots of thugs. Where do you go? It's natural. So it starts right after World War II.

We can follow the trail through the French Connection in Marseilles, trying to undermine the resistance in the unions, to the Golden Triangle in Laos, Burma, etc., and on to Afghanistan and all these places. The CIA has been involved, but as an agency of state policy. What I don't agree with, and here I differ from a lot of others, is I don't think the CIA is an independent agency. I think it does what it's told.

You can maybe find examples, but as far as I read the records, the CIA is basically the agency of the White House, carrying out operations that require plausible deniability. Take the source of the Webb story, which is fundamentally correct. Bob Parry and Brian Barger exposed a lot of it ten years ago. They were shut up very quickly. But their evidence was correct. The U.S. was involved in massive international terrorism throughout Central America.

It was clandestine to a large extent, meaning everybody knew about it, but it was below the surface enough so you could pretend you didn't. They needed the usual things: untraceable money and brutal thugs. They naturally turned right away to the narcotraffickers. Noriega was our great friend, remember, until he decided not to play a part in this any longer. He became too independent and had to be thrown out. But in the beginning he was fine, an ordinary thug, narcotrafficker, helping with the contras.

So, of course, there's a connection between the CIA and drugs. What Webb did was trace some of the details and find that one aspect of that connection was that cocaine got into the ghetto through such-and-such a passage. That's predictable. When the CIA says they didn't know anything about it, I assume they're right. Why should they know anything about it? It's not their business. The structure of the system, however, is very clear. And it's not just this case. It's many other cases. That it's going to end up in the ghettos is not a plot. It's just going to happen in the natural course of events. It's not going to sneak into well-defended communities which can protect themselves. It will break into communities that are being devastated, often by external social forces where people are alone and have to fight for survival. Kids aren't cared for because their parents are working to put food on the table. That's where it's going to break into.

You wrote to a mutual friend about when educated classes line up for a parade, a person of conscience has three options. Either one can join them and march in the parade or join the cheering and watch from the sidelines or speak out against it and expect to pay the price.

That's about right. That's been going on for a couple of thousand years, too.

Where do you see yourself in that structure?

It's a question of choice, but I would like to see myself with those who are not joining and not cheering. Incidentally, the origins of our own history are exactly that. Go back to the oldest recorded texts. Just notice what happens to people who didn't march in the parade, like what happened to Socrates. He wasn't treated very nicely. Or take the *Bible*. The *Bible* had intellectuals. They called them "prophets." They fell into the usual two classes. There were the ones who were flattering the kings and telling them how wonderful they were and leading the parade or cheering the parade. They were the ones who were honored and respected. A couple of hundred years later, a thousand years later they were called false prophets, but not at the time. There were other people, like, say, Amos who, incidentally, insisted: "I am not an intellectual," or, as he put it, "I am not a prophet. I am not the son of a prophet. I am a poor farmer." He had other things to say, as did many of the people who were much later honored as prophets. They

were imprisoned, persecuted, hated, and despised. Any surprise in that? If you don't join in the parade—remember the prophets were giving geo-political analysis as well as moral lessons—you're hated. The geopolitical analysis turned out to be pretty accurate. The moral prescriptions were often very elevated. Why were people in power going to like that? Of course they were going to drive them out. You might say, going back to your television producer about people watching what they want, yeah, it was the public who was driving them into the desert and imprisoning them.

They don't want to hear it either. Not because they're bad people, but for the usual reasons: short-term interest, manipulation, dependence on power. That's an image of what the world is like. Of course, that's a negative image. There are plenty of successes. The world is way better than it was. Go back to the 18th century, the way people were treating each other was an unbelievable horror. Go back 50 years and the circumstances were indescribably bad. Right now we're trying to defend a minimal healthcare system. Thirty years ago we weren't because there wasn't any. That's progress. Over a long period there were plenty of successes. They're cumulative. Nobody ever said that it was going to be easy.

José Ramos-Horta and Bishop Carlos Belo of East Timor were honored with the Nobel Prize.

That was great, a wonderful thing. I ran into José Ramos-Horta in Sao Paolo. I haven't seen his official speech yet, but certainly he was saying in public that the prize should have been given to Xanana Gusmao, who is the leader of the resistance to Indonesian aggression. He's in an Indonesian jail. But the recognition of the struggle is a very important thing, or will be an important thing if we can turn it into something. It will be suppressed as quickly as possible, polite applause, and let's forget about it. If that happens it's our fault, nobody else's. This gives an opportunity to keep this issue up front. Right now the Clinton administration is planning to send advanced arms to Indonesia. That doesn't have to work. But it will work unless there's a real public outcry. The granting of the Nobel Peace Prize offers a golden opportunity for people who care about the fate of a couple hundred thousand people to do something about it. But it's not going to happen by itself. In fact, some of the major issues about this have never even made it to the American press, like the oil issue. A large part of the reason for the Indonesian invasion and the U.S. and Australian support for it was that Timor has rich oil resources which are now being robbed in an outlandishly disgraceful Australian-Indonesian treaty, with U.S. oil companies involved. We can do something about that.

Didn't you go in the early 1980s to the New York Times *with a Portuguese Timorese?*

What actually happened was they were refusing to interview Timorese refugees in Lisbon and Australia, claiming they had no access to them.

The Times *was claiming this?*

Everybody was. We brought over some Timorese refugees. Actually I paid to bring them from Lisbon and tried to bring them to the editorial offices. It didn't work. The case you're mentioning was a little more complicated. The story has not been told because I'm not sure how much to tell of it. Someday it will be told. I arranged to have a Portuguese priest, Father Leoneto do Rego, interviewed by the *New York Times*. He was a very interesting man and a very credible witness. He had been living in the mountains with the Timorese resistance and had been driven out during the really near-genocidal campaign of 1978, when then-president Carter vastly increased the flow of weapons and Indonesia really smashed people. When they talk about hundreds of thousands of people being killed, that's then. A lot of people were driven out of the hills. He was one of them. He's Portuguese, so they didn't murder him. He was a classmate of the Archbishop of Boston, pretty hard to disregard. He

could describe what was happening. Nobody would talk to him. Finally, in a complicated way, I got the *Times* to agree to interview him. The interview by Kathleen Teltsch ran and it was an utter disgrace. It said almost nothing about what was happening. It had one line in it saying, Things aren't nice in Timor, or something like that. I think it must be that event that shamed the *Times* editors into running their first serious editorial on the problem. That's my strong suspicion. The transcript of that interview later leaked. I was working very hard to get the *Boston Globe* to cover the story. They were just publishing State Department handouts and apologetics from Indonesian generals. I finally got them to agree to look at the facts. They offered to let me write an op-ed. I said, "No, I don't want to write an op-ed. Get one of your reporters to look into it." So they didn't take it too seriously. They gave it to an extremely good local reporter. He was not an international reporter. The last I heard he was reporting on restaurants. He dug the way you dig into a local story, like investigating a corrupt judge, good reporting.

We helped him with some leads, but he picked it up and ran with the story. He wrote the best story on Timor that had ever appeared in the American press. One of the things he did was get to the State Department and find a guy who had been transferred away from the Indonesia desk because he didn't like what was going on. Somehow this guy leaked to him a transcript of the actual *New York Times* interview and he published good parts of it. It was a very powerful interview with Father Leoneto saying extremely important things. So that *Times* interview did appear in the *Boston Globe*. That must have been around 1981.

All this stuff was going on. Censorship had been total, and I mean total. In 1978, when the atrocities peaked and U.S. and British arms flow peaked, coverage was literally zero. The first article in the U.S., at least it's listed in the *Reader's Guide,* that specifically deals with Timor, is one of my own. It was from *Inquiry,* a right-wing libertarian journal where I was writing in those days. It was basically testimony that I had given in the UN on the suppression of the issue by the Western, primarily the U.S., press. There had been an earlier article by Arnold Kohen about Indonesia in the *Nation*, which had discussed this, and that's it for the journals. It's not that nobody noticed it. You go back to 1974-75, there was very extensive coverage in the context of the collapse of the Portuguese empire. It dropped to zero at the peak of the atrocities, started picking up again around 1979-80 as a result very largely of these activities.

Incidentally, here's a case where a very small number of people, the most important by far being Arnold Kohen, managed to get the issue to some extent into the public arena. It certainly saved tens of thousands of lives. The Red Cross was allowed in. There was some attention. The terror continued but lessened. And on to the present. Here's also a case where the Internet made a difference. The East Timor Action Network was a very small and scattered support group until the Internet came along. That was used very constructively by Charlie Scheiner and others to set up a wide base of support to bring the information to people who couldn't get it. I was getting information from the Australian press, but how many people have friends in Australia who send them the press? The movement grew and began to have an impact.

Does the Guatemala peace treaty that was signed signal the end to this three-decade-old bloodbath?

I'm sort of glad it's being signed, but it's a sad occasion. What it reflects is the great success of state terror, which has devastated any serious opposition, has intimidated people, has made it not only acceptable but even desirable for them to have the rule of ultra-right business interests, mostly foreign interests, in a peace treaty which

may, let's hope, put an end to the real horrors. So in the context a step forward, but in the broader picture a very ugly outcome of one of the biggest state terror operations of the modern period, which started in 1954 when the U.S. took part in overthrowing the one democratic government.

I'd like to end with an incident that you told me about.. Do you remember?

I remember it very well. My family was first generation, so we lived in Philadelphia, but there were two big branches of the family. My father's family was in Baltimore and my mother's family was in New York. The one in Baltimore was very religious. We were sort of observant, but not super-Orthodox. My brother and I, I was maybe six or seven, he was maybe two. We went there for the holidays. It was nice to see cousins. But there was always a tone of fear, the fear that I would do something wrong. I don't know what it is, but I'm going to do something wrong. Because I don't know the rules. It wasn't that they were harsh, it was just that you knew you were going to do something wrong and you were going to be ashamed of it. It's one of these things that's inevitable. The incident I remember was when my brother on Saturday turned on a radio very loud. Saturday is the big family day, everybody is sitting around the kitchen having fun and this radio starts blaring, driving everybody crazy. Of course, nobody could turn it down. You're not allowed to touch it on Saturday. He understood enough to know that he had done something really criminal. He had made everybody suffer this horrible noise all through Saturday. I was a few years older and I could perceive the criminality.

David Barsamian is a radio broadcaster, writer, and founder of Alternative Radio in Boulder, Colorado. His interviews have appeared in Z Magazine, *the* Progressive, *and the* Nation.

3

Imperial Presidency

The conception of presidential sovereignty
is so extreme that it has drawn unprecedented criticism

It goes without saying that what happens in the U.S. has an enormous impact on the rest of the world, and conversely, what happens in the rest of the world cannot fail to have an impact on the U.S., in several ways. First, it sets constraints on what even the most powerful state can do. Second, it influences the domestic U.S. component of "the second superpower," as the *New York Times* ruefully described world public opinion after the huge protests before the Iraq invasion. Those protests were a critically important historical event, not only because of their unprecedented scale, but also because it was the first time in hundreds of years of the history of Europe and its North American offshoots that a war was massively protested even before it was officially launched.

We may recall, by comparison, the war against South Vietnam launched by JFK in 1962, brutal and barbaric from the outset invoking bombing, chemical warfare to destroy food crops so as to starve out the civilian support for the indigenous resistance, programs to drive millions of people to virtual concentration camps or urban slums to eliminate its popular base. By the time protests reached a substantial scale, the highly respected and quite hawkish Vietnam specialist and military historian Bernard Fall wondered whether "Viet-Nam as a cultural and historic entity" would escape "extinction" as "the countryside literally dies under the blows of the largest military machine ever unleashed on an area of this size"—particularly South Vietnam, always the main target of the U.S. assault. When protest did finally develop, many years too late, it was mostly directed against the peripheral crimes: the extension of the war against the South to the rest of Indochina—hideous crimes, but lesser ones.

It's quite important to remember how much the world has changed since then. As almost always, not as a result of gifts from benevolent leaders, but through deeply committed popular struggle, far too late in developing, but ultimately effective. One con-

From Z Magazine, April 1997

sequence was that the U.S. government could not declare a national emergency, which should have been healthy for the economy, as during World War II when public support was very high. Johnson had to fight a "guns-and-butter" war, buying off an unwilling population, harming the economy, ultimately leading the business classes to turn against the war as too costly, after the Tet Offensive of January 1968 showed that it would go on a long time. There were also concerns among U.S. elites about rising social and political consciousness stimulated by the activism of the 1960s, much of it reaction to the miserable crimes in Indochina, then at last arousing popular indignation. We learn from the last sections of the *Pentagon Papers* that after the Tet offensive, the military command was reluctant to agree to the president's call for further troop deployments, wanting to be sure that "sufficient forces would still be available for civil disorder control" in the U.S., and fearing that escalation might run the risk of "provoking a domestic crisis of unprecedented proportions."

The Reagan administration assumed that the problem of an independent, aroused population had been overcome and, apparently, planned to follow the Kennedy model of the early 1960s in Central America. But they backed off in the face of unanticipated public protest, turning instead to "clandestine war," employing murderous security forces and a huge international terror network. The consequences were terrible, but not as bad as B-52s and mass murder operations of the kind that were peaking when John Kerry was deep in the Mekong Delta in the South, by then largely devastated. The popular reaction to even the "clandestine war," so called, broke entirely new ground. The solidarity movements for Central America, now in many parts of the world, are again something new in Western history.

State managers cannot fail to pay attention to such matters. Routinely, a newly elected president requests an intelligence evaluation of the world situation. In 1989, when Bush I took office, a part was leaked. It warned that when attacking "much weaker enemies"—the only sensible target—the U.S. must win "decisively and rapidly." Delay might "undercut political support," recognized to be thin, a great change since the Kennedy-Johnson years when the attack on Indochina, while never popular, aroused little reaction for many years.

The world is pretty awful today, but it is far better than yesterday, not only with regard to unwillingness to tolerate aggression, but also in many other ways, which we now tend to take for granted. There are very important lessons here, which should always be uppermost in our minds—for the same reason they are suppressed in the elite culture.

Without forgetting the very significant progress towards more civilized societies in past years, and the reasons for it, let's focus nevertheless on the notions of imperial sovereignty now being crafted. It is not surprising that as the population becomes more civilized, power systems become more extreme in their efforts to control the "great beast" (as the Founding Fathers called the people). And the great beast is indeed frightening.

The conception of presidential sovereignty crafted by the statist reactionaries of the Bush administration is so extreme that it has drawn unprecedented criticism in the most sober and respected establishment circles. These ideas were transmitted to the president by the newly appointed attorney-general, Alberto Gonzales—who is depicted as a moderate in the press.

They are discussed by the respected constitutional law professor Sanford Levinson in the summer 2004 issue of *Daedalus*, the journal of the American Academy of Arts and Sciences. Levinson writes that the conception is based on the principle, "There exists no norm that is applicable to chaos." The quote, Levinson comments, is from Carl Schmitt, the leading German philosopher of law during the Nazi period, who Levinson describes as "the true éminence grise of the Bush administration." The Administration, advised by Gonzales, articulated "a view of presidential authority that is all too close to the power that Schmitt was willing to accord his own

Führer," Levinson writes. One rarely hears such words from the heart of the establishment. The same issue of the journal carried an article by two prominent strategic analysts on the "transformation of the military," a central component of the new doctrines of imperial sovereignty, including the rapid expansion of offensive weaponry, including militarization of space, and other measures designed to place the entire world at risk of instant annihilation.

These elicited the anticipated reactions by Russia and recently China. The analysts concluded that these U.S. programs may lead to "ultimate doom." They express their hope that a coalition of peace-loving states will coalesce as a counter to U.S. militarism and aggressiveness, led by China. We've come to a pretty pass when such sentiments are voiced in sober respectable circles not given to hyperbole.

Going back to Gonzales, he transmitted to the president the conclusions of the Justice Department that the president has the authority to rescind the Geneva Conventions—the supreme law of the land, the foundation of modern international humanitarian law. Gonzales, who was then Bush's legal counsel, advised him that this would be a good idea because rescinding the Conventions "substantially reduces the threat of domestic criminal prosecution [of administration officials] under the War Crimes Act" of 1996, which carries the death penalty for "grave breaches" of Geneva Conventions.

We can see on the front pages why the Justice Department was right to be concerned that the president and his advisers might be subject to the death penalty under the laws passed by the Republican Congress in 1996—and under the principles of the Nuremberg Tribunal, if anyone took them seriously.

In early November, the *NY Times* featured a front-page story reporting the conquest of the Falluja General Hospital. It reported, "Patients and hospital employees were rushed out of rooms by armed soldiers and ordered to sit or lie on the floor while troops tied their hands behind their backs." An accompanying photograph depicted the scene. That was presented as an important achievement. "The offensive also shut down what officers said was a propaganda weapon for the militants—Falluja General Hospital, with its stream of reports of civilian casualties." These "inflated" figures—inflated because our Leader so declares—were "inflaming opinion throughout the country" and the region, driving up "the political costs of the conflict." The word "conflict" is a common euphemism for U.S. aggression, as when we read on the same pages that the U.S. must now rebuild "what the conflict just destroyed"—just "the conflict," with no agent, like a hurricane.

Let's go back to the *NYT* picture and story about the closing of the "propaganda weapon." There are some relevant documents, including the Geneva Conventions, which state, "Fixed establishments and mobile medical units of the Medical Service may in no circumstances be attacked, but shall at all times be respected and protected by the Parties to the conflict." So page one of the world's leading newspaper is cheerfully depicting war crimes for which the political leadership could be sentenced to death under U.S. law.

The world's greatest newspaper also tells us that the U.S. military "achieved nearly all their objectives well ahead of schedule," leaving "much of the city in smoking ruins." But it was not a complete success. There is little evidence of dead "packrats" in their "warrens" or the streets, which remains "an enduring mystery." The embedded reporters did find a body of a dead woman, though it is "not known whether she was an Iraqi or a foreigner," apparently the only question that comes to mind.

The front-page account quotes a Marine commander who says, "It ought to go down in the history books." Perhaps it should. If so, we know on just what page of history it will go down and who will be right beside it, along with those who praise or, for that matter, even tolerate it. At least, we know that if we are honesty.

One might mention some of the recent counterparts that immediately come to mind, like the

Russian destruction of Grozny ten years ago, a city of about the same size; or Srebrenica, almost universally described as "genocide" in the West. In that case—as we know in detail from a Dutch government report and other sources—the Muslim enclave in Serb territory, inadequately protected, was used as a base for attacks against Serb villages and, when the anticipated reaction took place, it was horrendous. The Serbs drove out all but military age men and then moved in to kill them. There are differences with Falluja. Women and children were not bombed out of Srebrenica, but trucked out and there will be no extensive efforts to exhume the last corpse of the packrats in their warrens in Falluja. There are other differences, arguably unfair to the Serbs.

It could be argued that all this is irrelevant. The Nuremberg Tribunal, spelling out the UN Charter, declared that initiation of a war of aggression is "the supreme international crime differing only from other war crimes in that it contains within itself the accumulated evil of the whole." Hence the war crimes in Falluja and Abu Ghraib, the doubling of acute malnutrition among children since the invasion (now at the level of Burundi, far higher than Haiti or Uganda), and all the rest of the atrocities. Those judged to have played any role in the supreme crime—for example, the German Foreign Minister—were sentenced to death by hanging. The *Tokyo Tribunal* was far more severe.

There is a very important book on the topic by Canadian international lawyer Michael Mandel, who reviews in convincing detail how the powerful are self-immunized from international law.

In fact, the Nuremberg Tribunal established this principle. To bring the Nazi criminals to justice, it was necessary to devise definitions of "war crime" and "crime against humanity." How this was done is explained by Telford Taylor, chief counsel for the prosecution and a distinguished international lawyer and historian: "Since both sides [in World War II] had played the terrible game of urban destruction—the Allies far more successfully—there was no basis for criminal charges against Germans or Japanese and, in fact, no such charges were brought.... Aerial bombardment had been used so extensively and ruthlessly on the Allied side, as well as the Axis side, that neither at Nuremberg nor Tokyo was the issue made a part of the trials."

The operative definition of "crime" is: "Crime that you carried out, but we did not." To underscore the fact, Nazi war criminals were absolved if the defense could show that their U.S. counterparts carried out the same crimes. Taylor concludes that "to punish the foe—especially the vanquished foe—for conduct in which the enforcer nation has engaged, would be so grossly inequitable as to discredit the laws themselves." That is correct, but the operative definition also discredits the laws themselves, along with all subsequent tribunals. Taylor provides this background as part of his explanation of why U.S. bombing in Vietnam was not a war crime. His argument is plausible, further discrediting the laws themselves.

Some of the subsequent judicial inquiries are discredited in perhaps even more extreme ways, such as the *Yugoslavia vs. NATO* case adjudicated by the International Court of Justice. The U.S. was excused, correctly, on the basis of its argument that it is not subject to the jurisdiction of the Court in this case. The reason is that when the U.S. finally signed the Genocide Convention (which is at issue) after 40 years, it did so with a reservation stating that it is not applicable to the United States.

In an outraged comment on the efforts of Justice Department lawyers to demonstrate that the president has the right to authorize torture, Yale Law School Dean Harold Koh said, "The notion that the president has the constitutional power to permit torture is like saying he has the constitutional power to commit genocide." The president's legal advisers and the new attorney-general should have little difficulty arguing that the president does have that right, if the second superpower permits him to exercise it. The sacred doctrine of self-immunization is sure to hold for the trial of Saddam Hussein, if it is ever held. We see that every time Bush, Blair, and other worthies in government and commentary lament over the terrible crimes of Saddam Hussein, always bravely omitting the words: "with our help, because we did not care." Surely no tribunal will be permitted to address the fact that U.S. presidents from Kennedy until today, along with French presidents, British prime ministers, and Western businesses, have been complicit in Saddam's crimes, sometimes in horrendous ways, including current incumbents and their mentors. In setting up the Saddam tribunal, the State Department consulted U.S. legal expert professor Charif Bassiouni, recently quoted as saying: "All efforts are being made to have a tribunal whose judiciary is not independent but controlled, and by controlled I mean that the political manipulators of the tribunal have to make sure the U.S. and other western powers are not brought in cause. This makes it look like victor's vengeance and it makes it seem targeted, selected, unfair. It's a subterfuge." We hardly need to be told.

The pretext for U.S.-UK aggression in Iraq is what is called the right of "anticipatory self-defense," now sometimes called "preemptive war" in a perversion of that concept. The right of anticipatory self-defense was affirmed officially in the Bush administration's National Security Strategy of September 2002, declaring Washington's right to resort to force to eliminate any potential challenge to its global dominance. The NSS was widely criticized among the foreign policy elite, beginning with an article in the main establishment journal *Foreign Affairs (FA)*, warning that "the new imperial grand strategy" could be very dangerous. Criticism continued at an unprecedented level, but on narrow grounds—not that the doctrine itself was wrong, but rather its style and manner of presentation. Clinton's Secretary of State Madeleine Albright summed the criticism up accurately, also in *FA*. She pointed out that every president has such a doctrine in his back pocket, but it is foolish to smash people in the face with it and to implement it in a manner that will infuriate even allies. That is threatening

to U.S. interests and therefore wrong. Albright knew, of course, that Clinton had a similar doctrine.

The Clinton doctrine advocated "unilateral use of military power" to defend vital interests, such as "ensuring uninhibited access to key markets, energy supplies and strategic resources," without even the pretexts that Bush and Blair devised. Taken literally, the Clinton doctrine is more expansive than Bush's NSS. But the more expansive Clinton doctrine was barely even reported. It was presented with the right style and implemented less brazenly.

Henry Kissinger described the Bush doctrine as "revolutionary," pointing out that it undermines the 17th century Westphalian system of international order and of course the UN Charter and international law. He approved of the doctrine, but with reservations about style and tactics and with a crucial qualification that it cannot be "a universal principle available to every nation." Rather, the right of aggression must be reserved to the U.S., perhaps delegated to chosen clients. We must forcefully reject the principle of universality—that we apply to ourselves the same standards we do to others, more stringent ones if we are serious. Kissinger is to be praised for his honesty in articulating prevailing doctrine, usually concealed in professions of virtuous intent and tortured legalisms. He understands his educated audience. As he doubtless expected, there was no reaction.

His understanding of his audience was illustrated, rather dramatically, when the Kissinger-Nixon tapes were released, over Kissinger's strong objections. There was a report in the world's leading newspaper. It mentioned, in passing, the orders to bomb Cambodia that Kissinger transmitted from Nixon to the military commanders. In Kissinger's words, "A massive bombing campaign in Cambodia. Anything that flies on anything that moves." It is rare for a call for horrendous war crimes—what we would not hesitate to call "genocide" if others were responsible—to be so stark and explicit. It would be interesting to see if there is anything like it in archival records. The publication elicited no reaction, refuting Dean Koh. Apparently, it is taken for granted in the elite culture that the president and his National Security adviser do have the right to order genocide.

Imagine the reaction if the prosecutors at the Milosevic Tribunal could find anything remotely similar. They would be overjoyed, the trial would be over, Milosevic would receive several life sentences, the death penalty if the Tribunal adhered to U.S. law. But that is them, not us.

Anticipator Self-Defense

The principle of universality is the most elementary of moral truisms. It is the foundation of "just war theory" and of every system of morality deserving of anything but contempt. Rejection of such moral truisms is so deeply rooted in the intellectual culture as to be invisible. To illustrate again how deeply entrenched it is, let's return to the principle of "anticipatory self-defense," adopted as legitimate by both political organizations in the U.S. and across virtually the entire spectrum of articulate opinion, apart from the usual margins. The principle has some immediate corollaries. If the U.S. is granted the right of "anticipatory self-defense" against terror, then, certainly, Cuba, Nicaragua, and a host of others have long been entitled to carry out terrorist acts within the U.S. because there is no doubt of its involvement in very serious terrorist attacks against them, extensively documented in impeccable sources and, in the case of Nicaragua, even condemned by the World Court and the Security Council (in two resolutions that the U.S. vetoed, with Britain loyally abstaining). The conclusion that Cuba and Nicaragua, among many others, have long had the right to carry out terrorist atrocities in the U.S. is, of course, utterly outrageous and advocated by no one. Thanks to our self-determined immunity from moral truisms, there is no fear that anyone will draw outrageous conclusions. There are still more outrageous ones. No one,

for example, celebrates Pearl Harbor day by applauding the fascist leaders of Imperial Japan. But by our standards, the bombing of military bases in the U.S. colonies of Hawaii and the Philippines seems rather innocuous.

The Japanese leaders knew that B-17 Flying Fortresses were coming off the Boeing production lines and were surely familiar with the public discussions in the U.S. explaining how they could be used to incinerate Japan's wooden cities in a war of extermination, flying from Hawaiian and Philippine bases—"to burn out the industrial heart of the Empire with fire-bombing attacks on the teeming bamboo ant heaps," as retired Air Force General Chennault recommended in 1940, a proposal that "simply delighted" President Roosevelt. That's a far more powerful justification for anticipatory self-defense than anything conjured up by Bush-Blair and their associates—and accepted, with tactical reservations, throughout mainstream articulate opinion.

Examples can be enumerated virtually at random. To add one last one, consider the most recent act of NATO aggression prior to the U.S.-UK invasion of Iraq: the bombing of Serbia in 1999. The justification is supposed to be that there were no diplomatic options and that it was necessary to stop ongoing genocide. It is not hard to evaluate these claims.

As for diplomatic options, when the bombing began, there were two proposals on the table, a NATO and a Serbian proposal. After 78 days of bombing, a compromise was reached between them—formally at least. It was immediately undermined by NATO. All of this quickly vanished into the mists of unacceptable history, to the limited extent that it was ever reported. What about ongoing genocide—to use the term that appeared hundreds of times in the press as NATO geared up for war? That is unusually easy to investigate. There are two major documentary studies by the State Department, offered to justify the bombing, along with extensive documentary records from the OSCE, NATO, and other Western sources—and a detailed British Parliamentary Inquiry. All agree on the basic facts: the atrocities followed the bombing, they were not its cause. Furthermore, that was predicted by the NATO command, as General Wesley Clark informed the press right away and confirmed in more detail in his memoirs. The Milosevic indictment, issued during the bombing—surely as a propaganda weapon, despite implausible denials—and relying on U.S.-UK intelligence as announced at once, yields the same conclusion: virtually all the charges are post-bombing. Such annoyances are handled quite easily. The Western documentation is commonly expunged in the media and even scholarship. The chronology is regularly reversed, so that the anticipated consequences of the bombing are transmuted into its cause.

There were indeed pre-bombing atrocities: about 2,000 were killed in the year before the March 1999 bombing, according to Western sources. The British, the most hawkish element of the coalition, made the astonishing claim —hard to believe just on the basis of the balance of forces—that until January 1999 most of the killings were by the Albanian KLA guerrillas attacking civilians and soldiers in cross-border raids in the hope of eliciting a harsh Serbian response that could be used for propaganda purposes in the West, as they candidly reported, apparently with CIA support in the last months. Western sources indicate no substantial change until the bombing was announced and the monitors withdrawn a few days before the March bombing.

In one of the few works of scholarship that even mentions the unusually rich documentary record, Nicholas Wheeler concludes that 500 of the 2,000 were killed by Serbs. He supports the bombing on the grounds that there would have been worse Serbian atrocities had NATO not bombed, eliciting the anticipated crimes. That's the most serious scholarly work. The press, and much of scholarship, chose the easier path of ignoring Western documentation and reversing the chronology. It is all too easy to continue. But the—unpleasantly consistent—record leaves open a crucial question: how does the "great beast" react, the domestic U.S. component of the second superpower? The conventional answer is that the population approves of all of this, as shown by the election of George Bush. But, as is often the case, a closer look is helpful.

Each candidate received about 30 percent of the electoral vote, Bush a bit more, Kerry a bit less. General voting patterns were close to the 2000 elections; almost the same "red" and "blue" states, in the conventional metaphor. A few percent shift in vote would have meant that Kerry would be in the White House. Neither outcome could tell us much of any significance about the mood of the country, even of voters. Issues of substance were, as usual, kept out of the campaign or presented so obscurely that few could understand.

It is important to bear in mind that political campaigns are designed by the same people who sell toothpaste and cars. Their professional concern in their regular vocation is not to provide information. Their goal, rather, is deceit, but deceit is expensive, requiring complex graphics showing the car with a sexy actor or a sports hero or climbing a sheer cliff or some other device to project an image that might deceive the consumer into buying this car instead of the virtually identical one produced by a competitor. The same is true of elections, run by the same public relations industry. The goal is to project images and deceive the public into accepting them, while sidelining issues—for good reasons.

The population seems to grasp the nature of the performance. Right before the 2000 elections, about 75 percent regarded it as virtually meaningless, some game involving rich contributors, party managers, and candidates who are trained to project images that conceal issues, but might pick up some votes. This is probably why the "stolen election" was an elite concern that did not seem to arouse much public interest. If elections have about as much significance as flipping a coin to pick the King, who cares if the coin was biased? Right before the 2004 election, about 10 percent of voters said their choice would be based on the candidate's "agendas/ideas/platforms/ goals"—6 percent for Bush voters, 13 percent for Kerry voters. For the rest, the choice would be based on what the industry calls "qualities" and "values." Does the candidate project the image of a strong leader, the kind of person you'd like to meet in a bar, someone who really cares about you and is just like you? It wouldn't be surprising to learn that Bush is carefully trained to say "nucular" and "misunderestimate" and the other silliness that intellectuals like to ridicule. That's probably about as real as the ranch constructed for him and the rest of the folksy manner. After all, it wouldn't do to present him as a spoiled frat boy from Yale who became rich and powerful thanks to his rich and powerful connections. Rather, the imagery has to be an ordinary guy just like us, who'll protect us, and who shares our "moral values," more so than the windsurfing goose-hunter who can be accused of faking his medals.

Bush received a large majority among voters who said they were concerned primarily with "moral values" and "terrorism." We learn all we have to know about the moral values of the Administration by reading the pages of the business press the day after the election, describing the "euphoria" in boardrooms—not because CEOs are opposed to gay marriage. Or by observing the principle, hardly concealed, that the very serious costs incurred by the Bush planners, in their dedicated service to power and wealth, are to be transferred to our children and grandchildren, including fiscal costs, environmental destruction, and perhaps "ultimate doom." These are the moral values, loud and clear. The commitment of Bush planners to "defense against terrorism" is illustrated most dramatically, perhaps, by their decision to escalate the threat of terror, as had been predicted even by their own intelligence agencies, not because they enjoy terrorist attacks against U.S. citizens, but because it is, plainly, a low priority for them—surely as compared with

> We learn from the last sections of the Pentagon Papers that after the Tet offensive, the military command was reluctant to agree to the president's call for further troop deployments, wanting to be sure that "sufficient forces would still be available for civil disorder control" in the U.S."

such goals as establishing secure military bases in a dependent client state at the heart of the world's energy resources, recognized since World War II as the "most strategically important area of the world," "a stupendous source of strategic power and one of the greatest material prizes in world history."

It is critically important to ensure that "profits beyond the dreams of avarice"—to quote a leading history of the oil industry—flow in the right directions, i.e., to U.S. energy corporations, the Treasury Department, U.S. high tech (militarized) industry, huge construction firms, and so on. Even more important was the stupendous strategic power. Having a firm hand on the spigot guarantees "veto power" over rivals, as George Kennan pointed out over 50 years ago. In the same vein, Zbigniew Brzezinski wrote that control over Iraq gives the U.S. "critical leverage" over European and Asian economies, a major concern of planners since World War II.

Rivals are to keep to their "regional responsibilities" within the "overall framework of order" managed by the U.S., as Kissinger instructed them in his "Year of Europe" address 30 years ago. That is even more urgent today, as the major rivals threaten to move in an independent course, maybe even united.

The EU and China became each other's leading trading partners in 2004 and those ties are becoming tighter, including the world's second largest economy, Japan. Critical leverage is more important than ever for world control in the tripolar world that has been evolving for over 30 years. In comparison, the threat of terror is a minor consideration—though the threat is known to be awesome. Long before 9/11 it was understood that, sooner or later, the Jihadist terror organized by the U.S. and its allies in the 1980s was likely to combine with WMDs, with horrifying consequences. Notice that the crucial issue with regard to Middle East oil—about two-thirds of estimated world resources and unusually easy to extract—is control, not access. U.S. policies towards the Middle East were the same when it was a net exporter of oil and remain the same today when U.S. intelligence projects that the U.S. will rely on more stable Atlantic Basin resources. Policies would be likely to be about the same if the U.S. were to switch to renewable energy. The need to control the "stupendous source of strategic power" and to gain "profits beyond the dreams of avarice" would remain. Jockeying over Central Asia and pipeline routes reflects similar concerns.

There are plenty of other illustrations of the same ranking of priorities. To mention one, the Treasury Department has a bureau (OFAC, Office of Foreign Assets Control) that is assigned the task of investigating suspicious financial transfers, a crucial component of the "war on terror." OFAC has 120 employees. Last April, the White House informed Congress that four are assigned to tracking the finances of Osama bin Laden and Saddam Hussein, while almost two dozen are dedicated to enforcing the embargo against Cuba—incidentally, declared illegal by every relevant international organization, even the usually compliant Organization of American States. From 1990 to 2003, OFAC informed Congress, there were 93 terrorism-related investigations with $9,000 in fines; and 11,000 Cuba-related investigations with $8 million in fines.

Why should the Treasury Department devote vastly more energy to strangling Cuba than to the war on terror? The basic reasons were explained in secret documents 40 years ago, when the Kennedy administration sought to bring "the terrors of the earth" to Cuba, as historian (and Kennedy confidante) Arthur Schlesinger recounted in his biography of Robert Kennedy, who ran the terror operations as his highest priority.

State Department planners warned that the "very existence" of the Castro regime is "successful defiance" of U.S. policies going back 150 years to the Monroe Doctrine—no Russians, but intolerable defiance of the master of the hemisphere. Furthermore, this successful defiance encourages others, who might be infected by the "Castro idea of taking matters into their own hands," Schlesinger had warned incoming President Kennedy, summarizing the report of the President's Latin American mission. These dangers are particularly grave, Schlesinger elaborated, when "the distribution of land and other forms of national wealth greatly favors the propertied classes…and the poor and underprivileged, stimulated by the example of the Cuban revolution, are demanding opportunities for a decent living."

The Great Beast

U.S. public opinion is studied with great care and depth. Studies released right before the election showed that those planning to vote for Bush assumed that the Republican Party shared their views, even though the Party explicitly rejected them. In brief, those who bothered to vote mostly accepted the imagery concocted by the PR industry, which had only the vaguest resemblance to reality. That's apart from the more wealthy who tend to vote their class interests. What about actual public attitudes? Again, right before the election, major studies were released reporting them—and we see right away why it is a good idea to base elections on deceit, very much as in the fake markets of the doctrinal system. A considerable majority believe the U.S. should:

- accept the jurisdiction of the International Criminal Court and the World Court

- sign the Kyoto protocols

- allow the UN to take the lead in international crises (including reconstruction, and political transition in Iraq)

- rely on diplomatic and economic measures more than military ones in the "war on terror," and use force only if there is "strong evidence that the country is in imminent danger of being attacked," thus rejecting the bipartisan consensus on "pre-emptive war" and adopting a rather conventional interpretation of the UN Charter

· give up the Security Council veto

Overwhelming majorities favor expansion of purely domestic programs: primarily health care (80 percent), but also aid to education and Social Security. Similar results have long been found in these studies, carried out by the most reputable organizations that monitor public opinion. In other mainstream polls, about 80 percent favor guaranteed health care even if it would raise taxes—a national health care system is likely to reduce expenses considerably, avoiding the heavy costs of bureaucracy, supervision, paperwork, etc., some of the factors that render the U.S. privatized system the most inefficient in the industrial world.

Public opinion has been similar for a long time, with numbers varying depending on how questions are asked. The facts are sometimes discussed in the press, with public preferences noted, but dismissed as "politically impossible." That happened again on the eve of the 2004 elections.

A few days before (October 31), the *NY Times* reported, "There is so little political support for government intervention in the health care market in the United States that Senator John Kerry took pains in a recent presidential debate to say that his plan for expanding access to health insurance would not create a new government program"—what the majority want, so it appears. But it is politically impossible and there is too little political support, meaning that the insurance companies, HMOs, pharmaceutical industries, Wall Street, etc., are opposed.

It is notable that these views are held by people in virtual isolation. Their preferences do not enter into the political campaigns and only mar-

> The pretext for U.S.-UK aggression in Iraq is what is called the right of "anticipatory self-defense," now sometimes called "pre-emptive war" in a perversion of that concept

ginally into articulate opinion in media and journals. The same extends to other domains and raises important questions about a "democratic deficit" in the world's most important state, to adopt the phrase we use for others. What would the results of the election have been if the parties, either of them, had been willing to articulate people's concerns on the issues they regard as vitally important? Or if these issues could enter into public discussion within the mainstream? We can only speculate about that, but we do know that it does not happen and that the facts are scarcely even reported. It seems reasonable to suppose that fear of the great beast is rather deep. The operative concept of democracy is revealed very clearly in other ways as well.

Perhaps the most extraordinary was the distinction between Old and New Europe in the run-up to the Iraq war. The criterion for membership was so clear that it took real discipline to miss it. Old Europe—the bad guys—were the governments that took the same stand as the large majority of the population.

New Europe—the exciting hope for a democratic future—were the Churchillian leaders like Berlusconi and Aznar who disregarded even larger majorities of the population and submissively took their orders from Crawford, Texas. The most dramatic case was Turkey, where, to everyone's surprise, the government followed the will of 95 percent of the population. The official administration moderate, Colin Powell, immediately announced harsh punishment for this crime. Turkey was bitterly condemned in the national press for lacking "democratic credentials." The most extreme example was Paul Wolfowitz, who berated the Turkish military for not compelling the government to follow Washington's orders and demanded that they apologize and publicly recognize that the goal of a properly functioning democracy is to help the U.S. In other ways, too, the operative concept of democracy is scarcely concealed. The lead think-piece in the *NY Times* on the death of Yasser Arafat opened by saying, "The post-Arafat era will be the latest test of a quintessentially American article of faith: that elections provide legitimacy even to the frailest institutions." In the final paragraph, on the continuation page, we read that Washington "resisted new national elections among the Palestinians" because Arafat would win and gain "a fresher mandate" and elections "might help give credibility and authority to Hamas" as well. In other words, democracy is fine if the results come out the right way—otherwise, to the flames. To take just one crucial current example, a year ago, after other pretexts for invading Iraq had collapsed, Bush's speech writers had to come up with something to replace them.. They settled on what the liberal press calls "the president's messianic vision to bring democracy" to Iraq, the Middle East, the whole world. The reactions were intriguing. They ranged from rapturous acclaim for the vision, which proved that this was the most noble war in history (David Ignatius, veteran *Washington Post* correspondent) to critics who agreed that the vision was noble and inspiring, but might be beyond our reach because Iraqi culture is just not ready for such progress towards our civilized values. We have to temper the messianic idealism of Bush and Blair with some sober realism, the *London Financial Times* advised.

The interesting fact is that it was presupposed uncritically across the spectrum that the messianic vision must be the goal of the invasion, not this silly business about WMDs and al-Qaeda, no longer credible to elite opinion. What is the evidence that the U.S. and Britain are guided by the messianic vision? There is indeed a single piece of evidence: our leaders proclaimed it. What more could be needed?

There is one sector of opinion that had a different view: the Iraqis. Just as the messianic vision was unveiled in Washington to reverent applause, a U.S.-run poll of Baghdadis was released. Some agreed with the near-unanimous stand of Western elite opinion that the goal of the invasion was to bring democracy to Iraq. One percent. Five percent thought the goal was to help Iraqis. The majority assumed the obvious: the U.S. wants to control Iraq's resources and use its base there to reorganize the region in its interest. Baghdadis agree that there is a problem of cultural backwardness, in the West, not in Iraq.

Actually, their views were more nuanced. Though 1 percent believed that the goal of the invasion was to bring democracy, about half felt that the U.S. wanted democracy, but would not allow Iraqis to run their democracy "without U.S. pressure and influence." They understand the quintessentially American faith very well, perhaps because it was the quintessentially British faith while Britain's boot was on their necks. They don't have to know the history of Wilsonian idealism or Britain's noble counterpart or France's civilizing mission or the even more exalted vision of Japanese fascists and many others—probably also close to a historical universal. Their own experience is enough.

At the outset, I mentioned the notable successes of popular struggles in the past decades. Both recent history and public attitudes suggest some straightforward strategies for short- term activism on the part of those who don't want to wait for China to save us from "ultimate doom." We enjoy great privilege and freedom, remarkable by comparative and historical standards. That legacy was not granted from above, it was won by dedicated struggle, which does not reduce to pushing a lever every few years. We can abandon that legacy and take the easy way of pessimism—everything is hopeless, so I'll quit. Or we can make use of that legacy to work to create—in part re-create—the basis for a functioning democratic culture in which the public

> The interesting fact is that it was presupposed uncritically across the spectrum that the messianic vision must be the goal of the invasion, not this silly business about WMDs and al-Qaeda, no longer credible to elite opinion.

plays some role in determining policies, not only in the political arena from which it is largely excluded, but also in the crucial economic arena, from which it is excluded in principle.

These are hardly radical ideas. They were articulated clearly, for example, by the leading 20th century social philosopher in the U.S., John Dewey, who pointed out that until "industrial feudalism" is replaced by "industrial democracy," politics will remain "the shadow cast by big business over society." Dewey was as "American as apple pie," in the familiar phrase. He was, in fact, drawing from a long tradition of thought and action that had developed in working class culture from the origins of the industrial revolution and can become a living part of our societies, cultures, and institutions. But like other victories for justice and freedom over the centuries, that will not happen by itself. One of the clearest lessons of history, including recent history, is that rights are not granted; they are won. The rest is up to us.

4.

Marketing Democracy in a Neo-Liberal Order

A new mission to consolidate the victory of democracy and open markets

I have been asked to speak on some aspect of academic or human freedom, an invitation that offers many choices. I will keep to some simple ones. Freedom without opportunity is a devil's gift and the refusal to provide such opportunities is criminal. The fate of the more vulnerable offers a sharp measure of the distance from here to something that might be called "civilization." While I am speaking, 1,000 children will die from easily preventable disease and almost twice that many women will die or suffer serious disability in pregnancy or childbirth for lack of simple remedies and care. UNICEF estimates that to overcome such tragedies, and to ensure universal access to basic social services, would require a quarter of the annual military expenditures of the "developing countries," about 10 percent of U.S. military spending. It is against the background of such realities as these that any discussion of human freedom should proceed.

It is widely held that the cure for such profound social maladies is within reach. The hopes have foundation. The past few years have seen the fall of brutal tyrannies, the growth of scientific understanding that offers great promise, and many other reasons to look forward to a brighter future. The discourse of the privileged is marked by confidence and triumphalism: the way forward is known and there is no other.

The basic theme, articulated with force and clarity, is that "America's victory in the Cold War was a victory for a set of political and economic principles: democracy and the free market." These principles are "the wave of the future—a future for which America is both the gatekeeper and the model." I am quoting the chief political commentator of the *New York Times*, but the picture is conventional, widely repeated throughout much of the world, and accepted as generally accurate even by critics.

It was also enunciated as the "Clinton Doctrine," which declared that our new mission is to "consolidate the victory of democracy and open markets" that had just been won. There remains

From a Davie Lecture at the University of Cape Town, May 1997. Published in Z Magazine, September 1997 a range of disagreement. At one extreme "Wilsonian idealists" urge continued dedication to the traditional mission of benevolence; at the other, "realists" counter that we may lack the means to conduct these crusades of "global meliorism," and should not neglect our own interests in the service of others. Within this range lies the path to a better world. Reality seems to me rather different. The current spectrum of public policy debate has as little relevance to actual policy as its numerous antecedents. Neither the United States nor any other power has been guided by "global meliorism." Democracy is under attack worldwide, including the leading industrial countries, at least, democracy in a meaningful sense of the term, involving opportunities for people to manage their own collective and individual affairs. Something similar is true of markets. The assaults on democracy and markets are furthermore related. Their roots lie in the power of corporate entities that are totalitarian in internal structure, increasingly interlinked and reliant on powerful states, and largely unaccountable to the public. Their immense power is growing as a result of social policy that is globalizing the structural model of the third world, with sectors of enormous wealth and privilege alongside an increase in "the proportion of those who will labor under all the hardships of life, and secretly sigh for a more equal distribution of its blessings," as the leading framer of American democracy, James Madison, predicted 200 years ago.

These policy choices are most evident in Anglo-American societies, but extend worldwide. They cannot be attributed to what "the free market has decided, in its infinite but mysterious wisdom," "the implacable sweep of 'the market revolution'," "Reaganesque rugged individualism," or a "new orthodoxy" that "gives the market full sway." The quotes are liberal-to-left, in some cases quite critical. The analysis is similar across the rest of the spectrum, but generally euphoric. The reality, on the contrary, is that state intervention plays a decisive role, as in the past, and the basic outlines of policy are hardly novel. Current versions reflect "capital's clear subjugation of labor" for more than 15 years, in the words of the business press, which often frankly articulates the perceptions of a highly class-conscious business community, dedicated to class war.

If these perceptions are valid, then the path to a world that is more just and more free lies well outside the range set forth by privilege and power. I cannot hope to establish such conclusions here, but only to suggest that they are credible enough to consider with care. And to suggest further that prevailing doctrines could hardly survive were it not for their contribution to "regimenting the public mind every bit as much as an army regiments the bodies of its soldiers," to borrow the dictum of the respected Roosevelt-Kennedy liberal Edward Bernays in his classic manual for the Public Relations industry, of which he was one of the founders and leading figures.

Bernays was drawing from his experience in Woodrow Wilson's state propaganda agency, the Committee on Public Information. "It was, of course, the astounding success of propaganda during the war that opened the eyes of the intelligent few in all departments of life to the possibilities of regimenting the public mind," he wrote. His goal was to adapt these experiences to the needs of the "intelligent minorities," primarily business leaders, whose task is "The conscious and intelligent manipulation of the organized habits and opinions of the masses." Such "engineering of consent" is the very "essence of the democratic process," Bernays wrote shortly before he was honored for his contributions by the American Psychological Association in 1949.

> I cannot hope to establish such conclusions here, but only to suggest that they are credible enough to consider with care. And to suggest further that prevailing doctrines could hardly survive were it not for their contribution to "regimenting the public mind every bit as much as an army regiments the bodies of its soldiers"

The importance of "controlling the public mind" has been recognized with increasing clarity as popular struggles succeeded in extending the modalities of democracy, thus giving rise to what liberal elites call "the crisis of democracy" as when normally passive and apathetic populations become organized and seek to enter the political arena to pursue their interests and demands, threatening stability and order. As Bernays explained the problem, with "universal suffrage and universal schooling...at last even the bourgeoisie stood in fear of the common people. For the masses promised to become king," a tendency fortunately reversed—so it has been hoped—as new methods "to mold the mind of the masses" were devised and implemented.

To discover the true meaning of the "political and economic principles" that are declared to be "the wave of the future," it is necessary to go beyond rhetorical flourishes and public pronouncements and to investigate actual practice and the internal documentary record. Close examination of particular cases is the most rewarding path, but these must be chosen carefully to give a fair picture. There are some natural guidelines. One reasonable approach is to take the examples chosen by the proponents of the doctrines themselves, as their "strongest case." Another is to investigate the record where influence is greatest and interference least, so that we see the operative principles in their purest form. If we want to determine what the Kremlin meant by "democracy" and "human rights," we will pay little heed to Pravda's solemn denunciations of racism in the United States or state terror in its client regimes, even less to protestation of noble motives. Far more instructive is the state of affairs in the "people's democracies" of Eastern Europe.

The point is elementary and applies to the self-designated "gatekeeper and model" as well. Latin America is the obvious testing ground, particularly the Central America-Caribbean region. Here Washington has faced few external challenges for almost a century, so the guiding principles of policy and of today's neoliberal "Washington consensus," are revealed most clearly when we examine the state of the region and how that came about. Washington's "crusade for democracy," as it is called, was waged with particular fervor during the Reagan years, with Latin America the chosen terrain. The results are commonly offered as a prime illustration of how the U.S. became "the inspiration for the triumph of democracy in our time," to quote the editors of the leading intellectual journal of American liberalism. The author, Sanford Lakoff, singles out the "historic North American Free Trade Agreement (NAFTA)" as a potential instrument of democratization. In the region of traditional U.S. influence, he writes, the countries are moving towards democracy, having "survived military intervention" and "vicious civil war."

The primary "barriers to implementation" of democracy, Lakoff suggests, are the "vested interests" that seek to protect "domestic markets" —that is, to prevent foreign (mainly U.S.) corporations from gaining even greater control over the society. We are to understand, then, that democracy is enhanced as significant decision-making shifts even more into the hands of unaccountable private tyrannies, mostly foreign-based. Meanwhile, the public arena is to shrink still further as the state is "minimized" in accordance with the neoliberal "political and economic principles" that have emerged triumphant. A study of the World Bank points out that the new orthodoxy represents "a dramatic shift away from a pluralist, participatory ideal of politics and towards an authoritarian and technocratic ideal," one that is very much in accord with leading elements of 20th century liberal and progressive thought, and in another variant, the Leninist model. The two are more similar than often recognized. Thinking through the tacit reasoning, we gain some useful insight into the concepts of democracy and markets, in the operative sense.

Lakoff does not look into the "revival of democracy" in Latin America, but he does cite a scholarly source that includes a contribution on Washington's crusade in the 1980s. The author is Thomas Carothers, who combines scholarship with an "insider's perspective," having worked on "democracy enhancement" programs in Reagan's State Department. Carothers regards Washington's "impulse to promote democracy" as "sincere," but largely a failure. Furthermore, the failure was systematic: where Washington's influence was least, in South America, there was real progress towards democracy, which the Reagan administration generally opposed, later taking credit for it when the process proved irresistible. Where Washington's influence was greatest, progress was least. Where it occurred, the U.S. role was marginal or negative. His general conclusion is that the U.S. sought to maintain "the basic order of...quite undemocratic societies" and to avoid "populist- based change," "inevitably [seeking] only limited, top-down forms of democratic change that did not risk upsetting the traditional structures of power with which the United States has long been allied."

The last phrase requires a gloss. The term "United States" is conventionally used to refer to structures of power within the United States. The "national interest" is the interest of these groups, which correlates only weakly with interests of the general population. So the conclusion is that Washington sought top-down forms of democracy that did not upset traditional structures of power with which the structures of power in the United States have long been allied.

To appreciate the significance of the fact, it is necessary to examine more closely the nature of parliamentary democracies. The United States is the most important case, not only because of its power, but because of its stable and long-standing democratic institutions. Furthermore, the United States was about as close to a model as one can find. America can be "as happy as she pleases," Thomas Paine remarked in 1776: "she has a blank sheet to write upon. The indigenous societies were largely eliminated. There is little residue of earlier European structures, one rea-

> Madison declared, "to protect the minority of the opulent against the majority." To achieve this goal, political power must rest in the hands of "the wealth of the nation," men who would "sympathize sufficiently" with property rights and "be safe depositories of power over them"

son for the relative weakness of the social contract and of support systems, which often had their roots in pre-capitalist institutions. And to an unusual extent, the socio-political order was consciously designed. In studying history, one cannot construct experiments, but the U.S. is as close to the "ideal case" of state capitalist democracy as can be found.

Furthermore, the leading framer of the constitutional system was an astute and lucid political thinker, James Madison, whose views largely prevailed. In the debates on the Constitution, Madison pointed out that in England, if elections "were open to all classes of people, the property of landed proprietors would be insecure. An agrarian law would soon take place," giving land to the landless. The system that he and his associates were designing must prevent such injustice, he urged, and "secure the permanent interests of the country," which are property rights. It is the responsibility of government, Madison declared, "to protect the minority of the opulent against the majority." To achieve this goal, political power must rest in the hands of "the wealth of the nation," men who would "sympathize sufficiently" with property rights and "be safe depositories of power over them," while the rest are marginalized and fragmented, offered only imited public participation in the political arena.

Among Madisonian scholars, there is a consensus that "The Constitution was intrinsically an aristocratic document designed to check the democratic tendencies of the period," delivering power to a "better sort" of people and excluding "those who were not rich, well born, or prominent from exercising political power."

These conclusions are often qualified by the observation that Madison, and the constitutional system generally, sought to balance the rights of persons against the rights of property. But the formulation is misleading. Property has no rights.

In both principle and practice, the phrase "rights of property" means the right to property, typically material property, a personal right which must be privileged above all others and is crucially different from others, in that one person's possession of such rights deprives another of them. When the facts are stated clearly, we can appreciate the force of the doctrine that "the people who own the country ought to govern it," "one of [the] favorite maxims" of Madison's influential colleague John Jay, his biographer observes.

One may argue, as some historians do, that these principles lost their force as the national territory was conquered and settled, the native population driven out or exterminated. Whatever one's assessment of those years, by the late 19th century the founding doctrines took on a new and much more oppressive form.

But the growth of the industrial economy, and the rise of corporate forms of economic enterprise, led to a completely new meaning of the term. In a current official document, "Person is broadly defined to include any individual, branch, partnership, associated group, association, estate, trust, corporation or other organization (whether or not organized under the laws of any State), or any government entity," a concept that doubtless would have shocked Madison and others with intellectual roots in the Enlightenment and classical liberalism—pre-capitalist, and anti-capitalist in spirit.

These radical changes in the conception of human rights and democracy were not introduced primarily by legislation, but by judicial decisions and intellectual commentary. Corporations, which previously had been considered artificial entities with no rights, were accorded all the rights of persons and, far more, since they are "immortal persons," and "persons" of extraordinary wealth and power. Furthermore, they were no longer bound to the specific purposes designated by state charter, but could act as they chose, with few constraints. The intellectual backgrounds for granting such extraordinary rights to "collectivist legal entities" lie in neo-He-

gelian doctrines that also underlie Bolshevism and fascism—the idea that organic entities have rights over and above those of persons. Conservative legal scholars bitterly opposed these innovations, recognizing that they undermine the traditional idea that rights inhere in individuals, and undermine market principles as well. But the new forms of authoritarian rule were institutionalized and along with them, the legitimation of wage labor, which was considered hardly better than slavery in mainstream American thought through much of the 19th century, not only by the rising labor movement, but by such figures as Abraham Lincoln, the Republican Party, and the establishment media.

These are topics with enormous implications for understanding the nature of market democracy. The material and ideological outcome helps explain the understanding that "democracy" abroad must reflect the model sought at home: "top-down" forms of control, with the public kept to a "spectator" role, not participating in the arena of decision-making, which must exclude these "ignorant and meddlesome outsiders," according to the mainstream of modern democratic theory. I happen to be quoting the essays on democracy by Walter Lippmann, one of the most respected American public intellectuals and journalists of the century. But the general ideas are standard and have solid roots in the constitutional tradition, radically modified in the new era of collectivist legal entities.

Returning to the "victory of democracy" under U.S. guidance, neither Lakoff nor Carothers asks how Washington maintained the traditional power structure of highly undemocratic societies. Their topic is not the terrorist wars that left tens of thousands of tortured and mutilated corpses, millions of refugees, and devastation perhaps beyond recovery—in large measure wars against the Church, which became an enemy when it adopted "the preferential option for the poor," trying to help suffering people to attain some measure of justice and democratic rights. It is more than symbolic that the terrible decade of the 1980s opened with the murder of an Archbishop who had become "a voice for the voiceless," and closed with the assassination of six leading Jesuit intellectuals who had chosen the same path, in each case by terrorist forces armed and trained by the victors of the "crusade for democracy." One should take careful note of the fact that the leading Central American dissident intellectuals were doubly assassinated: both murdered and silenced. Their words, indeed their very existence, are scarcely known in the United States, unlike dissidents in enemy states, who are greatly honored and admired; another cultural universal, I presume.

Such matters do not enter history as recounted by the victims. In Lakoff's study, which is not untypical in this regard, what survives are references to "military intervention" and "civil wars," with no external factor identified. These matters will not so quickly be put aside, however, by those who seek a better grasp of the principles that are to shape the future, if the structures of power have their way.

Particularly revealing is Lakoff's description of Nicaragua, again standard: "a civil war was ended following a democratic election and a difficult effort is underway to create a more prosperous and self-governing society." In the real world, the superpower attacking Nicaragua escalated its assault on the country's first democratic election of 1984, which was closely monitored and recognized as legitimate by the professional association of Latin American scholars (LASA), Irish and British Parliamentary delegations, and others, including a hostile Dutch government delegation that was remarkably supportive of Reaganite atrocities, as well as the leading figure of Central American democracy, Jose Figueres of Costa Rica, also critical observer, though regarding the elections as legitimate in this "invaded country," and calling on Washington to allow the Sandinistas "to finish what they started in peace—they deserve it."

The U.S. strongly opposed the holding of the elections and sought to undermine them, concerned that democratic elections might interfere with its terrorist war. But that concern was put to rest by the good behavior of the doctrinal system, which barred the reports with remarkable efficiency, reflexively adopting the state propaganda line that the elections were a meaningless fraud.

Overlooked as well is the fact that, as the next election approached on schedule, Washington left no doubt that unless the results came out the right way, Nicaraguans would continue to endure the illegal economic warfare and "unlawful use of force" that the World Court had condemned and ordered terminated, of course in vain. This time the outcome was acceptable and hailed in the U.S. with an outburst of exuberance that is highly informative. At the outer limits of critical independence, columnist Anthony Lewis of the *New York Times* was overcome with admiration for Washington's "experiment in peace and democracy," which showed that "we live in a romantic age."

The experimental methods were no secret. Thus *Time* magazine, joining in the celebration as "democracy burst forth" in Nicaragua, outlined them frankly: to "wreck the economy and prosecute a long and deadly proxy war until the exhausted natives overthrow the unwanted government themselves," with a cost to us that is "minimal," leaving the victim "with wrecked bridges, sabotaged power stations, and ruined farms," and providing Washington's candidate with "a winning issue," ending the "impoverishment of the people of Nicaragua," not to speak of the continuing terror, better left unmentioned. The methods of this "romantic age," and the reaction to them in enlightened circles, tell us more about the demo-

> One should take careful note of the fact that the leading Central American dissident intellectuals were doubly assassinated, both murdered and silenced. Their words, indeed their very existence, are scarcely known in the United States, unlike dissidents in enemy states, who are greatly honored and admired—another cultural universal, I presume

cratic principles that have emerged victorious. They also shed some light on why it is such a "difficult effort" to "create a more prosperous and self-governing society" in Nicaragua. It is true that the effort is now underway and is meeting with some success for a privileged minority, while most of the population faces social and economic disaster, all in the familiar pattern of Western dependencies.

We learn more about the victorious principles by recalling that these same representative figures of liberal intellectual life had urged that Washington's wars must be waged mercilessly, with military support for "Latin-style fascists...regardless of how many are murdered," because "there are higher American priorities than Salvadoran human rights." Elaborating, editor Michael Kinsley, who represented "the left" in mainstream commentary and TV debate, cautioned against unthinking criticism of Washington's official policy of attacking undefended civilian targets. Such international terrorist operations cause "vast civilian suffering," he acknowledged, but they may be "perfectly legitimate" if "cost-benefit analysis" shows that "the amount of blood and misery that will be poured in" yields "democracy," as the world rulers define it. Enlightened opinion insists that terror is not a value in itself, but must meet the pragmatic criterion. Kinsley later observed that the desired ends had been achieved: "impoverishing the people of Nicaragua was precisely the point of the contra war and the parallel policy of economic embargo and veto of international development loans," which "wreck[ed] the economy" and "creat[ed] the economic disaster [that] was probably the victorious opposition's best election issue." He then joined in welcoming the "triumph of democracy" in the "free election" of 1990. Client states enjoy similar privileges. Thus, commenting on yet another of Israel's attacks on Lebanon, foreign editor H.D.S.

> In response to John F. Kennedy's efforts to organize collective action against Cuba in 1961, a Mexican diplomat explained that Mexico could not go along because "If we publicly declare that Cuba is a threat to our security, forty million Mexicans will die laughing"

Greenway of the *Boston Globe*, who had graphically reported the first major invasion 15 years earlier, commented that "If shelling Lebanese villages, even at the cost of lives, and driving civilian refugees north would secure Israel's border, weaken Hezbollah, and promote peace, I would say go to it, as would many Arabs and Israelis. But history has not been kind to Israeli adventures in Lebanon. They have solved very little and have almost always caused more problems." By the pragmatic criterion, then, the murder of many civilians, expulsion of hundreds of thousand of refugees, and devastation of southern Lebanon is a dubious proposition.

Also revealing was the reaction to periodic Reagan administration allegations about Nicaraguan plans to obtain jet interceptors from the Soviet Union (the U.S. having coerced its allies into refusing to sell them). Hawks demanded that Nicaragua be bombed at once. Doves countered that the charges must first be verified, but if they were, the U.S. would have to bomb Nicaragua. Sane observers understood why Nicaragua might want jet interceptors—to protect its territory from CIA overflights that were supplying the U.S. proxy forces and providing them with up-to-the-minute information so that they could follow the directive to attack undefended "soft targets." The tacit assumption is that no country has a right to defend civilians from U.S. attack. The doctrine, which reigned unchallenged, is an interesting one. It might be illuminating to seek counterparts elsewhere.

The pretext for Washington's terrorist wars was self-defense, the standard official justification for just about any monstrous act, even the Nazi Holocaust. Indeed, Ronald Reagan, finding "that the policies and actions of the Government of Nicaragua constitute an unusual and extraordinary threat to the national security and foreign policy of the United States," declared "a national emergency to deal with that threat," arousing no

THE CHOMSKY Z COLLECTION

ridicule. Others react differently. In response to John F. Kennedy's efforts to organize collective action against Cuba in 1961, a Mexican diplomat explained that Mexico could not go along because "If we publicly declare that Cuba is a threat to our security, forty million Mexicans will die laughing." Enlightened opinion in the West takes a more sober view of the extraordinary threat to national security. By similar logic, the USSR had every right to attack Denmark, a far greater threat to its security, and surely Poland and Hungary when they took steps towards independence. The fact that such pleas can regularly be put forth is again an interesting comment on the intellectual culture of the victors and another indication of what lies ahead.

The substance of the Cold War pretexts is greatly illuminated by the case of Cuba, as are the real operative principles. These have emerged with much clarity once again in the past few weeks, with Washington's refusal to accept World Trade Organization adjudication of a European Union challenge to its embargo, which is unique in its severity and had already been condemned as a violation of international law by the Organization of American States and repeatedly by the United Nations, with near unanimity, more recently extended to severe penalties for third parties that disobey Washington's edicts, yet another violation of international law and trade agreements.

The official response of the Clinton administration, as reported by the Newspaper of Record, is that "Europe is challenging 'three decades of American Cuba policy that goes back to the Kennedy Administration,' and is aimed entirely at forcing a change of government in Havana." The Administration also declared that the WTO "has no competence to proceed" on an issue of American national security, and cannot "force the U.S. to change its laws."

The reasoning with regard to the WTO is reminiscent of the official U.S. grounds for dismissing World Court adjudication of Nicaragua's charges. In both cases, the U.S. rejected jurisdiction on the plausible assumption that rulings would be against the U.S. By simple logic, then, neither is a proper forum. The State Department Legal Adviser explained that when the U.S. accepted World Court jurisdiction in the 1940s, most members of the UN "were aligned with the United States and shared its views regarding world order." But now "A great many of these cannot be counted on to share our view of the original constitutional conception of the UN Charter" and "This same majority often opposes the United States on important international questions." Lacking a guarantee that it will get its way, the U.S. must now "reserve to ourselves the power to determine whether the Court has jurisdiction over us in a particular case," on the principle that "the United States does not accept compulsory jurisdiction over any dispute involving matters essentially within the domestic jurisdiction of the United States, as determined by the United States." The "domestic matters" in question were the U.S. attack against Nicaragua.

The media, along with intellectual opinion generally, agreed that the Court discredited itself by ruling against the United States. The crucial parts of its decision were not reported, including its determination that all U.S. aid to the contras is military and not humanitarian. It remained "humanitarian aid" across the spectrum of respectable opinion until Washington's terror, economic warfare, and subversion of diplomacy brought about the "victory for U.S. fair play."

Returning to the WTO case, we need not tarry on the allegation that the existence of the United States is at stake in the strangulation of the Cuban economy. More interesting is the thesis that the U.S. has every right to overthrow another government, in this case, by aggression, large-scale terror over many years, and economic strangulation. Accordingly, international law and trade agreements are irrelevant. The fundamental principles of world order that have emerged victorious again resound, loud and clear.

The Clinton administration declarations passed without challenge, though they were criticized on narrower grounds by historian Arthur Schlesinger. Writing "as one involved in the

Kennedy administration's Cuban policy," Schlesinger maintained that the Clinton administration had misunderstood Kennedy's policies. The concern had been Cuba's "troublemaking in the hemisphere" and "the Soviet connection," Schlesinger explained. But these are now behind us, so the Clinton policies are an anachronism, though otherwise unobjectionable, we are to conclude. Schlesinger did not explain the meaning of the phrases "troublemaking in the hemisphere" and "the Soviet connection," but he has elsewhere, in secret.

Reporting to incoming President Kennedy on the conclusions of a Latin American Mission in early 1961, Schlesinger spelled out the problem of Castro's "troublemaking"—what the Clinton administration calls Cuba's effort "to destabilize large parts of Latin America. It is "the spread of the Castro idea of taking matters into one's own hands," a serious problem, Schlesinger added, when "The distribution of land and other forms of national wealth greatly favors the propertied classes...[and] the poor and underprivileged, stimulated by the example of the Cuban revolution, are now demanding opportunities for a decent living." Schlesinger also explained the threat of the "Soviet connection": "Meanwhile, the Soviet Union hovers in the wings, flourishing large development loans, and presenting itself as the model for achieving modernization in a single generation." The "Soviet connection" was perceived in a similar light far more broadly in Washington and London from the origins of the Cold War 80 years ago.

With these (secret) explanations of Castro's "destabilization" and "troublemaking in the hemisphere," and of the "Soviet connection," we come closer to understanding the reality of the Cold War. It should come as no surprise that basic policies persist with the Cold War a fading memory, just as they were carried out before the Bolshevik Revolution: the brutal and destructive invasion of Haiti and the Dominican Republic, to mention one illustration of "global meliorism" —under the banner of "Wilsonian idealism." It should be added that the policy of overthrowing

the government of Cuba antedates the Kennedy administration. Castro took power in January 1959. By June, the Eisenhower administration had determined that his government must be overthrown. Terrorist attacks from U.S. bases began shortly after. The formal decision to overthrow Castro in favor of a regime "more devoted to the true interests of the Cuban people and more acceptable to the U.S." was taken in secret in March 1960, with the addendum that the operation must be carried out "in such a manner as to avoid any appearance of U.S. intervention" because of the expected reaction in Latin America and the need to ease the burden on doctrinal managers at home. At the time, the "Soviet connection" and "troublemaking in the hemisphere" were nil, apart from the Schlesingerian version. The CIA estimated that the Castro government enjoyed popular support (the Clinton administration has similar evidence today). The Kennedy administration also recognized that its efforts violated international law and the Charters of the UN and OAS, but such issues were dismissed without discussion, the declassified record reveals

Latin America As Chosen Terrain

Washington's "crusade for democracy" was waged with particular fervor during the Reagan years, with Latin America the chosen terrain. The results are commonly offered as a prime illustration of how the U.S. became "the inspiration for the triumph of democracy in our time." The most recent scholarly study of democracy describes "the revival of democracy in Latin America" as impressive, but not unprob- lematic. The barriers to implementation remain formidable, but can perhaps be overcome through closer integration with the United States. The author, Sanford Lakoff, singles out the "historic North American Free Trade Agreement (NAFTA)" as a potential instrument of democratization, alongside of other examples of the kind already discussed. A closer look at NAFTA is informative.

The NAFTA agreement was rammed through Congress over strenuous popular opposition but with overwhelming support from the business world and the media, which were full of joyous promises of benefits for all concerned, also confidently predicted by the U.S. International Trade Commission and leading economists equipped with the most up-to-date models (which had failed miserably to predict the consequences of the U.S.-Canada Free Trade Agreement, but were somehow going to work in this case).

Completely suppressed was the careful analysis by the Office of Technology Assessment (the research bureau of Congress), which concluded that the planned version of NAFTA would harm most of the population of North America, proposing modifications that could render the agreement beneficial beyond small circles of investment and finance. Still more instructive was the suppression of the official position of the U.S. labor movement.

Meanwhile labor was bitterly condemned for its "backward, unenlightened" perspective and "crude threatening tactics," motivated by "fear of change and fear of foreigners"; I am again sampling only from the far left of the spectrum, in this case, Anthony Lewis. The charges were demonstrably false, but they were the only word that reached the public in this inspiring exercise of democracy. Further details are most illuminating and reviewed in the dissident literature at the time and since, but kept from the public eye. By now, the tales about the wonders of NAFTA have quietly been shelved, as the facts have been coming in. One hears no more about the hundreds of thousands of new jobs and other great benefits in store for the people of the three countries. These good tidings have been replaced by the distinctly benign economic viewpoint—the "expert's view"—that NAFTA had no significant effects. The *Wall Street Journal* reports that "Administration officials feel frustrated by their inability to convince voters that the threat doesn't hurt them" and that job loss is "much less than predicted by Ross Perot," who was allowed into mainstream discussion (unlike the OTA, the Labor movement, economists who didn't echo the Party Line, and dissident analysts) because his claims were sometimes extreme and easily ridiculed. "It's hard to fight the critics" by telling the truth—that the trade pact "hasn't really done anything," an Administration official observes sadly. Forgotten is what 'the truth' was going to be when the impressive exercise in democracy was roaring full steam ahead. While the experts have downgraded NAFTA to "no significant effects," dispatching the earlier "experts view" to the memory hole, a less than 'distinctly benign economic viewpoint comes into focus if the national interest is widened in scope to include the general population.

Testifying before the Senate Banking Committee in February 1997, Federal Reserve Board Chair Alan Greenspan was highly optimistic about "sustainable economic expansion" thanks to atypical restraint on compensation increases [which] appears to be mainly the consequence of greater worker insecurity—an obvious desideratum for a just society. The February 1997 Economic Report of the President, taking pride in the Administration's achievements, refers more obliquely to changes in labor market institutions and practices as a factor in the "significant wage restraint" that bolsters the economy.

One reason for these benign changes is spelled out in a study commissioned by the NAFTA Labor Secretariat on the effects of the sudden closing of the plant on the principle of freedom of association and the right of workers to organize in the three countries. The study was carried out under NAFTA rules in response to a complaint by telecommunications workers on illegal labor practices by Sprint. The complaint was upheld by the U.S. National Labor Relations Board, which ordered trivial penalties after years of delay, the standard procedure. The NAFTA study, by Cornell University Labor economist Kate Bronfenbrenner, was authorized for release by Canada and Mexico, but delayed by the Clinton administration. It reveals a significant impact of NAFTA on strike-breaking. About half of union organizing efforts are disrupted by employer threats to transfer production abroad; for example, by placing signs reading "Mexico Transfer Job" in front of a plant where there is an organizing drive. The threats are not idle: when such organizing drives nevertheless succeed, employers close the plant in whole or in part at triple the pre-NAFTA rate (about 15 percent of the time). Plant-closing threats are almost twice as high in more mobile industries (manufacturing vs. construction).

Changes in Labor Market Institutions

These and other practices reported in the study are illegal, but that is a technicality, on a par with violations of international law and trade agreements when outcomes are unacceptable. The Reagan administration had made it clear to the business world that their illegal anti-union activities would not be hampered by the criminal state, and successors have kept to this stand. There has been a substantial effect on destruction of unions—or in more polite words, "changes in labor market institutions and practices" that contribute to "significant wage restraint" within an economic model offered with great pride to a backward world that has not yet grasped the victorious principles that are to lead the way to freedom and justice.

What was reported all along outside the mainstream media about the goals of NAFTA is also now quietly conceded. The real goal was to lock Mexico in to the reforms that had made it an "economic miracle," in the technical sense of this term—a miracle for U.S. investors and the Mexican rich, while the population sank into misery. The Clinton administration "forgot that the underlying purpose of NAFTA was not to promote trade but to cement Mexico's economic reforms," *Newsweek* correspondent Marc Levinson loftily declares, failing only to add that the contrary was loudly proclaimed to ensure the passage of NAFTA while critics who pointed out this underlying purpose were efficiently excluded

from the free market of ideas by its owners. Perhaps some day the reasons will be conceded too. "Locking Mexico in" to these reforms, it was hoped, would deflect the danger detected by a Latin America Strategy Development Workshop in Washington in September 1990. It concluded that relations with the brutal Mexican dictatorship were fine, though there was a potential problem since a "democracy opening" in Mexico could test the special relationship by bringing into office a government more interested in challenging the U.S. on economic and nationalist grounds—no longer a serious problem now that Mexico is "locked into the reforms" by treaty.

The threat is democracy, at home and abroad, as the chosen example again illustrates. Democracy is permissible, even welcome, but again, as judged by outcome, not process. NAFTA was considered to be an effective device to diminish the threat of democracy. It was implemented at home by effective subversion of the democratic process, and in Mexico by force, again over vain public protest. The results are now presented as a hopeful instrument to bring American-style democracy to benighted Mexicans. A cynical observer aware of the facts might agree.

Once again, the chosen illustrations of the triumph of democracy are natural ones and are interesting and revealing as well, though not quite in the intended manner.

Markets are always a social construction, and in the specific form being crafted by current social policy they should serve to restrict functioning democracy, as in the case of NAFTA, the WTO agreements, and other instruments that may lie ahead. One case that merits close attention is the Multilateral Agreement on Investment (MAI) that is now being forged by the OECD, the rich men's club, and the WTO (where it is the MIA). The apparent hope is that the agreement will be adopted without public awareness, as was the initial intention for NAFTA, not quite achieved, though the "information system" managed to keep the basic story under wraps. If the plans outlined in draft texts are implemented, the whole world may be "locked into" treaty arrangements that provide transnational corporations with still more powerful weapons to restrict the arena of democratic politics, leaving policy largely in the hands of huge private tyrannies that have ample means of market interference as well. The efforts may be blocked at the WTO because of the strong protests of the "developing countries," notably India and Malaysia, which are not eager to become wholly-owned subsidiaries of great foreign enterprises. But the OECD version may fare better, to be presented to the rest of the world as a fait accompli, with the obvious consequences. All of this proceeds in impressive secrecy, so far. The announcement of the Clinton Doctrine was accompanied by a prize example to illustrate the victorious principles: what the Administration had achieved in Haiti.

Since this is again offered as the strongest case, it would be appropriate to look at it. True, Haiti's elected president was allowed to return, but only after the popular organizations had been subjected to three years of terror by forces that retained close connections to Washington throughout; the Clinton administration still refuses to turn over to Haiti 160,000 pages of documents on state terror seized by U.S. military forces—"to avoid embarrassing revelations" about U.S. government involvement with the coup regime, according to Human Rights Watch. It was also necessary to put President Aristide through "a crash course in democracy and capitalism," as his leading supporter in Washington described the process of civilizing the troublesome priest.

As a condition on his return, Aristide was compelled to accept an economic program that directs the policies of the Haitian government to the needs of civil society, especially the private sector, both national and foreign. U.S. investors are designated to be the core of Haitian civil society, along with wealthy Haitians who backed the military coup, but not the Haitian peasants and slum-dwellers who organized a civil society so lively and vibrant that they were even able to elect their own president against overwhelming

odds, eliciting instant U.S. hostility and efforts to subvert Haiti's first democratic regime.

The unacceptable acts of the "ignorant and meddlesome outsiders" in Haiti were reversed by violence, with direct U.S. complicity, not only through contacts with the state terrorists in charge. The Organization of American States declared an embargo. The Bush and Clinton administrations undermined it from the start by exempting U.S. firms, and also by secretly authorizing the Texaco Oil Company to supply the coup regime and its wealthy supporters in violation of the official sanctions, a crucial fact that was prominently revealed the day before U.S. troops landed to "restore democracy," but has yet to reach the public, and is an unlikely candidate for the historical record.

Now democracy has been restored. The new government has been forced to abandon the democratic and reformist programs that scandalized Washington, and to follow the policies of Washington's candidate in the 1990 election, in which he received 14 percent of the vote.

Haitians seem to understand the lessons, even if doctrinal managers in the West prefer a different picture. Parliamentary elections in April 1997 brought forth "a dismal 5 percent" of voters, the press reported, thus raising the question "Did Haiti Fail U.S. Hope?" We have sacrificed so much to bring them democracy, but they are ungrateful and unworthy. One can see why realists urge that we stay aloof from crusades of "global meliorism." Similar attitudes hold throughout the hemisphere. Polls show that in Central America, politics elicits "boredom, distrust and indifference in proportions far outdistancing interest or enthusiasm among an apathetic public...which feels itself a spectator in its democratic system and has general pessimism about the future." The first Latin America survey, sponsored by the European Union, found much the same, "The survey's most alarming message," the Brazilian coordinator commented, was 'the popular perception that only the elite had benefited from the transition to democracy." Latin American scholars observe that the recent wave of democratization coincided with neo-liberal economic reforms, which have been very harmful for most people, leading to a cynical appraisal of formal democratic procedures. The introduction of similar programs in the richest country in the world has had similar effects. By the early 1990s, after 15 years of a domestic version of structural adjustment, over 80 percent of the U.S. population had come to regard the democratic system as a sham, with business far too powerful, and the economy as "inherently unfair." These are natural consequences of the specific design of market democracy under business rule. Let us return to the prevailing doctrine that "America's victory in the Cold War" was a victory for democracy and the free market.

With regard to democracy, the doctrine is partially true, though we have to understand what is meant by democracy—top-down control "to protect the minority of the opulent against the majority." What about the free market? Here too, we find that doctrine is far removed from reality, as several examples have illustrated.

Consider again the case of NAFTA, an agreement intended to lock Mexico into an an economic discipline that protects investors from the danger of a democracy opening. Its provisions tell us more about the economic principles that have emerged victorious. It is not a "free trade agreement," rather, it is highly protectionist, designed to impede East Asian and European competitors. Furthermore, it shares with the global agreements such anti-market principles as intellectual property rights restrictions of a sort rich societies never accepted during their period of development, but now intend to use to protect home-based corporations and to destroy the pharmaceutical industry in poorer countries, for example—and, incidentally, to block technological innovations, such as improved production processes for patented products. Progress is no more a desideratum than markets, unless it yields benefits for those who count. There are also questions about the nature of trade.

Over half of U.S. trade with Mexico is reported to consist of intrafirm transactions, up about 15 percent since NAFTA. For example, already a decade ago, mostly U.S.-owned plants in Northern Mexico employing few workers and with virtually no linkages to the Mexican economy produced more than one-third of engine blocks used in U.S. cars and three-fourths of other essential components. The post-NAFTA collapse of the Mexican economy in 1994, exempting only the very rich and U.S. investors (protected by U.S. government bailouts), led to an increase of U.S.-Mexico trade as the new crisis, driving the population to still deeper misery, "transformed Mexico into a cheap [i.e., even cheaper] source of manufactured goods, with industrial wages one-tenth of those in the U.S.," the business press reports.

Ten years ago, according to some specialists, half of U.S. trade worldwide consists of such centrally-managed transactions and much the same is true of other industrial powers, though one must treat with caution conclusions about institutions with limited public accountability. Some economists have plausibly described the world system as one of "corporate mercantilism," remote from the ideal of free trade. The OECD concludes that "Oligopolistic competition and strategic interaction among firms and governments rather than the invisible hand of market forces condition today's competitive advantage and international division of labor in high-technology industries," implicitly adopting a similar view.

Even the basic structure of the domestic economy violates the neoliberal principles that are hailed. The main theme of Alfred Chandler's standard work on U.S. business history is that "modern business enterprise took the place of market mechanisms in coordinating the activities of the economy and allocating its resources," handling many transactions internally, another large departure from market principles. There are many others. Consider, for example, the fate of Adam Smith's principle that free movement of people is an essential component of free trade —across borders, for example. When we move on to the world of transnational corporations, with strategic alliances and critical support from powerful states, the gap between doctrine and reality becomes substantial. Free market theory comes in two varieties: the official doctrine, and what we might call "really existing free market doctrine."

Market discipline is good for you, but I need the protection of the nanny state. The official doctrine is imposed on the defenseless, but it is "really existing doctrine" that has been adopted by the powerful since the days when Britain emerged as Europe's most advanced fiscal-military and developmental state, with sharp increases in taxation and efficient public administration as the state became "the largest single actor in the economy (historian John Brewer)" and its global expansion, establishing a model that has been followed to the present in the industrial world, surely by the United States, from its origins.

Britain did finally turn to liberal internationalism—in 1846, after 150 years of protectionism, violence, and state power had placed it far ahead of any competitor. But the turn to the market had significant reservations. Forty percent of British textiles continued to go to colonized India, and much the same was true of British exports generally. British steel was kept from U.S. markets by very high tariffs that enabled the United States to develop its own steel industry. But India and other colonies were still available, and remained so when British steel was priced out of international markets.

India is an instructive case as it produced as much iron as all of Europe in the late 18th century, and British engineers were studying more advanced Indian steel manufacturing techniques in 1820 to try to close "the technological gap." Bombay was producing locomotives at competitive levels when the railway boom began. But really existing free market doctrine destroyed these sectors of Indian industry just as it had destroyed textiles, ship-building, and other industries that were advanced by the standards of the day. The U.S. and Japan, in contrast, escaped European

> But really existing free market doctrine destroyed these sectors of Indian industry just as it had destroyed textiles, ship-building, and other industries that were advanced by the standards of the day

control and could adopt Britain's model of market interference. When Japanese competition proved to be too much to handle, England called off the game: the empire was effectively closed to Japanese exports, part of the background of World War II. Indian manufacturers asked for protection at the same time—but against England, not Japan. No such luck, under really existing free market doctrine.

With the abandonment of its restricted version of laissez-faire in the 1930s, the British government turned to more direct intervention into the domestic economy as well. Within a few years, machine tool output increased five times, along with a boom in chemicals, steel, aerospace, and a host of new industries, "an unsung new wave of industrial revolution," Will Hutton writes. State-controlled industry enabled Britain to outproduce Germany during the war, even to narrow the gap with the U.S., which was undergoing its own dramatic economic expansion as corporate managers took over the state-coordinated war-time economy.

A century after England turned to a form of liberal internationalism, the U.S. followed the same course. After 150 years of protectionism and violence, the U.S. had become by far the richest and most powerful country in the world, and like England before it, came to perceive the merits of a level playing field on which it could expect to crush any competitor. But like England, with crucial reservations.

One was that Washington used its power to bar independent development elsewhere, as England had done. In Latin America, Egypt, South Asia, and elsewhere, development was to be complementary, not competitive. There was also large-scale interference with trade. For example, Marshall Plan aid was tied to purchase of U.S. agricultural products, part of the reason why the U.S. share in world trade in grains increased from less than 10 percent before the war to more than half by 1950, while Argentine exports reduced by two-thirds. U.S. Food for Peace aid was also used both to subsidize U.S. agribusiness and shipping and to undercut foreign producers, among other measures to prevent independent development. The virtual destruction of Colombia's wheat growing by such means is one of the factors in the growth of the drug industry, which has been further accelerated throughout the Andean region by the neoliberal policies of the past few years.

Kenya's textile industry collapsed in 1994 when the Clinton administration imposed a quota, barring the path to development that has been followed by every industrial country, while African reformers are warned that they "must make more progress" in improving the conditions for business operations and "sealing in free-market reforms" with "'trade and investment policies" that meet the requirements of Western investors.

In December 1996 Washington barred exports of tomatoes from Mexico in violation of NAFTA and WTO rules (though not technically, because it was a sheer power play and did not require an official tariff), at a cost to Mexican producers of close to $1 billion annually. The official reason for this gift to Florida growers is that prices were "artificially suppressed by Mexican competition" and Mexican tomatoes were preferred by U.S. consumers. In other words, free market principles were working, but with the wrong outcome. These are only scattered illustrations.

High tech industry has always functioned by the same rules. A few weeks ago (September 29, 1997), an honest headline in the *Wall Street Journal* read: "In Effect, ITC's Steep Tariffs on Japan Protect US Makers of Supercomputers." The story reports the decision of the U.S. International Trade Commission to impose "steep antidumping duties on Japanese supercomputers," sending a clear message abroad—"foreign supercomputers, keep out." The ITC ruled that a proposed sale by Japan's NEC Corporation could damage U.S. industry, in particular Cray Research, the main U.S. manufacturer of supercomputers. Cray is called "private enterprise" as its technology has relied heavily on public subsidy

and its market has been the Pentagon and the Department of Energy, but profits and management are private. Japanese firms have yet to sell a single supercomputer to agencies funded by the U.S. government, while Japan is regularly bashed —accurately—for its efforts to protect its own industry and services. The whole farce is standard and natural under the rules of really existing free market capitalism. The biggest thug on the block basically does what he likes.

One revealing example is Haiti, along with Bengal, the world's richest colonial prize and the source of a good part of France's wealth, largely under U.S. control since Woodrow Wilson's Marines invaded 80 years ago, and by now such a catastrophe that it may scarcely be habitable in the not-too-distant future. In 1981, a USAID-World Bank development strategy was initiated, based on assembly plants and agroexport, shifting land from food for local consumption. USAID forecast "a historic change toward deeper market interdependence with the United States" in what would become "the Taiwan of the Caribbean." The World Bank concurred, offering the usual prescriptions for expansion of private enterprises and minimization of "social objectives," thus increasing inequality and poverty and reducing health and educational levels; it may be noted, for what it is worth, that these standard prescriptions are offered side-by-side with sermons on the need to reduce inequality and poverty and improve health and educational levels, while World Bank technical studies recognize that relative equality and high health and educational standards are crucial factors in economic growth.

In the Haitian case, the consequences were the usual ones: profits for U.S. manufacturers and the Haitian superrich, and a decline of 56 percent in Haitian wages through the 1980s—in short, an "economic miracle." Haiti remained Haiti, not Taiwan, which had followed a radically different course, as advisers must surely know. It was the effort of Haiti's first democratic government to alleviate the growing disaster that called forth Washington's hostility and the military coup and terror that followed. With democracy restored, USAID is withholding aid to ensure that cement and flour mills are privatized for the benefit of wealthy Haitians and foreign investors (Haitian civil society, according to the orders that accompanied the restoration of democracy), while barring expenditures for health and education. Agribusiness receives ample funding, but no resources are made available for peasant agriculture and handicrafts, which provide the income of the overwhelming majority of the population.

Foreign-owned assembly plants that employ workers (mostly women) at well below subsistence pay under horrendous working conditions benefit from cheap electricity, subsidized by the generous supervisor. But for the Haitian poor—the general population—there can be no subsidies for electricity, fuel, water, or food. These are prohibited by IMF rules on the principled grounds that they constitute price control. Before the reforms were instituted, local rice production supplied virtually all domestic needs, with important linkages to the domestic economy. Thanks to one-sided "liberalization," it now provides only 50 percent, with the predictable effects on the economy. The liberalization is, crucially, one-sided. Haiti must reform, eliminating tariffs in accord with the stern principles of economic science—which, by some miracle of logic, exempts U.S. agribusiness. It continues to receive huge public subsidies, increased by the Reagan administration to the point where they provided 40 percent of growers' gross incomes by 1987.

The natural consequences are understood and intended. A 1995 USAID report observes that the "export-driven trade and investment policy" that Washington mandates will "relentlessly squeeze the domestic rice farmer," who will be forced to turn to the more rational pursuit of agroexport for the benefit of U.S. investors, in accord with the principles of rational expecta- tions theory. By such methods, the most impoverished country in the hemisphere has been turned into a leading purchaser of U.S.-produced rice, enriching publicly-subsidized U.S. enterprises. Those lucky enough to have received a good Western education can doubtless explain that the benefits will trickle down to Haitian peasants and slumdwellers—ultimately. Africans may choose to follow a similar path, as currently advised by the leaders of "global meliorism" and local elites, and perhaps may see no choice under existing circumstances—questionable judgment, I suspect. But if they do, it should be with eyes open.

The last example illustrates the most important departures from official free trade doctrine, more significant in the modern era than protectionism, which was far from the most radical interference with the doctrine in earlier periods, either, though it is the one usually studied under the conventional breakdown of disciplines, which makes its own useful contribution to disguising social and political realities. To mention one obvious example, the industrial revolution depended on cheap cotton, just as the golden age of contemporary capitalism has depended on cheap energy, but the methods for keeping the crucial commodities cheap and available, which hardly conform to market principles, do not fall within the professional discipline of economics.

After World War II, the U.S. broke from its protectionist tradition and called for liberalization of the international economy, recognizing that the playing field was appropriately tilted—sharply in favor of U.S. firms. But business leaders intended to take no chances, as noted, and insisted on crucial reservations. One had to do with public subsidy.

It is a fundamental component of free trade theory that public subsidies are not allowed. It was, however, widely understood that high tech industry "cannot satisfactorily exist in a pure, competitive, unsubsidized, 'free enterprise economy'"and that "the government is their only possible savior," as the business press put the matter 50 years ago. The Pentagon system was quickly selected as the most efficient means to transfer public funds to private pockets. It is easy to sell to the public under the guise of security, and does not have the unwelcome side effects of social spending, which tends to be redistributive and democratizing, and is not a direct subsidy to corporate power. So the system has functioned to the present, with variations as needed. The peak of market interference was reached by the Reaganites, who preached the gospel of market discipline to the poor at home and abroad (Reaganite rugged individualism) while raising protection for U.S. manufacturers to postwar heights and conducting a "defense buildup [that] actually pushed military R&D spending (in constant dollars) past the record levels of the mid-1960s," Stuart Leslie notes.

The public was terrified with foreign threats, but the message to the business world was plain and clear. As soon as the Cold War ended, with the fall of the Berlin Wall in 1989, Washington informed Congress (and the business world) that military spending must continue with little change, in part to protect the "defense industrial base"—virtually all of high tech industry—offering dual-use technology to its beneficiaries to enable them to dominate commercial markets and enrich themselves at public expense.

All understand very well that free enterprise means that the public pays the costs and bears the risks if things go wrong; for example bank and corporate bailouts that have cost the public hundreds of billions of dollars in recent years. Profit is to be privatized, but cost and risk socialized, in really existing market systems. The centuries-old tale proceeds today without notable change, not only in the United States, of course. Another equally venerable tale is the refusal of the public to accept such outcomes.

Despite setbacks, popular struggles have made the world a far better place. There is no reason to doubt that the cycle can continue its generally upward course. Right now, popular movements are resilient and growing throughout the world, and can realistically aim for higher goals than seemed attainable not long ago. Skeptics who dismiss such thoughts as utopian and naive have only to cast their eyes on what has happened right here in South Africa in the last few years, an inspiring tribute to what the human spirit can achieve, and its limitless prospects—lessons that the world desperately needs to learn, and that should guide the next steps in the continuing struggle for justice and freedom here too, as the people of South Africa, fresh from one great victory, turn to the still more difficult tasks that lie ahead.

5.

Rogue States

Claiming the legal right to use unilateral force

The concept of "rogue state" plays a pre-eminent role today in policy planning and analysis. The current Iraq crisis is only the latest example. Washington and London declared Iraq a "rogue state," a threat to its neighbors and to the entire world, an "outlaw nation" led by a reincarnation of Hitler who must be contained by the guardians of world order, the United States and its British "junior partner"—to adopt the term ruefully employed by the British foreign office half a century ago. The concept merits a close look. But first, let's consider its application in the current crisis.

The most interesting feature of the debate over the Iraq crisis is that it never took place. True, many words flowed and there was dispute about how to proceed. But discussion kept within rigid bounds that excluded the obvious answer—the U.S. and UK should act in accord with their laws and treaty obligations.

The relevant legal framework is formulated in the Charter of the United Nations, a "solemn treaty" recognized as the foundation of international law and world order and under the U.S. Constitution, "the supreme law of the land." The Charter states that, "The Security Council shall determine the existence of any threat to the peace, breach of the peace, or act of aggression, and shall make recommendations, or decide what measures shall be taken in accordance with Articles 41 and 42," which detail the preferred "measures not involving the use of armed force" and permit the Security Council to take further action if it finds such measures inadequate. The only exception is Article 51, which permits the "right of individual or collective self-defense" against "armed attack...until the Security Council has taken the measures necessary to maintain international peace and security." Apart from these exceptions, member states "shall refrain in their international relations from the threat or use of force."

There are legitimate ways to react to the many threats to world peace. If Iraq's neighbors feel threatened, they can approach the Security Council to authorize appropriate measures to respond to the threat. If the U.S. and Britain feel threatened, they can do the same. But no state has the authority to make its own determinations on these mat-

From Z Magazine, April 1998

ters and to act as it chooses; the U.S. and UK would have no such authority even if their own hands were clean, hardly the case.

Outlaw states do not accept these conditions: Saddam's Iraq, for example, or the United States. Its position was forthrightly articulated by Secretary of State Madeleine Albright, then UN Ambassador, when she informed the Security Council during an earlier U.S. confrontation with Iraq that the U.S. will act "multilaterally when we can and unilaterally as we must," because, "We recognize this area as vital to U.S. national interests" and therefore accept no external constraints. Albright reiterated that stand when UN Secretary-General Kofi Annan undertook his February 1998 diplomatic mission: "We wish him well," she stated, "and when he comes back we will see what he has brought and how it fits with our national interest," which will determine how we respond.

When Annan announced that an agreement had been reached, Albright repeated the doctrine: "It is possible that he will come with something we don't like, in which case we will pursue our national interest." President Clinton announced that if Iraq fails the test of conformity (as determined by Washington), "everyone would understand that then the United States and, hopefully, all of our allies would have the unilateral right to respond at a time, place and manner of our own choosing," in the manner of other violent and lawless states.

The Security Council unanimously endorsed Annan's agreement, rejecting U.S./UK demands that it authorize their use of force in the event of non-compliance. The resolution warned of "severest consequences," but with no further specification. In the crucial final paragraph, the Council "decides, in accordance with its responsibilities under the Charter, to remain actively seized of the matter, in order to ensure implementation of this resolution and to ensure peace and security in the area." The Council, no one else, in accordance with the Charter.

The facts were clear and unambiguous. Headlines read: "An Automatic Strike Isn't Endorsed"

(*Wall St. Journal*); "U.N. Rebuffs U.S. on threat to Iraq if it Breaks Pact" (*New York Times*), etc. Britain's UN Ambassador "privately assured his colleagues on the council that the resolution does not grant the United States and Britain an 'automatic trigger' to launch strikes against Iraq if it impedes" UN searches. "It has to be the Security Council who determines when to use armed force," the Ambassador of Costa Rica declared, expressing the position of the Security Council.

Washington's reaction was different. U.S. Ambassador Bill Richardson asserted that the agreement "did not preclude the unilateral use of force" and that the U.S. retains its legal right to attack Baghdad at will. State Department spokesperson James Rubin dismissed the wording of the resolution as "not as relevant as the kind of private discussions that we've had": "I am not saying that we don't care about that resolution," but "we've made clear that we don't see the need to return to the Security Council if there is a violation of the agreement."

The president stated that the resolution "provides authority to act" if the U.S. is dissatisfied with Iraqi compliance and his press secretary made clear that that means military action. "U.S Insists It Retains Right to Punish Iraq," the *New York Times* headline read, accurately. The U.S. has the unilateral right to use force at will, period.

Some felt that even this stand strayed too close to our solemn obligations under international and domestic law. Senate majority leader Trent Lott denounced the Administration for having "subcontracted" its foreign policy "to others"—to the UN Security Council. Senator John McCain warned that "the United States may be subordinating its power to the United Nations," an obligation only for law-abiding states. Senator John Kerry added that it would be "legitimate" for the U.S. to invade Iraq outright if Saddam "remains obdurate and in violation of the United Nations resolutions, and in a position of threat to the world community," whether the Security Council so determines or not. Such unilateral U.S. action would be "within the framework of international law," as Kerry conceives it. A liberal dove who reached national prominence as an opponent of the Vietnam War, Kerry explained that his current stand was consistent with his earlier views. Vietnam taught him that the force should be used only if the objective is "achievable and it meets the needs of your country." Saddam's invasion of Kuwait was wrong for one reason—it was not "achievable," as matters turned out.

At the liberal-dovish end of the spectrum, Annan's agreement was welcomed, but within the narrow framework that barred the central issues. In a typical reaction, the *Boston Globe* stated that had Saddam not backed down, "the United States would not only have been justified in attacking Iraq—it would have been irresponsible not to," with no further questions asked. The editors also called for "a universal consensus of opprobrium" against "weapons of mass destruction" as "the best chance the world has of keeping perverted science from inflicting hitherto unimagined harm." A sensible proposal. One can think of easy ways to start, without the threat of force, but these are not what are intended.

Political analyst William Pfaff deplored Washington's unwillingness to consult "theological or philosophical opinion," the views of Thomas Aquinas and Renaissance theologian Francisco Suarez—as "a part of the analytical community" in the U.S. and UK had done "during the 1950s and 1960s," seeking guidance from "philosophy and theology." But not the foundations of contemporary international and domestic law, which are explicit, though irrelevant to the intellectual culture.

Another liberal analyst urged the U.S. to face the fact that if its incomparable power "is really being exercised for mankind's sake, mankind demands some say in its use," which would not be permitted by "the Constitution, the Congress nor television's Sunday pundits"; "And the other nations of the world have not assigned Washington the right to decide when, where and how their interests should be served" (Ronald Steel). The Constitution does happen to provide such mechanisms, namely, by declaring valid treaties "the supreme law of the land," particularly the most fundamental of them, the UN Charter.

It further authorizes Congress to "define and punish...offenses against the law of nations," undergirded by the Charter in the contemporary era. It is, furthermore, a bit of an understatement to say that other nations "have not assigned Washington the right." They have forcefully denied it that right, following the (at least rhetorical) lead of Washington, which largely crafted the Charter.

Reference to Iraq's violation of UN resolutions was regularly taken to imply that the two warrior states have the right to use force unilaterally, taking the role of "world policemen"—an insult to the police, who in principle are supposed to enforce the law, not tear it to shreds. There was criticism of Washington's "arrogance of power" and the like, not quite the proper terms for a self-designated violent outlaw state.

One might contrive a tortured legal argument to support U.S./UK claims, though no one really tried. Step one would be that Iraq has violated UN Resolution 687 of April 3, 1991, which declares a ceasefire "upon official notification by Iraq" that it accepts the provisions that are spelled out (destruction of weapons, inspection, etc.). This is probably the longest and most detailed Security Council on record, but it mentions no enforcement mechanism. Step two of the argument, then, would be that Iraq's noncompliance "reinvokes" Resolution 678 (November 29, 1990). That Resolution authorizes member states "to use all necessary means to uphold and implement Resolution 660" (August 2, 1990), which calls on Iraq to withdraw at once from Kuwait and for Iraq and Kuwait "to begin immediately intensive negotiations for the resolution of their differences," recommending the framework of the Arab League. Resolution 678 also invokes "all subsequent relevant resolutions" (listing them: 662, 664); these are "relevant" in that they refer to the occupation of Kuwait and Iraqi actions relating to it. Reinvoking 678 thus leaves matters as they were, with no authorization to use force to implement the later Resolution 687, which brings up completely different issues, authorizing nothing beyond sanctions. There is no need to debate the matter. The U.S. and UK could readily have settled all doubts by calling on the Security Council to authorize their "threat and use of force," as required by the Charter. Britain did take some steps in that direction, but abandoned them when it became obvious, at once, that the Security Council would not go along. But these considerations have little relevance in a world dominated by rogue states that reject the rule of law.

Suppose that the Security Council were to authorize the use of force to punish Iraq for violating the ceasefire UN Resolution 687. That authorization would apply to all states. For example, to Iran, which would therefore by entitled to invade southern Iraq to sponsor a rebellion. Iraq is a neighbor and the victim of U.S.-backed Iraqi aggression and chemical warfare, and could claim, not implausibly, that its invasion would have some local support. The U.S. and UK can make no such claim. Such Iranian actions, if imaginable, would never be tolerated, but would be far less outrageous than the plans of the self-appointed enforcers. It is hard to imagine such elementary observations entering public discussion in the U.S. and UK.

Contempt for the rule of law is deeply rooted in U.S. practice and intellectual culture. Recall, for example, the reaction to the judgment of the World Court in 1986 condemning the U.S. for "unlawful use of force" against Nicaragua, demanding that it desist and pay extensive reparations and declaring all U.S. aid to the contras, whatever its character, to be "military aid," not "humanitarian aid." The Court was denounced on all sides for having discredited itself. The terms of the judgment were not considered fit to print and were ignored. The Democrat-controlled Congress immediately authorized new funds to step up the unlawful use of force. Washington vetoed a Security Council resolution calling on all states to respect international law—not mentioning anyone, though the intent was clear.

When the General Assembly passed a similar resolution, the U.S. voted against it, effectively vetoing it, joined only by Israel and El Salvador; the following year, only the automatic Israeli vote could be garnered. Little of this received mention in the media or journals of opinion, let alone what it signifies.

Secretary of State George Shultz meanwhile explained (April 14, 1986) that "Negotiations are a euphemism for capitulation if the shadow of power is not cast across the bargaining table." He condemned those who advocate "utopian, legalistic means like outside mediation, the United Nations, and the World Court, while ignoring the power element of the equation"—sentiments not without precedent in modern history.

The open contempt for Article 51 is particularly revealing. It was demonstrated with remarkable clarity immediately after the 1954 Geneva accords on a peaceful settlement for Indochina, regarded as a "disaster" by Washington, which moved at once to undermine them. The National Security Council secretly decreed that even in the case of "local Communist subversion or rebellion not constituting armed attack," the U.S. would consider the use of military force, including an attack on China if it is "determined to be the source" of the "subversion" (NSC 5429/2; my emphasis). The wording, repeated verbatim annually in planning documents, was chosen so as to make explicit the U.S. right to violate Article 51. The same document called for remilitarizing Japan, converting Thailand into "the focal point of U.S. covert and psychological operations in Southeast Asia," undertaking "covert operations on a large and effective scale" throughout Indochina, and, in general, acting forcefully to undermine the Accords and the UN Charter. This critically important document was grossly falsified by the *Pentagon Papers* historians, and has largely disappeared from history.

The U.S. proceeded to define "aggression" to include "political warfare, or subversion" (by someone else, that is)—what Adlai Stevenson called "internal aggression" while defending JFK's escalation to a full-scale attack against

South Vietnam. When the U.S. bombed Libyan cities in 1986, the official justification was "self defense against future attack." *New York Times* legal specialist Anthony Lewis praised the Administration for relying "on a legal argument that violence [in this case] is justified as an act of self-defense," under this creative interpretation of Article 51 of the Charter, which would have embarrassed a literate high school student. The U.S. invasion of Panama was defended in the Security Council by Ambassador Thomas Pickering by appeal to Article 51, which, he declared, "provides for the use of armed force to defend a country, to defend our interests and our people," and entitles the U.S. to invade Panama to prevent its "territory from being used as a base for smuggling drugs into the United States." Educated opinion nodded sagely in assent.

In June 1993, Clinton ordered a missile attack on Iraq, killing civilians and greatly cheering the president, congressional doves, and the press, who found the attack "appropriate, reasonable, and necessary." Commentators were particularly impressed by Ambassador Albright's appeal to Article 51. The bombing, she explained, was in "self-defense against armed attack"—namely, an alleged attempt to assassinate former president Bush two months earlier, an appeal that would have scarcely risen to the level of absurdity even if the U.S. had been able to demonstrate Iraqi involvement; "Administration officials, speaking anonymously," informed the press "that the judgment of Iraq's guilt was based on circumstantial evidence and analysis rather than ironclad intelligence," the *New York Times* reported, dismissing the matter. The press assured elite opinion that the circumstances "plainly fit" Article 51 (*Washington Post*). "Any President has a duty to use military force to protect the nation's interests" (*New York Times*, while expressing some skepticism about the case in hand). "Diplomatically, this was the proper rationale to invoke," and "Clinton's reference to the UN charter conveyed an American desire to respect international law" (*Boston Globe*). Article 51 "permits states to respond militarily if they are threat-ened by a hostile power" (*Christian Science Monitor*). Article 51 entitles a state to use force "in self-defense against threats to one's nationals," British Foreign Secretary Douglas Hurd instructed Parliament, supporting Clinton's "justified and proportionate exercise of the right of self-defense." There would be a "dangerous state of paralysis" in the world, Hurd continued, if the U.S. were required to gain Security Council approval before launching missiles against an enemy that might—or might not—have ordered a failed attempt to kill an ex-President two months earlier.

The record lends considerable support to the concern widely voiced about "rogue states" that are dedicated to the rule of force, acting in the "national interest" as defined by domestic power; most ominously, rogue states that anoint themselves global judge and executioner.

The Narrow Construction

It is also interesting to review the issues that did enter the non-debate on the Iraq crisis. But first a word about the concept "rogue state." The basic conception is that although the Cold War is over, the U.S. still has the responsibility to protect the world—but from what? Plainly it cannot be from the threat of "radical nationalism"—that is, unwillingness to submit to the will of the powerful. Such ideas are only fit for internal planning documents, not the general public. From the early 1980s, it was clear that the conventional technique for mass mobilization was losing its effectiveness: the appeal to JFK's "monolithic and ruthless conspiracy," Reagan's "evil empire." New enemies were needed.

At home, fear of crime—particularly drugs —was stimulated by "a variety of factors that have little or nothing to do with crime itself," the National Criminal Justice Commission concluded, including media practices and "the role of government and private industry in stoking citizen fear," "exploiting latent racial tension for political purposes," with racial bias in enforcement and sentencing that is devastating black communities, creating a "racial abyss" and putting "the nation at risk of a social catastrophe." The results have been described by criminologists as "the American Gulag," "the new American Apartheid," with African Americans now a majority of prisoners for the first time in U.S. history, imprisoned at well over seven times the rate of whites, completely out of the range of arrest rates, which themselves target blacks far out of proportion to drug use or trafficking.

Abroad, the threats were to be "international terrorism," "Hispanic narcotraffickers," and most serious of all, "rogue states." A secret 1995 study of the Strategic Command, which is responsible for the strategic nuclear arsenal, outlines the basic thinking. Released through the Freedom of Information act, the study, "Essentials of Post-Cold War Deterrence," "shows how the United States shifted its deterrent strategy from the defunct Soviet Union to so-called rogue states such as Iraq, Libya, Cuba, and North Korea," AP reports. The study advocates that the U.S. exploit its nuclear arsenal to portray itself as "irrational and vindictive if its vital interests are attacked." That "should be a part of the national persona we project to all adversaries," particularly the "rogue states." "It hurts to portray ourselves as too fully rational and cool-headed," let alone committed to such silliness as international law and treaty obligations. "The fact that some elements" of the U.S. government "may appear to be potentially 'out of control' can be beneficial to creating and reinforcing fears and doubts within the minds of an adversary's decision makers." The report resurrects Nixon's "madman theory": our enemies should recognize that we are crazed and unpredictable, with extraordinary destructive force at our command, so they will bend to our will in fear. The concept was apparently devised in Israel in the 1950s by the governing Labor Party, whose leaders "preached in favor of acts of madness," Prime Minister Moshe Sharett records in his diary, warning that "we will go crazy" ("nishtagea") if crossed, a "secret weapon" aimed in part against the U.S., not con-

sidered sufficiently reliable at the time. In the hands of the world's sole superpower, which regards itself as an outlaw state and is subject to few constraints from elites within, that stance poses no small problem for the world.

Libya was a favorite choice as "rogue state" from the earliest days of the Reagan administration. Vulnerable and defenseless, it is a perfect punching bag when needed: for example, in 1986, when the first bombing in history orchestrated for prime time TV was used by the Great Communicator's speech writers to muster support for Washington's terrorist forces attacking Nicaragua, on grounds that the "archterrorist" Qaddafi "has sent $400 million and an arsenal of weapons and advisors into Nicaragua to bring his war home to the United States," which was then exercising its right of self-defense against the armed attack of the Nicaraguan rogue state.

After The Berlin Wall Fell

Immediately after the Berlin Wall fell, ending any resort to the Soviet threat, the Bush administration submitted its annual call to Congress for a huge Pentagon budget. It explained that, "In a new era, we foresee that our military power will remain an essential underpinning of the global balance, but...the more likely demands for the use of our military forces may not involve the Soviet Union and may be in the Third World, where new capabilities and approaches may be required," as "when President Reagan directed American naval and air forces to return to [Libya] in 1986" to bombard civilian urban targets, guided by the goal of "contributing to an international environment of peace, freedom, and progress within which our democracy—and other free nations—can flourish." The primary threat we face is the "growing technological sophistication" of the Third World. We must therefore strengthen "the defense industrial base" —aka high tech industry—creating incentives "to invest in new facilities and equipment as well as in research and development." And we must maintain intervention forces, particularly those targeting the Middle East, where the "threats to our interests" that have required direct military engagement "could not be laid at the Kremlin's door"—contrary to endless fabrication, now put to rest. As had occasionally been recognized in earlier years, sometimes in secret, the "threat" is now conceded officially to be indigenous to the region, the "radical nationalism" that has been a primary concern, not only in the Middle East.

At the time, the "threats to our interests" could not be laid at Iraq's door either. Saddam was then a favored friend and trading partner. His status changed a few months later, when he misinterpreted U.S. willingness to allow him to modify the border with Kuwait by force as authorization to take the country over—or from the perspective of the Bush administration—to duplicate what the U.S. had done in Panama.

> At the time, the "threats to our interests" could not be laid at Iraq's door either. Saddam was then a favored friend and trading partner. His status changed only a few months later, when he misinterpreted U.S. willingness to allow him to modify the border with Kuwait by force as authorization to take the country over.

At a high-level meeting immediately after Saddam's invasion of Kuwait, President Bush articulated the basic problem: "My worry about the Saudis is that they're...going to bug out at the last minute and accept a puppet regime in Kuwait." Chair of the Joint Chiefs Colin Powell posed the problem sharply: "The next few days Iraq will withdraw," putting "his puppet in" and "Everyone in the Arab world will be happy."

Historical parallels are never exact, of course. When Washington partially withdrew from Panama after putting its puppet in, there was great anger throughout the hemisphere, including Panama. Indeed throughout much of the world, compelling Washington to veto two Security Council resolutions and to vote against a General Assembly resolution condemning Washington's "flagrant violation of international law and of the independence, sovereignty and territorial integrity of states" and calling for the withdrawal of the "U.S. armed invasion forces from Panama." Iraq's invasion of Kuwait was treated differently, in ways remote from the standard version, but readily discovered in print.

The inexpressible facts shed interesting light on the commentary of political analysts: Ronald Steel, for example, who muses today on the "conundrum" faced by the U.S., which, "as the world's most powerful nation, faces greater constraints on its freedom to use force than does any other country." Hence Saddam's success in Kuwait as compared with Washington's inability to exert its will in Panama.

It is worth recalling that debate was effectively foreclosed in 1990-1991 as well. There was much discussion of whether sanctions would work, but none of whether they already had worked, perhaps shortly after Resolution 660 was passed. Fear that sanctions might have worked animated Washington's refusal to test Iraqi withdrawal offers from August 1990 to early January. With the rarest of exceptions, the information system kept tight discipline on the matter. Polls a few days before the January 1991 bombing showed 2-1 support for a peaceful settlement based on Iraqi withdrawal along with an international conference on the Israel-Arab conflict.

Few among those who expressed this position could have heard any public advocacy of it; the media had loyally followed the President's lead, dismissing "linkage" as unthinkable—in this unique case. It is unlikely that respondents knew that their views were shared by the Iraqi democratic opposition, barred from mainstream media. Or that an Iraqi proposal in the terms they advocated had been released a week earlier by U.S. officials who found it reasonable, and flatly rejected by Washington. Or that an Iraqi withdrawal offer had been considered by the National Security Council as early as mid-August, but dismissed, and effectively suppressed, apparently because it was feared that unmentioned Iraqi initiatives might "defuse the crisis," as the

New York Times diplomatic correspondent obliquely reported Administration concerns.

Since then, Iraq has displaced Iran and Libya as the leading "rogue state." Others have never entered the ranks. Perhaps the most relevant case is Indonesia, which shifted from enemy to friend when General Suharto took power in 1965, presiding over an enormous slaughter that elicited great satisfaction in the West. Since then Suharto has been "our kind of guy," as the Clinton administration described him, while carrying out murderous aggression, and endless atrocities against his own people; killing 10,000 Indonesians just in the 1980s, according to the personal testimony of "our guy," who wrote that "the corpses were left lying around as a form of shock therapy."

In December 1975, the UN Security Council unanimously ordered Indonesia to withdraw its invading forces from East Timor "without delay" and called upon "all States to respect the territorial integrity of East Timor as well as the inalienable right of its people to self-determination." The U.S. responded by (secretly) increasing shipments of arms to the aggressors; Carter accelerated the arms flow once again as the attack reached near-genocidal levels in 1978. In his memoirs, UN Ambassador Daniel Patrick Moynihan takes pride in his success in rendering the UN "utterly ineffective in whatever measures it undertook," following the instructions of the State Department, which "wished things to turn out as they did and worked to bring this about." The U.S. also happily accepts the robbery of East Timor's oil (with participation of a U.S. company), in violation of any reasonable interpretation of international agreements.

The analogy to Iraq/Kuwait is close, though there are differences: to mention only the most obvious, U.S.-sponsored atrocities in East Timor were vastly beyond anything attributed to Saddam Hussein in Kuwait.

There are many other examples, though some of those commonly invoked should be treated with caution, particularly concerning Israel. The civilian toll of Israel's U.S.-backed invasion of Lebanon in 1982 exceeded Saddam's in Kuwait, and it remains in violation of a 1978 Security Council resolution ordering it to withdraw forthwith from Lebanon, along with numerous others regarding Jerusalem, the Golan Heights, and other matters. There would be far more if the U.S. did not regularly veto such resolutions. But the common charge that Israel, particularly its current government, is violating UN 242 and the Oslo Accords, and that the U.S. exhibits a "double standard" by tolerating those violations, is dubious at best, based on serious misunderstanding of these agreements.

From the outset, the Madrid-Oslo process was designed and implemented by U.S.-Israeli power to impose a Bantustan-style settlement. The Arab world has chosen to delude itself about the matter, as have many others, but they are clear in the actual documents, and particularly in the U.S.-supported projects of the Rabin-Peres governments, including those for which the Likud government is now being denounced.

It is clearly untrue to claim that "Israel is not demonstrably in violation of Security Council decrees" (*New York Times*), but the reasons often given should be examined carefully.

Returning to Iraq, it surely qualifies as a leading criminal state. Defending the U.S. plan to attack Iraq at a televised public meeting on February 18, Secretaries Albright and Cohen repeatedly invoked the ultimate atrocity: Saddam was guilty of "using weapons of mass destruction against his neighbors as well as his own people," his most awesome crime. "It is very important for us to make clear that the United States and the civilized world cannot deal with somebody who is willing to use those weapons of mass destruction on his own people, not to speak of his neighbors," Albright emphasized in an angry response to a questioner who asked about U.S. support for Suharto. Shortly after, Senator Lott condemned Kofi Annan for seeking to cultivate a "human relationship with a mass murderer" and denounced the Administration for trusting a person who would sink so low. Ringing words. Putting aside their evasion of the question raised, Albright and

Cohen forgot to mention—and commentators have been kind enough not to point out—that the acts that they now find so horrifying did not turn Iraq into a "rogue state." And Lott failed to note that his heroes Reagan and Bush forged unusually warm relations with the "mass murderer." There were no passionate calls for a military strike after Saddam's gassing of Kurds at Halabja in March 1988. On the contrary, the U.S. and UK extended their strong support for the mass murderer, then also "our kind of guy." When ABC TV correspondent Charles Glass revealed the site of one of Saddam's biological warfare programs ten months after Halabja, the State Department denied the facts, and the story died. The Department "now issues briefings on the same site," Glass observes.

Expediting Saddam's Atrocities

The two guardians of global order also expedited Saddam's other atrocities—including his use of cyanide, nerve gas, and other barbarous weapons—with intelligence, technology, and supplies, joining with many others.

The Senate Banking Committee reported in 1994 that the U.S. Commerce Department had traced shipments of "biological materials" identical to those later found and destroyed by UN inspectors, Bill Blum recalls. These shipments continued at least until November 1989. A month later, Bush authorized new loans for his friend Saddam, to achieve the "goal of increasing U.S. exports and put us in a better position to deal with Iraq regarding its human rights record...," the State Department announced with a straight face, facing no criticism in the mainstream (or even report). Britain's record was exposed, at least in part, in an official inquiry (Scott Inquiry).

The British government has just now been compelled to concede that it continued to grant licenses to British firms to export materials usable for biological weapons after the Scott report was published, at least until December 1996. In a

February 28 review of Western sales of materials usable for germ warfare and other weapons of mass destruction, the *Times* mentions one example of U.S. sales in the 1980s, including "deadly pathogens," with government approval, some from the Army's center for germ research in Fort Detrick. Just the tip of the iceberg.

A common current pretense is Saddam's crimes were unknown, so we are now properly shocked at the discovery and must "make clear" that we civilized folk "cannot deal with" the perpetrator of such crimes (Albright). The posture is cynical fraud. UN Reports of 1986 and 1987 condemned Iraq's use of chemical weapons. U.S. Embassy staffers in Turkey interviewed Kurdish survivors of chemical warfare attacks, and the CIA reported them to the State Department. Human Rights groups reported the atrocities at Halabja and elsewhere at once. Secretary of State George Shultz conceded that the U.S. had evidence on the matter.

An investigative team sent by the Senate Foreign Relations Committee in 1988 found "overwhelming evidence of extensive use of chemical weapons against civilians," charging that Western acquiescence in Iraqi use of such weapons against Iran had emboldened Saddam to believe —correctly—that he could use them against his own people with impunity—actually against Kurds, hardly "the people" of this tribal-based thug. The chair of the Committee, Claiborne Pell, introduced the Prevention of Genocide Act of 1988, denouncing silence "while people are gassed" as "complicity," much as when "the world was silent as Hitler began a campaign that culminated in the near extermination of Europe's Jews," and warning that "we cannot be silent to genocide again." The Reagan administration strongly opposed sanctions and insisted that the matter be silenced, while extending its support for the mass murderer. In the Arab world, "the Kuwait press was among the most enthusiastic of the Arab media in supporting Baghdad's crusade against the Kurds," journalist Adel Darwish reports. In January 1991, while the war drums were beating, the International Commission of Jurists observed to the UN Human Rights Commission that "After having perpetrated the most flagrant abuses on its own population without a word of reproach from the UN, Iraq must have concluded it could do whatever it pleased"—UN in this context means U.S. and UK, primarily. That truth must be buried along with international law and other "utopian" distractions.

An unkind commentator might remark that recent U.S./UK toleration for poison gas and chemical warfare is not too surprising. The British used chemical weapons in their 1919 intervention in North Russia against the Bolsheviks, with great success according to the British command. As Secretary of State at the War Office in 1919, Winston Churchill was enthusiastic about the prospects of "using poisoned gas against uncivilized tribes"—Kurds and Afghans—and authorized the RAF Middle East command to use chemical weapons "against recalcitrant Arabs as experiment," dismissing objections by the India office as "unreasonable" and deploring the "squeamishness about the use of gas." "We cannot in any circumstances acquiesce in the non-utilization of any weapons which are available to procure a speedy termination of the disorder which prevails on the frontier," he explained—chemical weapons are merely "the application of Western science to modern warfare."

The Kennedy administration pioneered the massive use of chemical weapons against civilians as it launched its attack against South Vietnam in 1961-1962. There has been much rightful concern about the effects on U.S. soldiers, but not the incomparably worse effects on civilians. Here, at least.

In an Israeli mass-circulation daily, the respected journalist Amnon Kapeliouk reported on his 1988 visit to Vietnam, where he found that "Thousands of Vietnamese still die from the effects of American chemical warfare," citing estimates of one-quarter of a million victims in South Vietnam and describing the "terrifying" scenes in hospitals in the south with children dying of cancer and hideous birth deformities. It

was South Vietnam that was targeted for chemical warfare, not the North, where these consequences are not found," he reports. There is also substantial evidence of U.S. use of biological weapons against Cuba, reported as minor news in 1977 and, at worst, only a small component of continuing U.S. terror.

These precedents aside, the U.S. and UK are now engaged in a deadly form of biological warfare in Iraq. The destruction of infrastructure and banning of imports to repair it has caused disease, malnutrition, and early death on a huge scale, including 567,000 children by 1995, according to UN investigations; UNICEF reports 4,500 children dying a month in 1996. In a bitter condemnation of the sanctions (January 20, 1998), 54 Catholic Bishops quoted the Archbishop of the southern region of Iraq, who reports that "epidemics rage, taking away infants and the sick by the thousands" while "those children who survive disease succumb to malnutrition."

The Bishop's statement, reported in full in Stanley Heller's journal *The Struggle,* received scant mention in the press. The U.S. and Britain have taken the lead in blocking aid programs —for example, delaying approval for ambulances on the grounds that they could be used to transport troops, barring insecticides to prevent spread of disease and spare parts for sanitation systems. Meanwhile, western diplomats point out, "The U.S. had directly benefited from [the humanitarian] operation as much, if not more, than the Russians and the French," for example, by purchase of $600 million worth of Iraqi oil (second only to Russia) and sale by U.S. companies of $200 million in humanitarian goods to Iraq. They also report that most of the oil bought by Russian companies ends up in the U.S.

Washington's support for Saddam reached such an extreme that it was even willing to overlook an Iraqi air force attack on the *USS Stark,* killing 37 of the crew, a privilege otherwise enjoyed only by Israel (in the case of the *USS Liberty*). It was Washington's decisive support for Saddam, well after the crimes that now so shock the Administration and Congress, that led to Ira-

61

nian capitulation to "Baghdad and Washington," Dilip Hiro concludes in his history of the Iran-Iraq war. The two allies had "co-ordinate[d] their military operations against Teheran." The shooting down of an Iranian civilian airliner by the guided-missile cruiser *Vincennes* was the culmination of Washington's "diplomatic, military, and economic campaign" in support of Saddam, he writes.

Saddam was also called upon to perform the usual services of a client state. For example, train several hundred Libyans sent to Iraq by the U.S. so they could overthrow the Qaddafi government, former Reagan White House aide Howard Teicher revealed. It was not his massive crimes that elevated Saddam to the rank of "Beast of Baghdad." Rather, it was his stepping out of line, much as in the case of the far more minor criminal Noriega, whose major crimes were also committed while he was a U.S. client.

In passing, one might note that the destruction of Iran Air 655 in Iranian airspace by the *Vincennes* may come back to haunt Washington. The circumstances are suspicious, to say the least. In the Navy's official journal, Commander David Carlson wrote that he "wondered aloud in disbelief" as he observed from his nearby vessel as the *Vincennes*—then within Iranian territorial waters—shot down what was obviously a civilian airliner in a commercial corridor, perhaps out of "a need to prove the viability of Aegis," its high tech missile system. The commander and key officers "were rewarded with medals for their conduct," Marine Corps Colonel (retired) David Evans observes in the same journal in an acid review of the Navy Department cover-up of the affair. President Bush informed the UN that, "One thing is clear and that is that the *Vincennes* acted in self-defense...in the midst of a naval attack initiated by

> In passing, one might note that the destruction of Iran Air 655 in Iranian airspace by the Vincennes may come back to haunt Washington. The circumstances are suspicious, to say the least. In the Navy's official journal, Commander David Carlson wrote that he "wondered aloud in disbelief" as he observed from his nearby vessel as the Vincennes —then within Iranian territorial waters—shot down what was obviously a civilian airliner in a commercial corridor.

Iranian vessels"—all lies—Evans points out, though of no significance, given Bush's position that, "I will never apologize for the United States of America—I don't care what the facts are." A retired Army colonel who attended the official hearings concluded that, "our Navy is too dangerous to deploy."

It is difficult to avoid the thought that the destruction of Pan Am 103 over Lockerbie a few months later was Iranian retaliation, as stated explicitly by Iranian intelligence defector Abolhassem Mesbahi, also an aide to President Rafsanjani, "regarded as a credible and senior Iranian source in Germany and elsewhere," the *Guardian* reports. A 1991 U.S. intelligence document (National Security Agency), declassified in 1997, draws the same conclusion, alleging that Akbar Mohtashemi, a former Iranian interior minister, transferred $10 million "to bomb Pan Am 103 in retaliation for the U.S. shootdown of the Iranian Airbus," referring to his connections with "the Al Abas and Abu Nidal terrorist groups." It is striking that, despite the evidence and the clear motive, this is the only act of terrorism not blamed on Iran. Rather, the U.S. and UK have charged two Libyan nationals with the crime.

The charges against the Libyans have been widely disputed, including a detailed inquiry by Denis Phipps, former head of security at British Airways who served on the government's National Aviation Committee. The British organization of families of Lockerbie victims believe that there has been "a major coverup" (spokesperson Dr. Jim Swire) and regard as more credible the account given in Alan Frank-ovich's documentary *The Maltese Cross*, which provides evidence of the Iranian connection and a drug operation involving a courier working for the U.S. DEA. The film was shown at the British House of Commons and on British TV, but rejected here. The U.S. families keep strictly to Washington's version.

Also intriguing is the U.S./UK refusal to permit a trial of the accused Libyans. This takes the form of rejection of Libya's offer to release the accused for trial in some neutral venue to a judge nominated by the UN (December 1991), a trial at the Hague "under Scottish law," etc. These proposals have been backed by the Arab League and the British relatives organization but flatly rejected by the U.S./UK. In March 1992, the UN Security Council passed a resolution imposing sanctions against Libya, with five abtsentions: China, Morocco (the only Arab member), India, Zimbabwe, Cape Verde. There was considerable arm-twisting: thus China was warned that it would lose U.S. trade preferences if it vetoed the resolution. The U.S. press has reported Libya's offer to release the suspects for trial, dismissing it as worthless and ridiculing Qaddafi's "dramatic gesture" of calling for the surrender of U.S. pilots who bombed two Libyan cities, killing 37 people, including his adopted daughter. Plainly, that is as absurd as requests by Cuba and Costa Rica for extradition of U.S. terrorists.

It is understandable that the U.S./UK should want to ensure a trial they can control, as in the case of the Noriega kidnapping. Any sensible defense lawyer would bring up the Iranian connection in a neutral venue. How long the charade can continue is unclear. In the midst of the current Iraq crisis, the World Court rejected the U.S./UK claim that it has no jurisdiction over the matter, and intends to launch a full hearing (13-2, with the U.S. and British judges opposed), which may make it harder to keep the lid on.

The Court ruling was welcomed by Libya and the British families. Washington and the U.S. media warned that the World Court ruling might prejudice the 1992 UN resolution that demanded that, "Libya must surrender those accused of the Lockerbie bombing for trial in Scotland or the United States" (*New York Times*), that Libya "extradite the suspects to the United States and Britain" (AP). These claims are not accurate. The issue of transfer to Scotland or the U.S. never arose and is not mentioned in the UN Resolutions. Resolution 731 (21 January 1992), "Urges the Libyan Government immediately to provide a full and effective response" to requests "in connection with the legal procedures" related to attacks against Pan Am 103 and a French airliner. Resolution 748 (31 March 1992), "Decides that the Libyan Government must now comply without any further delay" with the request of Resolution 731 and that it renounce terrorism, calling for sanctions if Libya fails to do so. Resolution 731 was adopted in response to a U.S./UK declaration that Libya must "surrender for trial all those charged with the crime," with no further specification. Press reports at the time were similarly inaccurate. Thus, reporting the U.S. dismissal of the Libyan offer to turn the suspects over to a neutral country, the *New York Times* highlighted the words: "Again, Libya tries to avoid a UN order."

The *Washington Post* dismissed the offer as well, stating that, "The Security Council contends that the suspects must be tried in U.S. or British courts." Doubtless Washington prefers to have matters seen in this light. A correct account was given in a 1992 opinion piece by international legal authority Alfred Rubin of the Fletcher School (*Christian Science Monitor*), who noted that the Security Council resolution makes no mention of extradition to the U.S. and UK, and observes that its wording "departs so far from what the United States, Britain, and France are reported to have wanted that current public statements and press accounts reporting an American diplomatic triumph and UN pressures on Libya seem incomprehensible"; unfortunately, the performance is all too routine.

In the *NY Times*, British specialist on UN law Marc Weiler, in an op-ed, agreed with Rubin that the U.S. should follow the clear requirements of international law and accept Libya's proposal for World Court adjudication. Libya's response to the U.S./UK request was "precisely as mandated by international law," Weiler wrote, condemning the U.S./UK for having "flatly refused" to submit the issue to the World Court. Rubin and Weiler also ask obvious further questions: Suppose that New Zealand had resisted powerful French pressures to compel it to abandon its attempt to extradite the French government terrorists who had bombed the Rainbow Warrior in Auckland harbor? Or that Iran were to demand that the captain of the Vincennes be extradited? The World Court has now drawn the same conclusion as Rubin and Weiler.

The qualifications as "rogue state" are illuminated further by Washington's reaction to the uprisings in Iraq in March 1991, immediately after the cessation of hostilities. The State Department formally reiterated its refusal to have any dealings with the Iraqi democratic opposition and, as from before the Gulf War, they were virtually denied access to the major U.S. media. "Political meetings with them would not be appropriate for our policy at this time," State Department spokesperson Richard Boucher stated. "This time" happened to be March 14, 1991, while Saddam was decimating the southern opposition under the eyes of General Schwartzkopf, refusing even to permit rebelling military officers access to captured Iraqi arms. Had it not been for unexpected public reaction, Washington probably would not have extended even tepid support to rebelling Kurds, subjected to the same treatment shortly after.

Iraqi opposition leaders got the message. Leith Kubba, head of the London-based Iraqi Democratic Reform Movement, alleged that the U.S. favors a military dictatorship, insisting that "changes in the regime must come from within, from people already in power." London-based banker Ahmed Chalabi, head of the Iraqi National Congress, said that "the United States, covered by the fig leaf of non-interference in Iraqi affairs, is waiting for Saddam to butcher the insurgents in the hope that he can be overthrown later by a suitable officer," an attitude rooted in the U.S. policy of "supporting dictatorships to maintain stability."

Administration reasoning was outlined by *New York Times* chief diplomatic correspondent Thomas Friedman. While opposing a popular rebellion, Washington did hope that a military coup might remove Saddam, "and then Washington would have the best of all worlds: an ironfisted Iraqi junta without Saddam Hussein," a return to the days when Saddam's "iron fist...held Iraq together, much to the satisfaction of the American allies Turkey and Saudi Arabia," not to speak of Washington. Two years later, in another useful recognition of reality, he observed that "it has always been American policy that the iron-fisted Mr. Hussein plays a useful role in holding Iraq together," maintaining "stability." There is little reason to believe that Washington has modified the preference for dictatorship over democracy deplored by the ignored Iraqi democratic opposition, though it doubtless would prefer a different "iron fist" at this point. If not, Saddam will have to do.

The concept "rogue state" is highly nuanced. Thus, Cuba qualifies as a leading "rogue state" because of its alleged involvement in international terrorism, but the U.S. does not fall into the category despite its terrorist attacks against Cuba for close to 40 years, apparently continuing through last summer according to important investigative reporting of the *Miami Herald*, which failed to reach the national press (here; although it did in Europe). Cuba was a "rogue state" when its military forces were in Angola, backing the government against South African attacks supported by the U.S.

South Africa, in contrast, was not a rogue state then, nor during the Reagan years when it caused over $60 billion in damage and 1.5 million deaths in neighboring states according to a UN Commission, not to speak of some events at home—and with ample U.S./UK support. The same exemption applies to Indonesia and many others. The criteria are fairly clear: a "rogue state" is not simply a criminal state, but one that defies the orders of the powerful—who are, of course, exempt.

That Saddam is a criminal is undoubtedly true and one should be pleased, I suppose, that the U.S. and UK, and mainstream doctrinal institutions, have at last joined those who "prematurely" condemned U.S./UK support for the mass murderer. It is also true that he poses a threat to anyone within his reach. On the comparison of the threat with others, there is little unanimity outside the U.S. and UK, after their (ambiguous) transformation from August 1990. Their 1998 plan to use force was justified in terms of Saddam's threat to the region, but there was no way to conceal the fact that the people of the region objected to their salvation, so strenuously that governments were compelled to join in opposition.

Bahrein refused to allow U.S./British forces to use bases there. The president of the United Arab Emirates described U.S. threats of military action as "bad and loathsome," and declared that Iraq does not pose a threat to its neighbors. Saudi Defense Minister Prince Sultan had already stated that, "We'll not agree and we are against striking Iraq as a people and as a nation," causing Washington to refrain from a request to use Saudi bases. After Annan's mission, long-serving Saudi foreign minister Prince Saud al-Faisal reaffirmed that any use of Saudi air bases "has to be a UN, not a U.S. issue."

An editorial in Egypt's quasi-official journal *Al Ahram* described Washington's stand as "coercive, aggressive, unwise and uncaring about the lives of Iraqis, who are unnecessarily subjected to sanctions and humiliation," and denounced the planned U.S. "aggression against Iraq." Jordan's Parliament condemned "any aggression against Iraq's territory and any harm that might come to the Iraqi people"; the Jordanian army was forced to seal off the city of Maan after two days of pro-Iraq rioting. A political science professor at Kuwait University warned that, "Saddam has come to represent the voice of the voiceless in the Arab world," expressing popular frustration over the "New World Order" and Washington's advocacy of Israeli interests.

Even in Kuwait, support for the U.S. stance was at best "tepid" and "cynical over U.S. motives," the press recognized. "Voices in the streets of the Arab world, from Cairo's teeming slums to the Arabian Peninsula's shiny capitals, have been rising in anger as the American drumbeat of war against Iraq grows louder," *Boston Globe* correspondent Charles Sennott reported.

The Iraqi democratic opposition was granted a slight exposure in the mainstream, breaking the previous pattern. In a telephone interview with the *New York Times*, Ahmed Chalabi reiterated the position that had been reported in greater detail in London weeks earlier: "Without a political plan to remove Saddam's regime, military strikes will be counter-productive," he argued, killing thousands of Iraqis, leaving Saddam perhaps even strengthened along with his weapons of mass destruction and with "an excuse to throw out UNSCOM [the UN inspectors]," who have in fact destroyed vastly more weapons and production facilities than the 1991 bombing. U.S./UK plans would "be worse than nothing." Interviews with opposition leaders from several groups found "near unanimity" in opposing military action that did not lay the basis for an uprising to overthrow Saddam. Speaking to a Parliamentary committee, Chalabi held that it was "morally indefensible to strike Iraq without a strategy" for removing Saddam. In London, the opposition also outlined an alternative program:

- declare Saddam a war criminal

- recognize a provisional Iraqi government formed by the opposition

- unfreeze hundreds of millions of dollars of Iraqi assets abroad

- restrict Saddam's forces by a "no-drive zone" or extend the "no-flight zone" to cover the whole country

The U.S. should "help the Iraqi people remove Saddam from power," Chalabi told the Senate Armed Services Committee. Along with other opposition leaders, he "rejected assassination, covert U.S. operations, or U.S. ground troops," Reuters reported, calling instead for "a popular insurgency." Similar proposals have occasionally appeared in the U.S. Washington claims to have attempted support for opposition groups, but their own interpretation is different. Chalabi's view, published in England, is much as it was years earlier: "everyone says Saddam is boxed in, but it is the Americans and British who are boxed in by their refusal to support the idea of political change."

Regional opposition was regarded as a problem to be evaded, not a factor to be taken into account, any more than international law. The same was true of warnings by senior UN and other international relief officials in Iraq that the planned bombing might have a "catastrophic" effect on people already suffering miserably, and might terminate the humanitarian operations that have brought at least some relief. What matters is to establish that "What We Say Goes," as President Bush triumphantly proclaimed, announcing the New World Order as bombs and missiles were falling in 1991.

As Kofi Annan was preparing to go to Baghdad, former Iranian president Rafsanjani, "still a pivotal figure in Tehran, was given an audience by the ailing King Fahd in Saudi Arabia," British Middle East correspondent David Gardner reported, "in contrast to the treatment experienced by Madeleine Albright...on her recent trips to Riyadh seeking support from America's main Gulf ally."

As Rafsanjani's ten-day visit ended on March 2, foreign minister Prince Saud described it as "one more step in the right direction towards improving relations," reiterating that "the greatest destabilising element in the Middle East and the cause of all other problems in the region" is Israel's policy towards the Palestinians and U.S. support for it, which might activate popular forces that Saudi Arabia greatly fears, as well as undermining its legitimacy as "guardian" of Islamic holy places, including the Dome of the Rock in East Jerusalem, now effectively annexed by U.S./Israeli programs as part of their intent to extend "greater Jerusalem" virtually to the Jordan Valley, to be retained by Israel. Shortly before, the Arab states had boycotted a U.S.-sponsored economic summit in Qatar that was intended to advance the "New Middle East" project of Clinton and Peres. Instead, they attended an Islamic conference in Teheran in December, joined even by Iraq.

These are tendencies of considerable import, relating to the background concerns that motivate U.S. policy in the region—its insistence, since World War II, on controlling the world's major energy reserves. As many have observed, in the Arab world there is growing fear and resentment of the long-standing Israel-Turkey alliance that was formalized in 1996, now greatly strengthened. For some years, it had been a component of the U.S. strategy of controlling the region with "local cops on the beat," as Nixon's Defense Secretary put the matter. There is apparently a growing appreciation of the Iranian advocacy of regional security arrangements to replace U.S. domination. A related matter is the intensifying conflict over pipelines to bring Central Asian oil to the rich countries, one natural outlet being via Iran.

U.S. energy corporations will not be happy to see foreign rivals—now including China and Russia as well—gain privileged access to Iraqi oil reserves, second only to Saudi Arabia in scale, or to Iran's natural gas, oil, and other resources.

For the present, Clinton planners may well be relieved to have escaped temporarily from the "box" they had constructed that was leaving them no option, but a bombing of Iraq that could have been harmful even to the interests they represent. The respite is temporary. It offers opportunities to citizens of the warrior states to bring about changes of consciousness and commitment that could make a great difference in the not too distant future.

6.

Crisis in the Balkans

Bombing to "uphold our values"

On March 24, U.S.-led NATO forces launched cruise missiles and bombs at targets in Yugo-slavia, "plunging America into a military conflict that President Clinton said was necessary to stop ethnic cleansing and bring stability to Eastern Europe," lead stories in the press reported. In a televised address, Clinton explained that by bombing Yugoslavia, "we are upholding our values, protecting our interests, and advancing the cause of peace."

In the preceding year, according to Western sources, about 2,000 people had been killed in the Yugoslav province of Kosovo and there were several hundred thousand internal refugees. The humanitarian catastrophe was overwhelmingly attributable to Yugoslav military and police forces, the main victims being ethnic Albanian Kosovars, commonly said to constitute about 90 percent of the population. After three days of bombing, according to the UN High Commissioner for Refugees, several thousand refugees had been expelled to Albania and Macedonia, the two neighboring countries. Refugees reported that the terror had reached the capital city of Pristina, largely spared before, and provided credible accounts of large-scale destruction of villages, assassinations, and a radical increase in generation of refugees, perhaps an effort to expel a good part of the Albanian population. Within 2 weeks the flood of refugees had reached some 350,000, mostly from the southern sections of Kosovo adjoining Macedonia and Albania, while unknown numbers of Serbs fled north to Serbia to escape the increased violence from the air and on the ground.

On March 27, U.S.-NATO Commanding General Wesley Clark declared that it was "entirely predictable" that Serbian terror and violence would intensify after the NATO bombing. On the same day, State Department spokesperson James Rubin said that "The United States is extremely alarmed by reports of an escalating pattern of Serbian attacks on Kosovar Albanian civilians," now attributed in large part to paramilitary forces mobilized after the bombing. General Clark's phrase "entirely predictable" is an overstatement. Noth-

From Z Magazine, May 1999

ing is "entirely predictable," surely not the effects of extreme violence.

But he is correct in implying that what happened at once was highly likely. As observed by Carnes Lord of the Fletcher School of Law and Diplomacy, formerly a Bush administration national security adviser, "enemies often react when shot at," and "though Western officials continue to deny it, there can be little doubt that the bombing campaign has provided both motive and opportunity for a wider and more savage Serbian operation than what was first envisioned."

In the preceding months, the threat of NATO bombing—again, predictably—was followed by an increase in atrocities. The withdrawal of international observers, sharply condemned by the Serb Parliament, predictably had the same consequence. The bombing was then undertaken under the rational expectation that killing and refugee generation would escalate as a result, as indeed happened, even if the scale may have come as a surprise to some, though apparently not the commanding general.

Increase In Atrocities

Under Tito, Kosovars had had a considerable measure of self-rule. So matters remained until 1989, when Kosovo's autonomy was rescinded by Slobodan Milosevic, who established direct Serbian rule and imposed "a Serbian version of Apartheid," in the words of former U.S. government specialist on the Balkans James Hooper, no dove: he advocates direct NATO invasion of Kosovo. The Kosovars "confounded the international community," Hooper continues, "by eschewing a war of national liberation, embracing instead the nonviolent approach espoused by leading Kosovo intellectual Ibrahim Rugova and constructing a parallel civil society," an impressive achievement, for which they were rewarded by "polite audiences and rhetorical encouragement from Western governments." The nonviolent strategy "lost its credibility" at the

Dayton accords in November 1995, Hooper observes. At Dayton, the U.S. effectively partitioned Bosnia-Herzegovina between an eventual greater Croatia and greater Serbia, after having roughly equalized the balance of terror by providing arms and training for the forces of Croatian dictator Tudjman and supporting his violent expulsion of Serbians from Krajina and elsewhere. With the sides more or less balanced, and exhausted, the U.S. took over, displacing the Europeans who had been assigned the dirty work much to their annoyance. "In deference to Milosevic," Hooper writes, the U.S. "excluded Kosovo Albanian delegates" from the Dayton negotiations and "avoided discussion of the Kosovo problem." "The reward for nonviolence was international neglect"; more accurately, U.S. neglect.

Recognition that the U.S. understands only force led to "the rise of the guerrilla Kosovo Liberation Army (KLA) and expansion of popular support for an armed independence struggle." By February 1998, KLA attacks against Serbian police stations led to a "Serbian crackdown" and retaliation against civilians, another standard pattern. Israeli atrocities in Lebanon, particularly under Nobel Peace laureate Shimon Peres, are or should be a familiar example, though one that is not entirely appropriate.

These Israeli atrocities are typically in response to attacks on its military forces occupying foreign territory in violation of longstanding orders to withdraw. Many Israeli attacks are not retaliatory at all, including the 1982 invasion that devastated much of Lebanon and left 20,000 civilians dead (a different story is preferred in U.S. commentary, though the truth is familiar in Israel). We need scarcely imagine how the U.S. would respond to attacks on police stations by a guerrilla force with foreign bases and supplies.

Fighting in Kosovo escalated, the scale of atrocities corresponding roughly to the resources of violence. An October 1998 cease-fire, made possible the deployment of 2,000 European monitors. Breakdown of U.S.-Milosevic negotiations led to renewed fighting, which increased with the threat of NATO bombing and the with-drawal of the monitors, again as predicted. Officials of the UN refugee agency and Catholic Relief Services had warned that the threat of bombing "would imperil the lives of tens of thousands of refugees believed to be hiding in the woods," predicting "tragic" consequences if "NATO made it impossible for us to be here." Atrocities then sharply escalated as the late March bombing provided "motive and opportunity," as was surely "predictable," if not "entirely" so.

The bombing was undertaken, under U.S. initiative, after Milosevic had refused to accept a U.S. ultimatum—the Rambouillet agreement—of the NATO powers in February. There were disagreements within NATO, captured in a *New York Times* headline that reads: "Trickiest Divides Are Among Big Powers at Kosovo Talks." One problem had to do with deployment of NATO peace-keepers. The European powers wanted to ask the Security Council to authorize the deployment, in accord with treaty obligations and international law. Washington, however, refused to allow the "neuralgic word 'authorize'," the *New York Times* reported, though it did finally permit "endorse." The Clinton administration "was sticking to its stand that NATO should be able to act independently of the United Nations."

The discord within NATO continued. Apart from Britain (by now, about as much of an independent actor as the Ukraine was in pre-Gorbachev years), NATO countries were skeptical of Washington's preference for force, and annoyed by Secretary of State Albright's "saber-rattling," which they regarded as "unhelpful when negotiations were at such a sensitive stage," though "U.S. officials were unapologetic about the hard line."

Turning from generally uncontested fact to speculation, we may ask why events proceeded as they did, focusing on the decisions of U.S. planners—the factor that must be our primary concern on elementary moral grounds, and that is a leading if not decisive factor on grounds of equally elementary considerations of power. We may note at first that the dismissal of Kosovar democrats "in deference to Milosevic" is hardly surprising.

To mention another example, after Saddam Hussein's repeated gassing of Kurds in 1988, in deference to its friend and ally the U.S. barred official contacts with Kurdish leaders and Iraqi democratic dissidents, who were largely excluded from the media as well. The official ban was renewed immediately after the Gulf war, in March 1991, when Saddam was tacitly authorized to conduct a massacre of rebelling Shi'ites in the south and then Kurds in the north. The massacre proceeded under the steely gaze of Stormin' Norman Schwartzkopf, who explained that he was "suckered" by Saddam, not anticipating that Saddam might carry out military actions with the military helicopters he was authorized by Washington to use. The Bush administration explained that support for Saddam was necessary to preserve "stability," and its preference for a military dictatorship that would rule Iraq with an "iron fist" just as Saddam had done was sagely endorsed by respected U.S. commentators.

Tacitly acknowledging past policy, Secretary of State Albright announced in December 1998 that "we have come to the determination that the Iraqi people would benefit if they had a government that really represented them." A few months earlier, on May 20, Albright had informed Indonesian President Suharto that he was no longer "our kind of guy," having lost control and disobeyed IMF orders, so that he must resign and provide for "a democratic transition." A few hours later, Suharto transferred formal authority to his hand-picked vice-president. We now celebrate the May 1999 elections in Indonesia, hailed by Washington and the press as the first democratic elections in 40 years—but with-

> The official ban was renewed immediately after the Gulf War, in March 1991, when Saddam was tacitly authorized to conduct a massacre of rebelling Shi'ites in the south and then Kurds in the north

out a reminder of the major U.S. clandestine military operation 40 years ago that brought Indonesian democracy to an end, undertaken in large measure because the democratic system was unacceptably open, even allowing participation of the left.

We need not tarry on the plausibility of Washington's discovery of the merits of democracy in the past few months. The fact that the words can be articulated, eliciting no comment, is informative enough. In any event, there is no reason to be surprised at the disdain for non-violent democratic forces in Kosovo or at the fact that the bombing was undertaken with the likely prospect that it would undermine a courageous and growing democratic movement in Belgrade, now probably demolished as Serbs are "unified from heaven—but by the bombs, not by God," in the words of Aleksa Djilas, the historian son of Yugoslav dissident Milovan Djilas. "The bombing has jeopardized the lives of more than 10 million people and set back the fledgling forces of democracy in Kosovo and Serbia," having "blasted... [its] germinating seeds and insured that they will not sprout again for a very long time," according to Serbian dissident Veran Matic, editor in chief of the independent station Radio B-92 (now banned).

Former *Boston Globe* editor Randolph Ryan, who has been working for years in the Balkans and living in Belgrade, wrote, "Now, thanks to NATO, Serbia has overnight become a totalitarian state in a frenzy of wartime mobilization," as NATO must have expected, just as it "had to know that Milosevic would take immediate revenge by redoubling his attacks in Kosovo," which NATO would have no way to stop.

As to what planners "envisioned," Carnes Lord's confidence is hard to share. If the documentary record of past actions is any guide, planners probably were doing what comes naturally to those with a strong card—in this case violence. Namely, play it, and then see what happens. With the basic facts in mind, one may speculate about how Washington's decisions were made. Turbulence in the Balkans qualifies as a "hu-

manitarian crisis," in the technical sense. It might harm the interests of rich and privileged people, unlike slaughters in Sierra Leone or Angola, or crimes we support or conduct ourselves. The question, then, is how to control the authentic crisis. The U.S. will not tolerate the institutions of world order, so the problems have to be handled by NATO, which the U.S. pretty much dominates. The divisions within NATO are understandable: violence is Washington's strong card. It is necessary to guarantee the "credibility of NATO"—meaning, of U.S. violence—others must have proper fear of the global hegemon. "One unappealing aspect of nearly any alternative" to bombing, Barton Gellman observed in a *Washington Post* review of "the events that led to the confrontation in Kosovo," "was the humiliation of NATO and the United States."

National Security Adviser Samuel Berger "listed among the principal purposes of bombing 'to demonstrate that NATO is serious'." A European diplomat concurred. "Inaction would have involved 'a major cost in credibility, particularly at this time as we approach the NATO summit in celebration of its fiftieth anniversary'." "To walk away now would destroy NATO's credibility," Prime Minister Tony Blair informed Parliament. Blair is not concerned with the credibility of Italy or Belgium, and understands "credibility" in the manner of any Mafia Don.

Violence may fail, but planners can be confident that there is always more in reserve. Side benefits include an escalation of arms production and sales—the cover for the massive state role in the high tech economy for years. Just as bombing unites Serbs behind Milosevic, it unites Americans behind our leaders. These are standard effects of violence. They may not last for long, but planning is for the short term.

The Issues

There are two fundamental issues: What are the accepted and applicable "rules of world order?" How do these or other considerations apply in the case of Kosovo? There is a regime of international law and international order, binding on all states, based on the UN Charter and subsequent resolutions and World Court decisions. In brief, the threat or use of force is banned unless explicitly authorized by the Security Council after it has determined that peaceful means have failed, or in self-defense against "armed attack" (a narrow concept) until the Security Council acts.

There is, of course, more to say. Thus, there is at least a tension, if not an outright contradiction, between the rules of world order laid down in the UN Charter and the rights articulated in the Universal Declaration of Human Rights (UD), a second pillar of the world order established under U.S. initiative after World War II. The Charter bans force violating state sovereignty; the UD guarantees the rights of individuals against oppressive states. The issue of "humanitarian intervention" arises from this tension. It is the right of "humanitarian intervention" that is claimed by the U.S./NATO in Kosovo, with the general support of editorial opinion and news reports.

The question was addressed at once in a *New York Times* report headed, "Legal Scholars Support Case for Using Force." One example is offered: Allen Gerson, former counsel to the U.S. mission to the UN. Two other legal scholars are cited. One, Ted Galen Carpenter, "scoffed at the Administration argument" and dismissed the alleged right of intervention.

The third is Jack Goldsmith, a specialist on international law at Chicago Law school. He says that critics of the NATO bombing "have a pretty good legal argument," but "many people think [an exception for humanitarian intervention] does exist as a matter of custom and practice." That summarizes the evidence offered to justify the favored conclusion stated in the headline.

Goldsmith's observation is reasonable, at least if we agree that facts are relevant to the determination of "custom and practice." We may also bear in mind a truism: the right of humanitarian intervention, if it exists, is premised on the "good faith" of those intervening, and that assumption

is based not on their rhetoric but on their record, in particular their record of adherence to the principles of international law, World Court decisions, and so on. That is indeed a truism, at least with regard to others. Consider, for example, Iranian offers to intervene in Bosnia to prevent massacres at a time when the West would not do so. These were dismissed with ridicule (in fact, generally ignored); if there was a reason beyond subordination to power, it was because Iranian good faith could not be assumed.

A rational person then asks obvious questions: is the Iranian record of intervention and terror worse than that of the U.S.? And other questions, for example: How should we assess the "good faith" of the only country to have vetoed a Security Council resolution calling on all states to obey international law? What about its historical record? Unless such questions are prominent on the agenda of discourse, an honest person will dismiss it as mere allegiance to doctrine. A useful exercise is to determine how much of the literature—media or other—survives such elementary conditions as these.

When the decision was made to bomb, there had been a serious humanitarian crisis in Kosovo for a year. In such cases, outsiders have three choices:

(1) try to escalate the catastrophe

(2) do nothing

(3) try to mitigate the catastrophe

The choices are illustrated by other contemporary cases. Let's keep to a few of approximately the same scale and ask where Kosovo fits into the pattern.

Colombia. According to State Department estimates, the annual level of political killing by the government and its paramilitary associates is about at the level of Kosovo, and refugee flight primarily from their atrocities is well over a million, another 300,000 last year. Colombia has been the leading Western hemisphere recipient of U.S. arms and training as violence increased through the 1990s, and that assistance is now increasing, under a "drug war" pretext dismissed by almost all serious observers. The Clinton administration was particularly enthusiastic in its praise for President Gaviria, whose tenure in office was responsible for "appalling levels of violence," according to human rights organizations, even surpassing his predecessors. Details are readily available. In this case, the U.S. reaction is (1): escalate the atrocities.

Turkey. For years, Turkish repression of Kurds has been a major scandal. It peaked in the 1990s; one index is the flight of over a million Kurds from the countryside to the unofficial Kurdish capital Diyarbakir from 1990 to 1994, as the Turkish army was devastating the countryside. Two million were left homeless according to the Turkish State Minister for Human Rights, a result of "state terrorism" in part, he acknowledged. "Mystery killings" of Kurds (assumed to be death squad killings) alone amounted to 3,200 in 1993 and 1994, along with torture, destruction of thousands of villages, bombing with napalm, and an unknown number of casualties, generally estimated in the tens of thousands; no one was counting. The killings are attributed to Kurdish terror in Turkish propaganda, generally adopted in the U.S. as well.

Presumably Serbian propaganda follows the same practice. 1994 marked two records in Turkey: it was "the year of the worst repression in the Kurdish provinces," Jonathan Randal reported from the scene, and the year when Turkey became "the biggest single importer of American military hardware and thus the world's largest arms purchaser. Its arsenal, 80 percent American, included M-60 tanks, F-16 fighter-bombers, Cobra gunships, and Blackhawk 'slick' helicopters, all of which were eventually used against the Kurds." When human rights groups exposed Turkey's use of U.S. jets to bomb villages, the Clinton administration found ways to evade laws requiring suspension of arms deliveries, much as it was doing in Indonesia and elsewhere. Turkish aircraft have now shifted to bombing Serbia, while Turkey is lauded for its humanitarianism.

Colombia and Turkey explain their (U.S.-supported) atrocities on grounds that they are defending their countries from the threat of terrorist guerrillas. As does the government of Yugoslavia. Again, the example illustrates (1): act to escalate the atrocities.

Laos. Every year thousands of people, mostly children and poor farmers, are killed in the Plain of Jars in Northern Laos, the scene of the heaviest bombing of civilian targets in history it appears, and arguably the most cruel: Washington's furious assault on a poor peasant society had little to do with its wars in the region. The worst period was from 1968, when Washington was compelled to undertake negotiations (under popular and business pressure), ending the regular bombardment of North Vietnam. Kissinger-Nixon then shifted the planes to bombardment of Laos and Cambodia.

The deaths are from "bombies," tiny anti-personnel weapons, far worse than land-mines: they are designed specifically to kill and maim, and have no effect on trucks, buildings, etc. The Plain was saturated with hundreds of millions of these criminal devices, which have a failure-to-explode rate of 20 percent to 30 percent according to the manufacturer, Honeywell.

The numbers suggest either remarkably poor quality control or a rational policy of murdering civilians by delayed action. These were only a fraction of the technology deployed, including advanced missiles to penetrate caves where families sought shelter. Current annual casualties from "bombies" are estimated from hundreds a year to "an annual nationwide casualty rate of 20,000," more than half of them deaths, according to the veteran Asia reporter Barry Wain of the *Wall Street Journal* in its Asia edition. A conservative estimate, then, is that the crisis last year was approximately comparable to Kosovo, though deaths are far more highly concentrated among children over half—according to studies reported by the Mennonite Central Committee, which has been working there since 1977 to alleviate the continuing atrocities. There have been efforts to publicize and deal with the humanitarian catastrophe. A British-based Mine Advisory Group (MAG) is trying to remove the lethal objects, but the U.S. is "conspicuously missing from the handful of Western organisations that have followed MAG," the British press reports, though it has finally agreed to train some Laotian civilians. The British press also reports, with some annoyance, the allegation of MAG specialists that the U.S. refuses to provide them with "render harmless procedures" that would make their work "a lot quicker and a lot safer." These remain a state secret, as does the whole affair in the United States. The Bangkok press reports a very similar situation in Cambodia, particularly the Eastern region where U.S. bombardment from early 1969 was most intense.

> Madeleine Albright commented on national TV in 1996 when asked for her reaction to the killing of half a million Iraqi children in five years, but "we think the price is worth it."

In this case, the U.S. reaction is (2): do nothing. The reaction of the media and commentators is to keep silent, following the norms under which the war against Laos was designated a "secret war" meaning well-known, but suppressed, as in the case of Cambodia from March 1969. The level of self-censorship was extraordinary then, as is the current phase. The relevance of this shocking example should be obvious without further comment.

President Clinton explained to the nation that "there are times when looking away simply is not an option.... We can't respond to every tragedy in every corner of the world," but that doesn't mean that "we should do nothing for no one." But the President and commentators failed to add that the "times" are well-defined. The principle applies to "humanitarian crises," in the technical sense, discussed earlier when the interests of rich and privileged people are endangered. Accordingly, the examples just mentioned do not qualify as "humanitarian crises," so looking away and not responding are definitely options, if not obligatory. On similar grounds, Clinton's policies on Africa are understood by Western diplomats to be "leaving Africa to solve its own crises." For example, in the Republic of Congo—scene of a major war and huge atrocities. Clinton refused a UN request for a trivial sum for a battalion of peacekeepers, according to the UN's senior Africa envoy, the highly respected diplomat Mohamed Sahnoun, a refusal that "torpedoed" the UN proposal. In the case of Sierra Leone, "Washington dragged out discussions on a British proposal to deploy peacekeepers" in 1997, paving the way for another major disaster, but also of the kind for which "looking away" is the preferred option. In other cases too, "the United States has actively thwarted efforts by the United Nations to take on peacekeeping operations that might have prevented some of Africa's wars, according to European and UN diplomats," correspondent Colum Lynch reported as the plans to bomb Serbia reached the final stages.

I will skip other examples of (1) and (2), which abound and also contemporary atrocities of a different kind, such as the slaughter of Iraqi civilians by means of a vicious form of what amounts to biological warfare "a very hard choice," Madeleine Albright commented on national TV in 1996 when asked for her reaction to the killing of half a million Iraqi children in five years, but "we think the price is worth it." Current estimates remain about 5,000 children killed a month and it seems the price is still "worth it." These and other examples might be kept in mind when we read admiring accounts of how the "moral compass" of the Clinton administration is at last functioning properly in Kosovo (Columbia University professor of preventive diplomacy David Phillips). Kosovo is another illustration: acting in such a way as to escalate the violence, with exactly that expectation.

To find examples illustrating (3) is all too easy, at least if we keep to official rhetoric. The most extensive recent academic study of "humanitarian intervention" is by George Washington University law professor, Sean Murphy. He reviews the record after the Kellogg-Briand pact of 1928 which outlawed war and then, after the UN Charter, which strengthened and articulated these provisions. In the first phase, he writes, the most prominent examples of "humanitarian intervention" were Japan's attack on Manchuria, Mussolini's invasion of Ethiopia, and Hitler's occupation of parts of Czechoslovakia, all accompanied by uplifting humanitarian rhetoric and factual justifications as well. Japan was going to establish an "earthly paradise" as it defended Manchurians from "Chinese bandits," with the support of a leading Chinese nationalist, a far more credible figure than anyone the U.S. was able to conjure up during its attack on South Vietnam. Mussolini was liberating thousands of slaves as he carried forth the Western "civilizing mission." Hitler announced Germany's intention to end ethnic tensions and violence and "safeguard the national individuality of the German and Czech peoples," in an operation "filled with earnest desire to serve the true interests of the peoples dwelling in the area," in accordance with their will as the Slovakian President asked Hitler to declare Slovakia a protectorate.

Another useful intellectual exercise is to compare those obscene justifications with those offered for interventions, including "humanitarian interventions." In the post-UN Charter period, perhaps the most compelling example of (3) is the Vietnamese invasion of Cambodia in December 1978, terminating Pol Pot's atrocities, which were then peaking. Vietnam pleaded the right of self-defense against armed attack, one of the few post-Charter examples when the plea is plausible. The Khmer Rouge regime (Democratic Kampuchea, DK) was carrying out murderous attacks against Vietnam in border areas. The U.S. reaction is instructive. The press condemned the "Prussians" of Asia for their outrageous violation of international law. They were harshly punished for the crime of having ended Pol Pot's slaughters, first by a (U.S.-backed) Chinese invasion, then by U.S. imposition of extremely harsh sanctions. The U.S. recognized the expelled DK as the official government of Cambodia because of its "continuity" with the Pol Pot regime, the State Department explained. Not too subtly, the U.S. supported the Khmer Rouge in its continuing attacks in Cambodia.

The example tells us more about the "custom and practice" that underlies "the emerging legal norms of humanitarian intervention."

Another illustration of (3) is India's invasion of East Pakistan in 1971, which terminated an enormous massacre and refugee flight (over ten million, according to estimates at the time). The U.S. condemned India for aggression. Kissinger was particularly infuriated by India's action, in part it seems because it was interfering with a carefully staged secret trip to China. Perhaps this is one of the examples that historian John Lewis Gaddis had in mind in his fawning review of the latest volume of Kissinger's memoirs, when he reports admiringly that Kissinger "acknowledges here, more clearly than in the past, the influence of his upbringing in Nazi Germany, the examples set by his parents and the consequent impossibility, for him, of operating outside a moral framework." The logic is overpowering, as are the illustrations, too well-known to record. Again, the same lessons.

Despite the desperate efforts of ideologues to prove that circles are square, there is no serious doubt that the NATO bombings further undermined what remains of the fragile structure of international law. The U.S. made that clear in the debates that led to the NATO decision, as already discussed. The more closely one approaches the conflicted region, the greater the opposition to Washington's insistence on force, even within NATO (Greece and Italy). Again, that is not an unusual phenomenon. Another current example is the U.S./UK bombing of Iraq, undertaken in December with unusually brazen gestures of contempt for the Security Council Still another illustration, minor in context, is the destruction of half the pharmaceutical production of a small African country a few months earlier, another event that does not indicate that the "moral compass" is straying from righteousness, though comparable destruction of U.S. facilities by Islamic terrorists might evoke a slightly different reaction. It is unnecessary to emphasize that there is a far more extensive record that would be prominently reviewed right now if facts were considered relevant to determining "custom and practice."

Contempt For World Order

It could be argued, rather plausibly, that further demolition of the rules of world order is by now of no significance, as in the late 1930s. The contempt of the world's leading power for the framework of world order has become so extreme that there is little left to discuss. A review of the internal documentary record demonstrates that the stance traces back to the earliest days, even to the first memorandum of the newly-formed National Security Council in 1947. During the Kennedy years, the stance began to gain overt expression, as, for example, when the respected statesperson and Kennedy adviser Dean Acheson justified the blockade of Cuba in 1962 by informing the American Society for International Law that a situation in which our country's "power, position, and prestige" are involved cannot be treated as a "legal issue."

The main innovation of the Reagan-Clinton years is that defiance of international law and solemn obligations has become entirely open. It has also been backed with interesting explanations, which would be on the front pages and prominent in the school and university curriculum, if honesty and human consequences were considered significant values. The highest authorities explained that international law and agencies had become irrelevant because they no longer follow U.S. orders, as they did in the early postwar years, when U.S. power was overwhelming. When the World Court was considering what it later condemned as Washington's "unlawful use of force" against Nicaragua, Secretary of State

George Shultz derided those who advocate "utopian, legalistic means like outside mediation, the United Nations, and the World Court, while ignoring the power element of the equation." Clear, forthright, and by no means original. State Department Legal Adviser Abraham Sofaer explained that members of the UN can no longer "be counted on to share our view," and the "majority often opposes the United States on important international questions," so we must "reserve to ourselves the power to determine" how we will act. One can follow standard practice and ignore "custom and practice," or dismiss it on some absurd grounds ("change of course," "Cold War," and other familiar pretexts).

Or we can take custom, practice, and explicit doctrine seriously, departing from respectable norms, but at least opening the possibility of understanding what is happening in the world.

While the Reaganites broke new ground, under Clinton the defiance of world order has become so extreme as to be of concern even to hawkish policy analysts. In the current issue of the leading establishment journal, *Foreign Affairs*, Samuel Huntington warns that Washington is treading a dangerous course. In the eyes of probably most of the world, he suggests the U.S. is "becoming the rogue superpower," considered "the single greatest external threat to their societies." Realist "international relations theory," he argues, predicts that coalitions may arise to counterbalance the rogue superpower.

On pragmatic grounds, then, the stance should be reconsidered. Americans, who prefer a different image of their society might have other grounds for concern over these tendencies, but they are probably of little concern to planners, with their narrower focus and immersion in ideology. Where does that leave the question of what to do in Kosovo? It leaves it unanswered. The U.S. has chosen a course of action which, as it explicitly recognizes, escalates atrocities and violence; a course that strikes yet another blow against the regime of international order, which does offer the weak at least some limited protection from predatory states; a course that undermines, perhaps destroys, promising democratic developments within Yugoslavia, probably Macedonia as well. The longer-term, consequences are unpredictable.

One plausible observation is that "every bomb that falls on Serbia and every ethnic killing in Kosovo suggests that it will scarcely be possible for Serbs and Albanians to live beside each other in some sort of peace" (*Financial Times*). Other possible long-term outcomes are not pleasant to contemplate. The resort to violence has, again predictably, narrowed the options. Perhaps the least ugly that remains is an eventual partition of Kosovo, with Serbia taking the northern areas that are rich in resources and have the main historical monuments. The southern sector will become a NATO protectorate where some Albanians can live in misery. Another possibility is that, with much of the population gone, the U.S. might turn to the Carthaginian solution. If that happens, it would again be nothing new, as large areas of Indochina can testify.

A standard argument is that we had to do something as we could not simply stand by as atrocities continued. The argument is so absurd that it is rather surprising to hear it voiced. Suppose you see a crime in the streets and feel that you can't just stand by silently, so you pick up an assault rifle and kill everyone involved—criminal, victim, bystanders. Are we to understand that to be the rational and moral response?

One choice, always available, is to follow the Hippocratic principle: "First, do no harm." If you can think of no way to adhere to that elementary principle, then do nothing. At least that is preferable to causing harm. But there are always other ways that can be considered. Diplomacy and negotiations are never at an end. That was true right before the bombing, when the Serb Parliament, responding to Clinton's ultimatum, called for negotiations over an "international presence in Kosovo immediately after the signing of an accord for self-administration in Kosovo, which would be accepted by all national communities" living in the province, reported on wire services worldwide but scarcely noted here. Just what that meant we cannot know, since the two warrior states preferred to reject the diplomatic path in favor of violence.

Another argument, if one can call it that, has been advanced most prominently by Henry Kissinger. He believes that intervention was a mistake ("open-ended," quagmire, etc.). That aside, it is futile. "Through the centuries, these conflicts [in the Balkans] have been fought with unparalleled ferocity because none of the populations has any experience with and essentially no belief in Western concepts of toleration." At last we understand why Europeans have treated each other with such gentle solicitude "through the centuries," and have tried so hard over many centuries to bring to others their message of non-violence, toleration, and loving kindness.

Simply Unacceptable

One can always count on Kissinger for some comic relief, though in reality, he is not alone. He is joined by those who ponder "Balkan logic" as contrasted with the Western record of humane rationality. And those who remind us of the "distaste for war or for intervention in the affairs of others" that is "our inherent weakness," of our dismay over the "repeated violations of norms and rules established by international treaty, human rights conventions" (historian Tony Judt). We are to consider Kosovo as "A New Collision of East and West," a *Times* think piece is headlined, a clear illustration of Samuel Huntington's "Clash of Civilizations." "A democratic West, its humanitarian instincts repelled by the barbarous inhumanity of Orthodox Serbs," all of this "clear to Americans," but not to others, a fact that Americans fail to comprehend (Huntington, interview).

Or we may listen to the inspiring words of Secretary of Defense William Cohen, introducing the president at Norfolk Naval Air Station. He opened by quoting Theodore Roosevelt, speaking "at the dawn of this century, as America was awakening into its new place in the world." President Roosevelt said, "Unless you're willing to fight for great ideals, those ideals will vanish," and "today, at the dawn of the next century, we're joined by President Bill Clinton" who understands as well as Teddy Roosevelt that "standing on the sidelines...as a witness to the unspeakable horror that was about to take place, that would in fact affect the peace and stability of NATO countries, was simply unacceptable."

One has to wonder what must pass through the mind of someone invoking this famous racist fanatic and raving jingoist as a model of American values, along with the events that illustrated his cherished "great ideals" as he spoke—the slaughter of hundreds of thousands of Filipinos who had sought liberation from Spain, shortly after Roosevelt's contribution to preventing Cubans from achieving the same goal.

Wiser commentators will wait until Washington settles on an official story. After two weeks of bombing, the story is that they both knew and didn't know that a catastrophe would follow. On March 28, "when a reporter asked if the bombing was accelerating the atrocities, [President Clinton] replied, 'absolutely not'" (Adam Clymer). He reiterated that stand in his April 1 speech at Norfolk: "Had we not acted, the Serbian offensive would have been carried out with impunity." The following day, Pentagon spokesperson Kenneth Bacon announced that the opposite was true: "I don't think anyone could have foreseen the breadth of this brutality," the first acknowledgment by the Administration that "it was not fully prepared for the crisis," the press reported a crisis that was "entirely predictable," the Commanding General had informed the press a week earlier. From the start, reports from the scene were that "the Administration had been caught off guard" by the Serbian military reaction (Jane Perlez and many others).

The right of "humanitarian intervention" is likely to be more frequently invoked in coming years maybe with justification, maybe not now that Cold War pretexts have lost their efficacy. In such an era, it may be worthwhile to pay attention to the views of highly respected commentators—not to speak of the World Court, which ruled on the matter of intervention and "humanitarian aid" in a decision rejected by the United States, its essentials not even reported.

In the scholarly disciplines of international affairs and international law it would be hard to find more respected voices than Hedley Bull or Louis Henkin. Bull warned 15 years ago that "Particular states or groups of states that set themselves up as the authoritative judges of the world common good, in disregard of the views of others, are, in fact, a menace to international order and, thus, to effective action in this field." Henkin, in a standard work on world order, writes that the "pressures eroding the prohibition on the use of force are deplorable and the arguments to legitimize the use of force in those circumstances are unpersuasive and dangerous.... Violations of human rights are indeed all too common and if it were permissible to remedy them by external use of force, there would be no law to forbid the use of force by almost any state against almost any other. Human rights, I believe, will have to be vindicated, and other injustices remedied, by other, peaceful means, not by opening the door to aggression and destroying the principal advance in international law, the outlawing of war, and the prohibition of force."

7.

World Order and its Rules

A new world, led by the U.S., bent on using the right to intervene

Despite the desperate efforts of ideologues to prove that circles are square, there is no serious doubt that the NATO bombings further undermine what remains of the fragile structure of international law. The U.S. made that clear in the debates that led to the NATO decision. The more closely one approached the conflicted region, the greater in general was the opposition to Washington's insistence on force, even within NATO (Greece and Italy). Again, that is not an unusual phenomenon: another recent example is U.S./UK bombing of Iraq, undertaken in December 1998 with unusually brazen gestures of contempt for the Security Council—even the timing, coinciding with an emergency session to deal with the crisis. Still another illustration is Clinton's destruction of half the pharmaceutical production of a small African country a few months earlier. It was dismissed here as a marginal curiosity, though comparable destruction of U.S. facilities by Islamic terrorists might evoke a slightly different reaction. Perhaps this is an example of the kind of "creative deterrence" advised by the U.S. Strategic Command, 1995, aiming at what "is valued within a culture," such as the fate of children dying from easily curable disease.

It should be unnecessary to emphasize that there is a far more extensive record that would be prominently reviewed right now if facts were considered relevant to determining the "custom and practice" that is called upon to confer upon the most enlightened state the right "to do what it thinks right" by force.

It could be argued, rather plausibly, that further demolition of the rules of world order is by now of no significance, as in the late 1930s. The contempt of the world's leading power for the framework of world order has become so extreme that there is little left to discuss. A review of the internal documentary record demonstrates that the stance traces back to the earliest days, even to the first memorandum of the newly formed National Security Council in 1947. During the Kennedy years, the stance began to gain overt expression, as, for example, when the eminent statesman and Kennedy adviser Dean Acheson justified the blockade of Cuba in 1962 by informing the American Society of International Law that the "propriety" of a U.S. response to a "challenge...[to the]...power, position, and prestige of the United States...is not a legal issue." The real purpose of talking about international law was, for Acheson, sim-

An excerpt from Chomsky's The New Military Humanism (Common Courage, 1999); published in Z Magazine, October 1999

ply "to gild our positions with an ethos derived from very general moral principles which have affected legal doctrines"—when convenient.

The main innovation of the Reagan-Clinton years is that defiance of international law and solemn obligations has become entirely open, even widely lauded in the West as "the new internationalism" that heralds a wonderful new age, unique in human history. Unsurprisingly, the developments are perceived rather differently in the traditional domains of the enlightened states; and, for different reasons, are of concern even to some hawkish policy analysts.

The end of the Cold War made it possible to transcend even Achesonian cynicism. Bows to world order are unnecessary, even to be despised, as the enlightened states do as they please without concern for deterrence or world opinion. Doctrinal management suffices "to gild our positions with an ethos derived from very general moral principles," as recent developments show with much clarity.

"Innovative but justifiable extension of international law" (Mark Weller) can be devised at will by the powerful, to serve their special interests: "humanitarian intervention" by bombs in Kosovo, but no withdrawal of a huge flow of lethal arms for worthy ethnic cleansing and state terror within NATO, to cite only the most dramatic illustration. With "unpopular ideas silenced and inconvenient facts kept dark" in the style described by Orwell in his (silenced) observations on the free societies, all should proceed smoothly. Whatever happens is "a landmark in international relations" as the "enlightened states," led by an "idealistic New World bent on ending inhumanity," proceed to use military force where they "believe it to be just"—or as others see it, to devise "rules of the game" that accord them "the right to intervene with force to compel what seems to them to be justified," always "cloaked in moralistic righteousness," "as in the colonial era." From the perspective of the enlightened, the difference of interpretation reflects the sharp divide that separates their "normal world" from that of the backward peoples who lack "Western concepts of toleration" and have not yet overcome "the human capacity for evil," to the astonishment and dismay of the civilized world. In this context, it is hardly surprising that "international law is today probably less highly regarded in our country than at any time" since the founding of the American Society of International Law in 1908. Or that the editor of the leading professional journal of international law should warn of the "alarming exacerbation" of Washington's dismissal of treaty obligations.

The prevailing attitude towards institutions of world order was illustrated in a different way when Yugoslavia brought charges against NATO countries to the World Court, appealing to the Genocide Convention. The Court determined that it had no jurisdiction, while holding that "All parties must act in conformity with their obligations under the United Nations Charter," which clearly bars the bombing—"veiled language to say that the bombing was breaking international law," the *New York Times* reported. Of particular interest was the submission of the U.S. government, which presented an airtight legal argument, accepted by the Court, that its actions did not fall under Court jurisdiction. The U.S. had indeed ratified the Genocide Convention, after a very long delay, but with a reservation that "the specific consent of the United States is required" if charges are brought against it; and the United States refuses to give the "specific consent" that the reservation stipulates. Court rules require that both parties agree to its jurisdiction, Counsel John Crook reminded the Court, and U.S. ratification of the Convention was conditioned on its inapplicability to the United States.

It may be added that the reservation is more general. The U.S. ratifies few enabling conventions concerning human rights and related matters, and these few are conditioned by reservations that render them (effectively) inapplicable to the United States. The explanations offered for rejection of international obligations are interesting, and would be on the front pages, and prominent in the school and university curriculum, if honesty and human consequences were considered significant values. The highest authorities have made it clear that international law and agencies had become irrelevant because they no longer follow Washington's orders, as they did in the early postwar years, when U.S. power was overwhelming. When the World Court was considering what it later condemned as Washington's "unlawful use of force" against Nicaragua, Secretary of State George Shultz—honored as the Mr. Clean of the Reagan administration—derided those who advocate "utopian, legalistic means like outside mediation, the United Nations, and the World Court, while ignoring the power element of the equation." Clear and forthright and by no means original. State Department Legal Adviser Abraham Sofaer explained that members of the UN can no longer "be counted on to share our view," and the "majority often opposes the United States on important international questions," so we must "reserve to ourselves the power to determine" how we will act and which matters fall "essentially within the domestic jurisdiction of the United States, as determined by the United States"—in this case, Washington's "unlawful use of force" against Nicaragua.

It is all very well to speak abstractly of the "innovative but justifiable extension of international law" that creates a right of "humanitarian intervention," or to accord to the enlightened states the right to use military force where they "believe it to be just." But it should also be recognized that, hardly by accident, the states that are self-qualified as enlightened turn out to be those that can act as they please. And that in the real world, there are two options: (1) Some kind of framework of world order, perhaps the UN Charter, the International Court of Justice, and other existing institutions, or perhaps something better if it can be devised and broadly accepted; (2) The powerful do as they wish, expecting to receive the accolades that are the prerogative of power.

Abstract discussion may choose to consider other possible worlds, perhaps a fit topic for graduate seminars in philosophy. But for the present, at least, it is options (1) and (2) that identify the real world in which decisions that affect human affairs have to be made.

The fact that the operative choices reduce to (1) and (2) was recognized 50 years ago by the World Court: "The Court can only regard the alleged right of intervention as the manifestation of a policy of force, such as has, in the past, given rise to most serious abuses and such as cannot, whatever be the defects in international organization, find a place in international law...; from the nature of things, [Intervention] would be reserved for the most powerful states, and might easily lead to perverting the administration of justice itself."

One can adopt the stance of "intentional ignorance" and ignore "custom and practice," or dismiss them on some absurd grounds ("change of course," "Cold War," and other familiar pretexts). Or we can take custom, practice, and explicit doctrine seriously, along with the actual history of "humanitarian intervention," departing from respectable norms but at least opening the possibility of gaining some understanding of what is happening in the world.

Where does that leave the specific question of what should have been done in Kosovo? It leaves it unanswered. The answer cannot be simply deduced from abstract principle, still less from pious hopes, but requires careful attention to the circumstances of the real world.

A reasonable judgment, I think, is that the U.S. chose a course of action that—as anticipated—would escalate atrocities and violence; that strikes yet another blow against the regime of international order, which offers the weak at least some limited protection from predatory states; that undermines democratic developments within Yugoslavia, possibly Macedonia as well; and that sets back the prospects for disarmament and for some control of nuclear weapons and other weapons of mass destruction, indeed may leave others with "no choice" but to "obtain weapons of mass destruction" in self-defense. Of the three logically possible options, it chose (I) "act to escalate the catastrophe," rejecting the alternatives: (II) "do nothing," (III) "try to mitigate the catastrophe." Was option (III) realistic? One cannot know, but there are indications that it might have been. For Kosovo, one plausible observation from the outset was that "every bomb that falls on Serbia and every ethnic killing in Kosovo it will scarcely be possible for Serbs and Albanians to live beside each other in some sort of peace" (*Financial Times,* March 27).

Other possible long-term outcomes are not pleasant to contemplate. At best, NATO's immediate institution of its version of the official settlement leaves "staggering problems" to be addressed, most urgently those that are "the effect" of the bombing, as acknowledged.

A standard argument is that we had to do something: we could not simply stand by as atrocities continued. There was no alternative to the resort to force, Tony Blair declared, with many heads nodding in sober agreement: "to do nothing would have been to acquiesce in Milosevic's brutality." If option (III) ("mitigate the catastrophe") is excluded, as tacitly assumed, and we are left only with (I) ("escalate the catastrophe") or (II) ("do nothing"), then we must choose (I). That the argument can even be voiced is a tribute to the desperation of supporters of the bombing. Suppose you see a crime in the streets, and feel that you can't just stand by silently, so you pick up an assault rifle and kill everyone involved: criminal, victim, bystanders. Are we to understand that to be the rational and moral response, in accord with Blair's principle?

One choice, always available, is to follow the Hippocratic principle: "First, do no harm." If you can think of no way to adhere to that elementary principle, then do nothing; at least that is preferable to causing harm—the consequence recognized in advance to be "predictable" in the case of Kosovo, a prediction amply fulfilled. It may sometimes be true that the search for peaceful means is at an end, and that there is "no alterna-

tive" to doing nothing or causing vast harm. If so, anyone with even a minimal claim to being a moral agent will abide by the Hippocratic principle. That nothing constructive can be done must, however, be demonstrated. In the case of Kosovo, diplomatic options appeared to be open, and might have been productive and as is coming to be acknowledged, far too late.

The right of "humanitarian intervention" is likely to be more frequently invoked in coming years—maybe with justification, maybe not—now that the system of deterrence has collapsed (allowing more freedom of action) and Cold War pretexts have lost their efficacy (requiring new ones). In such an era, it may be worthwhile to pay attention to the views of highly respected commentators—not forgetting the World Court, which ruled on the matter of intervention and "humanitarian aid" in a decision rejected by the United States, its essentials not even reported.

In the scholarly disciplines of international affairs and international law it would be hard to find more respected voices than Hedley Bull or Louis Henkin. Bull warned 15 years ago that "Particular states or groups of states that set themselves up as the authoritative judges of the world common good, in disregard of the views of others, are in fact a menace to international order, and thus to effective action in this field." Henkin, in a standard work on world order,

> Even humanitarian intervention can too readily be used as the occasion or pretext for aggression.

writes that the "pressures eroding the prohibition on the use of force are deplorable, and the arguments to legitimize the use of force in those circumstances are unpersuasive and dangerous.... Even humanitarian intervention can too readily be used as the occasion or pretext for aggression. Violations of human rights are indeed all too common, and if it were permissible to remedy them by external use of force, there would be no law to forbid the use of force by almost any state against almost any other. Human rights, I believe, will have to be vindicated, and other injustices remedied, by other, peaceful means, not by opening the door to aggression and destroying the principal advance in international law, the outlawing of war and the prohibition of force."

These are reflections that should not be lightly disregarded. Recognized principles of international law and world order, treaty obligations, decisions by the World Court, considered pronouncements by respected commentators—these do not automatically yield general principles or solutions to particular problems. Each has to be considered on its merits. For those who do not adopt the standards of Saddam Hussein, there is a heavy burden of proof to meet in undertaking the threat or use of force.

Perhaps the burden can be met, but that has to be shown, not merely proclaimed. The consequences have to be assessed carefully—in particular, what we take to be "predictable." The reasons for the actions also have to be assessed—on rational grounds, with attention to historical fact and the documentary record, not simply by adulation of our leaders and the "principles and values" attributed to them by admirers.

8.

The Colombia Plan

Providing military aid for counterinsurgency forces

In 1999, Colombia became the leading recipient of U.S. military and police assistance, replacing Turkey (Israel and Egypt are in a separate category). The figure is scheduled to increase sharply with the anticipated passage of Clinton's Colombia Plan, a $1.6 billion "emergency aid" package for 2 years. Through the 1990s, Colombia has been the leading recipient of U.S. military aid in Latin America, and has also compiled the worst human rights record, in conformity with a well-established correlation.

We can often learn from systematic patterns, so let us focus for a moment on the previous champion, Turkey. As a major U.S. military ally and strategic outpost, Turkey has received substantial military aid from the origins of the Cold War. But arms deliveries began to increase sharply in 1984 with no Cold War connection at all. Rather, that was the year when Turkey initiated a large-scale counterinsurgency campaign in the Kurdish southeast, which also is the site of major U.S. air bases and the locus of regional surveillance, so that everything that happens there is well known in Washington. Arms deliveries peaked in 1997, exceeding the total from the entire period 1950-1983. U.S. arms amounted to about 80 percent of Turkish military equipment, including heavy armaments (jet planes, tanks, etc.).

By 1999, Turkey had largely suppressed Kurdish resistance by terror and ethnic cleansing, leaving some 2-3 million refugees, 3,500 villages destroyed (7 times Kosovo under NATO bombs), and tens of thousands killed. A huge flow of arms from the Clinton administration was no longer needed to accomplish these objectives. Turkey can therefore be singled out for praise for its "positive experiences" in showing how "tough counterterrorism measures plus political dialogue with non-terrorist opposition groups" can overcome the plague of violence and atrocities, so we learn from the lead article in the *New York Times* on the State Department's "latest annual report describing the administration's efforts to combat terrorism." Nevertheless, despite the great success achieved by some of the most extreme state terror of the

Published in Z Magazine, April 2000

1990s, military operations continue while Kurds are still deprived of elementary rights. On April 1, 10,000 Turkish troops began new ground sweeps in the regions that had been most devastated by the U.S.-Turkish terror campaigns of the preceding years, also launching another offensive into northern Iraq to attack Kurdish guerrilla forces—in a no-fly zone where Kurds are protected by the U.S. airforce from the (temporarily) wrong oppressor. As these new campaigns were beginning, Secretary of Defense William Cohen addressed the American-Turkish Council, a festive occasion with much laughter and applause, according to the government report. He praised Turkey for taking part in the humanitarian bombing of Yugoslavia, apparently without embarrassment, and announced that Turkey had been invited to join in co-production of the new Joint Strike Aircraft, just as it has been co-producing the F-16s that it used to such good effect in approved varieties of ethnic cleansing and atrocities within its own territory, as a loyal member of NATO.

In Colombia, however, the military armed and trained by the United States has not crushed domestic resistance, though it continues to produce its regular annual toll of atrocities. Each year, some 300,000 new refugees are driven from their homes, with a death toll of about 3,000 and many horrible massacres. The great majority of atrocities are attributed to the paramilitary forces that are closely linked to the military, as documented in detail once again in February 2000 by Human Rights Watch, and in April 2000 by a UN study which reported that the Colombian security forces that are to be greatly strengthened by the Colombia Plan maintain an intimate relationship with death-squads, organize paramilitary forces, and either participate in their massacres directly or, by failing to take action, have "undoubtedly enabled the paramilitary groups to achieve their exterminating objectives."

The Colombian Commission of Jurists reported in September 1999 that the rate of killings had increased by almost 20 percent over the preceding year, and that the proportion attributable to the paramilitaries had risen from 46 percent in 1995 to almost 80 percent in 1998, continuing through 1999. The Colombian government's Human Rights Ombudsman's Office (Defensoria del Pueblo) reported a 68 percent increase in massacres in the first half of 1999 as compared to the same period of 1998, reaching more than one a day, overwhelmingly attributed to paramilitaries.

We may recall that in the early months of 1999, while massacres were proceeding at over one a day in Colombia, there was also a large increase in atrocities (including many massacres) in East Timor carried out by Indonesian commandoes armed and trained by the U.S. In both cases, the conclusion drawn was exactly as in Turkey: support the killers. There was also one reported massacre in Kosovo, at Racak on January 15, the event that allegedly inspired such horror among Western humanitarians that it was necessary to bomb Yugoslavia 10 weeks later with the expectation, quickly fulfilled, that the consequence would be a sharp escalation of atrocities. The accompanying torrent of self-congratulation, which has few if any counterparts, heralded a "new era" in human affairs in which the "enlightened states" will selflessly dedicate themselves to the defense of human rights. Putting aside the actual facts about Kosovo, the performance was greatly facilitated by silence or deceit about the participation of the same powers in comparable or worse atrocities at the very same time.

Returning to Colombia, prominent human rights activists continue to flee abroad under death threats, including now the courageous head of the Church-based human rights group Justice and Peace, Fr. Javier Giraldo, who has played an outstanding role in defending human rights. The AFL-CIO reports that several trade unionists are murdered every week, mostly by paramilitaries supported by the government security forces. Forced displacement in 1998 was 20 percent above 1997 and increased in 1999 in some regions, according to Human Rights Watch. Colombia now has the largest displaced population in the world, after Sudan and Angola. Hailed as a leading democracy by Clinton and other U.S. leaders and political commentators, Colombia did at last permit an independent party (UP, Patriotic Union) to challenge the elite system of power-sharing.

The UP party, drawing in part from constituencies of the FARC guerrillas, faced certain difficulties, however, including the rapid assassination of about 3,000 activists, including presidential candidates, mayors, and legislators. The results taught lessons to the guerrillas about the prospects for entering the political system. Washington also drew lessons from these and other events of the same period. The Clinton administration was particularly impressed with the performance of President Cesar Gaviria who presided over the escalation of state terror and induced (some say compelled) the Organization of American States to accept him as secretary general on grounds that, "He has been very forward looking in building democratic institutions in a country where it was sometimes dangerous to do so"—which is surely true, in large measure because of the actions of his government. A more significant reason, perhaps, is that he was also "forward looking...on economic reform in Colombia and on economic integration in the hemisphere," code words that are readily interpreted.

Meanwhile, shameful socioeconomic conditions persist, leaving much of the population in misery in a rich country with concentration of wealth and land-ownership that is high even by Latin American standards. The situation became worse in the 1990s as a result of the "neoliberal reforms" formalized in the 1991 constitution.

The constitution reduced still further "the effective participation of civil society" in policy-formation, while, as in Latin America generally, the "neoliberal reforms have also given rise to alarming levels of poverty and inequality, approximately 55 percent of Colombia's population lives below the poverty level" and "this situation has been aggravated by an acute crisis in agriculture, itself a result of the neoliberal program" (Arlene Tickner, *Current History*, February 1998). The respected president of the Colombian Permanent Committee for Human Rights, former Minister of Foreign Affairs Alfredo Vasquez Carrizosa, writes that it is "poverty and insufficient land reform" that "have made Colombia one of the most tragic countries of Latin America," though as elsewhere, "violence has been exacerbated by external factors," primarily the initiatives of the Kennedy administration, which "took great pains to transform our regular armies into counterinsurgency brigades."

These initiatives ushered in "what is known in Latin America as the National Security Doctrine," which is not concerned with "defense against an external enemy," but rather "the internal enemy." The new "strategy of the death squads" accords the military "the right to fight and to exterminate social workers, trade unionists, men and women who are not supportive of the establishment and who are assumed to be communist extremists."

As part of its strategy of converting the Latin American military from "hemispheric defense" to "internal security"—meaning war against the domestic population—Kennedy dispatched a military mission to Colombia in 1962 headed by Special Forces General William Yarborough. He proposed "reforms" to enable the security forces to "as necessary execute paramilitary, sabotage and/or terrorist activities against known communist proponents"—the "communist extremists" to whom Vasquez Carrizosa alludes.

Again the broader patterns are worth noting. Shortly after, Lyndon Johnson escalated Kennedy's war against South Vietnam—what is called here "the defense of South Vietnam," just as Russia called its war against Afghanistan "the defense of Afghanistan." In January 1965, U.S. special forces in South Vietnam were issued standing orders "to conduct operations to dislodge VC-controlled officials, to include assassination," and more generally to use such "pacification" techniques as "ambushing, raiding, sabotaging, and committing acts of terrorism against known VC personnel," the counterparts of the "known Communist proponents" in Colombia. A Colombian governmental commission concluded that "the criminalization of social protest" is one of the "principal factors which permit and encourage violations of human rights" by the military and police authorities and their paramilitary collaborators. Ten years ago, as U.S.-backed state terror was increasing sharply, the Minister of Defense called for "total war in the political, economic, and social arenas," while another high military official explained that guerrillas were of secondary importance. "The real danger" is "what the insurgents have called the political and psychological war," the war "to control the popular elements" and "to manipulate the masses." The "subversives" hope to influence unions, universities, media, and so on. "Every individual who in one or another manner supports the goals of the enemy must be considered a traitor and treated in that manner," a 1963 military manual prescribed, as the Kennedy initiatives were moving into high gear. Since the official goals of the guerrillas are social democratic, the circle of treachery targeted for terror operations is wide.

In the years that followed, the Kennedy-Yarborough strategy was developed and applied broadly in "our little region over here," as it was described by FDR's Secretary of War Henry Stimson when he was explaining why the U.S. was entitled to control its own regional system while all others were dismantled. Violent repression spread throughout the hemisphere, beginning in the southern cone and reaching its awesome peak in Central America in the 1980s as the ruler of the hemisphere reacted with extreme violence to efforts by the Church and other "subversives" to confront a terrible legacy of misery and repression. Colombia's advance to first-rank among the criminal states in "our little region" is in part the result of the decline in Central American state terror, which achieved its primary aims as in Turkey ten years later, leaving in its wake a "culture of terror" that "domesticates the expectations of the majority" and undermines aspirations towards "alternatives that differ from those

of the powerful," in the words of Salvadoran Jesuits, who learned the lessons from bitter experience—those who survived the U.S. assault, that is. In Colombia, however, the problem of establishing approved forms of democracy and stability remains and is even becoming more severe. One approach would be to address the needs and concerns of the poor majority. Another is to send arms to keep things as they are.

Quite predictably, the announcement of the Colombia Plan led to countermeasures by the guerrillas, in particular, a demand that everyone with assets of more than $1 million pay a "revolutionary tax" or face the threat of kidnapping (as the FARC puts it, jailing for non-payment of taxes). The motivation is explained by the *London Financial Times:* "In the Farc's eyes, financing is required to fight fire with fire. The government is seeking $1.3 billion in military aid from the U.S., ostensibly for counter-drugs operations. Farc believes the new weapons will be trained on them. They appear ready to arm themselves for battle," which will lead to military escalation and undermining of the fragile but ongoing peace negotiations.

According to *New York Times* reporter Larry Rohter, "ordinary Colombians" are "angered" by the government's peace negotiations, which ceded control to FARC of a large region that they already controlled and the "embittered residents" of the region also oppose the guerrillas. No evidence is cited.

The leading Colombian military analyst Alfredo Rangel sees matters differently. He "makes a point of reminding interviewers that FARC has significant support in the regions where it operates," Alma Guillermoprieto reports. Rangel cites "FARC's ability to launch surprise attacks" in different parts of the country, a fact that is "politically significant" because "in each case, a single warning by the civilian population would be enough to alert the army, and it doesn't happen." On the same day that Rohter reported the anger of "ordinary Colombians," the *Financial Times* reported an "innovative forum" in the FARC-controlled region, one of many held there to allow "members of the public to participate in the current peace talks." They come from all parts of Colombia, speaking before TV cameras and meeting with senior FARC leaders. Included are union and business leaders, farmers, and others. A trade union leader from Colombia's second largest city, Cali, "gave heart to those who believe that talking will end the country's long-running conflict," addressing both the government and FARC leaders. He directed his remarks specifically to "Senor Marulanda," the long-time FARC peasant leader "who minutes earlier had entered to a rousing ovation," telling him that "unemployment is not a problem caused by the violence," but "by the national government and the businessmen of this country." Business leaders also spoke, but "were heckled by the large body of trade union representatives who had also come to speak." Against a background of "union cheers," a FARC spokesperson "put forward one of the clearest visions yet of his organization's economic program," calling for freezing of privatization, subsidizing energy, and agriculture as is done in the rich countries, and stimulation of the economy by protecting local enterprises. The government representative, who "emphasized export-led growth and private participation," nevertheless described the FARC statement as "raw material for the negotiations," though FARC, "bolstered by evident popular discontent with 'neoliberal' government policies," argues that those who "have monopolized power" must yield in the negotiations."

Of course, no one can say what "ordinary Colombians" (or "ordinary Americans") think, even under peaceful conditions, let alone when extreme violence and terror prevail, and much of the population seeks to survive under conditions of misery and repression.

The Colombia Plan is officially justified in terms of the "drug war," a claim taken seriously by few competent analysts. The U.S. Drug Enforcement Administration (DEA) reports that "all branches of government" in Colombia are involved in "drug-related corruption." In November 1998, U.S. Customs and DEA inspectors found 415 kg of cocaine and 6 kg of heroin in a Colombian Air Force plane that had landed in Florida, leading to the arrest of several Air Force officers and enlisted personnel. Other observers have also reported the heavy involvement of the military in narcotrafficking and the U.S. military has also been drawn in. The wife of Colonel James Hiett pleaded guilty to conspiracy to smuggle heroin from Colombia to New York, and shortly after it was reported that Colonel Hiett, who is in charge of U.S. troops "that trained Colombian security forces in counternarcotics operations," is "expected to plead guilty" to charges of complicity.

The paramilitaries openly proclaim their reliance on the drug business. However, the U.S. and Latin American press report, "the US-financed attack stays clear of the areas controlled by paramilitary forces," though "the leader of the paramilitaries [Carlos Castano] acknowledged in a television interview that the drug trade provided 70 percent of the group's funding." The targets of the Colombia Plan are guerrilla forces based on the peasantry and calling for internal social change, which would interfere with integration of Colombia into the global system on the terms that the U.S. demands, that is, dominated by elites linked to U.S. power interests that are accorded free access to Colombia's valuable resources, including oil.

In standard U.S. terminology, the FARC forces are "narco-guerrillas," a useful concept as a cover for counterinsurgency, but one that has been sharply criticized on factual grounds. It is agreed—and FARC leaders say—that they rely for funding on coca production, which they tax, as they tax other businesses. But "'The guerrillas are something different from the traffickers,' says Klaus Nyholm, who runs the UN Drug Control Program," which has agents throughout the drug producing regions. He describes the local FARC fronts as "quite autonomous." In some areas "they are not involved at all" in coca production and in others "they actively tell the farmers not to grow [coca]." Andean drug specialist Ricardo Vargas describes the role of the guerrillas as "primarily focused on taxation of illicit crops." They have called for "a development plan for the peasants" that would "allow eradication of coca on the basis of alternative crops." "That's all we want," their leader Marulanda has announced, as have other spokespersons.

But let us put these matters aside and consider a few other questions. Why do peasants in Colombia grow cocaine, not other crops? The reasons are well known. "Peasants grow coca and poppies," Vargas observes, "because of the crisis in the agricultural sector of Latin American countries, escalated by the general economic crisis in the region." He writes that peasants began colonizing the Colombian Amazon in the 1950s, "following the violent displacement of peasants by large landholders" and they found that coca was "the only product that was both profitable and easy to market." Pressures on the peasantry substantially increased as "ranchers, investors, and legal commercial farmers have created and strengthened private armies"—the para-militaries—that "serve as a means to violently expropriate land from indigenous people, peasants and settlers," with the result that "traffickers now control much of Colombia's valuable land." The counterinsurgency battalions armed and trained by the U.S.—do not attack traffickers, Vargas reports, but "have as their target the weakest and most socially fragile link of the drug chain: the production by peasants, settlers, and indigenous people." The same is true of the chemical and biological weapons that Washington employs, used experimentally in violation of manufacturer's specifications. These measures multiply the "dangers to the civilian population, the environment, and legal agriculture." They destroy "legal food crops like yucca and bananas, water sources, pastures, livestock, and all the crops included in crop substitution programs," including those of well-established Church-run development projects that have sought to develop alternatives to coca production. There are also uncertain, but potentially severe effects "on the fragile tropical rainforest environment."

Traditional U.S. programs, and the current Colombia Plan as well, primarily support the social forces that control the government and the military/paramilitary forces, and that have largely created the problems by their rapacity and violence. The targets are the usual victims.

There are other factors that operate to increase coca production. Colombia was once a major wheat producer. That was undermined in the 1950s by Food for Peace aid, a program that provided taxpayer subsidies to U.S. agribusiness and counterpart funds for U.S. client states, which they commonly used for military spending and counterinsurgency. A year before President Bush announced the "drug war" with great fanfare (once again), the international coffee agreement was suspended under U.S. pressure, on grounds of "fair trade violations." The result was a fall of prices of more than 40 percent within two months for Colombia's leading legal export.

Other factors are discussed by political economist Susan Strange in her last book. In the 1960s, the G77 governments (now 133, accounting for 80 percent of the world's population) initiated a call for a "new international economic order" in which the needs of the large majority of people of the world would be a prominent concern. Specific proposals were formulated by the UN Conference on Trade and Development (UNCTAD), which was established in 1964 "to create an international trading system consistent with the promotion of economic and social development." The UNCTAD proposals were summarily dismissed by the great powers, along with the call for a "new international order" generally; the U.S., in particular, insists that "development is not a right," and that it is "preposterous" and a "dangerous incitement" to hold otherwise in accord with the socioeconomic provisions of the

> The counterinsurgency battalions armed and trained by the U.S.—do not attack traffickers, Vargas reports, but "have as their target the weakest and most socially fragile link of the drug chain: the production by peasants, settlers, and indigenous people"

Universal Declaration of Human Rights, which the U.S. rejects. The world did move—or more accurately, was moved—towards a new international economic order, but along a different course, catering to the needs of a different sector, namely its designers—hardly a surprise, any more than one should be surprised that in standard doctrine the instituted form of "globalization" should be depicted as an inexorable process to which "there is no alternative," in Margaret Thatcher's cruel phrase.

One early UNCTAD proposal was a program for stabilizing commodity prices, a practice that is standard within the industrial countries by means of one or another form of subsidy, though it was threatened briefly in the U.S. when Congress was taken over in 1994 by ultra-rightists who seemed to believe their own rhetoric, much to the consternation of business leaders who understand that market discipline is for the defenseless.

The upstart free-market ideologues were soon taught better manners or dispatched back home, but not before Congress passed the 1996 Freedom to Farm Act to liberate American agriculture from the "East German socialist programs of the New Deal," as Newt Gingrich put it, ending market-distorting subsidies—which quickly tripled, reaching a record $23 billion in 1999, and scheduled to increase. The market has worked its magic, however, taxpayer subsidies go disproportionately to large agribusiness and the "corporate oligopolies" that dominate the input and output side, as Nicholas Kristof correctly observed. Those with market power in the food chain (from energy corporations to retailers) are enjoying great profits while the agricultural crisis, which is real, is concentrated in the middle of the chain, among smaller farmers, who produce the food.

One of the leading principles of modern economic history is that the devices used by the rich and powerful to ensure that they are protected by the nanny state are not to be available to the poor. Accordingly, the UNCTAD initiative to stabilize commodity prices was quickly shot down. The organization has been largely marginalized and tamed, along with others that reflect, to some extent at least, the interests of the global majority. Reviewing these events, Strange observes that farmers were therefore compelled to turn to crops for which there is a stable market. Large-scale agribusiness can tolerate fluctuation of commodity prices, compensating for temporary losses elsewhere. Poor peasants cannot tell their children: "don't worry, maybe you'll have something to eat next year." The result, Strange continues, was that drug entrepreneurs could easily "find farmers eager to grow coca, cannabis, or opium," for which there is always a ready market in the rich societies.

Other programs of the U.S. and the global institutions it dominates magnify these effects. The current Clinton plan for Colombia includes only token funding for alternative crops and none at all for areas under guerrilla control, though FARC leaders have repeatedly expressed their hope that alternatives will be provided so that peasants will not be compelled to grow coca. "By the end of 1999, the United States had spent a grand total of $750,000 on alternative development programs," the Center for International Policy reports, "all of it in heroin poppy-growing areas far from the southern plains" that are targeted in the Colombia Plan, which does, however, call for "assistance to civilians to be displaced by the push into southern Colombia," a section of the Plan that the Center rightly finds "especially disturbing." The Clinton administration also insists—over the objections of the Colombian government—that any peace agreement must permit crop destruction measures and other U.S. counternarcotics operations in Colombia. Constructive approaches are not barred, but they are someone else's business. The U.S. will concentrate on military operations—which, incidentally, happen to benefit the high-tech industries that produce military equipment and are engaged in "extensive lobbying" for the Colombia Plan, along with Occidental Petroleum, which has large investments in Colombia, and other corporations. Furthermore, IMF-World Bank programs demand that countries open their borders to a flood of (heavily subsidized) agricultural products from the rich countries, with the obvious effect of undermining local production. Those displaced are either driven to urban slums (thus lowering wage rates for foreign investors) or instructed to become "rational peasants," producing for the export market and seeking the highest prices—which translates as "coca, cannibis, opium." Having learned their lessons properly, they are rewarded by attack by military gunships while their fields are destroyed by chemical and biological warfare, courtesy of Washington.

Much the same is true throughout the Andean region. The issues broke through briefly to the public eye just as the Colombia Plan was being debated in Washington. On April 8, the government of Bolivia declared a state of emergency after widespread protests closed down the city of Cochabamba, Bolivia's third largest. The protests were over the privatization of the public water system and the sharp increase in water rates to a level beyond the reach of much of the population. In the background is an economic crisis attributed, in part, to the neoliberal policies that culminate in the drug war, which has destroyed more than half of the country's coca-leaf production, leaving the "rational peasants" destitute. A week later, farmers blockaded a highway near the capital city of La Paz to protest the eradication of coca leaf, the only mode of survival left to them under the "reforms," as implemented.

Reporting on the protests over water prices and the eradication programs, the *Financial Times* observes that, "The World Bank and the IMF saw Bolivia as something of a model," one of the great success stories of the "Washington consensus." But after the April protests we can see that "the success of eradication programs in Peru and Bolivia has carried a high social cost." The journal quotes a European diplomat in Bolivia who says that "Until a couple of weeks ago, Bolivia was regarded as a success story"—by some, at least; by those who "regard" a country while disregarding its people. But now, he continues, "the international community has to rec-

ognize that the economic reforms have not really done anything to solve the growing problems of poverty"; a bit euphemistic. The secretary of the Bolivian bishops' conference, which mediated an agreement to end the crisis, described the protest movement as "the result of dire poverty. The demands of the rural population must be listened to if we want lasting peace."

The Cochabamba protests were aimed at the World Bank and the San Francisco/London-based Bechtel corporation, the main financial power behind the transnational conglomerate that bought the public water system amid serious charges of corruption and give-away, and then doubled rates for many poor customers. Under Bank pressure, Bolivia has sold major assets to private (almost always foreign) corporations. The sale of the public water system and rate increases set off months of protest culminating in the demonstration that paralyzed the city.

Government policies adhered to World Bank recommendations that, "No subsidies should be given to ameliorate the increase in water tariffs in Cochabamba"; all users, including the very poor, must pay full costs. Using the Internet, activists in Bolivia called for international protests, which had a significant impact, presumably amplified by the Washington protests over World Bank-IMF policies then underway. Bechtel backed off and the government rescinded the sale. But a long and difficult struggle lies ahead.

As martial law was declared in Bolivia, a press report from southern Colombia described the spreading fears that fumigation planes were coming to "drop their poison on the coca fields, which would also kill the farmers' subsistence crops, cause massive social disruption, and stir up the ever-present threat of violence." The pervasive fear and anger reflect "the level of dread and confusion in this part of Colombia" as the U.S. carries out chemical and biological warfare to destroy coca production.

Another question lurks not too far in the background. Just what right does the U.S. have to carry out military operations and chemical-biological warfare in other countries to destroy a crop it doesn't like? We can put aside the cynical response that the governments requested this "assistance," or else. We therefore must ask whether others have the same extraterritorial right to violence and destruction that the U.S. demands.

The number of Colombians who die from U.S.-produced lethal drugs exceeds the number of North Americans who die from cocaine and is far greater, relative to population. In East Asia, U.S.-produced lethal drugs contribute to millions of deaths. These countries are compelled not only to accept the products, but also advertising for them, under threat of trade sanctions. The effects of "aggressive marketing and advertising by American firms is, in a good measure, responsible for...a sizeable increase in smoking rates for women and youth in Asian countries where doors were forced open by threat of severe U.S. trade sanctions," public health researchers conclude. The Colombian cartels, in contrast, are not permitted to run huge advertising campaigns in which a Joe Camel counterpart extols the wonders of cocaine.

We are, therefore, morally obligated, to ask whether Colombia, Thailand, China, and other targets of U.S. trade policies and lethal-export promotion have the right to conduct military, chemical, and biological warfare in North Carolina. And if not, why not?

We might also ask why there are no Delta Force raids on U.S. banks and chemical corporations, though it is no secret that they, too, are engaged in the narcotrafficking business. And why the Pentagon is not gearing up to attack Canada, now replacing Colombia and Mexico with high potency marijuana that has already become British Colombia's most valuable agricultural product and one of the most important sectors of the economy, joined by Quebec and closely followed by Manitoba, with a tenfold increase in just the past two years. Or to attack the United States, a

> We are, therefore, morally obligated, to ask whether Colombia, Thailand, China, and other targets of U.S. trade policies and lethal-export promotion have the right to conduct military, chemical, and biological warfare in North Carolina. And if not, why not?

major producer of marijuana with production expanding, including hydroponic groweries and the manufacture of high-tech illicit drugs (ATS, amphetamine-type stimulants), the fastest growing sector of drug abuse, with 30 million users worldwide, probably surpassing heroin and cocaine.

There is no need to review in detail the lethal effects of U.S. drugs. The Supreme Court recently concluded that it has been "amply demonstrated" that tobacco use is "perhaps the single most significant threat to public health in the United States," responsible for more than 400,000 deaths a year, more than AIDS, car accidents, alcohol, homicides, illegal drugs, suicides, and fires combined; the Court virtually called on Congress to legislate regulation. As use of this lethal substance has declined in the U.S., and producers have been compelled to pay substantial indemnities to victims, they have shifted to markets abroad, another standard practice. The death toll is incalculable. Oxford University epidemiologist Richard Peto estimated that in China alone, among children under 20 today 50 million will die of cigarette-related diseases, a substantial number because of highly selective U.S. "free trade" doctrine.

In comparison to the 400,000 deaths caused by tobacco every year in the United States, drug-related deaths reached a record 16,000 in 1997. Furthermore, only 4 out of 10 addicts who needed treatment received it, according to a White House report. These facts raise further questions about the motives for the drug war. The seriousness of concern over use of drugs was illustrated when a House Committee was considering the Clinton Colombia Plan. It rejected an amendment proposed by California Democrat Nancy Pelosi calling for funding of drug demand reduction services. It is well known that these are far more effective than forceful measures. A widely-cited Rand corporation study funded by the U.S. Army and Office of National Drug Control Policy found that funds spent on domestic drug treatment were 23 times as effective as "source country control" (Clinton's Colombia Plan), 11 times as effective as interdiction, and 7 times as effective as domestic law enforcement. But the inexpensive and effective path will not be followed. Rather, the drug war targets poor peasants abroad and poor people at home; by the use of force, not constructive measures to alleviate problems at a fraction of the cost.

While Clinton's Colombia Plan was being formulated, senior administration officials discussed a proposal by the Office of Budget and Management to take $100 million from the $1.3 billion then planned for Colombia, to be used for treatment of U.S. addicts. There was near-unanimous opposition, particularly from "drug czar" Barry McCaffrey, and the proposal was dropped. In contrast, when Richard Nixon—in many respects the last liberal president—declared a drug war in 1971, two-thirds of the funding went to treatment, which reached record numbers of addicts and there was a sharp drop in drug-related arrests and number of federal prison inmates, as well as crime rates. Since 1980, however, "the war on drugs has shifted to punishing offenders, border surveillance, and fighting production at the source countries," John Donnelly reports in the *Boston Globe*. One consequence is the enormous increase in drug-related (often victimless) crimes and an explosion in the prison population, reaching levels far beyond any industrial country and possibly a world record, with no detectable effect on availability or price of drugs.

Such observations, hardly obscure, raise the question of what the drug war is all about. It is recognized widely that it fails to achieve its stated ends and the failed methods are then pursued more vigorously while effective ways to reach the stated goals are rejected. It is, therefore, natural to conclude that the drug war, cast in the harshly punitive form implemented since 1980, is achieving its goals, not failing.

What are these goals? A plausible answer is implicit in a comment by Senator Daniel Patrick Moynihan, one of the few senators to pay close attention to social statistics. By adopting these measures, he observed, "we are choosing to have an intense crime problem concentrated among minorities." Criminologist Michael Tonry concludes that, "the war's planners knew exactly what they were doing." What they were doing is, first, getting rid of the "superfluous population," the "disposable people" ("desechables"), as they are called in Colombia, where they are eliminated by "social cleansing"; and second, frightening everyone else, not an unimportant task in a period when a domestic form of "structural adjustment" is being imposed, with significant costs for the majority of the population.

"While the War on Drugs only occasionally serves and more often degrades public health and safety," a well-informed and insightful review by Partners in Health researchers concludes, "it regularly serves the interests of private wealth, interests revealed by the pattern of winners and losers, targets and non-targets, well-funded, and underfunded," in accord with "the main interests of U.S. foreign and domestic policy generally" and the private sector that "has overriding influence on policy." One may debate the motivations, but the consequences in the U.S. and abroad seem reasonably clear.

9.

Voting Patterns and Abstentions

Almost half the electorate did not participate
and voting correlated with income

In the 2000 elections, as usual, almost half the electorate did not participate and voting correlated with income. It remains true that "voter turnout is among the lowest and most decisively class-skewed in the industrial world" (Thomas Ferguson and Joel Rogers). This feature of so-called "American exceptionalism" has been plausibly attributed to "the total absence of a socialist or laborite mass party as an organized competitor in the electoral market" (Walter Dean Burnham).

Higher-income voters favor Republicans, but class-skewed voting does not come close to accounting for the ability of the more openly pro-business party to garner half the vote. The voting bloc that provided Bush with his greatest electoral success provided the crucial contribution: middle-to-lower income white working class, particularly men, but women as well. By large margins they favored Gore on major policy issues, and among voters concerned more with policy issues than "qualities" Gore won handily. But the genius of the political system is to render policy irrelevant. Voter attention is to be focused on style, personality—anything but the issues that are of primary concern to the concentrated private power centers that largely finance campaigns and run the government. Their shared interests are off the agenda, in conformity with Ferguson's well-supported "investment theory of politics."

Crucially, questions of economic policy must not arise in the campaign. These are of great concern both to the general population and to private power and its political representatives, but with opposing preferences. The business world, not surprisingly, is overwhelmingly in favor of "neoliberal reforms," corporate-led "globalization," the investor-rights agreements called "free trade agreements," and other devices that concentrate wealth and power. Also not surprisingly, the public is generally opposed. It follows that such issues are not appropriate for political campaigns. For the public, the U.S. trade deficit had become the most important economic issue facing the country by 1998, outranking taxes or the budget deficit; people understand that it translates into loss of jobs, for example, when U.S. corporations establish plants abroad that export to the U.S. market.

For the business world, a high priority is free capital mobility: it increases profit and also provides a powerful weapon to undermine labor or-

From Z Magazine, February 2001

ganizing by threat of job transfer—technically illegal, but highly effective, as Kate Bronfenbrenner demonstrates in an important study extending her earlier research ("Uneasy Terrain: The Impact of Capital Mobility on Workers, Wages, and Union Organizing," Cornell 2000). Such threats contribute to the "growing worker insecurity" that has been hailed by Alan Greenspan and others as a significant factor in improving economic health by limiting wages, benefits, and inflation that would be unwelcome to financial interests. But such matters are not to intrude into the electoral process: the general population is induced to vote (if at all) on the basis of peripheral concerns.

This pattern too is familiar; I mentioned the example of 1984, when Reagan won a "landslide victory" while voters opposed his legislative program by a margin of 3-2. Such voting against interest is understandable among people who feel powerless, taking for granted that government is run by "a few big interests looking out for themselves"; half the population in 1984, rising to over 80 percent a few years later as the "neoliberal reforms" were more firmly instituted.

These "reforms" have the natural consequence of marginalizing the majority of the population, as decision-making is transferred further to unaccountable private power systems, while a "virtual Senate" of investors and lenders can exercise "veto power" over government decisions, thanks to financial liberalization. Regulation of capital flow and exchange rates under the Bretton Woods system established by the U.S. and Britain in the mid-1940s allowed for a form of "embedded liberalism," in which social democratic policies could be pursued within a liberalized international economy. The dismantling of the system 30 years later was one important element of the campaign to reverse the feared "excess of democracy" of the 1960s (to borrow the rhetoric of the 1975 Trilateral Commission report on "the crisis of democracy"), and to restore the population to passivity and acquiescence, perhaps even renewing the good old days when "Truman had been able to govern the country with the cooperation of a relatively small number of Wall Street lawyers and bankers," as the American rapporteur, Samuel Huntington, recalled with nostalgia.

The constitutional system was originally designed "to protect the minority of the opulent against the majority," in the words of the leading framer, James Madison. Political power, he explained, must be in the hands of "the wealth of the nation," men who can be trusted to "secure the permanent interests of the country"—the rights of the propertied—and to defend these interests against the "leveling spirit" of the general public.

In a modern version, the general public are considered "ignorant and meddlesome outsiders" who should be mere "spectators of action," not participants (Walter Lippmann); their role is only periodic choice among the "responsible men," who are to function in "technocratic insulation," in World Bank lingo, "securing the permanent interests." The doctrine, labeled "polyarchy" by democratic political theorist Robert Dahl, is given firmer institutional grounds by the reduction of the public arena under the "reforms." Democracy is to be construed as the right to choose among commodities.

Business leaders explain the need to impose on the population a "philosophy of futility" and "lack of purpose in life," to "concentrate human attention on the more superficial things that comprise much of fashionable consumption." People may then accept and even welcome their meaningless and subordinate lives, and forget ridiculous ideas about managing their own affairs. They will abandon their fate to the responsible people, the self-described "intelligent minorities" who serve and administer power—which of course lies elsewhere, a hidden, but crucial premise.

From this perspective, conventional in elite opinion, the latest elections do not reveal a flaw of American democracy, but rather its triumph.

10.

The War In Afghanistan

*Afghanistan refugees are describing scenes
of desperation and fear of a U.S. miliary attack*

The threat of international terrorism is surely severe. The horrendous events of September 11 had perhaps the most devastating instant human toll on record, outside of war. The word "instant" should not be overlooked. Regrettably, the crime is far from unusual in the annals of violence that falls short of war. The death toll may easily have doubled or more within a few weeks, as miserable Afghans fled—to nowhere—under the threat of bombing, and desperately-needed food supplies were disrupted and there were credible warnings of much worse to come.

The costs to Afghan civilians can only be guessed, but we do know the projections on which policy decisions and commentary were based, a matter of utmost significance. As a matter of simple logic, it is these projections that provide the grounds for any moral evaluation of planning and commentary or any judgment of appeals to "just war" arguments and, crucially, for a rational assessment of what may lie ahead.

Even before September 11, the UN estimated that millions were being sustained, barely, by international food aid. On September 16, the national press reported that Washington had "demanded [from Pakistan] the elimination of truck convoys that provided much of the food and other supplies to Afghanistan's civilian population." There was no detectable reaction in the U.S. or Europe to this demand to impose massive starvation, the plain meaning of the words. In subsequent weeks, the world's leading newspaper reported that, "The threat of military strikes forced the removal of international aid workers, crippling assistance programs" and refugees reaching Pakistan "after arduous journeys from Afghanistan are describing scenes of desperation and fear at home as the threat of American-led military attacks turns their long-running misery into a potential catastrophe." "The country was on a lifeline," one evacuated aid worker reported, "and we just cut the line." "It's as if a mass grave has been dug behind millions of people," an evacuated emergency officer for Christian Aid informed the press that, "We can drag

From Z Magazine, February 2002

them back from it or push them in. We could be looking at millions of deaths."

The UN World Food Program and others were able to resume some food shipments in early October, but were forced to suspend deliveries and distribution when the bombing began on October 7, resuming them later at a much lower pace. A spokesperson for the UN High Commissioner for Refugees warned that, "We are facing a humanitarian crisis of epic proportions in Afghanistan with 7.5 million short of food and at risk of starvation," while aid agencies leveled "scathing" condemnations of U.S. air drops that are barely concealed "propaganda tools" and may cause more harm than benefit, they warned.

A very careful reader of the national press could discover the estimate by the UN that "7.5 million Afghans will need food over the winter—2.5 million more than on September 11," a 50 percent increase as a result of the threat of bombing, then the actuality. In other words, Western civilization was basing its plans on the assumption that they might lead to the death of several million innocent civilians—not Taliban, whatever one thinks of the legitimacy of slaughtering Taliban recruits and supporters, but their victims. Meanwhile its leader, on the same day, once again dismissed with contempt offers of negotiation for extradition of the suspected culprit and the request for some credible evidence to substantiate the demands for capitulation.

The UN Special Rapporteur on the Right to Food pleaded with the U.S. to end the bombing that was putting "the lives of millions of civilians at risk," renewing the appeal of UN High Commissioner for Human Rights Mary Robinson, who warned of a Rwanda-style catastrophe. Both appeals were rejected, as were those of the major aid and relief agencies. And virtually unreported.

In late September, the UN Food And Agricultural Organization (FAD) warned that over seven million people were facing a crisis that could lead to widespread starvation if military action were initiated, with a likely "humanitarian catastrophe" unless aid were immediately resumed and the threat of military action terminated. After bombing began, the FAO advised that it had disrupted planting that provides 80 percent of the country's grain supplies, so that the effects next year are expected to be even more severe. All were ignored.

These unreported appeals happened to coincide with World Food Day, which was also ignored, along with the charge by the UN Special Rapporteur that the rich and powerful easily have the means, though not the will, to overcome the "silent genocide" of mass starvation in much of the world.

Let us return briefly to the ethical judgments and rational evaluation of what may lie ahead are grounded in the presuppositions of planning and commentary. An entirely separate matter, with no bearing on such judgments, is the accuracy of the projections on which planning and commentary were based. By year's end, there were hopes that unprecedented deliveries of food in December might "dramatically" revise the expectations at the time when planning was undertaken, implemented, and evaluated in commentary that these actions were likely to drive millions over the edge of starvation. Very likely, the facts will never be known, by virtue of a guiding principle of intellectual culture: We must devote enormous energy to exposing the crimes of official enemies, properly counting not only those literally killed, but also those who die as a consequence of policy choices, but we must take scrupulous care to avoid this practice in the case of our own crimes, on the rare occasions when they are investigated at all. Observance of the principle is all too well documented.

Another elementary point might also be mentioned. The success of violence evidently has no bearing on moral judgment with regard to its goals. In the present case, it seemed clear from the outset that the reigning superpower could easily demolish any Afghan resistance. My own view, for what it is worth, was that U.S. campaigns should not be too casually compared to the failed Russian invasion of the 1980s. The

Russians were facing a major army of perhaps 100,000 people or more, organized, trained, and heavily armed by the CIA and its associates. The U.S. is facing a ragtag force in a country that has already been virtually destroyed by 20 years of horror, for which we bear no slight share of responsibility. The Taliban forces, such as they are, might quickly collapse except for a small hardened core.

To my surprise, the dominant judgment—even after weeks of carpet bombing and resort to virtually every available device short of nuclear weapons ("daisy cutters," cluster bombs, etc.)—was confidence that the lessons of the Russian failure should be heeded, that airstrikes would be ineffective, and that a ground invasion would be necessary to achieve the U.S. war aims of eliminating bin Laden and al-Qaeda. Removing the Taliban regime was an afterthought. There had been no interest in this before September 11, or even in the month that followed. A week after the bombing began, the president reiterated that U.S. forces "would attack Afghanistan 'for as long as it takes' to destroy the Qaeda terrorist network of Osama bin Laden, but he offered to reconsider the military assault on Afghanistan if the country's ruling Taliban would surrender Mr. bin Laden."

"If you cough him up and his people today, then we'll reconsider what we are doing to your country," the president declared: "You still have a second chance."

When Taliban forces did finally succumb, after astonishing endurance, opinions shifted to triumphalist proclamations and exultation over the justice of our cause, now demonstrated by the success of overwhelming force against defenseless opponents.

Returning to the war, the airstrikes quickly turned cities into "ghost towns," the press reported, with electrical power and water supplies destroyed, a form of biological warfare. The UN reported that 70 percent of the population had fled Kandahar and Herat within two weeks, mostly to the countryside, where in ordinary times 10-20 people, many of them children, are killed or crippled daily by land mines. Those conditions became much worse as a result of the bombing. UN mine-clearing operations were halted, and unexploded U.S. ordnance, particularly the lethal bomblets scattered by cluster bombs, add to the torture, and are much harder to clear.

By late October, aid officials estimated that over a million had fled their homes, including 80 percent of the population of Jalalabad, only a "tiny fraction" able to cross the border, most scattering to the countryside where there was little food or shelter or possibility of delivering aid. Appeals from aid agencies to suspend attacks to allow delivery of supplies were again rejected by Blair, ignored by the U.S.

Destruction Of Lives

Months later, hundreds of thousands were reported to be starving in such "forgotten camps" as Maslakh in the North, having fled from "mountainous places to which the World Food Program was giving food aid, but stopped because of the bombing and now cannot be reached because the passes are cut off"—and who knows how many in places that no journalists found—though supplies were by then available and the primary factor hampering delivery was lack of interest and will.

By early January, the reported death toll in Maslakh alone—near Herat, therefore accessible to journalists—had risen to 100 a day, and aid officials warned that the camp is "on the on the brink of an Ethiopian-style humanitarian disaster" as the flight of refugees to the camp continued to increase, an estimated three-fourths of its population since September.

The destruction of lives is silent and mostly invisible, by choice; and can easily remain forgotten, also by choice. An even sorrier sight is denial—or worse, even ridicule—of the efforts to bring these tragedies to light so that pressures can be mounted to relieve them, which should be a very high priority whatever one thinks about what has happened. By the year's end, long after fighting ended, the occasional report noted that, "the delivery of food remains blocked or woefully inadequate," "a system for distributing food is still not in place," and even the main route to Uzbekistan "remains effectively closed to food trucks" over two weeks after it was officially opened with much fanfare.

The same was true of the crucial artery from Pakistan to Kandahar and others were so harassed by armed militias that the World Food Program, now with supplies available, still could not make deliveries, and had no place for storage because "most warehouses were destroyed or looted during the U.S. bombardment."

A detailed year-end review found that the U.S. war "has returned to power nearly all the same warlords who had misruled the country in the days before the Taliban" and some Afghans see the resulting situation as even "worse than it was before the Taliban came to power." The Taliban takeover of most of the country, with little combat, brought to an end a period described by Afghan and international human rights activists as "the blackest in the history of Afghanistan," "the worst time in Afghanistan's history," with vast destruction, mass rapes, other atrocities, and tens of thousands killed. These were the years of rule by warlords of the Northern Alliance and other Western favorites, such as the murderous Gulbuddin Hekmatyar, one of the few who has not reclaimed his fiefdom. There are indications that lessons have been learned both in Afghanistan and the world beyond.

Signs were mixed, at year's end. As anticipated, most of the population was greatly relieved to see the end of the Taliban, one of the most retrograde regimes in the world and relieved that there was no quick return to the atrocities of a decade earlier, as had been feared. The new government in Kabul showed considerably more promise than most had expected. The return of warlordism was a dangerous sign, as was the announcement by the new justice minister that the basic structure of sharia law as instituted by the Taliban, would remain in force,

though "there will be some changes. For example, the Taliban used to hang the victim's body in public for four days. We will only hang the body for a short time, say 15 minutes." Judge Ahamat Ullha Zarif added that some new location would be found for the regular public executions, not the Sports Stadium. "Adulterers, both male and female, would still be stoned to death, Zarif said, 'but we will use only small stones'," so that those who confess might be able to run away and others will be "stoned to death," as before.

As the year ended, desperate peasants, mostly women, were returning to the miserable labor of growing opium poppies so that their families could survive, reversing the Taliban ban. The UN reported in October that poppy production had already "increased threefold in areas controlled by the Northern Alliance," whose warlords "have long been reputed to control much of the processing and smuggling of opium" to Russia and the West, an estimated 75 percent of the world's heroin. The result of some poor woman's back-breaking labor is that "countless others thousands of miles away from her home in eastern Afghanistan will suffer and die."

Such consequences, and the devastating legacy of 20 years of brutal war and atrocities, could be alleviated by an appropriate international presence and well-designed programs of aid and reconstruction, were honesty to prevail, they would be called "reparations," at least from Russia and the U.S., which share primary responsibility for the disaster. The issue was addressed in a conference of the UN Development Program, World Bank, and Asian Development Bank in Islamabad in late November. Some guidelines were offered in a World Bank study that focused on Afghanistan's potential role in the development of the energy resources of the region. The study concluded that, "Afghanistan has a positive pre-war history of cost recovery for key infrastructure services like electric power and green field investment opportunities in sectors like telecommunications, energy, and oil/gas pipelines. It is extremely important that such services start out on the right track during reconstruction.

Options for private investment in infrastructure should be actively pursued. "

One may reasonably ask just whose needs are served by these priorities and what status they should have in reconstruction from the horrors of the past two decades. U.S. and British intellectual opinion, across the political spectrum, assured us that only radical extremists can doubt that, "this is basically a just war." Those who disagree can, therefore, be dismissed. Among them, for example, the 1,000 Afghan leaders who met in Peshawar in late October in a U.S.-backed effort to lay the groundwork for a post-Taliban regime led by the exiled King. They bitterly condemned the U.S. war, which is "beating the donkey rather than the rider," one speaker said to unanimous agreement.

The extent to which anti-Taliban Afghan opinion was ignored is rather striking—and not at all unusual. During the Gulf War, for example, Iraqi dissidents were excluded from press and journals, apart from "alternative media," though they were readily accessible. Without eliciting comment, Washington maintained its long standing official refusal to have any dealings with the Iraqi opposition even well after the war ended. In the present case, Afghan opinion is not as easily assessed, but the task would not have been impossible and the issue is of such evident significance that it merits at least a few comments.

We might begin with the gathering of Afghan leaders in Peshawar, some exiles, some who trekked across the border from within Afghanistan, all committed to overthrowing the Taliban regime. It was "a rare display of unity among tribal elders, Islamic scholars, fractious politicians, and former guerrilla commanders," the *New York Times* reported. They unanimously "urged the U.S. to stop the air raids," appealed to the international media to call for an end to

the "bombing of innocent people," and "demanded an end to the U.S. bombing of Afghanistan." They urged that other means be adopted to overthrow the hated Taliban regime, a goal they believed could be achieved without slaughter and destruction. Reported, but dismissed without further comment.

A similar message was conveyed by Afghan opposition leader Abdul Haq, who condemned the air attacks as a "terrible mistake." Highly regarded in Washington, Abdul Haq was considered to be "perhaps the most important leader of anti-Taliban opposition among Afghans of Pashtun nationality based in Pakistan." His advice was to "avoid bloodshed as much as possible." Instead of bombing, "we should undermine the central leadership, which is a very small and closed group and which is also the only thing which holds them all together. If they are destroyed, every Taliban fighter will pick up his gun and his blanket and disappear back home and that will be the end of the Taliban," an assessment that seems rather plausible in the light of subsequent events.

Several weeks later, Abdul Haq entered Afghanistan, apparently without U.S. support and was captured and killed. As he was undertaking this mission "to create a revolt within the Taliban," he criticized the U.S. for refusing to aid him and others in such endeavors, and condemned the bombing as "a big setback for these efforts." He reported contacts with second-level Taliban commanders and ex-Mujahidin tribal elders and discussed how further efforts could proceed, calling on the U.S. to assist them with funding and other support instead of under-mining them with bombs.

The U.S., Abdul Haq said, "is trying to show its muscle, score a victory, and scare everyone in the world. They don't care about the suffering of the Afghans or how many people we will lose.

> The U.S., Abdul Haq said, "is trying to show its muscle, score a victory, and scare everyone in the world. They don't care about the suffering of the Afghans or how many people we will lose. And we don't like that. Because Afghans are now being made to suffer for these Arab fanatics, but we all know who brought these Arabs to Afghanistan in the 1980s, armed them, and gave them a base. It was the Americans and the CIA."

And we don't like that. Because Afghans are now being made to suffer for these Arab fanatics, but we all know who brought these Arabs to Afghanistan in the 1980s, armed them, and gave them a base. It was the Americans and the CIA. And the Americans who did this all got medals and good careers, while all these years Afghans suffered from these Arabs and their allies. Now, when America is attacked, instead of punishing the Americans who did this, it punishes the Afghans."

We can also look elsewhere for enlightenment about Afghan opinions. A beneficial consequence of the latest Afghan war is that it elicited some belated concern about the fate of women in Afghanistan, even reaching the First Lady. Perhaps it will be followed some day by concern for the plight of women elsewhere in Central and South Asia, which, unfortunately, is often not very different from life under the Taliban, including in the most vibrant democracies. Of course, no sane person advocates foreign military intervention to rectify these and other injustices. The problems are severe, but should be dealt with from within, with assistance from outsiders if it is constructive and honest.

Since the harsh treatment of women in Afghanistan has at last gained some well-deserved attention, one might expect that attitudes of Afghan women towards policy options should be a primary concern. A natural starting point for an inquiry is Afghanistan's "oldest political and humanitarian organisation," RAWA (Revolutionary Association of the Women of Afghanistan), which has been "foremost in the struggle" for women's rights since its formation in 1977. RAWA's leader was assassinated by Afghan collaborators with the Russians in 1987, but they continued their work within Afghanistan at risk of death and in exile nearby.

RAWA has been quite outspoken. Thus, a week after the bombing began, RAWA issued a public statement entitled: "Taliban should be overthrown by the uprising of Afghan nation." It continued as follows: "Again, due to the treason of fundamentalist hangmen, our people have been caught in the claws of the monster of a vast war and destruction. America, by forming an international coalition against Osama and his Taliban-collaborators and in retaliation for the 11th September terrorist attacks, has launched a vast aggression on our country...what we have witnessed for the past seven days leaves no doubt that this invasion will shed the blood of numerous women, men, children, young and old of our country."

The statement called for "the eradication of the plague of Taliban and Al Qaeda" by "an overall uprising" of the Afghan people themselves, which alone "can prevent the repetition and recurrence of the catastrophe that has befallen our country." In another declaration on November 25, at a demonstration of women's organizations in Islamabad on the International Day for the Elimination of Violence against Women, RAWA condemned the U.S./Russian-backed Northern Alliance for a "record of human rights violations as bad as that of the Taliban's," and called on the UN to "help Afghanistan, not the Northern Alliance." RAWA issued similar warnings at the national conference of the All India Democratic Women's Association.

Also Ignored

One might note that this is hardly the first time that the concerns of advocates of women's rights in Afghanistan have been dismissed. Thus, in 1988 the UNDP senior adviser on women's rights in Afghanistan warned that the "great advances" in women's rights she had witnessed there were being imperilled by the "ascendant fundamentalism" of the U.S.-backed radical Islamists. Her report was submitted to the *New York Times* and *Washington Post*, but not published. Her account of how the U.S. "contributed handsomely to the suffering of Afghan women" remains unknown. The issue of "just war" should not be confused with a wholly different question: Should the perpetrators of the atrocities of September 11 be punished for their crimes—"crimes against humanity"—as they were called by Robert Fisk, Mary Robinson, and others. On this there is virtually unanimous agreement, though notoriously, the principles do not extend to the agents of even far worse crimes who are protected by power and wealth. The question is how to proceed.

The approach favored by Afghans who were ignored had considerable support in much of the world. Many in the South would surely have endorsed the recommendations of the UN representative of the Arab Women's Solidarity Association: "providing the Taliban with evidence (as it has requested) that links bin Laden to the September 11 attacks, employing diplomatic pressures to extradite him, and prosecuting terrorists through international tribunals," and generally adhering to international law, following precedents that exist even in much more severe cases of international terrorism. Adherence to international law had scattered support in the West as well, including the preeminent Anglo-American military historian Michael Howard, who delivered a "scathing attack" on the bombardment, calling instead for an international "police operation" and international court rather than "trying to eradicate cancer cells with a blow torch."

Washington's refusal to call for extradition of the suspected criminals or to provide the evidence that was requested, was entirely open, and generally approved. Its own refusal to extradite criminals remains effectively secret, however. There has been debate over whether U.S. military actions in Afghanistan were authorized under ambiguous Security Council resolutions, but it avoids the central issue that Washington plainly did not want Security Council authorization, which it surely could have obtained, clearly and unambiguously. Since it lost its virtual monopoly over UN decisions, the U.S. has been far in the lead in vetoes, Britain second, France a distant third, but none of these powers would have opposed a U.S.-sponsored resolution. Nor would Russia or China, eager to gain U.S. authorization for their own atrocities and repression (in Chechnya and western China, particularly). But Washington insisted on not obtaining Security Council authorization, which would entail that there is some higher authority to which it should defer. Systems of power resist that principle if they are strong enough to do so. There is even a name for that stance in the literature of diplomacy and international affairs scholarship: establishing "credibility," a justification commonly offered for the threat or use of force.

11.

What Makes Mainstream Media Mainstream?

The real mass media are basically trying to divert people

P art of the reason why I write about the media is because I am interested in the whole intellectual culture and the part of it that is easiest to study is the media. It comes out every day. You can do a systematic investigation. You can compare yesterday's version to today's version. There is a lot of evidence about what's played up and what isn't and the way things are structured. My impression is the media aren't very different from scholarship or from, say, journals of intellectual opinion. There are some extra constraints, but it's not radically different. They interact, which is why people go up and back quite easily among them.

You look at the media, or at any institution you want to understand. You ask questions about its internal institutional structure. You want to know something about their setting in the broader society. How do they relate to other systems of power and authority? If you're lucky, there is an internal record from leading people in the information system, which tells you what they are up to (it is sort of a doctrinal system). There is quite a lot of interesting documentation.

Those are three major sources of information about the nature of the media. You want to study them the way, say, a scientist would study some complex molecule. You take a look at the structure and then make some hypothesis based on the structure as to what the media product is likely to look like. Then you investigate the media product and see how well it conforms to the hypotheses. Virtually all work in media analysis is this last part—trying to study carefully just what the media product is and whether it conforms to obvious assumptions about the nature and structure of the media.

Well, what do you find? First of all, you find that there are different media which do different things, like entertainment/Hollywood, soap operas, and so on, or even most of the newspapers in the country (the overwhelming majority of them). They are directing the mass audience.

From a talk given at Z Media Institute, 2002. Published in Z Magazine, May 2014

There is another sector of the media, the elite media, sometimes called the agenda-setting media, because they are the ones with the big resources and they set the framework in which everyone else operates. The *New York Times* and CBS, that kind of thing, their audience is mostly privileged people. The people who read the *New York Times*—people who are wealthy or part of what is sometimes called the political class—they are actually involved in the political system in an ongoing fashion. They are basically managers of one sort or another. They can be political managers, business managers (like corporate executives), doctoral managers (like university professors), or other journalists who are involved in organizing the way people think and look at things.

The elite media set a framework within which others operate. If you are watching the Associated Press, which grinds out a constant flow of news; in the mid-afternoon it breaks and there is something that comes along every day that says "Notice to Editors: Tomorrow's *New York Times* is going to have the following stories on the front page." The point of that is, if you're an editor of a newspaper in Dayton, Ohio and you don't have the resources to figure out what the news is, or you don't want to think about it anyway, this tells you what the news is.

These are the stories for the quarter page that you are going to devote to something other than local affairs or diverting your audience. These are the stories that you put there because that's what the *New York Times* tells us is what you're supposed to care about tomorrow. If you are an editor in Dayton, Ohio, you would have to do that because you don't have much else in the way of resources. If you get off line, if you're producing stories that the big press doesn't like, you'll hear about it pretty soon. In fact, what just happened at *San Jose Mercury News* is a dramatic example of this. So there are a lot of ways in which power plays can drive you back into line and if you move out, if you try to break the mold, you're not going to last long. That framework works pretty well and it is understandable that it is just a reflection of obvious power structures.

The real mass media are basically trying to divert people. Let them do something else, but don't bother us (us being the people who run the show). Let them get interested in professional sports, for example. Let everybody be crazed about professional sports or sex scandals or personalities and their problems or something like that. Anything, as long as it isn't serious. Of course, the serious stuff is for the big guys.

What are the elite media, the agenda-setting ones? The *New York Times* and CBS, for example. Well, first of all, they are major, very profitable, corporations. Furthermore, most of them are either linked to or outright owned by, much bigger corporations, like General Electric, Westinghouse, and so on. They are at the top of the power structure of the private economy, which is a very tyrannical structure. Corporations are basically hierarchic tyrannies controlled from above. If you don't like what they are doing, you get out. The major media are part of that system.

What about the institutional setting? Well, that's more or less the same. What they interact with and relate to is other major power centers—the government, other corporations, or the universities. Because the media are a doctrinal system they interact closely with the universities. Say you are writing a story on Southeast Asia or Africa. You're supposed to go over to the big university and find an expert who will tell you what to write. Or else go to one of the foundations, like Brookings Institute or American Enterprise Institute and they will give you the words to say. These outside institutions are very similar to the media.

The universities, for example, are not independent institutions. There may be independent people scattered around in them, but that is true of the media as well. And it's generally true of corporations. It's true of Fascist states, for that matter. But the institution itself is parasitic. It's dependent on outside sources of support and those sources of support, such as private wealth, big corporations with grants, and the government (which is so closely interlinked with corporate power you can barely distinguish them), they are essentially what the universities are in the middle of. People within them, who don't adjust to that structure, who don't accept it and internalize it (you can't really work with it unless you internalize and believe it). People who don't do that are likely to be weeded out along the way, starting from kindergarten, all the way up. There are all sorts of filtering devices to get rid of people who are a pain in the neck and think independently. Those of you who have been through college know that the educational system is very highly geared to rewarding conformity and obedience; if you don't do that, you are a troublemaker. So, it is kind of a filtering device which ends up with people who honestly (they aren't lying) internalize the framework of belief and attitudes of the surrounding power system in the society. The elite institutions like, say, Harvard and Princeton and the small up-scale colleges, for example, are very much geared to socialization. If you go through a place like Harvard, most of what goes on there is teaching manners—how to behave like a member of the upper classes, how to think the right thoughts.

> There are all sorts of filtering devices to get rid of people who are a pain in the neck and think independently. Those of you who have been through college know that the educational system is very highly geared to rewarding conformity and obedience; if you don't do that, you are a troublemaker.

Censorship

If you've read George Orwell's *Animal Farm* which he wrote in the mid-1940s, it was a satire on the Soviet Union, a totalitarian state. It was a big hit. Everybody loved it. Turns out he wrote an introduction to *Animal Farm* which was suppressed. It only appeared 30 years later. Someone had found it in his papers. The introduction to *Animal Farm* was about "Literary Censorship in England" and what it says is that obviously this book is ridiculing the Soviet Union and its totalitarian structure. But he said England is not all that different. We don't have the KGB on our neck, but the end result comes out pretty much the same. People who have independent ideas or who think the wrong kind of thoughts are cut out. He talks a little, only two sentences, about the institutional structure. He asks, why does this happen? Well, one, because the press is owned by wealthy people who only want certain things to reach the public. The other thing he says is that when you go through the elite education system, when you go through the proper schools in Oxford, you learn that there are certain things it's not proper to say and there are certain thoughts that are not proper to have. That is the socialization role of elite institutions and if you don't adapt to that, you're usually out. Those two sentences more or less tell the story.

When you critique the media and you say, look, here is what Anthony Lewis or somebody else is writing, they get very angry. They say, quite correctly, "nobody ever tells me what to write. I write anything I like. All this business about pressures and constraints is non-sense because I'm never under any pressure." This is true, but the point is that they wouldn't be there unless they had already demonstrated that nobody has to tell them what to write because they are going say the right thing. If they had started off at the Metro desk and had pursued the wrong kind of stories, they never would have made it to the position where they can now say anything they like. The same is mostly true of university faculty in the more ideological disciplines. They have been through the socialization system.

Okay, you look at the structure of that whole system. What do you expect the news to be like? Well, it's pretty obvious. The *New York Times* is a corporation and sells a product. The product is audiences. They don't make money when you buy the newspaper. They are happy to put it on the worldwide web for free. They actually lose money when you buy the newspaper.

But the audience is the product. The product is privileged people, just like the people who are writing the newspapers—top-level decision-making people in society. You have to sell a product to a market and the market is, of course, advertisers (that is, other businesses). Whether it is television or newspapers, or whatever, they are selling audiences. Corporations sell audiences to other corporations. In the case of the elite media, it's big business.

What do you expect to happen? What would you predict about the nature of the media product, given that set of circumstances? The obvious assumption is that the product of the media—what appears, what doesn't appear, the way it is slanted—will reflect the interest of the buyers and sellers, the institutions, and the power systems that are around them. If that wouldn't happen, it would be kind of a miracle.

Then comes the hard work. You ask, does it work the way you predict? Well, you can judge for yourselves. There's lots of material on this obvious hypothesis, which has been subjected to the hardest tests anybody can think of and still stands up remarkably well. You never find anything in the social sciences that so strongly supports any conclusion, which is not a big surprise, because it would be miraculous if it didn't hold up given the way the forces are operating.

The next thing you discover is that this whole topic is completely taboo. If you go to the Kennedy School of Government or Stanford or somewhere, and you study journalism and communications or academic political science, these questions are not likely to appear. That is, the hypothesis that anyone would come across without even knowing anything that is not allowed to be expressed and the evidence bearing on it cannot be discussed. Well, you predict that too. If you look at the institutional structure, you would say, yeah, sure, that's got to happen because why should these guys want to be exposed? Why should they allow critical analysis of what they are up to take place? The answer is, there is no reason why they should allow that and, in fact, they don't. Again, it is not purposeful censorship. It is just that you don't make it to those positions. That includes the left (what

> You have to sell a product to a market and the market is, of course, advertisers (that is, other businesses). Whether it is television or newspapers, or whatever, they are selling audiences. Corporations sell audiences to other corporations. In the case of the elite media, it's big business.

is called the left), as well as the right. Unless you have been adequately socialized and trained so that there are some thoughts you just don't have because if you did have them, you wouldn't be there. So you have a second order of prediction which is that the first order of prediction is not allowed into the discussion.

The Doctrinal Framework

The last thing to look at is the doctrinal framework in which this proceeds. Do people at high levels in the information system—including the media, advertising, and academic political science and so on—do these people have a picture of what ought to happen when they are writing for each other (not when they are making graduation speeches)? When you make a commencement speech, it is pretty words and stuff. But when they are writing for one another, what do people say about it?

There are basically three currents to look at. One is the public relations industry, the main business propaganda industry. So what are the leaders of the PR industry saying? Second place to look is at what are called public intellectuals, big thinkers, people who write the "op eds" and that sort of thing. What do they say? The people who write impressive books about the nature of democracy and that sort of business. The third thing you look at is the academic stream, particularly that part of political science which is concerned with communications and information and that stuff that has been a branch of political science for the last 70 or 80 years.

So, look at those three things and see what they say and look at the leading figures who have written about this. They all say (I'm partly quoting), the general population is "ignorant and meddlesome outsiders." We have to keep them out of the public arena because they are too stupid and if they get involved they will just make trouble. Their job is to be "spectators," not "participants."

They are allowed to vote every once in a while, pick out one of us smart guys. But then they are supposed to go home and do something else like watch football or whatever it may be. But the "ignorant and meddlesome outsiders" have to be observers not participants. The participants are what are called the "responsible men" and, of course, the writer is always one of them. You never ask the question, why am I a "responsible man" and somebody else is in jail? The answer is pretty obvious. It's because you are obedient and subordinate to power and that other person may be independent. But you don't ask, of course. So there are the smart guys who are supposed to run the show and the rest of them are supposed to be out and we should not succumb to (I'm quoting from an academic article) "democratic dogmatisms about men being the best judges of their own interest." They are not. They are terrible judges of their own interests so we have do it for them for their own benefit.

Actually, it is very similar to Leninism. We do things for you and we are doing it in the interest of everyone. I suspect that's part of the reason why it's been so easy historically for people to shift up and back from being sort of enthusiastic Stalinists to being big supporters of U.S. power. People switch very quickly from one position to the other and my suspicion is that it's because basically it is the same position. You're not making much of a switch. You're just making a different estimate of where power lies.

How did all this evolve? It has an interesting history. A lot of it comes out of the first World War, which is a big turning point. It changed the position of the United States in the world considerably. In the 18th century the U.S. was already the richest place in the world. The quality of life, health, and longevity was not achieved by the upper classes in Britain until the early 20th century, let alone anybody else in the world. The U.S. was extraordinarily wealthy, with huge advantages,

and, by the end of the 19th century, it had by far the biggest economy in the world. But it was not a big player on the world scene. U.S. power extended to the Caribbean Islands, parts of the Pacific, but not much farther.

During the first World War, the relations changed. And they changed more dramatically during the second World War. After the second World War, the U.S. more or less took over the world. But after the first World War there was already a change and the U.S. shifted from being a debtor to a creditor nation. It wasn't huge, like Britain, but it became a substantial actor in the world for the first time. That was one change, but there were other changes.

Organized State Propaganda

The first World War was the first time there was highly organized state propaganda. The British had a Ministry of Information, and they really needed it because they had to get the U.S. into the war or else they were in bad trouble. The Ministry of Information was mainly geared to sending propaganda, including huge fabrications about "Hun" atrocities. They were targeting American intellectuals on the reasonable assumption that these are the people who are most gullible and most likely to believe propaganda. They are also the ones that disseminate it through their own system. So it was mostly geared to American intellectuals and it worked very well. The British Ministry of Information documents (a lot have been released) show their goal was, as they put it, to control the thought of the entire world, a minor goal, but mainly the U.S. They didn't care much what people thought in India. This Ministry of Information was extremely successful in deluding hot shot American intellectuals into accepting British propaganda fabrications. They were very proud of that. Properly so, it saved their lives. They would have lost the first World War otherwise. In the U.S., there was a counterpart. Woodrow Wilson was elected in 1916 on an anti-war platform. The

U.S. was a very pacifist country. It has always been. People don't want to go fight foreign wars. The country was very much opposed to the first World War and Wilson was, in fact, elected on an anti-war position.

"Peace without victory" was the slogan. But he was intending to go to war. So the question was, how do you get the pacifist population to become raving anti-German lunatics so they want to go kill all the Germans? That requires propaganda. So they set up the first and really only major state propaganda agency in U.S. history. The Committee on Public Information (nice Orwellian title), also called the Creel Commission—the guy who ran it was named Creel. The task of this commission was to propagandize the population into a jingoist hysteria. It worked incredibly well. Within a few months there was war hysteria and the U.S. was able to go to war.

A lot of people were impressed by these achievements. One person impressed—and this had some implications for the future—was Hitler. If you read *Mein Kampf,* he concludes, with some justification, that Germany lost the first World War because it lost the propaganda battle. They could not begin to compete with British and American propaganda which overwhelmed them. He pledges that next time around they'll have their own propaganda system, which they did during the second World War. More important for us, the American business community was also very impressed with the propaganda effort. They had a problem at that time. The country was becoming formally more democratic. A lot more people were able to vote and that sort of thing. The country was becoming wealthier and more people could participate and a lot of new immigrants were coming in.

So what do you do? It's going to be harder to run things as a private club. Therefore, you have to control what people think. There had been public relation specialists, but there was never a public relations industry. There was a guy hired to make Rockefeller's image look prettier and that sort of thing. But this huge public relations industry, which is a U.S. invention and a mon-

strous industry, came out of the first World War. The leading figures were people in the Creel Commission. In fact, the main one, Edward Bernays, comes right out of the Creel Commission. He has a book that came out right afterwards called *Propaganda*. The term "propaganda," incidentally, did not have negative connotations in those days. It was during the second World War that the term became taboo because it was connected with Germany and all those bad things. But in this period, the term propaganda just meant information or something like that. So he wrote *Propaganda* around 1925, and it starts off by saying he is applying the lessons of the first World War. The propaganda system of the first World War and this commission that he was part of showed, he says, it is possible to "regiment the public mind every bit as much as an army regiments their bodies." These new techniques of regimentation of minds, he said, had to be used by the intelligent minorities in order to make sure that the slobs stay on the right course. We can do it now because we have these new techniques.

This is the main manual of the public relations industry. Bernays is kind of the guru. He was an authentic Roosevelt/Kennedy liberal. He also engineered the public relations effort behind the U.S.-backed coup that overthrew the democratic government of Guatemala.

His major coup, the one that really propelled him into fame in the late 1920s, was getting women to smoke. Women didn't smoke in those days and he ran huge campaigns for Chesterfield. You know all the techniques—models and movie stars with cigarettes coming out of their mouths and that kind of thing. He got enormous praise for that. So he became a leading figure of the industry and his book was the real manual.

Another member of the Creel Commission was Walter Lippmann, the most respected figure in American journalism for about half a century (I mean serious American journalism, serious think pieces). He also wrote what are called progressive essays on democracy, regarded as progressive back in the 1920s. He was, again, applying the lessons of the work on propaganda very explicitly. He says there is a new art in democracy called manufacture of consent. That is his phrase. Edward Herman and I borrowed it for our book, but it comes from Lippmann. He says, there is this new art in the method of democracy, "manufacture of consent." By manufacturing consent, you can overcome the fact that a lot of people have the right to vote. We can make it irrelevant because we can manufacture consent and make sure that their choices and attitudes will be structured in such a way that they will always do what we tell them, even if they have a formal way to participate. So we'll have a real democracy. It will work properly. That's applying the lessons of the propaganda agency.

Academic social science and political science comes out of the same thing. The founder of what's called communications and academic political science is Harold Glasswell. His main achievement was a book, a study of propaganda. He says, very frankly, the things I was quoting before—those things about not succumbing to democratic dogmatism, that comes from academic political science (Lasswell and others). Again, drawing the lessons from the war time experience, political parties drew the same lessons, especially the conservative party in England. Their early documents, just being released, show they also recognized the achievements of the British Ministry of Information. They recognized that the country was getting more democratized and it wouldn't be a private men's club. So the conclusion was, as they put it, politics has to become political warfare, applying the mechanisms of propaganda that worked so brilliantly during the first World War towards controlling people's thoughts.

That's the doctrinal side and it coincides with the institutional structure. It strengthens the predictions about the way the thing should work. And the predictions are well confirmed. But these conclusions, also, are not allowed to be discussed. This is all now part of mainstream literature, but it is only for people on the inside. When you go to college, you don't read the classics about how to control peoples minds.

Just like you don't read what James Madison said during the Constitutional Conven- tion about how the main goal of the new system has to be "to protect the minority of the opulent against the majority" and has to be designed so that it achieves that end. This is the founding of the constitutional system, so nobody studies it. You can't even find it in the academic scholarship unless you really look hard.

That is roughly the picture, as I see it, of the way the system is institutionally, the doctrines that lie behind it, the way it comes out. There is another part directed to the "ignorant meddlesome" outsiders. That is mainly using diversion of one kind or another. From that, I think, you can predict what you would expect to find.

> Just like you don't read what James Madison said during the Constitutional Convention about how the main goal of the new system has to be "to protect the minority of the opulent against the majority" and has to be designed so that it achieves that end.

12.

Confronting the Empire

The U.S. intends to rule the world by force

We are meeting at a moment of world history that is in many ways unique—a moment that is ominous, but also full of hope. The U.S., the most powerful state in history, has proclaimed, loud and clear, that it intends to rule the world by force, the dimension in which it reigns supreme. Apart from the conventional bow to noble intentions that is the standard (hence meaningless) accompaniment of coercion, its leaders are committed to pursuit of their "imperial ambition," as it is frankly described in the leading journal of the foreign policy establishment—critically, an important matter. They have also declared that they will tolerate no competitors, now or in the future. They evidently believe that the means of violence in their hands are so extraordinary that they can dismiss with contempt anyone who stands in their way. There is good reason to believe that the war with Iraq is intended, in part, to teach the world some lessons about what lies ahead when the empire decides to strike a blow—though "war" is hardly the proper term, given the array of forces.

The doctrine is not entirely new or unique to the U.S., but it has never before been proclaimed with such brazen arrogance—at least not by anyone we would care to remember. I am not going to try to answer the question posed for this meeting: How to confront the empire? The reason is that most of you know the answers as well or better than I do, through your own lives and work. The way to "confront the empire" is to create a different world, one that is not based on violence and subjugation, hate and fear. That is why we are here, and the World Social Forum [WSF] offers hope that these are not idle dreams.

Yesterday, I had the rare privilege of seeing some very inspiring work to achieve these goals at the international gathering of the Via Campesina at a community of the MST, which I think is the most important and exciting popular movement in the world. With constructive local actions such as those of the MST, and international organization of the kind illustrated by the Via Campesina and the WSF, with sympathy and solidarity and mutual aid, there is real hope for a decent future.

I have also had some other recent experiences that give a vivid picture of what the world may be like if imperial violence is not limited and dismantled. Last month, I was in southeastern Turkey, the scene of some of the worst atrocities of the grisly 1990s, still continuing.

A talk at the World Social Forum, January 27, 2003. Published in Z Magazine, March 2003

A few hours ago we were informed of renewed atrocities by the army near Diyarbakir, the unofficial capital of the Kurdish regions.

Through the 1990s, millions of people were driven out of the devastated countryside, with tens of thousands killed and every imaginable form of barbaric torture. They try to survive in caves outside the walls of Diyarbakir, in condemned buildings in miserable slums in Istanbul, or wherever they can find refuge, barred from returning to their villages despite new legislation that theoretically permits return. Eighty percent of the weapons came from the U.S. In 1997 alone, Clinton sent more arms to Turkey than in the entire Cold War period combined up to the onset of the state terror campaign —called "counterterror" by the perpetrators and their supporters, another convention. Turkey became the leading recipient of U.S. arms as atrocities peaked (apart from Israel-Egypt, a separate category).

> In 1997 alone, Clinton sent more arms to Turkey than in the entire Cold War period combined up to the onset of the state terror campaign— called "counterterror" by the perpetrators and their supporters, another convention

In 1999, Turkey relinquished this position to Colombia. The reason is that in Turkey, U.S.-backed state terror had largely succeeded, while in Colombia it had not. Colombia had the worst human rights record in the Western hemisphere in the 1990s and was by far the leading recipient of U.S. arms and military training, and now leads the world. It also leads the world by other measures, for example, murder of labor activists —more than half of those killed worldwide in the last decade were in Colombia. Close to one-half million people were driven from their land, a new record. The displaced population is now estimated at 2.7 million. Political killings rose to 20 a day.

I visited Cauca in southern Colombia, which had the worst human rights record in the country in 2001. There I listened to hours of testimony by peasants who were driven from their lands by chemical warfare—called "fumigation" under the pretext of a U.S.-run "drug war" that few take seriously and that would be obscene if that were the intent. Their lives and lands are destroyed, children are dying and they suffer from sickness and wounds.

Peasant agriculture is based on a rich tradition of knowledge and experience gained over many centuries, in much of the world passed on from mother to daughter. Though a remarkable human achievement, it is very fragile and could be destroyed forever in a single generation. Also being destroyed is some of the richest biodiversity in the world, similar to neighboring regions of Brazil. Campesinos, indigenous people, Afro-Colombians can join the millions in rotting slums and camps. With the people gone, multinationals can come in to strip the mountains for coal, extract oil and other resources, and convert what is left of the land to monocrop agroexport, using laboratory-produced seeds in an environment shorn of its treasures and variety.

The scenes in Cauca and Southeastern Turkey are very different from the celebrations of the Via Campesina gathering at the MST community. But Turkey and Colombia are inspiring and hopeful in different ways because of the courage and dedication of people struggling for justice and freedom and confronted the empire.

These are some of the signs of the future if "imperial ambition" proceeds on its normal course, now to be accelerated by the grand strategy of global rule by force. None of this is inevitable and among the good models for ending these crimes are the ones I mentioned: the MST, the Via Campesina, and the WSF.

Two Main Themes

At the WSF, the range of issues and problems under intense discussion is very broad, remarkably so, but I think we can identify two main themes. One is global justice, the other is life after capitalism—or to put it more simply, life, because it is not so clear that the human species can survive very long under existing state capitalist institutions. In Davos, the *New York Times* tells us, "the mood has darkened." For the "movers and shakers," it is not "global party time" anymore.

In fact, the founder of the WEF has conceded defeat: "The power of corporations has completely disappeared," he said. So we have won. There is nothing left for us to do but pick up the pieces—not only to talk about a vision of the future that is just and humane, but to move on to create it.

Of course, we should not let the praise go to our heads. There are still a few difficulties ahead. The main theme of the WEF is Building Trust. There is a reason for that. The "masters of the universe," as they liked to call themselves in more exuberant days, know that they are in serious trouble. They recently released a poll showing that trust in leaders has severely declined.

Only the leaders of NGOs had the trust of a clear majority, followed by UN and spiritual/religious leaders, then leaders of Western Europe and economic managers, below them corporate executives, and well below them, at the bottom, leaders of the U.S., with about 25 percent trust. That may well mean virtually no trust because when people are asked whether they trust leaders with power, they usually say "Yes," out of habit.

It gets worse. A few days ago a poll in Canada found that over one-third of the population regard the U.S. as the greatest threat to world peace. The U.S. ranks more than twice as high as Iraq or North Korea and far higher than al-Qaeda as well. A poll—without careful controls—by *Time* magazine, found that over 80 percent of respondents in Europe regarded the U.S. as the greatest threat to world peace, compared with less than 10 percent for Iraq or North Ko-

rea. Even if these numbers are wrong by some substantial factor, they are dramatic.

The coming war with Iraq is undoubtedly contributing to these interesting and important developments. Opposition to the war is without historical precedent. In Europe it is so high that Secretary of "Defense" Donald Rumsfeld dismissed Germany and France as just the "old Europe," plainly of no concern because of their disobedience. The "vast numbers of other countries in Europe [are] with the United States," he assured foreign journalists. These vast numbers are the "new Europe," symbolized by Italy's Berlusconi, soon to visit the White House, praying that he will be invited to be the third of the "three Bs": Bush-Blair-Berlusconi—assuming that he can stay out of jail. Italy is on board, the White House tells us. It is apparently not a problem that over 80 percent of the Italian public is opposed to the war, according to recent polls. That just shows that the people of Italy also belong to the "old Europe" and can be sent to the ashcan of history along with France and Germany and others who do not know their place. Spain is hailed as another prominent member of the new Europe—with 75 percent opposed to the war, according to an international Gallup poll. According to the leading foreign policy analyst of *Newsweek*, pretty much the same is true of the most hopeful part of the new Europe, the former communist countries that are counted on (quite openly) to serve U.S. interests and undermine Europe's despised social market and welfare states. He reports that in Czechoslovakia, two-thirds of the population oppose participation in a war, while in Poland only one-fourth would support a war even if the UN inspectors "prove that Iraq possesses weapons of mass destruction." The Polish press reports 37 percent approval in this case, still extremely low, at the heart of the "new Europe." New Europe soon identified itself in an open let-

> A poll—without careful controls—by *Time* magazine, found that over 80 percent of respondents in Europe regarded the U.S. as the greatest threat to world peace, compared with less than 10 percent for Iraq or North Korea. Even if these numbers are wrong by some substantial factor, they are dramatic.

ter in the *Wall Street Journal*—along with Italy, Spain, Poland, and Czechoslovakia—the leaders, that is, not the people—it includes:

- Denmark (with popular opinion on the war about the same as Germany, therefore "old Europe")

- Portugal (53 percent opposed to war under any circumstances, 96 percent opposed to war by the U.S. and its allies unilaterally)

- Britain (40 percent opposed to war under any circumstances, 90 percent opposed to war by the U.S. and its allies unilaterally)

- Hungary (no figures available)

The exciting "new Europe" consists of some leaders who are willing to defy their populations. Old Europe reacted with some annoyance to Rumsfeld's declaration that they are "problem" countries, not modern states. Their reaction was explained by "thoughtful" U.S. commentators. Keeping just to the national press, we learn that "world-weary European allies" do not appreciate the "moral rectitude" of the president. The evidence for his "moral rectitude" is that "his advisors say the evangelical zeal" comes directly from the simple man who is dedicated to driving evil from the world. Since that is surely the most reliable and objective evidence that can be imagined, it would be improper to express slight skepticism, let alone to react as we would to similar performances by others.

The cynical Europeans, we are told, misinterpret Bush's purity of soul as "moral naiveté" —without a thought that the Administration's PR specialists might have a hand in creating imagery that will sell. We are informed further that there is a great divide between world-weary Europe and the "idealistic New World bent on ending inhumanity."

That this is the driving purpose of the idealistic New World we also know for certain, because so our leaders proclaim. What more in the way of proof could one seek? The rare mention of public opinion in the new Europe treats it as a problem of marketing. The product being sold is necessarily right and honorable, given its source. The willingness of the leaders of the new Europe to prefer Washington to their own populations "threatens to isolate the Germans and French," who are exhibiting retrograde democratic tendencies, and shows that Germany and France cannot "say that they are speaking for Europe." They are merely speaking for the people of old and new Europe, who—the same commentators acknowledge—express "strong opposition" to the policies of the new Europe.

The official pronouncements and the reaction to them are illuminating. They demonstrate with some clarity the contempt for democracy that is rather typical, historically, among those who feel that they rule the world by right. There are many other illustrations. When German Chancellor Gerhard Schroeder dared to take the position of the overwhelming majority of voters in the last election, it was described as a shocking failure of leadership, a serious problem that Germany must overcome if it wants to be accepted in the civilized world. The problem lies with Germany, not elites of the Anglo-American democracies. Germany's problem is, "the government lives in fear of the voters and that is causing it to make mistake after mistake" (says the spokesperson for the right-wing Christian Social Union party, who understands the real nature of "democracy").

The case of Turkey is even more revealing. As throughout the region, Turks are very strongly opposed to the war—about 90 percent according to the most recent polls. So far the government has irresponsibly paid some attention to the people who elected it. It has not bowed completely to the intense pressure and threats that Washington is exerting to compel it to heed the master's voice. This reluctance of the elected government to follow orders from on high proves that its leaders are not true democrats. For those who may be too dull to comprehend these subtleties, they are explained by former Ambassador to Turkey Morton Abramowitz, now a distinguished senior statesperson and commentator. Ten years ago, he explained, Turkey was governed by a real democrat, Turgut Ozal, who "overrode his countrymen's [sic] pronounced preference to stay out of the Gulf war." But democracy has "declined" in Turkey.

The current leadership "is following the people," revealing its lack of "democratic credentials." "Regrettably," he says, "for the U.S. there is no Ozal around." So it will be necessary to bring authentic democracy to Turkey by economic strangulation and other coercive means, regrettably, but that is demanded by what the elite press calls our "yearning for democracy." Brazil is witnessing another exercise of the real attitudes towards democracy among the masters of the universe. In the most free election in the hemisphere, a large majority voted for policies that are strongly opposed by international finance and investors, by the IMF, and the U.S. Treasury Department. In earlier years, that would have been the signal for a military coup installing a murderous National Security State, as in Brazil 40 years ago. Now that will not work. The populations of South and North have changed and will not easily tolerate it. Furthermore, there are now simpler ways to undermine the will of the people, thanks to the neoliberal instruments that have been put in place—economic controls, capital flight, attacks on currency, privatization, and other devices that are well-designed to reduce the arena of popular choice. These, it is hoped, may compel the government to follow the dictates of what international economists call the "virtual parliament" of investors and lenders, who make the decisions, coercing the population, an irrelevant nuisance according to the reigning principles of democracy.

When I was just about to leave for the airport, I received another of the many inquiries from the press about why there is so little anti-war protest in the U.S. The impressions are instructive. In fact, protest in the U.S., as elsewhere, is at levels

> It will be necessary to bring authentic democracy to Turkey by economic strangulation and other coercive means, regrettably, but that is demanded by what the elite press calls our "yearning for democracy."

that have no historical precedent—not just demonstrations, teach-ins, and other public events. To take an example of a different kind, last week the Chicago City Council passed an anti-war resolution, 46-1, joining 50 other cities and towns. The same is true in other sectors, including those that are the most highly trusted, as the WEF learned to its dismay: NGOs and religious organizations and figures, with few exceptions. Several months ago the biggest university in the U.S. passed a strong antiwar resolution—the University of Texas, right next door to George W's ranch. It's easy to continue.

Why the widespread judgment among elites that the tradition of dissent and protest has died? Invariably, comparisons are drawn to Vietnam, a very revealing fact. We have just passed the 40th anniversary of the public announcement that the Kennedy administration was sending the U.S. Air Force to bomb South Vietnam and initiating plans to drive millions of people into concentration camps and chemical warfare programs to destroy food crops. There was no pretext of defense, except in the sense of official rhetoric: defense against the "internal aggression" of South Vietnamese in South Vietnam and their "assault from the inside" (President Kennedy and his UN ambassador, Adlai Stevenson). Protest was non-existent. It did not reach any meaningful level for several years. By that time hundreds of thousands of U.S. troops had joined the occupying army, densely populated areas were being demolished by saturation bombing, and the aggression had spread to the rest of Indochina. Protest among elite intellectuals kept primarily to "pragmatic grounds": the war was a "mistake" that was becoming too costly to the U.S. In sharp contrast, by the late 1960s, the great majority of the public had come to oppose the war as "fundamentally wrong and immoral," not "a mistake," figures that have held steady until the present. Today, in dramatic contrast to the 1960s, there is large scale, committed, and principled popular protest all over the U.S. before the war has been officially launched. That reflects a steady increase over these years in unwillingness to tolerate aggression and atrocities, one of many such changes, worldwide, in fact. That's part of the background for what is taking place in Porto Alegre and part of the reason for the gloom in Davos.

The political leadership is well aware of these developments. When a new Administration comes into office, it receives a review of the world situation compiled by the intelligence agencies. It is secret; we learn about these things many years later. But when Bush #1 came into office in 1989, a small part of the review was leaked, a passage concerned with "cases where the U.S. confronts much weaker enemies"—the only kind one would think of fighting. Intelligence analysts advised that in conflicts with "much weaker enemies" the U.S. must win "decisively and rapidly" or popular support will collapse.

It's not like the 1960s when the population would tolerate a murderous and destructive war for years without visible protest. That's no longer true. The activist movements of the past 40 years have had a significant civilizing effect. By now, the only way to attack a much weaker enemy is to construct a huge propaganda offensive, depicting it as about to commit genocide, maybe even a threat to our very survival, then to celebrate a miraculous victory over the awesome foe, while chanting praises to the courageous leaders who came to the rescue just in time. That is the current scenario in Iraq.

Polls reveal more support in the U.S. for the planned war than elsewhere, but the numbers are misleading. It is important to bear in mind that the U.S. is the only country outside Iraq where Saddam Hussein is not only reviled, but also feared. There is a flood of lurid propaganda warning that if we do not stop him today he will destroy us tomorrow. The next evidence of his weapons of mass destruction may be a "mushroom cloud," so National Security Adviser Condoleezza Rice announced in September—

presumably over New York. No one in Iraq's neighborhood seems overly concerned, much as they may hate the murderous tyrant. Perhaps that is because they know that as a result of the sanctions "the vast majority of the country's population has been on a semi-starvation diet for years," as the World Health Organization reported and that Iraq is one of the weakest states in the region. Its economy and military expenditures are a fraction of Kuwait's, which has 10 percent of Iraq's population and much farther below others nearby.

But the U.S. is different. When Congress granted the president authority to go to war last October, it was "to defend the national security of the United States against the continuing threat posed by Iraq." We must tremble in fear before this awesome threat, while countries nearby seek to reintegrate Iraq into the region, including those who were attacked by Saddam when he was a friend and ally of those who now run the show in Washington—and who were happily providing him with aid including the means to develop WMD, at a time when he was far more dangerous than today and had already committed by far his worst crimes.

A serious measure of support for war in the U.S. would have to extricate this "fear factor," which is genuine and unique to the U.S. The residue would give a more realistic measure of support for the resort to violence and would show, I think, that it is about the same as elsewhere.

It is also rather striking that strong opposition to the coming war extends right through the establishment. The current issues of the two major foreign policy journals feature articles opposing the war by leading figures of foreign policy elites. The very respectable American Academy of Arts and Sciences released a long monograph on the war, trying to give the most sympathetic possible account of the Bush administration position, then dismantling it point by point. One respected analyst they quote is a Senior Associate of the Carnegie Endowment for International Peace who warns that the U.S. is becoming "a menace to itself and to mankind [sic]" under its current leadership. There are no precedents for anything like this.

We should recognize that these criticisms tend to be narrow. They are concerned with threats to the U.S. and its allies. They do not take into account the likely effects on Iraqis: the warnings of the UN and aid agencies that millions may be at very serious risk in a country that is at the edge of survival after a terrible war that targeted its basic infrastructure—which amounts to biological warfare—and a decade of devastating sanctions that have killed hundreds of thousands of people and blocked any reconstruction, while strengthening the brutal tyrant who rules Iraq.

It is also interesting that the criticisms do not even take the trouble to mention the lofty rhetoric about democratization and liberation. Presumably, the critics take for granted that the rhetoric is intended for intellectuals and editorial writers—who are not supposed to notice that the drive to war is accompanied by a dramatic demonstration of hatred of democracy, just as they are supposed to forget the record of those who are leading the campaign. That is also why none of this is ever brought up at the UN. Nevertheless, the threats that do concern establishment critics are very real. They were surely not surprised when the CIA informed Congress last October that they know of no link between Iraq and al Qaeda-style terrorism, but that an attack on Iraq would probably increase the terrorist threat to the West, in many ways. It is likely to inspire a new generation of terrorists bent on revenge and it might induce Iraq to carry out terrorist actions that are already in place, a possibility taken very seriously by U.S. analysts.

A high-level task force of the Council on Foreign Relations just released a report warning of likely terrorist attacks that could be far worse than 9/11, including possible use of WMD within the U.S.—dangers that become "more urgent by the prospect of the U.S. going to war with Iraq." They provide many illustrations, virtually a cookbook for terrorists. It is not the first, as similar ones were published by prominent strategic analysts long before 9/11.

It is also understood that an attack on Iraq may lead not just to more terror, but also to proliferation of WMD, for the simple reason that potential targets of the U.S. recognize that there is no other way to deter the most powerful state in history, which is pursuing "America's Imperial Ambition," posing serious dangers to the U.S. and the world, the author warns in the main establishment journal, *Foreign Affairs*. Prominent hawks warn that a war in Iraq might lead to the "greatest proliferation disaster in history."

They know that if Iraq has chemical and biological weapons, the dictatorship keeps them under tight control. They understand further that, except as a last resort if attacked, Iraq is highly unlikely to use any WMD it has, thus inviting instant incineration.

It is also highly unlikely to leak them to the Osama bin Ladens of the world, which would be a terrible threat to Saddam Hussein, quite apart from the reaction if there is even a hint that this might take place. But under attack, the society would collapse, including the controls over WMD. These would be "privatized," terrorism experts point out and offered to the huge "market for unconventional weapons where they will have no trouble finding buyers." That really is a "nightmare scenario," just as the hawks warn.

Even before the Bush administration began beating the war drums about Iraq, there were plenty of warnings that its adventurism was going to lead to proliferation of WMD, as well as terror, simply as a deterrent. Right now, Washington is teaching the world a very ugly and dangerous lesson: if you want to defend yourself from us, you had better mimic North Korea and pose a credible military threat, including WMD. Otherwise, we will demolish you in pursuit of the new "grand strategy" that has caused shudders not only among the usual victims and in "old Europe," but right at the heart of the U.S. foreign policy elite, who recognize that "commitment of the U.S. to active military confrontation for decisive national advantage will leave the world more dangerous and the U.S. less secure"—again, quoting respected figures in elite journals.

Evidently, the likely increase of terror and proliferation of WMD is of limited concern to planners in Washington in the context of their real priorities. Without too much difficulty, one can think of reasons why this might be the case.

The nature of the threats was dramatically underscored last October at the summit meeting in Havana on the 40th anniversary of the Cuban missile crisis, attended by key participants from Russia, the U.S., and Cuba. Planners knew at the time that they had the fate of the world in their hands, but new information released at the Havana summit was truly startling. We learned that the world was saved from nuclear devastation by one Russian submarine captain, Vasily Arkhipov, who blocked an order to fire nuclear missiles when Russian submarines were attacked by U.S. destroyers near Kennedy's "quarantine" line. Had Arkhipov agreed, the nuclear launch would have almost certainly set off an interchange that could have "destroyed the Northern hemisphere," as Eisenhower had warned.

Regime Change

The dreadful revelation is particularly timely because of the circumstances. The roots of the missile crisis lay in international terrorism aimed at "regime change," two concepts very much in the news today. U.S. terrorist attacks against Cuba began shortly after Castro took power and were sharply escalated by Kennedy, leading to a very plausible fear of invasion, as Robert McNamara has acknowledged. Kennedy resumed the terrorist war immediately after the crisis was over. Terrorist actions against Cuba, based in the U.S., peaked in the late 1970s continued 20 years later. Putting aside any judgment about the behavior of the participants in the missile crisis, the new discoveries demonstrate with brilliant clarity the terrible and unanticipated risks of attacks on a "much weaker enemy" aimed at "regime change"—risks to survival, it is no exaggeration to say. As for the fate of the people of Iraq, no one can predict with any con-

fidence: not the CIA, not Donald Rumsfeld, not those who claim to be experts on Iraq, no one.

Possibilities range from the frightening prospects for which the aid agencies are preparing to the delightful tales spun by administration PR specialists and their chorus. One never knows. These are among the many reasons why decent human beings do not contemplate the threat or use of violence, whether in personal life or international affairs, unless reasons have been offered that have overwhelming force. Surely nothing remotely like that has been offered in the present case, which is why opposition to the plans of Washington and London has reached such scale and intensity. The timing of the Washington-London propaganda campaign was so transparent that it, too, has been a topic of discussion, and sometimes ridicule, right in the mainstream. The campaign began in September of last year.

Before that, Saddam was a terrible guy, but not an imminent threat to the survival of the U.S. The "mushroom cloud" was announced in early September. Since then, fear that Saddam will attack the U.S. has been running at about 60-70 percent of the population. "The desperate urgency about moving rapidly against Iraq that Bush expressed in October was not evident from anything he said two months before," the chief political analyst of United Press International observed, drawing the obvious conclusion. September marked the opening of the political campaign for the mid-term congressional elections. The Administration, he continued, was "campaigning to sustain and increase its power on a policy of international adventurism, new radical preemptive military strategies, and a hunger for a politically convenient and perfectly timed confrontation with Iraq." As long as domestic issues were in the forefront, Bush and his cohorts were losing ground—naturally enough, because they were conducting a serious assault against the general population. "But lo and behold. Though there have been no new terrorist attacks or credible indications of imminent threats, since the beginning of September, national security issues have been in the driver's seat," not just al Qaeda but the awesome and threatening military power of Iraq.

Many others have made the same observations. The Carnegie Endowment Senior Associate I quoted before writes that Bush and Co. are following "the classic modern strategy of an endangered right-wing oligarchy, which is to divert mass discontent into nationalism," inspired by fear of enemies about to destroy us. That strategy is of critical importance if the "radical nationalists" setting policy in Washington hope to advance their announced plan for "unilateral world domination through absolute military superiority," while conducting a major assault against the interests of the large majority of the domestic population.

The Fall 2002 election was won by a small number of votes, but enough to hand Congress to the executive. Analyses of the election found that voters maintained their opposition to the Administration on social and economic issues, but suppressed these issues in favor of security concerns, which typically lead to support for the figure in authority—the brave cowboy who must ride to our rescue, just in time. As history shows, it is all too easy for unscrupulous leaders to terrify the public, with consequences that have not been attractive. That is the natural method to divert attention from the fact that tax cuts for the rich and other devices are undermining prospects for a decent life for a large majority of the population and for future generations.

When the presidential campaign begins, Republican strategists surely do not want people to be asking questions about their pensions, jobs, health care, and other such matters. Rather, they should be praising their heroic leader for rescuing them from imminent destruction by a foe of "colossal power" and marching on to confront the next powerful force bent on our destruction. It could be Iran or conflicts in the Andean coun-

tries. There are lots of choices, as long as the targets are defenseless. These ideas are second nature to the current political leaders, most of them recycled from the Reagan administration. They are replaying a familiar script: drive the country into deficit so as to be able to undermine social programs, declare a "war on terror" (as they did in 1981), and conjure up one devil after another to frighten the population into obedience. In the 1980s, it was Libyan hit-men prowling the streets of Washington to assassinate our leader, then the Nicaraguan army only two-days march from Texas, a threat to survival so severe that Reagan had to declare a national emergency. Or an airfield in Grenada that the Russians were going to use to bomb us (if they could find it on a map); Arab terrorists seeking to kill Americans everywhere while Qaddafi plans to "expel America from the world," Reagan wailed, or Hispanic narco-traffickers were seeking to destroy the youth and on and on.

Meanwhile, the political leadership was able to carry out domestic policies that had generally poor economic outcomes, but did create wealth for narrow sectors while harming a considerable majority of the population—the script that is being followed once again. Since the public knows it, they have to resort to "the classic modern strategy of an endangered right-wing oligarchy" if they hope to carry out the domestic and international programs to which they are committed, perhaps even to institutionalize them so they will be hard to dismantle when they lose control.

The September 11 terrorist atrocities provided an opportunity and pretext to implement plans to take control of Iraq's immense oil wealth, a central component of the Persian Gulf resources that the State Department, in 1945, described as "a stupendous source of strategic power and one of the greatest."

13.

Iraq As Trial Run

Establishing the doctrine of preventive war

V. K. RAMACHANDRAN: Does the present aggression on Iraq represent a continuation of United States' international policy in recent years or a qualitatively new stage in that policy?

NOAM CHOMSKY: It represents a significantly new phase. It is not without precedent, but significantly new nevertheless. This should be seen as a trial run. Iraq is considered an extremely easy and totally defenseless target. It is assumed, probably correctly, that the society will collapse, that the soldiers will go in, and that the U.S. will be in control and will establish the regime of its choice and military bases. They will go on to the harder cases. The next case could be the Andean region, it could be Iran, it could be others.

The trial run is to try and establish what the U.S. calls a "new norm" in international relations. The new norm is "preventive war." Notice that new norms are established only by the United States. So, for example, when India invaded East Pakistan to terminate horrendous massacres, it did not establish a new norm of humanitarian intervention because India is the wrong country and, besides, the U.S. was strenuously opposed to that action.

This is not pre-emptive war as there is a crucial difference. Pre-emptive war has a meaning, it means that, for example, if planes are flying across the Atlantic to bomb the United States, the United States is permitted to shoot them down even before they bomb and may be permitted to attack the air bases from which they came. Pre-emptive war is a response to ongoing or imminent attack. The doctrine of preventive war is totally different. It holds that the United States—alone, since nobody else has this right—has the right to attack any country that it claims to be a potential challenge to it. The doctrine of preventive war was announced explicitly in the National Security Strategy last September. It sent shudders around the world, including through the U.S.

V. K. Ramachandran interviews Chomsky.
Published in Z Magazine, May 2003

118

establishment, where, I might say, opposition to the war is unusually high. The Security Strategy said, in effect, that the U.S. will rule the world by force, which is the only dimension in which it is supreme. Furthermore, it will do so for the indefinite future because, if any potential challenge arises to U.S. domination, the U.S. will destroy it before it becomes a challenge.

This is the first exercise of that doctrine. If it succeeds on these terms, as it presumably will, because the target is so defenseless, then international lawyers and Western intellectuals and others will begin to talk about a new norm in international affairs. It is important to establish such a norm if you expect to rule the world by force for the foreseeable future.

I shall mention one precedent, just to show how narrow the spectrum is. In 1963, Dean Acheson, who was a much respected elder statesperson and senior adviser of the Kennedy administration, gave an important talk to the American Society of International Law, in which he justified the U.S. attacks against Cuba. The attack by the Kennedy administration on Cuba was large-scale international terrorism and economic warfare. The timing was interesting—it was right after the Missile Crisis when the world was very close to terminal nuclear war. In his speech, Acheson said that no "legal issue" arises when the United States responds to a challenge to its "power, position, or prestige," or words approximating that.

Is it a new phase in that the U.S. has not been able to carry others with it?

That is not new. In the case of the Vietnam War, for example, the United States did not even try to get international support. Nevertheless, you are right in that this is unusual. This is a case in which the United States was compelled, for political reasons, to try to force the world to accept its position and was not able to. Usually, the world succumbs.

So does it represent a "failure of diplomacy?"

I wouldn't call it diplomacy—it's a failure of coercion. Compare it with the first Gulf War. In the first Gulf War, the U.S. coerced the Security Council into accepting its position, although much of the world opposed it. NATO went along and the one country in the Security Council that did not—Yemen—was immediately and severely punished. In any legal system that you take seriously, coerced judgments are considered invalid, but in the international affairs conducted by the powerful, coerced judgments are fine—they are called diplomacy. What is interesting about this case is that the coercion did not work. There were countries—in fact, most of them—who stubbornly maintained the position of the vast majority of their populations.

The most dramatic case is Turkey. Turkey is vulnerable to U.S. punishment and inducements. Nevertheless, the new government, I think to everyone's surprise, maintained the position of about 90 percent of its population. Turkey is bitterly condemned for that here, just as France and Germany are bitterly condemned because they took the position of the overwhelming majority of their populations. The countries that are praised are countries like Italy and Spain, whose leaders agreed to follow orders from Washington over the opposition of maybe 90 percent of their populations.

That is another new step. I cannot think of another case where hatred and contempt for democracy have so openly been proclaimed, not just by the government, but also by liberal commentators and others. There is now a whole literature trying to explain why France, Germany, the so-called "old Europe," Turkey, and others are trying to undermine the United States. It is inconceivable to the pundits that they are doing so because they take democracy seriously and they think that when the overwhelming majority of a population has an opinion, a government ought to follow it.

That is real contempt for democracy; just as what has happened at the United Nations is total contempt for the international system. There are now calls—from the *Wall Street Journal*, people in government, and others—to disband the United Nations.

Fear of the United States around the world is extraordinary. It is so extreme that it is even being discussed in the mainstream media. The cover story of the upcoming issue of Newsweek *is about why the world is so afraid of the United States. The* Post *had a cover story about this as well.*

Of course, this is considered to be the world's fault, that there is something wrong with the world with which we have to deal somehow, but also something that has to be recognized. The idea that Iraq represents any kind of clear and present danger is, of course, without substance.

Nobody pays any attention to that accusation, except, interestingly, the population of United States. In the last few months, there has been a spectacular achievement of government/media propaganda, very visible in the polls. The international polls show that support for the war is higher in the United States than in other countries. That is, however, quite misleading, because if you look a little closer, you find that the United States is also different in another respect from the rest of the world. Since September 2002, the United States is the only country in the world where 60 percent of the population believes that Iraq is an imminent threat—something that people do not believe, even in Kuwait or Iran.

After the September 11 attack, the figure was about 3 percent. Government media propaganda managed to raise that to about 50 percent. If people genuinely believe that Iraq has carried out major terrorist attacks against the United States and is planning to do so again, well, in that case people will support the war.

This happened after September 2002 when the government media campaign began and also when the mid-term election campaign began. The Bush administration would have been smashed in the election if social and economic issues had been in the forefront, but it managed to suppress those issues in favor of security is-

sues—and people huddle under the umbrella of power. This is exactly the way the country was run in the 1980s.

Remember that these are almost the same people as in the Reagan and the senior Bush administrations. Through the 1980s they carried out domestic policies that were harmful to the population and which, as we know from extensive polls, the people opposed. But they managed to maintain control by frightening the people. So the Nicaraguan army was two days' march from Texas and the airbase in Grenada was one from which the Russians would bomb us. It was one thing after another, every year, every one of them ludicrous. The Reagan administration actually declared a national emergency in 1985 because of the threat to the security of the United States posed by the government of Nicaragua.

If somebody were watching this from Mars, they would not know whether to laugh or to cry. They are doing exactly the same thing now and will probably do something similar for the presidential campaign. There will have to be a new dragon to slay because, if the Administration lets domestic issues prevail, it is in deep trouble.

You have written that this war of aggression has dangerous consequences with respect to international terrorism and the threat of nuclear war.

I cannot claim any originality for that opinion. I am just quoting the CIA, other intelligence agencies, and virtually every specialist in international affairs and terrorism. *Foreign Affairs, Foreign Policy,* the study by the American Academy of Arts and Sciences, and the high-level Hart-Rudman Commission on terrorist threats to the United States all agree that it is likely to increase terrorism and the proliferation of weapons of mass destruction.

The reason is simple, partly for revenge, but partly for self-defense. There is no other way to protect oneself from U.S. attack. The United States is making the point very clearly and is teaching the world an extremely ugly lesson.

Compare North Korea and Iraq. Iraq is defenseless and weak, the weakest regime in the region. While there is a monster running it, it does not pose a threat to anyone else. North Korea, on the other hand, does pose a threat. North Korea, however, is not attacked for the very simple reason that it has a deterrent. It has amassed artillery aimed at Seoul and if the United States attacks it, it can wipe out a large part of South Korea.

So the United States is telling the countries of the world: if you are defenseless, we are going to attack you when we want, but if you have a deterrent, we will back off, because we only attack defenseless targets. It is telling countries that they had better develop a terrorist network and weapons of mass destruction or some other credible deterrent. If not, they are vulnerable to "preventive war." For that reason alone, this war is likely to lead to the proliferation of both terrorism and weapons of mass destruction.

How do you think the U.S. will manage the human and humanitarian consequences of the war?

No one knows, of course. That is why honest and decent people do not resort to violence—because one simply does not know. The aid agencies and medical groups that work in Iraq have pointed out that the consequences can be very severe. Everyone hopes not, but it could affect up to millions of people. To undertake violence when there is even such a possibility is criminal. There is already—that is, even before the war—a humanitarian catastrophe. By conservative estimates, ten years of sanctions have killed hundreds of thousands of people. If there were any honesty, the U.S. would pay reparations just for the sanctions.

The situation is similar to the bombing of Afghanistan. It was obvious the United States was never going to investigate the consequences.

Or invest the kind of money that was needed. No. First, the question is not asked, so no one has an idea of what the consequences of the bombing were for most of the country. Then almost nothing comes in. Finally, it is out of the news and no one remembers it any more. In Iraq, the United States will make a show of humanitarian reconstruction and will put in a regime that it will call democratic, which means that it follows Washington's orders. Then it will forget about what happens later and will go on to the next one.

How have the media lived up to their propaganda model reputation this time?

Right now it is cheerleading for the home team. Look at CNN, which is disgusting—and it is the same everywhere. That is to be expected in wartime—the media are worshipful of power. More interesting is what happened in the build-up to war. The fact that government media propaganda was able to convince the people that Iraq is an imminent threat and that Iraq was responsible for September 11 is a spectacular achievement and, as I said, was accomplished in about four months. If you ask people in the media about this, they will say, "Well, we never said that," and it is true, they did not. There was never a statement that Iraq is going to invade the United States or that it carried out the World Trade Center attack. It was just insinuated, hint after hint, until they got people to believe it.

Look at the resistance. Despite the denigration of the United Nations, they haven't carried the day.

The United Nations is in a very hazardous position. The United States might move to dismantle it. I don't really expect that, but at least to diminish it, because when it isn't following orders, of what use is it?

What are your impressions of the present resistance to U.S. aggression?

There is nothing like it. Opposition throughout the world is enormous and unprecedented and the same is true of the United States. Recently, for example, I was in demonstrations in downtown Boston. The first time I participated in a demonstration there, at which I was to speak, was after the United States had started bombing South Vietnam. Half of South Vietnam had been destroyed and the war had been extended to North Vietnam. At that time, we couldn't hold a demonstration because it was physically attacked, mostly by students, with the support of the liberal press and radio, who denounced these people who were daring to protest against an American war.

On this occasion [2003], however, there were massive protests before the war was launched and once again on the day it was launched —with no counter-demonstrators. That is a radical difference. If it were not for the fear factor that I mentioned, there would be much more opposition. The government knows that it can-not carry out long-term aggression and destruction as in Vietnam because the population will not tolerate it. There is only one way to fight a war now. First of all, pick a much weaker enemy, one that is defenseless. Then build it up in the propaganda system as either about to commit aggression or as an imminent threat. Next, you need a lightning victory. An important leaked document of the first Bush administration in 1989 described how the U.S. would have to fight war. It said that the U.S. had to fight much weaker enemies and that victory must be rapid and decisive, as public support will quickly erode. It is no longer like the 1960s, when a war could be fought for years with no opposition at all.

In many ways, the activism of the 1960s and subsequent years has made a lot of the world, including this country, much more civilized in many domains.

14.

U.S. & Haiti

A self-serving portrait by the establishment press

Those who have any concern for Haiti will naturally want to understand how its most recent tragedy has been unfolding. For those who have had the privilege of any contact with the people of this tortured land, it is not just natural, but inescapable. Nevertheless, we make a serious error if we focus too narrowly on the events of the recent past or even on Haiti alone. The crucial issue for us is what we should be doing about what has taken place. That would be true even if our options and our responsibility were limited, far more so when they are immense and decisive, as in the case of Haiti. And even more so because the course of the terrible story was predictable years ago—if we failed to act to prevent it—and fail we did. The lessons are clear and so important that they would be the topic of daily front-page articles in a free press.

Reviewing what was taking place in Haiti shortly after Clinton "restored democracy" in 1994, I was compelled to conclude, unhappily, in *Z Magazine,* that "It would not be very surprising, then, if the Haitian operations become another catastrophe" and, if so, "It is not a difficult chore to trot out the familiar phrases that will explain the failure of our mission of benevolence in this failed society." The reasons were evident to anyone who chose to look. The familiar phrases again resound, sadly and predictably.

There has been much solemn discussion explaining, correctly, that democracy means more than flipping a lever every few years. Functioning democracy has preconditions. One is that the population should have some way to learn what is happening in the world. The real world, not the self-serving portrait offered by the "establishment press," which is disfigured by its "subservience to state power" and "the usual hostility to popular movements"—the accurate words of Paul Farmer, whose work on Haiti is, in its own way, perhaps even as remarkable as what he has accomplished within the country. Farmer was writing in 1993, reviewing mainstream commentary and reporting on Haiti, a disgraceful record that goes back to the days of Wilson's vicious and destructive invasion in 1915 and on to the present. The facts are extensively documented, appalling, and shameful. They are deemed irrelevant for the usual reasons that they do not conform to the required self-image and so are efficiently dispatched deep into the mem-

From Z Magazine, April 2004

ory hole, though they can be unearthed by those who have some interest in the real world.

They will rarely be found, however, in the "establishment press." Keeping to the more liberal and knowledgeable end of the spectrum, the standard version is that in "failed states" like Haiti and Iraq, the U.S. must become engaged in benevolent "nation-building" to "enhance democracy," a "noble goal," but one that may be beyond our means because of the inadequacies of the objects of our solicitude. In Haiti, despite Washington's dedicated efforts from Wilson to FDR while the country was under Marine occupation, "the new dawn of Haitian democracy never came." "Not all America's good wishes, nor all its Marines, can achieve [democracy today] until the Haitians do it themselves" (H.D.S. Greenway, *Boston Globe*). As *New York Times* correspondent R.W. Apple recounted two centuries of history in 1994, reflecting on the prospects for Clinton's endeavor to "restore democracy" then underway, "Like the French in the 19th century, like the Marines who occupied Haiti from 1915 to 1934, the American forces who are trying to impose a new order will confront a complex and violent society with no history of democracy."

Apple does appear to go a bit beyond the norm in his reference to Napoleon's savage assault on Haiti, leaving it in ruins, in order to prevent the crime of liberation in the world's richest colony, the source of much of France's wealth. But perhaps that undertaking, too, satisfies the fundamental criterion of benevolence. It was supported by the United States, which was naturally outraged and frightened by "the first nation in the world to argue the case of universal freedom for all humankind, revealing the limited definition of freedom adopted by the French and American revolutions." So Haitian historian Patrick Bellegarde-Smith writes, accurately describing the terror in the slave state next door, which was not relieved even when Haiti's successful liberation struggle, at enormous cost, opened the way to the expansion to the West by compelling Napoleon to accept the Louisiana Purchase. The U.S. continued to do what it could to strangle Haiti, even supporting France's insistence that Haiti pay a huge indemnity for the crime of liberating itself, a burden it has never escaped —and France, of course, dismissed with elegant disdain Haiti's request, recently under Aristide, that it at least repay the indemnity, forgetting the responsibilities that a civilized society would accept.

The basic contours of what led to the current tragedy are pretty clear. Just beginning with the 1990 election of Aristide (far too narrow a time frame), Washington was appalled by the election of a populist candidate with a grass-roots constituency, just as it had been appalled by the prospect of the hemisphere's first free country on its doorstep two centuries earlier. Washington's traditional allies in Haiti naturally agreed. "The fear of democracy exists, by definitional necessity, in elite groups who monopolize economic and political power," Bellegarde-Smith observes in his perceptive history of Haiti—whether in Haiti or the U.S. or anywhere else.

The threat of democracy in Haiti in 1991 was even more ominous because of the favorable reaction of the international financial institutions (World Bank, IADB) to Aristide's programs, which awakened traditional concerns over the "virus" effect of successful independent development. These are familiar themes in international affairs: U.S. independence aroused similar concerns among European leaders. The dangers are commonly perceived to be particularly grave in a country like Haiti, which had been ravaged by France and then reduced to utter misery by a century of U.S. intervention. If even people in such dire circumstances can take their fate into their own hands, who knows what might happen elsewhere as the "contagion spreads."

The Bush I administration reacted to the disaster of democracy by shifting aid from the democratically elected government to what are called "democratic forces." The wealthy elites and the business sectors, who, along with the murderers and torturers of the military and paramilitaries, had been lauded by the current incumbents in Washington, in their Reaganite phase, for their progress in "democratic development," justifying lavish new aid. The praise came in response to ratification by the Haitian parliament of a law granting Washington's client killer and torturer Baby Doc Duvalier the authority to suspend the rights of any political party without reasons. The law passed by a majority of 99.98 percent. It, therefore, marked a positive step towards democracy as compared with the 99 percent approval of a 1918 law granting U.S. corporations the right to turn the country into a U.S. plantation, passed by 5 percent of the population after the Haitian Parliament was disbanded at gunpoint by Wilson's Marines when it refused to accept this "progressive measure," essential for "economic development." Their reaction to Baby Doc's encouraging progress towards democracy was characteristic—worldwide—on the part of the visionaries who are now entrancing educated opinion with their dedication to bringing democracy to a suffering world—although, to be sure, their actual exploits are being tastefully rewritten to satisfy current needs.

> The praise came in response to ratification by the Haitian parliament of a law granting Washington's client killer and torturer Baby Doc Duvalier the authority to suspend the rights of any political party without reasons. The law passed by a majority of 99.98 percent

Refugees fleeing to the U.S. from the terror of the U.S.-backed dictatorships were forcefully returned, in gross violation of international humanitarian law. The policy was reversed when a democratically elected government took office. Though the flow of refugees reduced to a trickle, they were mostly granted political asylum.

The policy returned to normal when a military junta overthrew the Aristide government after seven months and state terrorist atrocities rose to new heights. The perpetrators were the army—the inheritors of the National Guard left by Wilson's invaders to control the population—and its paramilitary forces. The most important of these, FRAPH, was founded by CIA asset Emmanuel Constant, who now lives happily in Queens, New York. Clinton, and Bush II dismissed extradition requests because he would reveal U.S. ties to the murderous junta, it is widely assumed. Constant's

contributions to state terror were, after all, meager—merely prime responsibility for the murder of 4,000 to 5,000 poor blacks. Recall the core element of the Bush doctrine, which has "already become a de facto rule of international relations," Harvard's Graham Allison writes in *Foreign Affairs:* "those who harbor terrorists are as guilty as the terrorists themselves," in the President's words, and must be treated accordingly by large-scale bombing and invasion.

When Aristide was overthrown by the 1991 military coup, the Organization of American States (OAS) declared an embargo. Bush I announced that the U.S. would violate it by exempting U.S. firms. He was thus "fine tuning" the embargo for the benefit of the suffering population, the *New York Times* reported. Clinton authorized even more extreme violations of the embargo. U.S. trade with the junta and its wealthy supporters sharply increased. The crucial element of the embargo was, of course, oil. While the CIA solemnly testified to Congress that the junta "probably will be out of fuel and power very shortly" and "Our intelligence efforts are focused on detecting attempts to circumvent the embargo and monitoring its impact," Clinton secretly authorized the Texaco Oil Company to ship oil to the junta illegally, in violation of presidential directives. This remarkable revelation was the lead story on the AP wires the day before Clinton sent the Marines to "restore democracy," impossible to miss—I happened to be monitoring AP wires that day and saw it repeated prominently over and over—and, obviously, it was of enormous significance for anyone who wanted to understand what was happening. It was suppressed with truly impressive discipline, though reported in industry journals along with scant mention buried in the business press.

Also efficiently suppressed were the crucial conditions that Clinton imposed for Aristide's return, that he adopt the program of the defeated

U.S. candidate in the 1990 elections, a former World Bank official who had received 14 percent of the vote. We call this "restoring democracy," a prime illustration of how U.S. foreign policy has entered a "noble phase" with a "saintly glow," the national press explained. The harsh neo-liberal program that Aristide was compelled to adopt was virtually guaranteed to demolish the remaining shreds of economic sovereignty, extending Wilson's progressive legislation and similar U.S.-imposed measures since.

As democracy was thereby restored, the World Bank announced, "The renovated state must focus on an economic strategy centered on the energy and initiative of Civil Society, especially the private sector, both national and foreign." That has the merit of honesty. Haitian Civil Society includes the tiny rich elite and U.S. corporations, but not the vast majority of the population, the peasants and slum-dwellers who had committed the grave sin of organizing to elect their own president. World Bank officers explained that the neoliberal program would benefit the "more open, enlightened, business class" and foreign investors, but assured us that the program "is not going to hurt the poor to the extent it has in other countries" subjected to structural adjustment because the Haitian poor already lacked minimal protection from proper economic policy, such as subsidies for basic goods.

Aristide's minister in charge of rural development and agrarian reform was not notified of the plans to be imposed on this largely peasant society, to be returned by "America's good wishes" to the track from which it veered briefly after the regrettable democratic election in 1990.

Matters then proceeded in their predictable course. A 1995 USAID report explained that the "export-driven trade and investment policy" that Washington imposed will "relentlessly squeeze the domestic rice farmer," who will be forced to turn to agroexport, with incidental benefits to U.S. agribusiness and investors. Despite their extreme poverty, Haitian rice farmers are quite efficient, but cannot possibly compete with U.S.

agribusiness, even if it did not receive 40 percent of its profits from government subsidies, sharply increased under the Reaganites who are again in power, still producing enlightened rhetoric about the miracles of the market. We now read that Haiti cannot feed itself, another sign of a "failed state."

A few small industries were still able to function making chicken parts. But U.S. conglomerates have a large surplus of dark meat and demanded the right to dump their excess products in Haiti. They tried to do the same in Canada and Mexico, too, but there illegal dumping could be barred. Not in Haiti, compelled to submit to efficient market principles by the U.S. government and the corporations it serves.

One might note that the Pentagon's proconsul in Iraq, Paul Bremer, ordered a very similar program to be instituted there, with the same beneficiaries in mind. That's also called "enhancing democracy." In fact, the record, highly revealing and important, goes back to the 18th century. Similar programs had a large role in creating today's third world. Meanwhile the powerful ignored the rules, except when they could benefit from them and were able to become rich developed societies. Dramatically the U.S., which led the way in modern protectionism and, particularly since World War II, has relied crucially on the dynamic state sector for innovation and development, socializing risk and cost.

The punishment of Haiti became much more severe under Bush II—there are differences within the narrow spectrum of cruelty and greed. Aid was cut and international institutions were pressured to do likewise, under pretexts too outlandish to merit discussion. They are extensively reviewed in Paul Farmer's *The Uses of Haiti* and in some current press commentary, notably by Jeffrey Sachs *(Financial Times)* and Tracy Kidder *(New York Times)*. Putting details aside, what has happened since is eerily similar to the overthrow of Haiti's first democratic government in 1991.

The Aristide government, once again, was undermined by U.S. planners, who understood, under Clinton, that the threat of democracy can be overcome if economic sovereignty is eliminated and presumably also understood that economic development will also be a faint hope under such conditions, one of the best-confirmed lessons of economic history. Bush II planners are even more dedicated to undermining democracy and independence and despised Aristide and the popular organizations that swept him to power with perhaps even more passion than their predecessors. The forces that reconquered the country are mostly inheritors of the U.S.-installed army and paramilitary terrorists.

Those who are intent on diverting attention from the U.S. role will object that the situation is more complex—as is always true—and that Aristide too was guilty of many crimes. Correct, but if he had been a saint the situation would hardly have developed very differently, as was evident in 1994, when the only real hope was that a democratic revolution in the U.S. would make it possible to shift policy in a more civilized direction. What is happening now is awful, maybe beyond repair, and there is plenty of short-term responsibility on all sides. But the right way for the U.S. and France to proceed is very clear. They should begin with payment of enormous reparations to Haiti (France is perhaps even more hypocritical and disgraceful in this regard than the U.S.).

That, however, requires construction of functioning democratic societies in which, at the very least, people have a prayer of knowing what's going on. Commentary on Haiti, Iraq, and other "failed societies" is quite right in stressing the importance of overcoming the "democratic deficit" that substantially reduces the significance of elections. It does not, however, draw the obvious corollary that the lesson applies in spades to a country where "politics is the shadow cast on society by big business," in the words of America's leading social philosopher, John Dewey, describing his own country in days when the blight had spread nowhere near as far as it has today.

For those who are concerned with the substance of democracy and human rights, the basic tasks at home are also clear enough. They have been carried out before, with no slight success, and under incomparably harsher conditions elsewhere, including the slums and hills of Haiti. We do not have to submit, voluntarily, to living in a failed state suffering from an enormous democratic deficit.

Part Two: 2007-2014

15.

Cold War II

Containing Iran

These are exciting days in Washington, as the government directs its energies to the demanding task of "containing Iran" in what *Washington Post* correspondent Robin Wright, joining others, calls "Cold War II." During Cold War I, the task was to contain two awesome forces. The lesser and more moderate force was "an implacable enemy whose avowed objective is world domination by whatever means and at whatever cost." Hence "if the United States is to survive," it will have to adopt a "repugnant philosophy" and reject "acceptable norms of human conduct" and the "long-standing American concepts of 'fair play'" that had been exhibited with such searing clarity in the conquest of the national territory, the Philippines, Haiti, and other beneficiaries of "the idealistic new world bent on ending inhumanity," as the newspaper of record describes our noble mission.

The judgments about the nature of the super-Hitler and the necessary response are those of General Jimmy Doolittle, in a critical assessment of the CIA commissioned by President Eisenhower in 1954. They are quite consistent with those of Truman administration liberals, the "wise men" who were "present at the creation," notoriously in NSC 68, but, in fact, quite consistently.

In the face of the Kremlin's unbridled aggression in every corner of the world, it is perhaps understandable that the U.S. resisted in defense of human values with a savage display of torture, terror, subversion, and violence while doing "everything in its power to alter or abolish any regime not openly allied with America," as Tim Weiner summarizes the doctrine of the Eisenhower administration in his recent history of the CIA. Just as the Truman liberals easily matched their successors in fevered rhetoric about the implacable enemy and its campaign to rule the world, so did John F. Kennedy, who bitterly condemned the "monolithic and ruthless conspiracy," and dismissed the proposal of its leader (Khrushchev) for sharp mutual cuts in offensive weaponry, then reacted to his unilateral implementation of these proposals with a huge military build-up. The Kennedy brothers also quickly surpassed Eisenhower in violence and terror, as they "unleashed covert action with an unprecedented intensity" (Wiener), doubling Eisenhower's annual record of major CIA covert operations, with horrendous consequences world wide, even a close brush with terminal nuclear war.

From Z Magazine, August 2007

But at least it was possible to deal with Russia, unlike the fiercer enemy, China. The more thoughtful scholars recognized that Russia was poised uneasily between civilization and barbarism. As Henry Kissinger later explained in his academic essays, only the West has undergone the Newtonian revolution and is therefore "deeply committed to the notion that the real world is external to the observer," while the rest still believe "that the real world is almost completely internal to the observer," the "basic division" that is "the deepest problem of the contemporary international order." But Russia, unlike third word peasants who think that rain and sun are inside their heads, was perhaps coming to the realization that the world is not just a dream, Kissinger felt.

Not so the still more savage and bloodthirsty enemy, China, which for liberal Democrat intellectuals at various times rampaged as a "a Slavic Manchukuo," a blind puppet of its Kremlin master, or a monster utterly unconstrained as it pursued its crazed campaign to crush the world in its tentacles, or whatever else circumstances demanded.

The remarkable tale of doctrinal fanaticism from the 1940s to the 1970s, which makes contemporary rhetoric seem rather moderate, is reviewed by James Peck in his highly revealing study of the national security culture, Washington's China.

In later years, there were attempts to mimic the valiant deeds of the defenders of virtue from the two villainous global conquerors and their loyal slaves—for example, when the Gipper strapped on his cowboy boots and declared a National Emergency because Nicaraguan hordes were only two days from Harlingen Texas, though, as he courageously informed the press, despite the tremendous odds, "I refuse to give up. I remember a man named Winston Churchill who said, 'Never give in. Never, never, never.' So we won't." With consequences that need not be reviewed.

Even with the best of efforts, however, the attempts never were able to recapture the glorious days of Cold War I. But now those heights might be within reach, as another implacable enemy bent on world conquest has arisen, which we must contain before it destroys us all: Iran.

Recovering The Heady Cold War Days

Perhaps it's a lift to the spirits to be able to recover those heady Cold War days when at least there was a legitimate force to contain, however dubious the pretexts and disgraceful the means. But it is instructive to take a closer look at the contours of Cold War II as they are being designed by "the former Kremlinologists now running U.S. foreign policy, such as Rice and Gates" (Wright).

The task of containment is to establish "a bulwark against Iran's growing influence in the Middle East," Mark Mazzetti and Helene Cooper explain in the *New York Times* (July 31). To contain Iran's influence we must surround Iran with U.S. and NATO ground forces, along with massive naval deployments in the Persian Gulf and, of course, incomparable air power and weapons of mass destruction. And we must provide a huge flow of arms to what Condoleezza Rice calls "the forces of moderation and reform" in the region, the brutal tyrannies of Egypt and Saudi Arabia and, with particular munificence, Israel, by now virtually an adjunct of the militarized high-tech U.S. economy. All to contain Iran's influence. A daunting challenge indeed.

And daunting it is. In Iraq, Iranian support is welcomed by much of the majority Shi'ite population. In an August visit to Teheran, Iraqi Prime Minister Nouri al-Maliki met with the supreme leader Ali Khamenei, President Ahmadinejad, and other senior officials, and thanked Tehran for its "positive and constructive" role in improving security in Iraq, eliciting a sharp reprimand from President Bush, who "declares Teheran a regional peril and asserts the Iraqi leader must understand," to quote the headline of the *Los*

Angeles Times report on al-Maliki's intellectual deficiencies. A few days before, also greatly to Bush's discomfiture, Afghan President Hamid Karzai, Washington's favorite, described Iran as "a helper and a solution" in his country. Similar problems abound beyond Iran's immediate neighbors. In Lebanon, according to polls, most Lebanese see Iranian-backed Hezbollah "as a legitimate force defending their country from Israel," Wright reports. In Palestine, Iranian-backed Hamas won a free election, eliciting savage punishment of the Palestinian population by the U.S. and Israel for the crime of voting "the wrong way," another episode in "democracy promotion."

But no matter. The aim of U.S. militancy and the arms flow to the moderates is to counter "what everyone in the region believes is a flexing of muscles by a more aggressive Iran," according to an unnamed senior U.S. government official—"everyone" being the technical term used to refer to Washington and its more loyal clients. Iran's aggression consists in its being welcomed by many within the region, and allegedly supporting resistance to the U.S. occupation of neighboring Iraq.

It's likely, though little discussed, that a prime concern about Iran's influence is to the East, where in mid-August, "Russia and China today host Iran's President Mahmoud Ahmadinejad at a summit of a Central Asian security club designed to counter U.S. influence in the region," the business press reports. The "security club" is the Shanghai Cooperation Organization (SCO), which has been slowly taking shape in recent years. Its membership includes not only the two giants Russia and China, but also the energy-rich Central Asian states Kyrgyzstan, Uzbekistan, Kazakhstan, and Tajikistan. Hamid Karzai of Afghanistan was a guest of honor at the August meeting. "In another unwelcome development for the Americans, Turkmeni-stan's President Gurbanguly Berdymukham-medov also accepted an invitation to attend the summit," another step in its improvement of relations with Russia, particularly in energy, revers-

ing a long-standing policy of isolation from Russia. "Russia in May secured a deal to build a new pipeline to import more gas from Turkmenistan, bolstering its dominant hold on supplies to Europe and heading off a competing U.S.-backed plan that would bypass Russian territory."

Along with Iran, there are three other official observer states: India, Pakistan, and Mongolia. Washington's request for similar status was denied. In 2005, the SCO called for a timetable for termination of any U.S. military presence in Central Asia. The participants at the August meeting flew to the Urals to attend the first joint Russia-China military exercises on Russian soil.

Association of Iran with the SCO extends its inroads into the Middle East, where China has been increasing trade and other relations with the jewel in the crown, Saudi Arabia. There is an oppressed Shi'ite population in Saudi Arabia that is also susceptible to Iran's influence—and happens to sit on most of Saudi oil. About 40 percent of Middle East oil is reported to be heading East, not West. As the flow Eastward increases, U.S. control declines over this lever of world domination, a "stupendous source of strategic power," as the State Department described Saudi oil 60 years ago.

In Cold War I, the Kremlin had imposed an iron curtain and built the Berlin Wall to contain Western influence. In Cold War II, Wright reports, the former Kremlinologists framing policy are imposing a "green curtain" to bar Iranian influence. In short, government-media doctrine is that the Iranian threat is rather similar to the Western threat that the Kremlin sought to contain and the U.S. is eagerly taking on the Kremlin's role in the thrilling new Cold War.

All of this is presented without noticeable concern. Nevertheless, the recognition that the U.S. government is modeling itself on Stalin and his successors in the new Cold War must be arousing at least some flickers of embarrassment. Perhaps that is how we can explain the ferocious *Washington Post* editorial announcing that Iran has escalated its aggressiveness to a Hot War: "the Revolutionary Guard, a radical state within Iran's Islamic state, is waging war against the United States and trying to kill as many American soldiers as possible." The U.S. must therefore "fight back," the editors thunder, finding quite "puzzling...the murmurs of disapproval from European diplomats and others who say they favor using diplomacy and economic pressure, rather than military action, to rein in Iran," even in the face of its outright aggression. The evidence that Iran is waging war against the U.S. is now conclusive. After all, it comes from an Administration that has never deceived the American people, even improving on the famous stellar honesty of its predecessors.

If the Charges Are True

Suppose that for once Washington's charges happen to be true and Iran really is providing Shi'ite militias with roadside bombs that kill U.S. forces, perhaps even making use of some of the advanced weaponry lavishly provided to the Revolutionary Guard by Ronald Reagan in order to fund the illegal war against Nicaragua, under the pretext of arms for hostages (the number of hostages tripled during these endeavors).

If the charges are true, then Iran could properly be charged with a minuscule fraction of the iniquity of the Reagan administration, which provided Stinger missiles and other high-tech military aid to the "insurgents" seeking to disrupt Soviet efforts to bring stability and justice to Afghanistan, as they saw it. Perhaps Iran is even guilty of some of the crimes of the Roosevelt administration, which assisted terrorist partisans attacking peaceful and sovereign Vichy France in 1940-41, and had thus declared war on Germany even before Pearl Harbor.

One can pursue these questions. The CIA station chief in Pakistan in 1981, Howard Hart, reports that "I was the first chief of station ever sent abroad with this wonderful order: 'Go kill Soviet soldiers.' Imagine! I loved it." Of course "the mission was not to liberate Afghanistan," Tim Wiener writes in his history of the CIA, repeating the obvious. But "it was a noble goal," he writes. Killing Russians, with no concern for the fate of Afghans, is a "noble goal," but support for resistance to a U.S. invasion and occupation would be a vile act and declaration of war. Without irony, the Bush administration and the media charge that Iran is "meddling" in Iraq, otherwise presumably free from foreign interference.

The evidence is partly technical. Do the serial numbers on the Improvised Explosive Devices really trace back to Iran? If so, does the leadership of Iran know about the IEDs, or only the Iranian Revolutionary Guard. Settling the debate, the White House plans to brand the Revolutionary Guard as a "specially designated global terrorist" force, an unprecedented action against a national military branch, authorizing Washington to undertake a wide range of punitive actions. Watching in disbelief, much of the world asks whether the U.S. military, invading and occupying Iran's neighbors, might better merit this charge—or its Israeli client, about to receive a huge increase in military aid to commemorate 40 years of harsh occupation and illegal settlement, and its fifth invasion of Lebanon a year ago.

It is instructive that Washington's propaganda framework is reflexively accepted, apparently without notice, in U.S. and other Western commentary and reporting, apart from the marginal fringe of what is called "the loony left." What is considered "criticism" is skepticism as to whether all of Washington's charges about Iranian aggression in Iraq are true. It might be an interesting research project to see how closely the propaganda of Russia, Nazi Germany, and other aggressors and occupiers matched the standards of today's liberal press and commentators. The comparisons are, of course, unfair.

Unlike German and Russian occupiers, American forces are in Iraq by right, on the principle, too obvious even to enunciate—that the U.S. owns the world. Therefore, as a matter of elementary logic, the U.S. cannot invade and occupy another country. The U.S. can only defend and liberate others. No other category exists. Predecessors, including the most monstrous, have commonly sworn by the same principle, but again there is an obvious difference: they were wrong and we are right—QED.

An Important Study

Another comparison comes to mind, which is studiously ignored when we are sternly admonished of the ominous consequences that might follow withdrawal of U.S. troops from Iraq. The preferred analogy is Indochina, highlighted in a shameful speech by the president on August 22. That analogy can perhaps pass muster among those who have succeeded in effacing from their minds the record of U.S. actions in Indochina, including the destruction of much of Vietnam and the murderous bombing of Laos and Cambodia as the U.S. began its withdrawal from the wreckage of South Vietnam. In Cambodia, the bombing was in accord with Kissinger's genocidal orders: "anything that flies on anything that moves"—actions that drove "an enraged populace into the arms of an insurgency [the Khmer Rouge] that had enjoyed relatively little support before the Kissinger-Nixon bombing was inaugurated," as Cambodia specialists Owen Taylor and Ben Kiernan observe in a highly important study that passed virtually without notice, in which they reveal that the bombing was five times the incredible level reported earlier, greater than all allied bombing in World War II. Completely suppressing all relevant facts, it is then possible for the president and many commentators to present Khmer Rouge crimes as a justification for continuing to devastate Iraq.

But although the grotesque Indochina analogy receives much attention, the obvious analogy is ignored: the Russian withdrawal from Afghanistan, which, as Soviet analysts predicted, led to shocking violence and destruction as the country was taken over by Reagan's favorites, who amused themselves by such acts as throwing acid in the faces of women in Kabul they regarded as too liberated and who then virtually destroyed the city and much else, creating such havoc and terror that the population actually welcomed the

Taliban. That analogy could indeed be invoked without utter absurdity by advocates of "staying the course," but evidently it is best forgotten.

Under the heading "Secretary Rice's Mideast mission: contain Iran," the press reports Rice's warning that Iran is "the single most important single-country challenge to...U.S. interests in the Middle East." That is a reasonable judgment. Given the long-standing principle that Washington must do "everything in its power to alter or abolish any regime not openly allied with America," Iran does pose a unique challenge, and it is natural that the task of containing Iranian influence should be a high priority.

As elsewhere, Bush administration rhetoric is relatively mild in this case. For the Kennedy administration, "Latin America was the most dangerous area in the world" when there was a threat that the progressive Cheddi Jagan might win a free election in British Guiana, overturned by CIA shenanigans that handed the country over to the thuggish racist Forbes Burnham. A few years earlier, Iraq was "the most dangerous place in the world" (CIA director Allen Dulles) after General Abdel Karim Qassim broke the Anglo-American condominium over Middle East oil, overthrowing the pro-U.S. monarchy, which had been heavily infiltrated by the CIA.

A primary concern was that Qassim might join Nasser, then the supreme Middle East devil, in using the incomparable energy resources of the Middle East for the domestic population. The issue for Washington was not so much access as control. At the time and for many years after, Washington was purposely exhausting domestic oil resources in the interests of "national security," meaning security for the profits of Texas oil men, like the failed entrepreneur who now sits in the Oval Office. But as high-level planner George Kennan had explained well before, we cannot relax our guard when there is any interference with "protection of our resources" (which happen to be somewhere else). Unquestionably, Iran's government merits harsh condemnation, though it has not engaged in worldwide terror, subversion, and aggression, following the U.S. model—which extends to today's Iran as well, if ABC news is correct in reporting that the U.S. is supporting Pakistan-based Junullah, which is carrying out terrorist acts inside Iran. The sole act of aggression attributed to Iran is the conquest of two small islands in the Gulf—under Washington's close ally the Shah. In addition to internal repression—heightened, as Iranian dissidents regularly protest, by U.S. militancy—the prospect that Iran might develop nuclear weapons also is deeply troubling. Though Iran has every right to develop nuclear energy, no one—including the majority of Iranians—wants it to have nuclear weapons. That would add to the threat of survival, posed much more seriously by its near neighbors Pakistan, India, and Israel, all nuclear armed with the blessing of the U.S., which most of the world regards as the leading threat to world peace.

Iran rejects U.S. control of the Middle East, challenging fundamental policy doctrine, but it hardly poses a military threat. On the contrary, it has been the victim of outside powers for years: in recent memory, when the U.S. and Britain overthrew its parliamentary government and installed a brutal tyrant in 1953, and when the U.S. supported Saddam Hussein's murderous invasion, slaughtering hundreds of thousands of Iranians, many with chemical weapons, without the "international community" lifting a finger—something that Iranians do not forget as easily as the perpetrators. And then under severe sanctions as a punishment for disobedience.

Israel regards Iran as a threat. Israel seeks to dominate the region with no interference and Iran might be some slight counterbalance, while also supporting domestic forces that do not bend to Israel's will. It may, however, be useful to bear in mind that Hamas has accepted the international consensus on a two-state settlement on the international border and Hezbollah, along with Iran, has made clear that it would accept any outcome approved by Palestinians, leaving the U.S. and Israel isolated in their traditional rejectionism. But Iran is hardly a military threat to Israel. And whatever threat there might be could

be overcome if the U.S. would accept the view of the great majority of its own citizens and of Iranians and permit the Middle East to become a nuclear-weapons free zone, including Iran and Israel, and U.S. forces deployed there. One may also recall that UN Security Council Resolution 687 of April 3, 1991, to which Washington appeals when convenient, calls for "establishing in the Middle East a zone free from weapons of mass destruction and all missiles for their delivery." It is widely recognized that use of military force in Iran would risk blowing up the entire region, with untold consequences beyond. We know from polls that in the surrounding countries, where the Iranian government is hardly popular—Turkey, Saudi Arabia, Pakistan—nevertheless large majorities prefer even a nuclear-armed Iran to any form of military action against it.

Outlaw State

The rhetoric about Iran has escalated to the point where both political parties and practically the whole U.S. press accept it as legitimate and, in fact, honorable, that "all options are on the table," to quote Hillary Clinton and everybody else, possibly even nuclear weapons. "All options on the table" means that Washington threatens war. The UN Charter outlaws "the threat or use of force." The United States, which has chosen to become an outlaw state, disregards international laws and norms. We're allowed to threaten anybody we want—and to attack anyone we choose.

Washington's feverish new Cold War "containment" policy has spread to Europe. Washington intends to install a "missile defense system" in the Czech Republic and Poland, marketed to Europe as a shield against Iranian missiles. Even if Iran had nuclear weapons and long-range missiles, the chances of its using them to attack Europe are perhaps on a par with the chances of Europe's being hit by an asteroid, so perhaps Europe would do as well to invest in an asteroid de-

135

fense system. Furthermore, if Iran were to indicate the slightest intention of aiming a missile at Europe or Israel, the country would be vaporized. Of course, Russian planners are gravely upset by the shield proposal. We can imagine how the U.S. would respond if a Russian anti-missile system were erected in Canada. The Russians have good reason to regard an anti-missile system as part of a first-strike weapon against them. It is generally understood that such a system could never block a first strike, but it could conceivably impede a retaliatory strike. On all sides, "missile defense" is therefore understood to be a first-strike weapon, eliminating a deterrent to attack. A small initial installation in Eastern Europe could easily be a base for later expansion. More obviously, the only military function of such a system with regard to Iran, the declared aim, would be to bar an Iranian deterrent to U.S. or Israel aggression.

Not surprisingly, in reaction to the "missile defense" plans, Russia has resorted to its own dangerous gestures, including the recent decision to renew long-range patrols by nuclear-capable bombers after a 15-year hiatus, in one recent case near the U.S. military base on Guam. These actions reflect Russia's anger "over what it has called American and NATO aggressiveness, including plans for a missile-defense system in the Czech Republic and Poland, analysts said" (Andrew Kramer, *NYT*).

The shield ratchets the threat of war a few notches higher, in the Middle East and elsewhere, with incalculable consequences, and the potential for a terminal nuclear war. The immediate fear is that by accident or design, Washington's war planners or their Israeli surrogate might decide to escalate their Cold War II into a hot one—in this case a real hot war.

16.

Kicking Away the Ladder

U.S. real wages are about the lowest in the industrial world

My days are often full of interviews on all sorts of topics, ranging from literal threats to human survival, which are quite real, to catastrophes all over the world, some known, like Iraq; some not known, like Western Sahara, the last literal colony in Africa. Many of these are tainted by the realization that the U.S. shares a lot of responsibility for misery, suffering, and possible disaster, often by action, sometimes by inaction. With that in front of us, it feels to me, and may seem to you, a little bit cold and bloodless to do what I'm now going to do and that is ignore the torment, misery, and threats to survival, and so on, and talk about problems of democracy and development. I think the implications for day-to-day life are actually quite direct.

Just to illustrate with one example—I'm sure you have read the many commentaries on the death of Milton Friedman. A typical one was the front-page story in the *Wall Street Journal* full of accolades, among them that the intellectual foundations of the Reagan administration were provided by Friedman's work—reliance on market forces and fiscal conservatism, all of which led to the grand economy that we have been enjoying for the last 30 years.

The problem is it is the exact opposite of the truth in every crucial respect. As for the grand economy, the last 30 years have been probably the major economic failure in U.S. history, the so called "neo-liberal period." There have been no serious depressions, no other major disasters, but the majority of the population has seen real wages and incomes stagnate or even decline. One stunning figure is that the bottom 40 percent of the population has seen a decline in their net worth. There has been economic growth through this period. There has been increased productivity, but the benefits are for the few.

You may have seen a couple of front-page articles in the *New York Times* on the "suffering" of the ultra rich because they're so envious of the super ultra rich, which is surely the great problem of the day—for some, at least. If you go back 30 years, the beginning of the so-called "neo-liberal period" in the United States, wages were the highest in the industrial world, the working hours were the least—exactly what you would expect in the richest county in the world. But now it is reversed. Real wages are about the lowest in the industrial world, working hours are the highest,

Parts 1 and 2 from Z Magazine,
May and June 2007

or close to it. Benefits, which were never very strong, have declined, debt has soared, and security has declined severely. Much of that, incidentally, was planned. Fed chair Alan Greenspan, when he testified to Congress about the wonders of the economy that he was organizing and running, pointed out very frankly that one of the major reasons for the health of the economy was what he called "growing worker insecurity." What happened is not some kind of accident, it was organized.

For example, during the Reagan years it seems that about $700 million was spent on trying to encourage corporations to shift from the United States to the Caribbean. One phase of it was discovered in a great sting operation by Charlie Kernaghan and the National Labor Committee that he runs—it even hit national television. They pretended to set up a fake company and were able to catch USAID officials explaining to them how beneficial it would be for this fake company to shift their operations to the Caribbean—very cheap labor, very exploited, no benefits, mostly women so you can control them easily, kick them out if they make a fuss or get pregnant, no environmental constraints, things we all know about.

Also the Reagan administration openly pioneered illegal labor practices. This was well recorded in *Business Week*, which pointed out that the Reagan administration effectively instructed the business world that his adminiatration was not going to enforce the laws, which led to a sharp increase in illegal company actions to prevent union organizing. That was continued by Clinton who had another way of doing it called NAFTA.

One of the predicted effects of NAFTA was that it would undermine union organizers by giving employers a way to threaten workers who were trying to organize and if you keep trying we'll move to Mexico. That worked too. It's is illegal, but when you have a criminal state, and the business world knows that it enjoys the benefits of a criminal state it can carry these activities out. But unions not only improve the lives of working people, they're a powerful democratizing force. So threatening them harms working people and also harms democracy. What about the miracle of the market under Reagan? Well, that's a standard line too—overlooking the fact that Reagan was the most protectionist president in post-war U.S. history. In fact, he practically doubled protective barriers, more than all post-war presidents combined. There is a reason for that. If you go back to, say, the late 1970s there was a great deal of concern in the business world that U.S. companies could not compete with superior Japanese manufacturers. U.S. managers hadn't understood the new techniques of production-on-time and other measures that had developed in Japan. U.S. industry was falling apart and there were calls in the business press to "reindustrialize America." Well, how do you do that? You do it by keeping out superior Japanese and South Korean products and by calling on the usual savior, namely, the Pentagon. Which has happened before.

Factory Of The Future

A century earlier the biggest business operation in the United States was railroads. It was beyond the competence of private industries and the Pentagon took it over. Of course I say the Pentagon, but the U.S. Army took it over. It has often happened before and it happened again with Reagan who called on the Pentagon to design what they called "the factory of the future," a modern factory. This would teach backward U.S. corporate managers how to use computers, on time production, and all of the techniques that the Japanese had invented.

This has many advantages, calling on the Pentagon. For one, they could design the factory of the future so that it empowers managers and de-skills workers. That has been pretty well studied. David Noble, who was on the faculty of MIT, did major work on this, particularly with regard to automation. He showed that under military auspices, automation was designed to insure that decisions were taken away from skilled mechanics and put in the hands of supervisors and managers to de-skill the workforce and empower management. There was no reason—efficiency or even profit, as it sometimes harmed profit. It did not matter. It was very important for class war to ensure that the working class was de-skilled and passive and that power was in the hands of the managers and supervisors.

There is nothing new about that either. It goes right through history. I'm sure you heard of "Taylorism," a concept that was introduced about a century ago essentially to turn working people into robots, in effect control every motion to make sure everything is maximally "efficient." It was designed in U.S. military production, armories, and so on. That gives you plenty of funding to do whatever you like—no controls, no constraints—and you can implement class war very efficiently. The Reagan administration broke new records in this.

Let's turn to a broader look at democracy and development. The two concepts are closely related in many respects. One respect is that they have a common enemy—loss of sovereignty. In a world of nation-states it is true by definition that decline of sovereignty leads to the decline of democracy and the decline in the ability to conduct economic and social policy. That in turn harms development, a conclusion that is very well confirmed by several centuries of economic history. That same economic history shows quite consistently that loss of sovereignty leads to imposed liberalization—imposed, of course, in the interest of the designers, not the subjects.

In recent years the imposed regime is commonly called "neo-liberalism." It is the reigning economic orthodoxy of the past decades. It's not a very good term, incidentally, as it is by no means new and it is not liberal, at least not in the sense of "liberal" as understood by classical liberals—Adam Smith and others.

The very design of neo-liberal principles is a direct attack on democracy. One component is privatization. You take something out of the public domain, put it into the hands of totalitarian systems, which is what corporations are and, obviously, that reduces democracy. Let's move to the current primary theme, what is called "trade in services." It has nothing to do with trade in the usual sense. It's privatization of services. It's called "trade" so they can fit it into the trade agreement. It just means selling off services.

What are services? Well, services are anything that a human being could be interested in—education, health, water, air, energy, and so on. "Trade in services" now means putting all of these into the hands of unaccountable totalitarian institutions. If that is achieved, you can have formal democracy quite openly—clean elections, etc.—but it doesn't matter much because there is nothing for people to have any decisions about, nothing that matters, at least. It's somewhere else in the hands of unaccountable institutions under the name of "General Agreement on Trade in Services." That is the leading theme of the current trade negotiations.

Financial Liberalization

Another component of the neo-liberal package is financial liberalization. It means governments, for example, can't control capital flight, currencies aren't regulated, and so on. It's very well understood by economists what that leads to. Financial liberalization creates what some international economists have called a "virtual senate" of investors and lenders who carry out a "moment-by-moment referendum" on social and economic policies. If they don't like those policies, they destroy the economy by capital flight, by attacks on currencies, by selling bonds, and so on. The policies that the virtual senate doesn't like are anything that is "irrational." "Irrational" means it's helpful to people, not to profits, and the virtual senate keeps an eye on this second by second. If the government makes the mistake of being irrational, you get huge capital flight, attacks on currency, and so on. It happens all the time and it keeps the countries in line. It means that governments have what is sometimes called a "dual constituency," one of them is the voters and the other is the virtual senate. You can guess who wins. All of this is coming to a head right now in what are called "free trade negotiations," which have practically nothing to do with free trade.

There is what is called the Doha Round. Poor countries, the so-called "developing countries" —a euphemism for the former colonial countries—are trying to escape the grip of imperial violence and destruction. They are called "developing countries" whether they are developing or not. They have blocked the Doha Round. But in the West, among the rich, it's considered a kind of no-brainer; of course we have to implement the Doha Round, we have to bring it to a successful conclusion. Popular opinion is generally opposed, often strongly opposed, in the rich countries too and that is no surprise. If you look at the proposals, which are usually kind of secret—people are not supposed to look at them—they provide great benefits for investors, lenders, and management who are free to set working people against one another all over the world. It's called "globalization." The main theme is to set working people against one another so it will naturally follow that wages are lowered, benefits decline, working conditions are harmed, environment is destroyed. It's a problem for our grandchildren, but planners don't worry about it. There are also tremendous privileges for management. One component of these agreements is what is called "national treatment." It means that if General Motors invests in Mexico, they have to be treated like a Mexican company. Better than a Mexican company, because the treatment of General Motors has to meet international trade conditions.

In contrast, if a Mexican comes to the United States, a Mexican of flesh and blood, he or she cannot demand national treatment, obviously. Try that and you might end up in Guantanamo, if you're lucky. But corporations are different; they have the rights of persons, granted by state power, but rights far beyond those as persons. The so-called "free trade agreements" extend those rights in numerous ways. What all of this means for the so-called "developing countries," often, is to lock them in to their current state of underdevelopment, if they follow the rules.

Climbing The Ladder

There is a name for this in economic theory. It's called kicking away the ladder. First climb up the ladder of development yourself and then kick it away. You make sure no one else uses the measures you used to climb to the top—protection of domestic industries, targeted investment, reliance on the state sector for research and development, production and procurement, and a whole bunch of other devices. It's called free trade.

What the developing countries are supposed to do is pursue comparative advantage. It is supposed to be a wonderful thing. The problem is that "development" means changing comparative advantage, not pursuing it. Development is changing your comparative advantage to a different comparative advantage. Take the history of the United States right after it won independence. Suppose it had followed the advice and pursued its comparative advantage in exporting fur and fish and so on. The scattered population that would live here today would be doing that. But they did not pursue their comparative advantage, they did not follow the rules. What they did was create very high tariffs to prevent superior British textiles from coming in, later superior British steel, and superior industrial machinery. That way the United States was able to change their comparative advantage and become the world's leading industrial society.

In the 19th century, right up to the mid-20th century, the United States was far in the lead in protectionism, violating all the rules, far more than other industrial countries. That is consistent throughout history. So consistent that a leading economic historian has actually concluded that protectionism enhances trade. It sounds kind of like a paradox, but it seems to work and has a rationale. Protectionism increases growth and growth increases trade. So protectionism seems to enhance trade. A similar conclusion, incidentally, holds into the post-WWII period when other forms of market interference became more prominent. The United States, by pursuing not only protectionist policies, but reliance on the state sector for research and development, became by far the world's leading economic power.

By 1950 the United States was the richest and most powerful state in history. U.S.-based corporations, and the state that caters to their interest, at that point were willing to sponsor limited free trade, knowing the playing field was not level and they were going to win—so maybe free trade would be okay. But that commitment was hedged with crucial restrictions to insure that the powerful would prevail.

The most extreme restriction, which is rarely discussed by economists, is reliance on a dynamic state sector as the engine of growth. It covers practically the whole high-tech economy—computers, Internet, lasers, commercial aircraft. You can go across the board and find that the state sector is critical in development. In the case of computers and the Internet, they were basically in the state sector for about 30 years before being handed over to private power.

It may not be what you learn in economics courses, but this is how the world works. And it makes a lot of sense. When research and development and production and procurement are in the state sector, it means that the public is paying for it and taking the risk. If something works out, maybe 30 years later, like in the case of computers and the Internet, you hand it over to private power to make profits. It's known as market society, free markets, capitalism, it's the way things really work.

Narco-Trafficking

The United States did not invent it. If you look at the global dominance of England, that is the way they handled it. In 1846 England shifted to free trade after 150 years of protectionism, state intervention, and imperial violence, which had placed England far in the lead in industrialization, twice as high per capita as any other country. It seemed that competition would be relatively safe, like for the U.S. a century later. But, like the U.S., the British hedged their bets. One way was to keep some protected markets, like India, to insure profits. One of the main reasons for conquering India was another form of market interference, trying to monopolize opium production. They did not quite make it—Yankee merchants got a piece of it—but the British came pretty close to monopolizing opium production.

That was extremely important because England was unable to break into the Chinese market. China did not want British goods because they felt their own were superior and British agents were complaining about that. But England hit on a brilliant way to do it, by developing by far the largest narco-trafficking industry in history. Colombia doesn't even come close. They tried to monopolize opium production and then forced it on China with gunboats. The enterprise succeeded brilliantly.

The China market was opened by what was called "the poison trade" and "the pig trade." The poison trade meant opium brought in at gunpoint, which turned the country into a nation of opium addicts, creating a market for British exports. The pig trade brought kidnapped Chinese workers to the United States to build the railroads—making a big contribution to U.S. economic development in the 19th century (as well as providing the term "Shanghaied"). The profits from the narco-trafficking racket were enormous.

They paid the cost of the Royal Navy, which was the mainstay of imperialism. They paid for administering India, a colony. They paid for the purchase of U.S. cotton—which fueled the industrial revolution, like oil today. That also was not exactly a free market miracle. It was created by extermination of the indigenous population and slavery, rather radical forms of market interference. But by the 1920s, England was facing a situation like the United States did 50 years later—superior Japanese products were driving British products out of the market. Britain handled it the way Reagan did and they closed the empire to Japanese imports. Notice it's similar to the Reaganite intervention to reindustrialize America in the face of Japanese competition in the 1970s. The general point is that free trade and democracy are just fine when you can make sure that the results come out the right way, otherwise you get rid of them. History is full of that.

After World War II the picture pretty much conforms to the historical pattern. There have been two phases, roughly 1950 to 1975 and 1975 to the present, not exact, but approximately. The first phase was designed under great popular pressure for social democracy, for much more radical measures of democracy and social welfare.

The system was designed to leave these options open. The system was designed with capital controls, regulated currencies, and government programs in the third world to stimulate production. It was called "import substitution" and continued roughly into the 1970s. That is a period that economists call "the golden age of capitalism," state capitalism is a more accurate term.

Economic results were better than ever before in history—and ever since. Take the United States. From roughly 1950 to 1975 this was the highest growth period ever in U.S. history and it was egalitarian—about the same for the lowest and highest quintile. An interesting and important fact is that the social indicators that measure the health of the society—infant mortality, child abuse, and a whole collection of measures—rose along with growth. That continued until 1975. Since then social indicators have declined, though growth has gone up, not as fast, but it has gone up. Social indicators declined by the year 2000 to the level of 1960—that is after the very brief and shallow Clinton boom. But since then the record has become much worse in all respects. One startling fact that was just revealed in the business press is that during the current Bush years, the private sector has added no jobs outside of the health sector. One reason there are added jobs there is because it is a total catastrophe, it is the most inefficient public health system in the industrial world. But outside of that no new jobs.

It's the same in much of the world. In the mid-1970s we switch to the neo-liberal period. There has been a sharp decline in almost every economic dimension—growth of the economy, growth of productivity, and others. The so-called Asian tigers, like Taiwan and South Korea, ignored the rules and grew very fast. The decline is correlated closely with following the rules, following the programs. The countries that followed the rules most rigorously have the worst records, like Latin America. Probably worst in their history.

India is a poster child. According to Thomas Friedman, the greatest place in the world, etc., and since 1990 it has partially followed the rules and there has been improvement for a substantial minority of the population—also in the number of billionaires. It's now eighth in the world. There is also something called the UN ranking for Human Development. Prior to this period in 1990, India was 124th. Now it has sunk to 127th. So much for the "grand economy."

If you look at the state sector in the United States, your taxes have been funding growth for years. Now the funding is shifting. Pentagon funding is declining and funding for the National Institute of Health and other health-related parts of the government is going up. Take a look at MIT, take a look at the funding that is going on. There is a pretty of good reason for it. In the early post-war period, the first 25 years, the cutting edge of the economy was electronics-based and the way to fool the public into paying for that was to scream, "The Russians are coming" or "Grenada is coming" or somebody. Then we have to have a big defense system and fund the computers and Internet and microelectronics and so on, and later hand it over to private corporations for profit. But now the cutting edge of the economy is biology-based, so therefore government funding has to shift—you have to have some other excuse for government funding and we will cure cancer, whatever it is. Meanwhile you have engineering and biotechnology being paid for by the same people, namely, you, with the profits going to whatever private corporations will be able to milk them when something is developed.

There are a lot of different devices. Like one critical part of the trade agreements is what is called Intellectual Property Rights and that is a fancy term that means "state guaranteed monopoly pricing rights." Pharmaceutical corporations can charge very high prices because they have a monopoly and that monopoly is given to them by state power under the pretext of free trade.

They claim that they need it for research and development, but that is a fraud. It has been well investigated by Dean Baker, an excellent economist. You can get some information on this from a book he just wrote, which is actually free if you go online. It is called *The Conservative Nanny State*, which is about the real economy. One part of that has to do with the production of drugs. Baker calculated that if you increase the state subsidy to 100 percent and force the companies on the market, drug savings would be a huge benefit for consumers. But that is not the way existing capitalism works.

Let's turn to NAFTA in 1994. Something happened in 1994. It was called "Operation Gatekeeper," instituted by the Clinton administration. It militarized the U.S./Mexican border. Previously, it was a fairly open border. Like most borders it was established by conquest. But pretty much the same people lived on both sides and moved across the borders in both directions, but that was not going to work anymore after NAFTA. They had to militarize it. Why? Well, it was understood what the effect of NAFTA was

going to be for Mexico. Mexican farmers were not going to be able to compete with state-subsidized U.S. agribusiness. So people were going to flee and a lot of them were going to flee to the United States. They were going to be joined by people fleeing from the wreckage of Washington's terrorist wars in Central America in the 1980s. So what is the solution? The solution is to build a wall. First, destroy their economy and then keep them out.

There is a real solution—promote or at least permit development. But that is counter to the interest of those who pretty much rule the world, or, at least, own it, or hope to.

Well, control of Latin America has been the earliest and major goal of U.S. foreign policy—and it remains very central. That is partly for resource and market investment, as well as for ideological reasons. These are discussed in internal records where planners point out that we cannot expect to achieve a successful order elsewhere in the world unless we control Latin America. So it's important to keep it under control. There are traditional methods of control—violence and economic strangulation. But they are losing their effectiveness.

U.S. military coups used to be routine. The most recent attempt was 2002 in Venezuela, and Washington, of course, supported the coup and probably instigated it. The coup installed a rich businessperson and his first act was to disband Parliament, eliminate the Supreme Court, and get rid of every other vestige of democracy—that's what the U.S. calls "democracy promotion." The coup was quickly reversed in a popular uprising, restoring the elected government. Washington had to turn to subversion, a propaganda war, and very substantial aid to the supporters of the coup, under the guise of democracy promotion. For example, the opposition candidate in the election

Something happened in 1994. It was called "Operation Gatekeeper," instituted by the Clinton administration. It militarized the U.S./Mexican border. Previously, it was a fairly open border. Like most borders it was established by conquest. But pretty much the same people lived on both sides and moved across the borders in both directions, but that was not going to work anymore after NAFTA. They had to militarize it.

143

supported the coup. Can you imagine what would happen in the United States if there was a military coup and one of its supporters then ran for president?

Well, Central America was pretty much subdued, at least temporarily, by Reaganite terror throughout the 1980s, but the region from Venezuela to Argentina is now falling out of control. Venezuela is forging closer relations with China. It's planning to sell increasing amounts of oil to China. That is part of its effort to diversify exports and reduce its dependence on the openly hostile U.S. government. In fact, Latin America as a whole is increasing trade and other relations with China and also Europe. But China is more worrisome to the United States, with very likely expansion for the raw material exporters like Brazil and Chile. China is investing in Latin America and challenging U.S. dominance.

If you look at U.S. public documents, China is regarded as the main potential threat, but not a military threat. Of the major powers it's been the most restrained in military expenditures. But it is a threat. The threat is it can't be intimidated. When the U.S. shakes its fist at Europe and tells them to stop investing in Iran, Europeans immediately pull out. China just moves in. They have been there for 3,000 years. They cannot be intimidated, which is very frightening to the U.S. Put yourself in the situation of a Mafia Don and suppose there is somebody that can't be intimidated. And international affairs are pretty much like the Mafia. In Latin America, China is just moving along.

You might recall last spring the Bush administration decided to insult the president of China. He came to visit Washington and they insulted him by not inviting him to a state dinner, only to a state lunch. He took it pretty calmly and he then flew to Saudi Arabia where he entered into new trade investment relations with Saudi Arabia, which is the oldest and most valued U.S. ally in the Middle East.

Getting back to Venezuela, it joined a South American economic bloc and was welcomed as opening a new chapter in integration. Venezuela supplied Argentina with fuel oil to help stave off an energy crisis and bought about a third of the Argentine debt. That is one element of a region-wide effort to free the countries from the controls of the International Monetary Fund. This is after two decades of disastrous effects of conformity to its rules. The way Argentine President Kirchner put it, "The IMF has acted towards our country as a promoter and vehicle of policies that cause poverty and pain among the Argentine people." That is approximately what he said when he announced his decision to pay almost a trillion dollars, in his words, "to rid Argentina of the IMF forever." And by radically violating IMF rules, Argentina did enjoy a substantial economic recovery from the disaster that was left by IMF policies. Other countries are going in the same direction.

Steps towards Latin American independence advanced further with the election of Evo Morales in Bolivia—a real democratic election, the kind that does not take place in the West. The election of Rafael Correa in Ecuador was another step. Morales moved very quickly to reach a series of energy agreements with Venezuela and he committed himself to reversing the neoliberal policies that Bolivia had pursued rigorously for 25 years, leaving the country with lower per capita income than at the outset.

In Brazil, now considered by the U.S. as one of the good guys, it was necessary to ignore the fact that the first thing President Lula did after his re-election was fly to Venezuela to offer his support to Chavez in the upcoming election there and also to promote regional integration by inaugurating a joint Venezuelan-Brazilian-built bridge across the Orinoco river and overseeing work by Brazil's state oil companies.

In addition, the indigenous populations are becoming much more active and influential and many of them want oil and gas—and other resources—to be domestically controlled. In some cases, they oppose production altogether. Some are even calling for an Indian nation in South America, which challenges the race/class divide that goes back to the Spanish conquests. The

144

elite that run the place are mostly white, European. The population are mostly Indians, black, mixed race. That is a fairly sharp distinction. Internal economic integration is also taking place for the first time since the Spanish conquest. Elites in the past, the white elites, have been linked to the imperial powers, but not to one another, and that is beginning to change.

Latin America is now, I think, the most exciting part of the world and there are opportunities for cooperative development and interchange that are quite real. One step towards that is the solidarity movements that developed in the United States in the 1980s and 1990s. That was something new. During hundreds of years of Western imperialism, no one in France ever thought to live in an Algerian village and no one ever thought of going to a Vietnamese village to live with the people to help them and support them and protect them with a white face. But that started in the 1980s on a substantial scale. Thousands of people, many of them from churches, organized what is now a mass popular movement all over the world.

The internal developments in much of Latin America, as you know, are strongly influenced by mass popular movements, which are coming together in the global justice movement. Where this will lead, nobody can say. But there are definitely opportunities now for real progress towards more freedom and justice in cooperation across the hemisphere—and beyond.

17.

Wars, Bailouts, and Elections

Revving up the slander and vilification machine

BARSAMIAN: Given the unpopularity of Bush, the wars, and the tumbling economy, why isn't Obama way ahead of McCain?

CHOMSKY: That's an interesting question. Most of the models that political scientists use predict that the Democrats should be way ahead. In fact, by and large they are way ahead, except on the presidential vote. So you have to look for other factors. One is probably race. It's well known that when people are asked on polls whether they have questions about racial prejudice, they deny that they have it. But when you see their behavior, you see that they're underestimating their own racial prejudice. Another element is class. The Republican public relations propaganda system, which is quite a formidable apparatus, has succeeded, as they succeeded in 2004, in portraying the Democrats and Obama as the representative of the elitist liberals who run the world and have contempt for common folk like you and me. And their candidate is kind of like an ordinary guy. It happens he can't remember how many houses he owns, but let's forget about that.

George Bush, a spoiled brat who went to Yale, is the kind of guy you would like to meet in a bar and wants to go cut brush on his ranch, an ordinary, simple guy. I think they succeeded in doing that with Obama, in making him so he's presented as, first of all, black and, secondly, somehow strange, not like one of us—us meaning white, working-class Americans, with blue eyes. They haven't even gotten started revving up their slander and vilification machine, but it's an impressive apparatus. One good example, which has been studied in some detail by Ed Herman and David Peterson, is the way they've used the Jeremiah Wright case. They have a detailed article in the September *Monthly Review.* This was the main story in the press for weeks, what Jeremiah Wright said. First of all, almost everything he said is entirely reasonable, even if it's unacceptable to mainstream ideology. But even the parts that merit criticism—like the U.S. organized AIDS to kill blacks or whatever it is—it's a marginal part of his message. The white preachers who support McCain have said similar or

David Barsamian interviews Chomsky. Published in Z Magazine, November 2008

146

worse things. So, for example, Falwell and Robertson, I think, blamed 9/11 on the ACLU, gays, and so on. How could you get more outrageous than that?

Pat Robertson called for the assassination of Hugo Chavez.

That probably is considered acceptable. When Wright said the chickens are coming home to roost, incidentally—I think, quoting an American ambassador—that was considered horrendous. But when Falwell and Robertson say it's the ACLU and gays who are responsible, the press didn't make a fuss about that.

The other thing, which is sort of in the background, is that American elections systematically keep away from issues and focus on personality, character, and what are called values, whatever that means. They're pretty frank about it. McCain's campaign manager stated, this election is not about issues, it's about personality and character. And the press has always had a love affair with him. They portray him as a maverick, for which there is no evidence in his record. Also as a hero and an expert at national security. That part is interesting, too.

Let's imagine that, say, someone in Russia now running for office who was a pilot in the invasion of Afghanistan and was shot down while he was bombing heavily populated urban areas in Kabul, civilian areas, and was then tortured by Reagan's freedom fighters. We should sympathize with him for his fate at the hands of the people who tortured him.

But how does that make you a hero and a specialist on national security? On the other hand, that's exactly what's being done with McCain. His expertise in national security is precisely that. But you can't raise that matter here because the jingoism and the commitment to the nobility of our military efforts is so high across the spectrum.

Just recently I read a column by James Carroll in the Boston Globe—*he's their kind of pacifist, for-*

mer priest, moral critic. He starts off by saying McCain is a man of honor with a heroic career. He says that antiwar activists felt that they had to go to McCain to apologize for their opposition to the war. Does some Russian who is opposed to the war in Afghanistan have to apologize for his opposition to the war in Afghanistan?

Let's take the invasion of Iraq. Compare it to, say, Putin's invasion of Chechnya. There are a lot of differences, but let's compare it. The Russians invaded Chechnya, destroyed Grozny, carried out massacres, terror. They pacified it. C.J. Chivers of the *New York Times* was there a couple months ago to report that Grozny is now a booming city, there is building all over, everybody has electricity run by Chechens, you don't see Russian soldiers around. Do we praise Putin for his achievement? No. In fact, we condemn him for it. I suppose that if Petraeus could achieve even a fraction of what Putin achieved in Chechnya, he would be crowned king.

Surely, Obama couldn't have any objection to it. His criticism of the war is completely unprincipled. To him, it was strategic error and we should have put our resources elsewhere. Therefore, if the U.S. succeeds in achieving what Putin achieved in Chechnya, we should all be applauding. In fact, he's kind of silenced even at the limited achievement. It distinguishes him sharply from his base, a lot of which has principled objections to the war. He made sure to tell them that he didn't really mean it, for example, by picking Biden as his vice president. Biden was one of the strongest supporters of the war in the Senate. I should say, incidentally, that I think picking Palin was a master stroke.

Why do you say that?

For one thing, she can't be criticized. If you criticize, it's sexist. Therefore, you have to kind of lay off. For another, she can effectively present herself, as she did, as a kind of hockey mom, five children, one of them is going to Iraq on September 11, her husband is a snowmobile champion, she hunts moose or whatever it is. It kind of hits all the right bases for ordinary, hard-working, mainstream Americans as distinct from these "Cambridge elitists" on the other side.

One thing about McCain, the bombing campaign that he was participating in as a naval pilot was called Rolling Thunder. What was that exactly?

The U.S. basically attacked South Vietnam in 1962. But it was unable to crush the resistance. The Johnson administration tried to put pressure on North Vietnam by bombing them. That's Rolling Thunder. So it started bombing North Vietnam to try to get them to compel the South Vietnamese guerillas to call off their resistance. It went up stage by stage. We know a lot about the planning because the *Pentagon Papers* and other documents have come out. I think McCain was shot down bombing Hanoi, so it's urban areas. It's against this background that you have to look at the issue of war hero, national security expert, commentator on Iraq, and so on. The picture is so skewed in the direction of jingoist nationalism that elite, educated discussion, articulate discussion, can't even begin to be rational about the matter.

It's interesting that both candidates say the U.S. should lead the world.

Because we're so wonderful. They don't say we should lead the world by example, by doing good things. They mean run the world. And they're not inventing it. In some respects it traces back to the founding fathers. This is the only country in the world that was founded as, I think Washington's phrase was, a "nascent empire." By World War II and since, U.S. policy has been quite explicit—that the U.S. would emerge from the war as the world's dominant power. It should organize a world system that's conducive to U.S. interests and it should block sovereignty by others that interfere with U.S. interests. And the core of it should be military force. I can't quote the exact words, but that was the gist of it. That has been the doctrine of every president.

It became pretty dramatic in 1990 when the Soviet Union collapsed. The pretext all those years was, well, we didn't want to do it, but we had to defend ourselves against this menace. Then it collapsed. How did the first Bush administration respond to the collapse of the Soviet Union?

It turns out that there was a national security strategy that was promulgated. There was a military spending program. What they said is almost ignored, probably because it's so interesting. What they said is that everything is going to go on exactly as before, with one change. Now it is not the Russian menace that we're defending against. We have to defend ourselves against what they call the technological sophistication of Third World powers. I don't know if they laughed hysterically when they wrote that, but that's what they said. What about the military system, what they call the defense industrial base? That's a euphemism for high-tech industry. It has to be exactly as before.

What about our intervention forces, primarily aimed toward the Middle East? They have to stay exactly the same. And they add an interesting phrase. They still have to be aimed toward the Middle East where the problems that might have called for military intervention "could not have been laid at the Kremlin's door." Nice phrase. That means, sorry, folks, we've been lying to you for 50 years, but now we can't lie anymore. The clouds have lifted so the problems could not have been laid at the Kremlin's door, but we still have to have those forces there because that's the world's major energy resource and we've got to control it.

That was when Bush I said, "What we say goes."

That's right. It's interesting that all of this passed with almost no comment. Some did comment. For example, there was an interesting article by Dimitri Simes, a Russian specialist, in the *New*

148

York Times (December 27, 1988) in which he said—this is right before the fall of the Berlin Wall—this is going to be great for the United States. We'll now be able to be much more free in our military actions everywhere. We'll be able to resist the pressure of the Third World countries that are oppressing us by all their demands for aid and so on.

Bush I's first action after the fall of the Berlin Wall, within weeks, was to invade Panama and probably kill a couple of thousand people. Nobody knows because we don't investigate our crimes. But the Costa Rican-based Central American Human Rights Agency investigated and I think they estimated 3,000 killed, mostly from bombing the El Chorrillo slums in Panama City. The Catholic bishops in Panama issued a pastoral letter condemning the bombing. Panama still observes a national day of mourning every December.

Elliott Abrams made an interesting comment about it. He said this is the first time that the United States has been able to—he probably didn't say invade—maybe liberate a country or something, without concern that the Russians might cause some trouble anywhere. Now, fortunately, the Russian deterrent is gone. It wasn't that we were deterring them. They were deterring us. Now the deterrent is gone, so we're much freer to act in accord with our long-standing commitments.

They had to reshape NATO. That was an interesting development, which is on the front pages today.

Because of Georgia and Ukraine, the Czech Republic, and Poland. What actually happened is that NATO had been presented as a U.S.-run military force that was going to defend the world against the terrible Russians. The Russians are gone. Now what's NATO? Gorbachev—I suspect naïvely, maybe he really believed it—suggested that the collapse of the Soviet Union should mean a period of partnership to seek peace. No victors, no vanquished. Let's just work together to set up a peaceful world. The Rus-

sians actually proposed a nuclear-weapons-free zone from the Arctic to the Black Sea as a step towards establishing peaceful relations.

Gorbachev made an astonishing concession. He agreed to let Germany be unified and to join NATO. He's allowing Germany to join a hostile military alliance. Look at the history of the century. Germany alone had practically destroyed Russia, killing tens of millions of people, twice, and he's saying, okay, a unified Germany can join a hostile military alliance. It's an incredible concession.

There was a quid pro quo. The Bush administration promised that NATO would not expand to the east. Jack Matlock, who was Reagan and Bush's ambassador to Russia, has just recently written about this. He said that Secretary of State Baker told Foreign Secretary Shevardnadze that NATO would not extend one inch further. He claims those are the words he used. That was the agreement, that we were going to have cooperation and peace. Clinton came in. One of his first acts was to renege on the promise.

Of course, the U.S. completely rejected the idea of a nuclear-weapons-free zone. The reason, pointed out by a former NATO planner, British analyst Michael McGwire, is that it would have interfered with extending NATO to the east, in violation of the firm commitments. Clinton expanded it to the east. The Clinton programs were highly triumphalist—no cooperation among equals, just forced peace of the victors. The programs were designed to essentially destroy the Russian economy, which they did, with the cooperation of the Russian leaders, who were pleased to become the counterpart to the Third World gangsters who run their countries and enrich themselves.

Explain "programs were designed." Is this the IMF and World Bank?

Plus the standard neoliberal programs, which cut back the Russian economy by some huge amount, maybe 50 percent, led to millions of deaths—the number of deaths probably wasn't all that different from Stalin's purges, there are various estimates—devastated the country, and enriched the leadership, which is what they wanted. That was their goal. We'll become rich while increasing the security threats by expanding NATO to the east.

All of this is described as if it were benign. Strobe Talbott, who was the highest official in the Clinton administration responsible for Eastern Europe and an honest, authentic liberal, recently described this on NPR, in which he said that it was a difficult decision, but we concluded that it was a benign thing to do because NATO is not a military alliance, it's just a friendly alliance. So, for example, if the Warsaw Pact had survived and they were bringing in Canada and Mexico, we would think that it's just a Quaker meeting, so what do we care.

Bush II came along and extended it. The so-called missile defense systems, which have nothing to do with missile defense—they're understood on both sides to be essentially first-strike weapons, not as they now stand, but as they potentially might develop. They're a strategic threat to Russia. Strategic analysts on the U.S. side recognize that and have written about it. Step after step was taken to show the Russians that we're going to kick you in the face. We won. Your problem. Now we're going to kick you in the face and take everything.

Finally, as Matlock (Reagan's and Bush's ambassador) pointed out, the Russians decided they're not going to take any more and they put their foot down. That's what happened in Georgia.

I think I was in India when Putin's comments in Munich at a G8 summit got a lot of coverage. This is over a year ago where he said a certain power was behaving in a way that is very reminiscent of Nazi Germany.

Indians understand it. India is playing a mixed game. It's on the one hand trying to strengthen its relations with the United States, but on the other hand it's not England. It doesn't just follow blindly along like a camp follower. So it's also pursuing its own independent course. For example, India joined the nonaligned countries, of which it's a leading member, in endorsing Iran's right to enrich uranium to develop nuclear energy. That doesn't get reported here. But the majority of the countries of the world support Iran on this, not the United States. Here we read that Iran is defying the world, the international community. But that's a funny definition of world.

To get back to U.S. domestic issues, you talk about institutional structures and how they frame and inhibit policies. So, realistically, whichever candidate is elected, can a president make a difference?

Oh, yes. Presidents make differences. In fact, over time there are systematic differences between Republicans and Democrats. So, for example, if you look over a long stretch, fairly consistently, when there is a Democratic president, there is a level of benefits for the majority of the population. Wages are a little better, benefits are a little better, for the large majority. When the Republicans are in office, it's the other way around. There are benefits, but for the super rich. The same is true of civil rights and other things. It's a consistent difference, even though they're within a narrow spectrum.

The same is true on international affairs. So for Reagan, Russia was the evil empire, for Kennedy it was the monolithic and ruthless conspiracy, but the behavior was somewhat different—not necessarily in Kennedy's favor, I should say. I don't doubt that there would be some difference between an Obama and a McCain presidency. The McCain presidency you can't predict very well because he's a loose cannon. It could be pretty threatening.

What about the lesser-of-two-evils argument?

It depends whether you care about human beings and their fate. If you care about human beings and their fate, you will support the lesser of the two evils, not mechanically, because there are other considerations. For example, there could be an argument for a protest vote if it were a step towards building a significant alternative to the choice between two factions of the business party, both of them to the right of the population on most issues. If there were such an alternative, there could be an argument either for not voting or for voting for the third alternative. But it's a delicate judgment. On the other hand, there is nothing immoral about voting for the lesser of two evils. In a powerful system like ours, small changes can lead to big consequences.

One of those institutional structures is the Electoral College, which seems by definition undemocratic. This is not talked about.

Basically, these technical changes wouldn't affect the core issue about American elections, which is that fundamentally they don't take place. The population is not misled about this. The press won't report it, but the polls these days show —and have for a long time—that about 80 percent of the population says the country is run by a few big interests looking out for themselves, not for the benefit of the people.

The latest polls I saw, by about 3 to 1, the population criticized the campaigns because they avoid issues and keep to personalities and marginal phenomena. The public is not misled, at least so the polls indicate. Those are critical facts: that elections are extravaganzas, essentially run by the public relations industry with the goal of marginalizing issues and voters. As compared with that, the technical details, like do the voting machines work or the Electoral College, just don't amount to much. Even if you fixed up those technical details, the fundamental problem would remain.

Talk about the bailout.

The people who are going to pay for it are the American taxpayers. One of the major economic correspondents, Martin Wolf, who is a good

economist, writes for the *Financial Times* and is a believer in markets, had a pretty strong column condemning it. He said, yes, it has to be done because of the disaster we're in, but it's outrageous. First the public is compelled to assume the risks of mortgage lending, then it's required to pay the costs when the whole system implodes. So probably there isn't any choice right now, given the nature of the disaster, but the whole system is an outrage. Why should the public have assumed the risks for financial managers, who are basically unregulated?

Part of the dominant ideology of the last couple of decades is that you should dismantle government regulation. Fine. So you dismantle government regulation, you have catastrophe after catastrophe. Now the public is called in to pay the costs of that ideology.

Remember, the first of them, I think it was Fannie Mae, was established in the New Deal and it was a public entity, I think, until 1968. It was part of the government. It was regulated within the government. The other one, Freddie Mac, was set up and it became essentially privatized, but with a government guarantee, which tells the managers and investors and so on that they can play whatever game we want. The government is going to come in and save us, meaning the taxpayer will. That's what happened. That's Milton Friedman-style economics. It's called free market economics, with the nanny state there to make sure that the public takes the risks and pays the costs.

Former Labor Secretary Robert Reich calls it "socialized capitalism."

He does, but it's much too narrow, because that's true of just about all of capitalism. The whole high-tech economy runs that way. It's kind of interesting to watch the outrage about it, but the same outrage should be expressed about the rest of the advanced economy as well. The financialization is a particularly egregious case, but so are, say, the pharmaceutical or electronics industry.

In the seven years since 2001, the United States has invaded and occupied two countries, Afghanistan and Iraq, bombed Somalia, bombed and attacked Pakistan. Do you have any information on what the U.S. is doing militarily in Iran?

We have the information that's being leaked from government sources to very good journalists like Seymour Hersh and others at ABC News and elsewhere. The news that's being leaked or that some journalists in the field are picking up is that the United States is supporting or carrying out what we would call terrorist operations, if someone else were doing it, either in or against Iran.

Using proxies or U.S. forces directly?

Let me first say we don't know that this information is correct as it's coming from government sources. And anything that's coming from intelligence sources or unidentified diplomats and always should be taken with a grain of skepticism. They're not in the business of telling people the truth, they're in the business of telling people what they want them to believe.

So it may be accurate or it may be psychological warfare against Iran. But I suspect it's accurate. There is good reason to suspect it on both the Iranian borders—Balochistan and the western borders. So it's very possible that the United States is indeed supporting terrorist groups, secessionist movements, trying to disrupt Iranian society. Maybe there are U.S. special forces or small groups inside, but mostly it appears, other anti-government factions.

Your estimate of the likelihood of a U.S. attack on Iran, before Bush leaves office or even after? Is Israel influencing U.S. policy on Iran and would Israel carry out a unilateral attack?

Israel has become a pretty crazy state, one which is hard to make judgments about. There was an incredible op-ed published in the *New York Times* by Benny Morris, one of Israel's leading

historians, in which he said, essentially, that Iran should welcome an Israeli bombing because if Israel doesn't bomb them conventionally, it's going to wipe the country out with nuclear bombing. Therefore, if Israel bombs them, they should cheer. Try to translate that into an Iranian columnist talking about Israel. The world would be totally outraged. This passed quietly. He's making all kinds of claims. He says that we know Iran is producing nuclear weapons. Actually, you can read that in the Nation, too. We know that Iran is producing nuclear weapons.

This is established as a "fact."

That's just a fact. We refer to it. But in the *Nation* they still say we shouldn't bomb, we should talk. But are they developing nuclear weapons? Is the National Intelligence Estimate of the United States just a bunch of liars?

The December 2007 Intelligence estimate said that Iran had stopped its nuclear weapons program.

It said that they stopped it. In fact, it never showed that they had it. Maybe they are, maybe they're not. But the point is, it's become a "fact." And then the question is how to stop them. It couldn't be that they're trying to develop nuclear energy, even though there are good reasons why they should want to do so.

But would Israel bomb? I doubt that they would do it without U.S. authorization, but it's a little difficult to predict. There is a doctrine in Israel, which goes back to the 1950s, which is what they call the Samson complex. In the 1950s, very high-level officials were saying, If anyone crosses us, we will go crazy. We'll show 'em. We'll bring the temple walls down. So the idea of an Iranian threat against Israel is pretty fantastic, actually. If Iran were ever to seriously threaten Israel, the country would be wiped out.

The United States would wipe them out in five minutes. What they really mean by the Iranian threat is that Iran is supporting Hezbollah and Hamas. Hamas won a democratic election and the United States and Israel reacted instantly by crushing Palestinians for daring to vote the wrong way in a democratic election. Iran is undoubtedly supporting Hamas so that makes them "terrorists" that support a political organization that won a democratic election. Hezbollah is defending Lebanon from Israeli attack. That's considered a crime. How can you dare defend a country from a U.S.-backed Israeli attack? That's another terrorist act. It's not to say that Hezbollah and Hamas and Iran are nice guys. That's a separate question. But the idea of a threat has to be understood. The threat is that they are daring to stand up against the master and that is terrorism and cannot be tolerated.

I was interested in a letter that I saw in In These Times *about the root cause of terrorism, kind of posing that question rhetorically. And the answer he gave was, "Terrorists are over here because we are over there."*

Terrorists are here for one reason. Because we are carrying out terrorism over there. So John Negroponte, for example, is here. In fact, he was appointed anti-terrorism czar. He's one of the leading terrorists of the late 20th century. He was ambassador to Honduras in the late 1980s, coordinating Reagan's terrorist wars and covering up for Honduran state terrorism, which was pretty atrocious, so that funds would keep flowing to maintain the terrorist wars that he was organizing. That's pretty serious terrorism. But that's not called terrorism, because we were doing it. Juan Bosch and Luis Posada Carriles are happily dining right now in some restaurant in

Miami, I suppose, two leading international terrorists. Not my judgment. It's the judgment of the FBI and the Justice Department, which accused Bosch of participation in 30 terrorist acts. George Bush I said: He's fine. We'll keep him here. Terrorists are here because we're protecting them while they carry out terrorist actions over there. But what the letter writer was talking about is what you hear from people like Michael Scheuer, who was head of the CIA unit under Clinton that was tracking Osama bin Laden. No dove, incidentally. But what he points out, and it's accurate, is that the terrorists who we call terrorists, namely the ones attacking us, are essentially defending themselves from our actions.

You've cited Justice Robert Jackson, the chief prosecutor of the Germans at Nuremberg. He said to the tribunal, "To pass these defendants," talking about the Nazis in the dock, "a poison chalice is to put it to our own lips as well." What was he talking about there?

He was saying, we have passed sentence on the Nazi war criminals, in fact, a death sentence, and there were principles that led us to do that. We are handing them a poison chalice in the sense that if we carry out similar acts, we must be subject to the same judgment. If not, the trial is a farce as it's just punishment by victors, not a step towards justice. Well, we can ask how have we dealt with that poison chalice? That's a question that can't be raised in the West because the answer is too incriminating.

18.

Domestic Constituencies

Undermining democracy

Let's begin with some simple points, assuming conditions that now prevail—not, of course, the terminus of the unending struggle for freedom and justice. There is a "public arena" in which, in principle, individuals can participate in decisions that involve the general society—how public revenues are obtained and used, what foreign policy will be, etc. In a world of nation-states, the public arena is primarily governmental, at various levels. Democracy functions insofar as individuals can participate meaningfully in the public arena, meanwhile running their own affairs, individually and collectively, without illegitimate interference by concentrations of power. Functioning democracy presupposes relative equality in access to resources—material, informational, and other—a truism as old as Aristotle. In theory, governments are instituted to serve their "domestic constituencies" and are to be subject to their will. A measure of functioning democracy, then, is the extent to which the theory approximates reality and the "domestic constituencies" approximate the population.

In state capitalist democracies, the public arena has been extended and enriched by long and bitter popular struggle. Meanwhile, concentrated private power has labored to restrict it. These conflicts form a good part of modern history. The most effective way to restrict democracy is to transfer decision-making from the public arena to unaccountable institutions such as kings and princes, priestly castes, military juntas, party dictatorships, or modern corporations. The decisions reached by the directors of GE affect the general society substantially, but citizens play no role in them, as a matter of principle (we may put aside a transparent myth about market and stock-holder "democracy"). Systems of unaccountable power do offer some choices to citizens. They can petition the King or the CEO or join the ruling Party. They can try to rent themselves to GE or buy its products. They can struggle for rights within tyrannies, state and private, and in solidarity with others, can seek to limit or dismantle illegitimate power, pursuing traditional ideals, including those that animated the U.S. labor movement: that those who work in the mills should own and run them.

From Z Magazine, May 2008

154

The "corporatization of America" during the past century was an attack on democracy—and on markets, part of the shift from something resembling "capitalism" to the highly administered markets of the modern state/corporate era. A current variant is called "minimizing the state," that is, transferring decision-making power from the public arena to somewhere else: "to the people," in the rhetoric of power; to private tyrannies, in the real world. All such measures are designed to limit democracy and to tame the "rascal multitude," as the population was called by the self-designated "men of best quality" during the first upsurge of democracy in the modern period, in 17th century England; the "responsible men," as they call themselves today. The basic problems persist, constantly taking new forms, calling forth new measures of control and marginalization, and leading to new forms of popular struggle.

The so-called "free trade agreements" are one such device for undermining democracy. They are designed to transfer decision-making about people's lives and aspirations into the hands of private tyrannies that operate in secret and without public supervision or control. Not surprisingly, the public doesn't like them. The opposition is almost instinctive, a tribute to the care that is taken to insulate the rascal multitude from relevant information and understanding.

Much of the picture is tacitly conceded. We've just witnessed yet another illustration: the effort of the past months to pass "Fast Track" legislation that would permit the Executive to negotiate trade agreements without congressional oversight and public awareness; a simple Yes or No will do. "Fast Track" had near-unanimous support within power systems, but as the Wall St. Journal ruefully observed, its opponents may have an "ultimate weapon": the majority of the population. The public continued to oppose the legislation despite the media barrage, foolishly believing that they ought to know what is happening to them and have a voice in determining it. Similarly, NAFTA was rammed through over public opposition, which remained firm despite the near unanimous and enthusiastic backing of state and corporate power, including their media, which refused even to allow the position of the prime opponents (the labor movement) to be expressed while denouncing them for various invented misdeeds.

Fast Track was portrayed as a free trade issue, but that is inaccurate. The most ardent free trader would strongly oppose Fast Track if s/he happened to believe in democracy—the issue at stake. That aside, the planned agreements hardly qualify as "free trade agreements" any more than NAFTA or the GATT/WTO treaties, matters discussed elsewhere.

The official reason for Fast Track was articulated by Deputy U.S. Trade Representative Jeffrey Lang: "the basic principle of negotiations is that only one person [the President] can negotiate for the U.S." The role of Congress is to rubber stamp; the role of the public is to watch—preferably, to watch something else.

The "basic principle" is real enough, but its scope is narrow. It holds for trade, but not for other matters like human rights, for example. Here the principle is the opposite as members of Congress must be granted every opportunity to ensure that the U.S. maintains its record of non-ratification of agreements, one of the worst in the world. The few enabling conventions to reach Congress have been held up for years, and even the rare endorsements are burdened with conditions rendering them inoperative in the United States—they are "non self-executing" and have specific reservations.

Trade is one thing, torture and rights of women and children another. The distinction holds more broadly. China is threatened with severe sanctions for failing to adhere to Washington's protectionist demands, or for interfering with its punishment of Libyans. But terror and torture elicit a different response, in this case, sanctions would be "counterproductive." They would hamper our efforts to extend our human rights crusade to suffering people in China and its domains, just as reluctance to train Indonesian military officers "diminishes our ability to posi-

155

tively influence [their] human rights policies and behavior," as the Pentagon recently explained. The missionary effort in Indonesia therefore must proceed, evading Congressional orders. That is only reasonable. It suffices to recall how U.S. military training "paid dividends" in the early 1960s, and "encouraged" the military to carry out their necessary tasks, as Defense Secretary McNamara informed Congress and the President after the huge army-led massacres of 1965, which left hundreds of thousands of corpses in a few months, a "staggering mass slaughter" (*New York Times*) that elicited unconstrained euphoria among the "men of best quality" (the *Times* included), and rewards for the "moderates" who had conducted it. Mc-Namara had particular praise for the training of Indonesian military officers in U.S. universities, "very significant factors" in setting the "new Indonesian political elite" (the military) on the proper course.

In crafting its human rights policies for China, the Administration might have also recalled the constructive advice of a Kennedy military mission to Colombia: "as necessary, execute paramilitary, sabotage and/or terrorist activities against known communist proponents" (a term that covers peasants, union organizers, human rights activists, etc.). The pupils learned the lessons well, compiling the worst human rights record of the 1990s in the hemisphere by the recommended means, to be rewarded by increasing military aid and training under "drug war" pretexts dismissed as "a myth" by Amnesty International, Colombian human rights activists (those who survive), and other competent observers.

Reasonable people can easily understand, then, that it would be counterproductive to press China too hard on such matters as torture of dissidents or atrocities in Tibet. That might even cause China to suffer the "harmful effects of a society isolated from American influence," the reason adduced by a group of corporate executives for removing the U.S. trade barriers that keep them from Cuban markets where they could labor to restore the "helpful effects of

American influence" that prevailed from the "liberation" 100 years ago through the Batista years—the same influences that have proven so benign in Haiti, El Salvador, and other contemporary paradises—by accident, yielding profits as well.

Such subtle discriminations must be part of the armory of those who aspire to respectability and prestige. Having mastered them, we can see why investors' rights and human rights require such different treatment. The contradiction about the "basic principle" is only apparent.

Black Holes

It is always enlightening to seek out what is omitted in propaganda campaigns. Fast Track received enormous publicity. But several crucial issues disappeared into the black hole that is reserved for topics rated unfit for public consumption. One is the fact, already mentioned, that the issue was not trade agreements, but rather democratic principle. In any event, the agreements were not about free trade. Still more striking was that throughout the intense campaign, there appears to have been no public mention of the upcoming treaty that must have been at the forefront of concern for every knowledgeable participant—the Multilateral Agreement on Investment (MAI), a far more significant matter than bringing Chile into NAFTA or other tidbits served up to illustrate why the President alone must negotiate trade agreements, without public interference.

The MAI has powerful support among financial and industrial institutions. Why then the silence? A plausible reason comes to mind. Few political and media leaders doubt that were the public to be informed, it would be less than overjoyed about the MAI. Opponents might once again brandish their "ultimate weapon," if the facts break through. It only makes sense, then, to conduct the negotiations under a "veil of secrecy," to borrow the term used by the former Chief Justice of Australia's High Court, Sir Anthony Mason, condemning his government's decision to remove from public scrutiny the negotiations over "an agreement which could have a great impact on Australia if we ratify it."

No similar voices were heard here. It would have been superfluous: the veil of secrecy remained impenetrable, defended with much greater vigilance in our free institutions.

Within the United States, readers of this journal are among the lucky few who know something about the MAI, which has been under intensive negotiation in the OECD ("the rich men's club") since May 1995. The original target date was May 1997. Had the goal been reached, the public would have known as much about the MAI as they do about the Telecommunications Act of 1996, another huge public gift to concentrated private power, kept largely to the business pages. But the OECD countries could not reach agreement on schedule, and the target date was delayed a year.

The original and preferred plan was to forge the treaty in the World Trade Organization. But that effort was blocked by Third World countries, particularly India and Malaysia, which recognized that the measures being crafted would deprive them of the devices that had been employed by the rich to win their own place in the sun. Negotiations were then transferred to the safer quarters of the OECD, where, it was hoped, an agreement would be reached "that emerging countries would want to join," as the *London Economist* delicately put it—on pain of being barred from the markets and resources of the rich, the familiar concept of "free choice" in systems of vast inequality of power and wealth.

For almost three years, the rascal multitude has been kept in blissful ignorance of what is taking place. But not entirely. In the Third World, it was a live issue by early 1997. In Australia, the news broke in January 1998 in the business pages, eliciting a flurry of reports and controversy in the national press; hence Sir Anthony's condemnation, speaking at a convention in Melbourne. The opposition party "urged the government to refer the agreement to the Parliamen-

tary committee on treaties before signing it," the press reported. The government refused to provide Parliament with detailed information or to permit parliamentary review. Our "position on the MAI is very clear," the Government responded: "We will not sign anything unless it is demonstrably in Australia's national interest to do so." In brief, "We'll do as we choose"—or more accurately, as our masters tell us, and following the regular convention, the "national interest" will be defined by power centers, operating in closed chambers.

Under pressure, the Government agreed a few days later to allow a Parliamentary committee to review MAI. Editors reluctantly endorsed the decision as it was necessary in reaction to the "xenophobic hysteria" of the "scare-mongerers" and the "unholy alliance of aid groups, trade unions, environmentalists and the odd conspiracy theorist." They warned, however, that after this unfortunate concession, it is "vitally important that the Government does not step back any further from its strong commitment" to the MAI. The Government denied the charge of secrecy, noting that a draft of the treaty was available on the internet—thanks to the activist groups that placed it there, after it was leaked to them. We can be heartened as democracy flourishes in Australia after all.

The derisive dismissal of the charge of secrecy, a device that might be adopted by more cynical U.S. commentators when they finally agree to mention the issue, has consequences that merit some thought. It entails that the media should gracefully exit the stage. After all, any meaningful evidence they use could be discovered by ordinary folk with diligent search and analysis/commentary are declared irrelevant.

In Canada, now facing a form of incorporation into the United States, accelerated by "free trade, the "unholy alliance" achieved much greater success. For a year, the treaty had been discussed in leading dailies and news weeklies, on prime time national TV, and in public meetings. The Province of British Columbia announced in the House of Commons that it "is strongly opposed" to the treaty, noting its "unacceptable restrictions" on elected governments at the federal, provincial, and local levels as well as its harmful impact on social programs (health care, etc.) and on environmental protection and resource management; the extraordinary scope of the definition of "investment"; and other attacks on democracy and human rights. The provincial government was particularly opposed to provisions that allow corporations to sue governments while they remain immune from any liability, and to have their charges settled in "unelected and unaccountable dispute panels," which are to be constituted of "trade experts," operating without rules of evidence or transparency, and with no possibility of appeal.

The veil of secrecy having been shredded by the rude noises from below, it became necessary for the Canadian government to reassure the public that ignorance is in their best interest. The task was undertaken in a national CBC TV debate by Canada's Federal Minister of International Trade, Sergio March. He "would like to think that people feel reassured," he said, by the "honest approach that I think is exuded by our Prime Minister" and "the love of Canada that he has." That ought to settle the matter. So democracy is healthy north of the border too.

According to CBC, the Canadian government—like Australia—"has no plans at this time for any legislation on the MAI," and "the trade minister says it may not be necessary," since the MAI "is just an extension of NAFTA."

There has been discussion in the national media in England and France, but I do not know whether there or elsewhere in the Free World it was felt necessary to assure the public that their interests are best served by faith in the leaders who "love them," "exude honesty," and steadfastly defend "the national interest."

Not too surprisingly, the tale has followed a unique course in the world's most powerful state, where "the men of best quality" declare themselves the champions of freedom, justice, human rights, and—above all—democracy. Media leaders have surely known all along about the MIA

and its broad implications, as have public intellectuals and the standard experts.

The business world has been intimately involved in planning and implementation from the outset: for example, the United States Council for International Business, which, in its own words, "advances the global interests of American business both at home and abroad." In January 1996, the Council even published *A Guide to the Multilateral Agreement on Investment,* available to its business constituencies and their circles, surely to the media. But in a most impressive show of self-discipline, the Free Press has succeeded in keeping those who rely on it in the dark—no simple task in a complicated world. We return to details.

The corporate world overwhelmingly supports the MAI. Though silence precludes citation of evidence, it is a fair guess that the sectors of the corporate world devoted to "enlightening the public" are no less enthusiastic. But once again, they understand that the the the "ultimate weapon" may well be unsheathed if the rascal multitude gets wind of the proceedings. The dilemma has a natural solution. We've been observing it now for almost three years.

Worthy & Unworthy Constituencies

Defenders of the MAI have one strong argument: critics do not have enough information to make a fully convincing case. The purpose of the "veil of secrecy" has been to guarantee that outcome, and the efforts have had some success. That is most dramatically true in the United States, which enjoys the world's most stable and long-lasting democratic institutions and can properly claim to be the model for state-capitalist democracy. Given this experience and status, it is not surprising that the principles of democracy are clearly understood in the United States, and lucidly articulated in high places. For example, by the distinguished Harvard political scientist Samuel Huntington, in his text American Politics, where he observes that power must remain invisible if it is to be effective: "The architects of power in the United States must create a force that can be felt but not seen. Power remains strong when it remains in the dark; exposed to the sunlight it begins to evaporate." He illustrated the thesis in the same year (1981) while explaining the function of the "Soviet threat": "you may have to sell [intervention or other military action] in such a way as to create the misimpression that it is the Soviet Union that you are fighting. That is what the United States has been doing ever since the Truman Doctrine."

Within these bounds—"creating misimpressions" to delude the public, and excluding them entirely—responsible leaders are to pursue their craft in democratic societies.

Nonetheless, it is unfair to charge the OECD powers with conducting the negotiations in secret. After all, activists did succeed in putting a draft version on the internet, having illicitly obtained it. Readers of the "alternative press" and Third World journals, and those infected by the "unholy alliance," have been following the proceedings since early 1997 at least. And keeping to the mainstream, there is no gainsaying the direct participation of the organization that "advances the global interests of American businesses," and their counterparts in other rich countries.

But there are a few sectors that have somehow been overlooked: the U.S. Congress, for example. Last November, 25 House representatives sent a letter to President Clinton stating that the MAI negotiations had "come to our attention"—presumably, through the efforts of activists and public interest groups. They asked the President to answer three simple questions.

"First, given the Administration's recent claims that it cannot negotiate complicated, multisectoral, multilateral agreements without fast track authority, how has the MAI nearly been completed," with a text "as intricate as NAFTA or GATT" and with provisions that "would require significant limitations on U.S. laws and policy concerning federal, state and local regulation of investment?"

Second, "how has this agreement been under negotiation since May 1995, without any Congressional consultation or oversight, especially given Congress' exclusive constitutional authority to regulate international commerce?"

"Third, the MAI provides expansive takings language that would allow a foreign corporation or investor to directly sue the U.S. government for damages if we take any action that would restrain 'enjoyment' of an investment. This language is broad and vague and goes significantly beyond the limited concept of takings provided in U.S. domestic law. Why would the U.S. willingly cede sovereign immunity and expose itself to liability for damages under vague language such as that concerning taking any actions 'with an equivalent effect' of an 'indirect' expropriation?"

On point three, the signatories might have had in mind the suit by the Ethyl Corporation —famous as the producer of leaded gasoline— against Canada, demanding $250 million to cover losses from "expropriation" and damages to Ethyl's "good reputation" caused by pending Canadian legislation to ban a gasoline additive that Canada regards as a dangerous toxin and significant health risk—in agreement with the U.S. Enironmental Protection Agency, which has sharply restricted its use, and the State of California, which has banned it entirely. Or perhaps the signers were thinking of the suit against Mexico by the U.S. hazardous-waste management firm Metalclad, asking $90 in damages for "expropriation" because a site they intended to use for hazardous wastes was declared part of an ecological zone.

These suits are proceeding under NAFTA rules. The intention presumably is to explore and if possible expand their (vague) limits. In part they are probably just intimidation, a standard and often effective device available to those with deep pockets to obtain what they want through legal threats that may be completely frivolous. "Considering the enormity of the MAI's potential implications," the congressional letter to the President concluded, "we eagerly await your answers to these questions." An answer reached the signers a few months later, saying nothing. The media were advised of all of this, but I know of no coverage.

Another segment of the population that has been overlooked, along with Congress, is the population. Apart from trade journals, the first articles in the mainstream appeared at the end of 1997, in local journals. The *Chicago Tribune* (December 4, 1997) reviewed some of the terms of the MAI and noted that the matter has "received no public attention or political debate," apart from Canada. In the U.S., "this obscurity seems deliberate," the *Tribune reports*. "Government sources say the administration...is not anxious to stir up more debate about the global economy." In the light of the public mood, secrecy is the best policy, relying on the collusion of the information system.

The Newspaper of Record broke its silence a few months later, permitting a paid advertisement by the International Forum on Globalization, which opposes the treaty (February 13, 1998). The ad quotes *Business Week* (February 9), which described the MAI as "The most explosive trade deal you've never heard of...[it] would rewrite the rules of foreign ownership, affecting everything from factories to real estate and even securities. But most lawmakers have never even heard of the Multilateral Agreement on Investment," let alone the public. Why not, the Forum asks, implicitly answering with a review of the basic features of the treaty.

A few days later (February 16), NPR's "Morning Edition" ran a segment on the MAI, and NPR has had further coverage since. A week later, the *Christian Science Monitor* ran a (rather thin) piece. The *New Republic* had already taken notice of rising public concern over the MAI. The issue had not been properly covered in respectable sectors, TNR concluded, because "the mainstream press," while "generally skewed to the left...is even more deeply skewed toward internationalism." Press lefties therefore failed to recognize the public opposition to Fast Track in time and have not noticed that the same

troublemakers "are already girding [for] battle" against the MAI. The press should confront its responsibilities more seriously and launch a pre-emptive strike against the "MAI paranoia" that has "ricocheted through the Internet" and even led to public conferences. Mere ridicule of "the flat earth and black helicopter crowd" may not be enough. Silence may not be the wisest stance if the rich countries are to be able to "lock in the liberalization of international investment law just as GATT codified the liberalization of trade."

Perhaps in reaction to the congressional letter or the surfacing of the crazies, Washington issued an official statement on the MAI on February 17 1998. The statement, by Under Secretary of State Stuart Eizenstat and Deputy U.S. Trade Representative Jeffrey Lang, received no notice to my knowledge. The statement is boilerplate, but deserves front-page headlines by the standards of what had already appeared (essentially nothing). The virtues of the MAI are taken as self-evident; no description or argument is offered. On such matters as labor and the environment, "takings," etc., the message is the same as the one delivered by the governments of Canada and Australia: "Trust us, and Shut Up."

Of greater interest is the good news that the U.S. has taken the lead at the OECD in ensuring that the agreement "complements our broader efforts," hitherto unknown, "in support of sustainable development and promotion of respect for labor standards." Eizenstat and Lang "are pleased that participants agree with us" on these matters. Furthermore, the other OECD countries now "agree with us on the importance of working closely with their domestic constituencies to build a consensus" on the MAI. They join us in understanding "that it is important for domestic constituencies to have a stake in this process. In the interest of greater transparency," the official statement adds, "the OECD has agreed to make public the text of the draft agreement," perhaps even before the deadline is reached. Here we have, at last, a ringing testimonial to democracy and human rights. The Clinton administration is leading the world, it proclaims, in ensuring that its "domestic constituencies" play an active role in "building a consensus" on the MAI.

Who are the "domestic constituencies?" The question is readily answered by a look at the uncontested facts. The business world has had an active role throughout, as we learn, for example, from the publications of the U.S. Council for International Business. Congress has not been informed. The annoying public—the "ultimate weapon"—has been consigned to ignorance. A straightforward exercise in elementary logic informs us exactly who the Clinton administration takes to be its "domestic constituencies."

That is a useful lesson. The operative values of the powerful are rarely articulated with such candor and precision. To be fair, they are not a U.S. monopoly.

The values are shared by state/private power centers in other parliamentary democracies, and by their counterparts in societies where there is no need to indulge in rhetorical flourishes about "democracy." The lessons are crystal clear. It would take real talent to miss them, and to fail to see how well they illustrate Madison's warnings over 200 years ago, when he deplored "the daring depravity of the times" as the "stock-jobbers will become the pretorian band of the government—at once its tools and its tyrant; bribed by its largesses, and overawing it by clamors and combinations." These observations reach to the core of the MAI. Like much of public policy in recent years, particularly in the Anglo-American societies, the treaty is designed to undercut democracy and rights of citizens by transferring even more decision-making authority to unaccountable private institutions, the governments for whom they are "the domestic constituencies," and the international organizations that serve their interests at public expense.

The Terms of The MAI

What do the terms of the MAI actually state, and portend? If the facts and issues were allowed to reach the public arena, what would we discover? There can be no definite answer to such questions.

Even if we had the full text of the MAI, a detailed list of the reservations introduced by signatories, and the entire verbatim record of the proceedings, we would not know the answers. The reason is that the answers are not determined by words, but by the power relations that impose their interpretations. Two centuries ago, in the leading democracy of his day, Oliver Goldsmith observed that "laws grind the poor, and rich men make the law"—the operative law, that is, whatever fine words may say. The principle remains valid.

These are, again, truisms, with broad application. In the U.S. Constitution and its Amendments, one can find nothing that authorizes the grant of human rights (speech, freedom from search and seizure, the right to buy elections, etc.) to what legal historians call "collectivist legal entities," organic entities that have the rights of "immortal persons"—rights far beyond those of real persons, when we take into account their power. One will search the U.N. Charter in vain to discover the basis for the authority claimed by Washington to use force and violence to achieve "the national interest," as defined by the immortal persons who cast over society the shadow called "politics," in John Dewey's evocative phrase. The U.S. Code defines "terrorism" with great clarity, and U.S. law provides severe penalties for the crime. But one will find no wording that exempts "the architects of power" from punishment for their exercises of state terror, not to speak of their monstrous clients (as long as they enjoy Washington's good graces): Suharto, Saddam Hussein, Mobutu, Noriega, and others great and small. As the leading Human Rights organizations point out year after year, virtually all U.S. foreign aid is illegal, from the leading recipient on down the list, because the law bars aid to countries that engage in "systematic torture." That may be law, but is it the meaning of the law?

The MAI falls into the same category. There is a "worst case" analysis, which will be the right analysis if "power remains in the dark," and the corporate lawyers who are its hired hands are able to establish their interpretation of the purposely convoluted and ambiguous wording of the draft treaty. There are less threatening interpretations, and they could turn out to be the right ones, if the "ultimate weapon" cannot be contained and democratic procedures influence outcomes. Among these possible outcomes is the dismantling of the whole structure and the illegitimate institutions on which it rests. These are matters for popular organization and action, not words.

Here one might raise some criticism of critics of the MAI (myself included). The texts spell out the rights of "investors," not citizens, whose rights are correspondingly diminished. Critics accordingly call it an "investor rights agreement," which is true enough, but misleading. Just who are the "investors?"

Half the stocks in 1997 were owned by the wealthiest 1 percent of households, and almost 90 percent by the wealthiest tenth (concentration is still higher for bonds and trusts, comparable for other assets); adding pension plans leads only to slightly more even distribution among the top fifth of households. The enthusiasm about the radical asset inflation of recent years is understandable, considering which voices are heard, sometimes believed. And effective control of the corporation lies in very few institutional and personal hands, with the backing of law, after a century of judicial activism.

The innocent talk of "investors" should not conjure up pictures of Joe Doakes on the plant floor, but of the Caterpillar corporation, which has just succeeded in breaking a major strike by reliance on the foreign investment that is so highly lauded: using the remarkable profit growth it shares with other "domestic constituencies" to create excess capacity abroad to undermine efforts by working people in Illinois to resist the erosion of their wages and working conditions. These developments result in no slight measure from the "financial liberalization" of the past 25 years, which is to be enhanced by the

MAI; it is worth noting too that this era of financial liberalization has been one of unusually slow growth (including the current "boom," the poorest recovery in postwar history), low wages, high profits—and, incidentally, trade restrictions by the rich.

A better term for the MAI and similar endeavors is not "investor rights agreements" but "corporate rights agreements."

The relevant "investors" are collectivist legal entities, not persons as understood by common sense and the tradition, before the days when modern judicial activism created contemporary corporate power. That leads to another criticism. Opponents of the MAI often allege that the agreements grant too many rights to corporations. But to speak of granting too many rights to the king, or the dictator, or the slaveowner, is to give away too much ground. Why should they have any rights at all? Rather than "corporate rights agreements," these measures might be termed, more accurately, "corporate power agreements," since it is hardly clear why such institutions should have any rights at all.

When the corporatization of the state capitalist societies took place a century ago, in part in reaction to massive market failures, conservatives—a breed that no longer exists—bitterly objected to this attack on the fundamental principles of classical liberalism. And rightly so. One may recall Adam Smith's critique of the "joint stock companies" of his day, particularly if management is granted a degree of independence; and his attitude toward the inherent corruption of private power, probably a "conspiracy" against the public when businessmen meet for lunch, in his acid view, let alone when they form collectivist legal entities and alliances among them, with extraordinary rights granted by state power.

With these provisos in mind, let us recall some of the intended features of the MAI, relying on what information has reached the concerned public, thanks to the "unholy alliance."

"Investors" are accorded the right to move assets freely, including production facilities and financial assets, without "government interference" (meaning a voice for the public). By modes of chicanery familiar to the business world and corporate lawyers, the rights granted to "foreign investors" transfer easily to "domestic investors" as well. Among democratic choices that might be barred are those calling for local ownership, sharing of technology, local managers, corporate accountability, living wage provisions, preferences (for deprived areas, minorities, women, etc), labor-consumer-environmental protection, restrictions on dangerous products, small business protection, support for strategic and emerging industries, land reform, community and worker control (that is, the foundations of authentic democracy), labor actions (which could be construed as illegal threats to order), and so on.

"Investors" are permitted to sue governments at any level for infringement on the rights granted them. There is no reciprocity: citizens and governments cannot sue "investors." The Ethyl and Metalclad suits are exploratory initiatives. No restrictions are allowed on investment in countries with human rights violations: South Africa in the days of "constructive engagement," Burma today, etc. It is to be understood, of course, that the Don will not be hampered by such constraints. The powerful stand above treaties and laws. Constraints on capital flow are barred: for example, the conditions imposed by Chile to discourage inflows of short-term capital, widely credited with having insulated Chile somewhat from the destructive impact of highly volatile financial markets subject to unpredictable herd-like irrationality. Or more far-reaching measures that might well reverse the deleterious consequences of liberalizing capital flows. Serious proposals to achieve these ends have been on the table for years, but have never reached the agenda of the "architects of power." It may well be that the economy is harmed by financial liberalization, as the evidence suggests. But that is a matter of little moment in comparison with the advantages conferred by the liberalization of financial flows for a quarter-century, initiated by the governments of the U.S. and U.K., primarily. These advantages are substantial. Financial liberalization contributes to concentration of wealth and provides powerful weapons to undermine social programs. It helps bring about the "significant wage restraint" and "atypical restraint on compensation increases [which] appears to be mainly the consequence of greater worker insecurity," which so encourage Fed chair Alan Greenspan and the Clinton administation, sustaining the "economic miracle" that arouses awe among its beneficiaries and deluded observers, particularly abroad.

Enthusiasm for these wonders is ebbing, however, among the managers of the global economy, as the near-disasters that have accelerated since financial flows were liberalized from the 1970s have begun to threaten the "domestic constituencies" as well as the general public. Chief economist of the World Bank Joseph Stiglitz, the editors of the London *Financial Times*, and others close to the centers of power have begun to call for steps to regulate capital flow, following the lead of such bastions of respectability as the Bank for International Settlements. The World Bank has also somewhat reversed course. Not only is the global economy very poorly understood, but serious weaknesses are becoming harder to ignore and patch over. There may be changes, in unpredictable directions. Returning to the MAI, signatories are to be "locked in" for 20 years.

That is a "U.S. government proposal" according to the spokesperson for the Canadian Chamber of Commerce, who doubles as senior adviser of Investment and Trade for IBM Canada, and is selected to represent Canada in public debate.

The Treaty has a built-in "ratchet" effect, a consequence of provisions for "standstill" and "rollback." "Standstill" means that no new legis-

> Like much of public policy in recent years, particularly in the Anglo-American societies, the treaty is designed to undercut democracy and rights of citizens by transferring even more decision-making authority to unnacountable private institutions.

lation is permitted that is interpreted as "non-conforming" to the MAI. "Rollback" means that governments are expected to eliminate legislation already on the books that is interpreted as "non-conforming." Interpretation, in all cases, is by you-know-who. The goal is to "lock countries into" arrangements which, over time, will shrink the public arena more and more, transferring power to the approved "domestic constituencies" and their international structures. These include a rich array of corporate alliances to administer production and trade, relying on powerful states that are to maintain the system while socializing cost and risk for nationally-based transnational corporations—virtually all TNCs, according to recent technical studies.

The current target date for the MAI is April 27, but further delays are likely because of disputes within the club. According to rumors filtering through the organs of power (mainly the foreign business press), these include efforts by the European Union and the United States to allow certain rights to constituent states (perhaps affording the EU something like the vast internal market that U.S.-based corporations enjoy), reservations by France and Canada to maintain some control over their cultural industries (a still greater problem for smaller countries), and European objections to the more extreme and arrogant forms of U.S. market interference, such as the Helms-Burton act.

The *Economist* reports further problems. Labor and environmental issues, which "barely featured at the start," are becoming harder to suppress. It is becoming more difficult to ignore the paranoids and flat-earthers who "want high standards written in for how foreign investors treat workers and protect the environment." Worse still, "their fervent attacks, spread via a network of internet websites, have left negotiators unsure how to proceed." One possibility would be to pay attention to what the public wants. But, quite properly, that option is not mentioned: it is excluded in principle, since it would undermine the point of the enterprise.

Even if the deadline isn't met and the MAI is abandoned, that wouldn't show that it has "all been for nothing," the *Economist* informs its constituency. Progress has been made, and "with luck, parts of MAI could become a blueprint for a global WTO accord on investment," which the recalcitrant "developing countries" may be more willing to accept—after a few years of battering by market irrationalities, the subsequent discipline imposed on the victims by the world rulers, and growing awareness by elite elements that they can share in concentrated privilege by helping to disseminate the doctrines of the powerful, however fraudulent they may be, however others may fare; and we can expect "parts of MAI" to take shape elsewhere, perhaps in the IMF, which is suitably secretive. From another point of view, further delays give the rascal multitude more opportunity to rend the veil of secrecy.

It is important for the general population to discover what is being planned for them. The efforts of governments and media to keep it all under wraps, except for their officially-recognized "domestic constituencies," are surely understandable. But such barriers have been overcome by vigorous public action before, and can be again.

19.

Coups, UNASUR, and the U.S.

Restoring Washington's capacity for military intervention

The last time I had the opportunity to speak in Caracas—at long-distance that time—was about a year ago, right after the UNASUR (Union of South American Nations) meeting in Santiago in September 2009. That meeting was called "with the purpose of considering the situation in the Republic of Bolivia," after an uprising backed by the traditional elites who had lost power in the impressive democratic elections of 2005. UNASUR condemned the violence and the massacre of peasants by the quasi-secessionist elements, and declared, "Their fullest and decided support for the constitutional government of President Evo Morales, whose mandate was ratified by a wide margin in the recent referendum." These are the words of the final Declaration, which also warned that the participating governments—all of the South American Republics—"energetically reject and do not recognize any situation that implies an intent of civil coup d'état, the rupture of institutional order, or that compromises the territorial integrity of the Republic of Bolivia." In response, President Morales thanked UNASUR for its support and observed that, "For the first time in South America's history, the countries of our region are deciding how to resolve our problems, without the presence of the United States."

True, and a fact of historic significance. It is instructive to compare the Charter of the Organization of American States (OAS) with that of the African Union (AU). The latter permits intervention by African states within the Union itself in exceptional circumstances. In contrast, the Charter of the OAS bars intervention "for any reason whatever, in the internal or external affairs of any other state." The reasons for the difference are clear. The OAS Charter seeks to deter intervention from the "colossus of the North"—and has failed to do so. That is an enduring problem in the Western hemisphere, nowhere near solution, though there has been significant progress. After the collapse of the apartheid states, the AU has faced no comparable problem.

Last year's UNASUR meeting in Santiago took a step forward in the difficult process of integration that is taking place in South America. This process has two aspects: external and internal. The external process establishes bonds among countries that had been largely separated from one another since the early European conquests,

From a talk given in Caracas, Venezuela.
Published in Z Magazine, October 2009

each one oriented towards the West. The internal process seeks to integrate the vast impoverished and oppressed majorities into the societies that took shape under colonial and neocolonial domination. These societies have typically been ruled by small Europeanized elites who had amassed enormous wealth and were linked to the imperial societies in many ways: export of capital, import of luxury goods, education, and many other dimensions.

The ruling sectors assumed little responsibility for the fate of their own countries and their suffering people. These critical factors sharply distinguish Latin America from the developmental states of East Asia. The processes of internal integration in South America, quite naturally, are arousing great concern among the traditional rulers at home and abroad, and strong opposition if they go beyond minor reforms of the worst abuses.

In early August, UNASUR met in Ecuador, which assumed the presidency of the organization. The announced goal of the meeting was to carry forward the process of integration, but the meeting took place under the shadow of renewed U.S. military intervention.

Colombia did not attend, in reaction to broad concern in the region over its decision to accept U.S. military bases. The host of the meeting, President Correa of Ecuador, had announced that the U.S. military would no longer be permitted to use its Manta base, the last major U.S. base remaining in South America.

Bases and Coups

Establishing U.S. bases in Colombia is only one part of a much broader effort to restore Washington's capacity for military intervention. In recent years, total U.S. military and police aid in the hemisphere has come to exceed economic and social aid. That is a new phenomenon. Even at the height of the Cold War, economic aid far exceeded military aid. Predictably, these programs have "strengthened military forces at the expense of civilian authorities, exacerbated human rights problems and generated significant social conflict and even political instability," according to a study by the Washington Office on Latin America. By 2003, the number of Latin Americans troops trained by U.S. programs had increased by more than 50 percent. It has probably become higher since. Police are trained in light infantry tactics. The U.S. Southern Military Command (SOUTH-COM) has more personnel in Latin America than most key civilian federal agencies combined. That again is a new development. The focus now is on street gangs and "radical populism": I do not have to explain what that phrase means in the Latin American context. Military training is being shifted from the State Department to the Pentagon. That shift is of some importance. It frees military training from human rights and democracy condition- alities under congressional supervision, which has always been weak, but was at least a deterrent to some of the worst abuses.

Military bases are also being established where possible to support what are called "forward operations"—meaning military intervention of one or another sort. In a related development, the U.S. Fourth Fleet, disbanded in 1950, was reactivated a few weeks after Colombia's invasion of Ecuador in March 2008. With responsibility for the Caribbean, Central and South America, and the surrounding waters, the Fleet's "various operations...include counter-illicit trafficking, Theater Security Cooperation, military-to-military interaction and bilateral and multinational training," the official announcement says. Quite properly, these moves elicited protest and concern from the governments of Brazil, Venezuela, and others.

In past years the U.S. routinely helped carry out military coups in Latin America or invaded outright. Examples are too numerous and familiar to review and are awful to contemplate. That capacity has declined, but has not disappeared. In the new century there have already been three military coups: in Venezuela, Haiti, and now Honduras. The first, in Venezuela, was openly supported by Washington. After a popular uprising restored the elected government, Washington immediately turned to a second plan to undermine the elected government: by funding groups of its choice within Venezuela, while refusing to identify recipients. Funding after the failed coup reached $26 million by 2006. The facts were reported by wire services, but ignored by the mainstream media. Law professor Bill Monning of the Monterey Institute of International Studies in California said that, "We would scream bloody murder if any outside force were interfering in our internal political system." He is, of course, correct: such actions would never be tolerated for a moment. But the imperial mentality allows them to proceed, even with praise, when Wash- ington is the agent.

The pretext, invariably, is "supporting democracy." In the real world, the measures employed have been a standard device to undermine democracy. Examples are numerous. To mention just a few, that is how the ground was prepared for the U.S.-backed military coup in Haiti after its first democratic election in 1990, bitterly opposed by Washington. And in another part of the world, it is happening right now in Palestine where the outcome of a free election in January 2006 was counter to Washington's wishes. At once, the U.S. and Israel, with Europe tagging politely along as usual, turned to severe punishment of the population for the crime of voting "the wrong way" in a free election, and also began to institute the standard devices to undermine an unwanted government: "democracy promotion" and military force. In this case, the military force is a collaborationist paramilitary army under the command of U.S. General Keith Dayton, trained in Jordan with Israeli participation. The Dayton army received great acclaim from liberals in the government and the press when it succeeded in suppressing protests in the West Bank during the murderous and destructive U.S.-backed Israeli military campaign in Gaza earlier this year. Senator John Kerry, chair of the Senate Foreign Relations committee, was one of many close to the Obama administration

who saw in this success a sign that Israel may at last have a "legitimate negotiating partner" for its U.S.-backed programs of taking over what is of value in the occupied territories, under the guise of a "political settlement."

All of this is routine, and very familiar in Latin America, where U.S. invasions have regularly left what remains of the country under the rule of brutal National Guards and collaborationist elites. The policies were initially developed with considerable sophistication a century ago after the U.S. conquest of the Philippines, which left hundreds of thousands of corpses. And these measures have often been successful for long periods. In the original testing ground, the Philippines, the impact still remains a century later, one reason for the continuing ugly record of state violence, and the failure of the Philippines to join the remarkable economic development of East and Southeast Asia in recent years.

Returning to coups in Latin America in the new millennium, the first one, in Venezuela, was unsuccessful. The second was in Haiti two years later. The U.S. and France intervened to remove the elected president and dispatched him off to Central Africa, actions that precipitated yet another reign of terror in this tortured country, once the richest colony in the world and the source of much of France's wealth, destroyed over the centuries by France and then the U.S. I should add that the harrowing history, in Haiti and elsewhere, is almost unknown in the U.S.—worse, it is replaced by fairy tales of noble missions that have sometimes failed because of the unworthiness of the beneficiaries. These are among the prerogatives of power, and facts that cannot be ignored by the traditional victims.

The third coup is of course the one taking place right now in Honduras, where an openly class-based military coup ousted left-leaning President Zelaya. This coup was unusual in that the U.S. did not carry it out or directly support it, but rather joined the Organization of American States in criticizing it, though weakly. Washington did not withdraw its ambassador in protest as Latin American and European countries did and made only limited use of its military and economic influence, as it could easily have done by simple means—for example by canceling all U.S. visas and freezing U.S. bank accounts of leaders of the coup regime.

A group of leading U.S. Latin American scholars recently reported that "not only does the administration continue to prop up the regime with aid money through the Millennium Challenge Account and other sources, but the U.S. continues to train Honduran military students at the Western Hemispheric Institute for Security Cooperation—the notorious institution formerly known as the School of the Americas," from which much of the top Honduran military has graduated.

Amnesty International has just released a long and detailed account of extremely serious human rights violations by the coup regime. If such a report were issued concerning an official enemy, it would be front-page news. In this case it was scarcely reported, consistent with the down-playing of coups to which U.S. political and economic power centers are basically sympathetic, as in this case.

The U.S. surely hopes to maintain and probably expand its military base at Soto Cano (Palmerola) in Honduras, a major base for the U.S.-run terrorist war in Nicaragua in the 1980s. There are unconfirmed rumors of plans for other bases. (The best source of information and analysis is the consistently outstanding work by Mark Weisbrot at the Center for Economic and Policy Research, who also reviews the media's refusal to rise to minimal journalistic standards by reporting the basic facts.)

Imperial Mentality

The justification offered for the new military bases in Colombia is the "war on drugs." The fact that the justification is even offered is remarkable. Suppose, for example, that Colombia, or China, or many others claimed the right to establish military bases in Mexico to implement their programs to eradicate tobacco in the U.S., by fumigation in North Carolina and Kentucky, interdiction by sea and air forces, and dispatch of inspectors to the U.S. to ensure it was eradicating this poison—which is, in fact, far more lethal even than alcohol, which in turn is far more lethal than cocaine or heroin, incomparably more than cannabis. The toll of tobacco use is truly fearsome, including "passive smokers" who are seriously affected though they do not use tobacco themselves. The death toll overwhelms the lethal effects of other dangerous substances.

The idea that outsiders should interfere with U.S. production and distribution of these murderous poisons is plainly unthinkable. Nevertheless, the U.S. justification for carrying out such policies in South America is accepted as plausible. The fact that it is even regarded as worthy of discussion is yet another illustration of the depth of the imperial mentality, and the abiding truth of the doctrine of Thucydides that the strong do as they wish and the weak suffer as they must—while the intellectual classes spin tales about the nobility of power. Leading themes of history, to the present day.

Despite the outlandish assumptions, let us agree to adopt the imperial mentality that reigns in the West—virtually unchallenged, in fact, not even noticed. Even after this extreme concession, it requires real effort to take the "war on drugs" pretext seriously. The war has been waged for close to 40 years and intensively for a decade in Colombia. There has been no notable impact on drug use or even street prices. The reasons are reasonably well understood. Studies by official and quasi-official governmental organizations provide good evidence that prevention and treatment are far more effective than forceful measures in reducing drug abuse: one major study finds prevention and treatment to have been 10 times as effective as drug interdiction and 23 times as effective as "supply-side" out-of-country operations, such as fumigation in Colombia, more accurately described as chemical warfare. The historical record supports these conclusions. There is ample evidence that changes in cultural attitudes and perceptions have been very effective in curtailing harmful practices. Nevertheless, despite what is known, policy is overwhelmingly directed to the least effective measures, with the support of the doctrinal institutions.

These and other facts leave us with only 2 credible hypotheses: either U.S. leaders have been systematically insane for the past 40 years; or the purpose of the drug war is quite different from what is proclaimed. We can exclude the possibility of collective insanity. To determine the real reasons we can follow the model of the legal system, which takes predictable outcome to be evidence of intent, particularly when practices persist over a long period and in the face of constant failure to approach the announced objectives. In this case, the predictable outcome is not obscure, both abroad and at home.

Abroad, the "supply-side approach" has been the basis for U.S.-backed counterinsurgency strategy in Colombia and elsewhere, with a fearful toll among victims of chemical warfare and militarization of conflicts, but enormous profits for domestic and foreign elites. Colombia has a shocking record of human rights violations, by far the worst in the hemisphere since the end of Reagan's Central American terror wars in the 1980s, and also the second-largest internal displacement of populations in the world, after Sudan. Meanwhile, domestic elites and multinationals profit from the forced displacement of peasants and indigenous people, which clears land for mining, agribusiness production and ranching, infrastructure development for industry, and much else. There is a great deal more to say about this, but I will put it aside. At home, the drug war coincided with the initiation of neoliberal programs, the financialization of the economy, and the attack on government social welfare systems, real, even though limited by international standards.

One immediate consequence of the war on drugs has been the extraordinary growth in scale and severity of incarceration in the past 30 years, placing the U.S. far in the lead worldwide. The victims are overwhelmingly African-American males and other minorities, a great many of them sentenced on victimless drug charges. Drug use is about the same as in privileged white sectors, which are mostly immune.

In short, while abroad the war on drugs is a thin cover for counterinsurgency, at home it functions as a civilized counterpart to Latin America limpieza social cleansing, removing a population that has become superfluous with the dismantling of the domestic productive system in the course of the neoliberal financiali- zation of the economy. A secondary gain is that like the "war on crime," the "war on drugs" serves to frighten the population into obedience as domestic policies are implemented to benefit extreme wealth at the expense of the large majority, leading to staggering inequality that is breaking historical records, and stagnation of real wages for the majority while benefits decline and working hours increase.

These processes conform well to the history of prohibition, which has been well studied by legal scholars. I cannot go into the very interesting details here, but quite generally, prohibition has been aimed at control of what are called "the dangerous classes"—those who threaten the rights and well-being of the privileged dominant minorities. These observations hold worldwide, where the topics have been studied. They have special meaning in the U.S. in the context of the history of African-Americans, much of which remains generally unknown. It is, of course, known that slaves were formally freed during the American Civil War, and that after ten years of relative freedom, the gains were mostly obliterated by 1877 as Reconstruction was brought to an end. But the horrifying story is only now being researched seriously, most recently in a study called "Slavery by another name" by *Wall Street Journal* editor Douglas Blackmon.

His work fills out the bare bones with shocking detail, showing how after Reconstruction African-American life was effectively criminalized, so that black males virtually became a permanent slave labor force. Conditions, however, were far worse than under slavery, for good capitalist reasons. Slaves were property, a capital investment, and were therefore cared for by their masters. Those criminalized for merely existing are similar to wage laborers, in that the masters have no responsibility for them, except to make sure that enough are available. That was one of the arguments used by slave owners to claim that they were more moral than those who hired labor. The argument was understood well enough by northern workers, who regarded wage labor as preferable to literal slavery only in that it was temporary, a position shared by Abraham Lincoln, among others.

Criminalized black slavery provided much of the basis for the American industrial revolution of the late 19th and early 20th century. It continued until World War II, when free labor was needed for war industry. During the postwar boom, which relied substantially on the dynamic state sector that had been established under the successful semi-command economy of World War II, African-American workers gained a certain degree of freedom for the first time since post-Civil War Reconstruction. But since the 1970s that process is being reversed, thanks in no small measure to the "war on drugs," which in some respects is a contemporary analogue to the criminalization of black life after the Civil War—and also provides a fine disciplined labor force, often in private prisons, in gross violation of international labor regulations.

For such reasons as these, we can expect that the "war on drugs" will continue until popular understanding and activism reach a point where the fundamental driving factors can be discerned and seriously addressed. Last February, the Latin American Commission on Drugs and Democracy issued its analysis of the U.S. "war on drugs" in the past decades.

The Commission, led by former Latin American presidents Cardoso, Zedillo, and Gavíria, concluded that the drug war had been a complete failure and urged a drastic change of policy, away from criminalization and "supply-side" operations and towards much less costly and more effective measures of education, prevention, and treatment. Their report had no detectable impact, just as earlier studies and the historical record have had none. That again reinforces the natural conclusion that the "drug war"—like the "war on crime" and "the war on terror"—has quite sensible goals, which are being achieved, and therefore continue in the face of a costly failure of announced goals.

Returning to the UNASUR meeting, a dose of realism, and skepticism about propaganda, would be helpful in evaluating the pretexts offered for the establishment of U.S. military bases in Colombia, retention of the base in Honduras, and the accompanying steps towards militarization. It is very much to be hoped that South America will bar moves towards militarization and intervention, and will devote its energies to the programs of integration in both their external and internal aspects—establishing effective political and economic organizations, overcoming the terrible internal problems of deprivation and suffering, and strengthening varied links to the outside world. But Latin America's problems go far beyond. The countries cannot hope to progress without overcoming their reliance on primary product exports, including crucially oil, but also minerals and food products. And all these problems, challenging enough in themselves, are overshadowed by a critical global concern: the looming environmental crisis. Current warnings by the best-informed investigators rely on the British Stern report, which is very highly regarded by leading scientists and numerous Nobel laureates in economics. On this basis, some have concluded, realistically, that "2009 may well turn out to be the decisive year in the human relationship with our home planet." In December, a conference in Copenhagen is "to sign a new global accord on global warming," which will tell us "whether or not our political systems are up to the unprecedented challenge that climate change represents." I am quoting Bill McKibben, one of the most knowledgeable researchers. He is mildly hopeful, but that may be optimistic unless there are really large-scale public campaigns to overcome the insistence of the managers of the state-corporate sector on privileging short-term

170

gain for the few over the hope that their grandchildren will have a decent future. At least some of the barriers are beginning to crumble, in part, because the business world perceives new opportunities for profit in alternative energy. Even the *Wall Street Journal*, one of the most stalwart deniers, has recently published a supplement with dire warnings about "climate disaster," urging that none of the options being considered may be sufficient and that it may be necessary to undertake more radical measures of geoengineering, "cooling the planet" in some manner.

Meanwhile, however, the energy industries are vigorously pursuing their own agenda. They are organizing major propaganda campaigns to defeat even the mild proposals being considered in Congress. They are quite openly following the script of the corporate campaigns that have virtually destroyed the very limited health care reforms proposed by the Obama administration so effectively that the business press now exults that the insurance companies have won—and everyone else will suffer.

The picture might be much grimmer even than what the Stern report predicts. A group of MIT scientists have just released the results of what they describe as, "The most comprehensive modeling yet carried out on the likelihood of how much hotter the Earth's climate will get in this century, [showing] that without rapid and massive action, the problem will be about twice as severe as previously estimated six years ago —and could be even worse than that [because the model] does not fully incorporate other positive feedbacks that can occur, for example, if increased temperatures caused a large-scale melting of permafrost in arctic regions and subsequent release of large quantities of methane." The leader of the project, a prominent earth scientist, says that, "There's no way the world can or should take these risks," and that, "The least-cost option to lower the risk is to start now and steadily transform the global energy system over the coming decades to low or zero greenhouse gas-emitting technologies." There is little sign of that. While new technologies are essential, the

problems go far beyond. It will be necessary to reverse the huge state-corporate social engineering projects of the post-World War II period, or at least severely ameliorate their harmful effects.

These projects quite purposefully promoted an energy-wasting and environmentally destructive fossil fuel-based economy. The state-corporate programs, which included massive projects of suburbanization along with destruction and then gentrification of inner cities, began with a conspiracy by manufacturing and energy industries to buy up and destroy efficient electric public transportation systems in Los Angeles and dozens of other cities; they were convicted of criminal conspiracy and given a light tap on the wrist. The Federal government then joined in, relocating infrastructure and capital stock to suburban areas and creating the interstate highway system, under the usual pretext of "defense." Railroads were displaced by government-subsidized motor and air transport.

The public played almost no role, apart from choice within the narrowly structured framework of options designed by state-corporate managers. One result is atomization of society and entrapment of isolated individuals with self-destructive ambitions and crushing debt. A central component of these processes is the vigorous campaign of the business world to "fabricate consumers," in the words of the distinguished political economist Thorstein Veblen, and to direct people "to the superficial things of life, like fashionable consumption." The campaign grew out of the recognition a century ago that it was no longer as easy as before to discipline the population by force, and that it would be necessary to resort to propaganda and indoctrination to curtail democratic achievements and ensure that the "opulent minority" is protected from the "ignorant and meddlesome outsiders," the population. These are crucial features of really existing democracy under contemporary state capitalism, a "democratic deficit" at the root of many of today's crises. While state-corporate power was promoting privatization of life and maximal waste of energy, it was also undermining the efficient choices that the market does not provide—another destructive built-in market inefficiency. To put it simply, if I want to get home from work, the market offers me a choice between a Ford and a Toyota, but not between a car and a subway. That's a social decision and in a democratic society would be the decision of an organized public. But that's just what the dedicated elite attack on democracy seeks to undermine.

The consequences are right before our eyes, in ways that are sometimes surreal—no less surreal than the huge resources being poured into militarization of the world while a billion people are going hungry and the rich countries are cutting back sharply on financing meager food aid. The business press recently reported that Obama's transportation secretary is in Europe seeking to contract with Spanish and other European manufacturers to build high-speed rail projects in the U.S., using federal funds that were authorized by Congress to stimulate the U.S. economy. Spain and other European countries are hoping to get U.S. taxpayer funding for the high-speed rail and related infrastructure that is badly needed in the U.S. At the same time, Washington is busy dismantling leading sectors of U.S. industry, ruining the lives of the workforce, families, and communities. It is difficult to conjure up a more damning indictment of the economic system that has been constructed by state-corporate managers, particularly during the neoliberal era. Surely the auto industry could be reconstructed to produce what the country needs, using its highly skilled workforce—and soon, if we are to have some hope of averting major catastrophe. It has been done before, after all. During World War II, the semi-command economy not only ended the Great Depression, but also initiated the most spectacular period of growth in economic history.

In a sane world, workers and communities would take over the abandoned factories, convert them to socially useful production, and run the factories themselves. That has been tried, but was blocked in the courts. To succeed, such efforts would require a level of popular support and working class consciousness that is not manifest in recent years, but that could be reawakened and could have large-scale effects.

These issues should be very prominent here in Venezuela, as in other oil-producing countries. They were discussed by President Chavez at the meeting of the UN General Assembly in September 2005. I will quote his words, which unfortunately were not reported, at least in the U.S. press: "Ladies and gentlemen, we are facing an unprecedented energy crisis in which an unstoppable increase of energy is perilously reaching record highs, as well as the incapacity of increased oil supply and the perspective of a decline in the proven reserves of fuel worldwide.... It is unpractical and unethical to sacrifice the human race by appealing in an insane manner to the validity of a socioeconomic model that has a galloping destructive capacity. It would be suicidal to spread it and impose it as an infallible remedy for the evils which are caused precisely by them." These words point in the right direction. To avoid the suicide of the species there must be coordinated efforts of producers and users, and radical changes in prevailing socioeconomic models and global organization. These are very large and urgent challenges. There can be no delay in recognizing and understanding them, and acting decisively to address them.

20.

The Obama-Netanyahu-Abbas Meetings

A turning point in U.S. Middle East policy

The Obama-Netanyahu-Abbas meetings in 2009, followed by Obama's speech in Cairo, have been widely interpreted as a turning point in U.S. Middle East policy, leading to consternation in some quarters, exuberance in others. Fairly typical is Middle East analyst Dan Fromkin of the *Washington Post*, who sees "signs Obama will promote a new regional peace initiative for the Middle East, much like the one championed by Jordan's King Abdullah....[and also] the first distinct signs that Obama is willing to play hardball with Israel" (*WP*, May 29). A closer look, however, suggests considerable caution.

King Abdullah insists that, "There is no change to the Arab Peace Initiative and there is no need to amend it. Any talk about amending it, is baseless" (AFP, May 16). Abbas, regularly described as the president of the Palestinian Authority (his term expired in January), firmly agrees. The Arab Peace Initiative reiterates the long-standing international consensus that Israel must withdraw to the international border, perhaps with "minor and mutual adjustments," to adopt official U.S. terminology before it departed sharply from world opinion in 1971, endorsing Israel's rejection of peace with Egypt in favor of settlement expansion (in the northeast Sinai). Furthermore, the consensus calls for a Palestinian state to be established in Gaza and the West Bank after Israel's withdrawal. The Arab Initiative adds that the Arab states should then normalize relations with Israel. The Initiative was later adopted by the Organization of Islamic States, including Iran (Akiva Eldar, *Ha'aretz*, June 1).

Obama has praised the Initiative and called on the Arab states to proceed to normalize relations with Israel. But he has so far scrupulously evaded the core of the proposal, thus implicitly maintaining the U.S. rejectionist stand that has blocked a diplomatic settlement since the 1970s, along with its Israeli client, in virtual isolation. There are no signs that Obama is willing even to consider the Arab Initiative, let alone "promote" it. That was under-

From Z Magazine, July 2009

scored in Obama's much heralded address to the Muslim world in Cairo on June 4.

Palestinian State:
Or "Fried Chicken?"

The U.S.-Israel confrontation—with Abbas on the sidelines—turns on two phrases: "Palestinian state" and "natural growth of settlements." Let's consider these in turn.

Obama has indeed pronounced the words "Palestinian state," echoing Bush. In contrast, the (unrevised) 1999 platform of Israel's governing party, Netanyahu's Likud, "flatly rejects the establishment of a Palestinian Arab state west of the Jordan river." Nevertheless, it was Netanyahu's 1996 government that was the first to use the phrase. It agreed that Palestinians can call whatever fragments of Palestine are left to them "a state" if they like—or they can call them "fried chicken" (David BarIllan, director of Communications and Policy Planning; Interview, *Palestine-Israel Journal*, Summer/Autumn 1996).

The 1996 Netanyahu government's contemptuous reference to Palestinian aspirations was a shift towards accommodation in U.S.-Israeli policy. As he left office shortly before, Shimon Peres forcefully declared that there will never be a Palestinian state (Amnon Barzilai, *Ha'aretz*, October 24, 1995). Peres was reaffirming the official 1989 position of the U.S. (Bush-Baker) and the Israeli coalition government (Shamir-Peres) that there can be no "additional Palestinian state" between Israel and Jordan—the latter declared to be a Palestinian state by U.S.-Israeli fiat. In the Peres-Shamir-Baker plan, barely reported (if at all) in the U.S., the fate of the occupied territories was to be settled in terms of the guidelines established by the government of Israel, and Palestinians were permitted to take part in negotiations only if they accepted these guidelines, which rule out Palestinian national rights.

Contrary to much misunderstanding, the Oslo agreements of September 1993—the "Day of Awe," as the press described it—changed little in this regard. The Declaration of Principles accepted by all participants established that the end point of the process would be realization of the goals of UN 242, which accords no rights to Palestinians. And by then, the U.S. had withdrawn its earlier interpretation of 242 as requiring Israeli withdrawal from the territories conquered in 1967, leaving the matter open.

The Peres-Shamir-Baker declarations of 1989 were in response to the official Palestinian acceptance of the international consensus on a two-state solution in 1988. That proposal was first formally enunciated in 1976 in a Security Council resolution introduced by the major Arab states with the tacit support of the PLO, vetoed by the U.S. (again in 1980). Since then, U.S.-Israeli rejectionism has persisted unchanged, with one brief but significant exception, in President Clinton's final month in office.

Clinton recognized that the terms he had offered at the failed 2000 Camp David meetings were not acceptable to any Palestinians and, in December, proposed his "parameters," inexplicit but more forthcoming. He then announced that both sides had accepted the parameters, though both had reservations. Israeli and Palestinian negotiators met in Taba Egypt to iron out the differences and made considerable progress. A full resolution could have been reached in a few more days, they announced in their final joint press conference. But Israel called off the negotiations prematurely and they have not been formally resumed.

The single exception suggests that if an American president were willing to tolerate a meaningful diplomatic settlement, it might very well be reached. The facts are well documented in Hebrew and English sources (see Chomsky, *Failed States*). But like much of the relevant history, they are regularly reshaped to suit doctrinal needs; for example by Jeffrey Goldberg, who writes that, "By December of 2000, Israel had accepted President Bill Clinton's 'parameters,' offering the Palestinians all of the Gaza Strip, 94 percent to 96 percent of the West Bank and sovereignty over Arab areas of East Jerusalem. Arafat again rejected the deal" (*NYT*, May 24). That is a convenient tale, false or seriously misleading in all particulars, and another useful contribution to U.S.-Israeli rejectionism.

International Consensus Or "Fried Chicken?"

Returning to the phrase "Palestinian state," the crucial question on the U.S. side is whether Obama means the international consensus or "fried chicken." So far, that remains unanswered, except by studious omission, and—crucially—by Washington's steady funding of Israel's programs of settlement and development in the West Bank. All of these programs violate international law, as Israeli Defense Minister Moshe Dayan conceded in 1967 and as has been reaffirmed by the Security Council and the World Court. Probably Netanyahu would still accept his 1996 position.

The contours of "fried chicken" are being carved into the landscape daily by U.S.-backed Israeli programs. The general goals were outlined by Prime Minister Olmert in May 2006 in his "Convergence program," later expanded to "Convergence-plus." Under "Convergence," Israel was to take over the territory within the illegal "separation wall" along with the Jordan Valley, thus imprisoning what is left, which is broken into cantons by several salients extending to the East. Israel also takes over Greater Jerusalem, the site of most of its current construction projects, driving out many Arabs. These Jerusalem projects not only violate international law, as do all the others, but also Security Council resolutions (at the time, still backed by the U.S.).

The plans being executed right now are designed to leave Israel in control of the most valuable land in the West Bank, with Palestinians

> The plans being executed right now are designed to leave Israel in control of the most valuable land in the West Bank, with Palestinians confined to unviable fragments, all separated from Jerusalem, the traditional center of Palestinian life

confined to unviable fragments, all separated from Jerusalem, the traditional center of Palestinian life. The "separation wall" also establishes Israeli control of the West Bank aquifer. Hence Israel will be able to continue to ensure that Palestinians receive one-fourth as much water as Israelis, as the World Bank reported in April, in some cases below minimum recommended levels. In the other part of Palestine, Gaza, regular Israeli bombardment and the cruel siege reduce consumption far below minimum standards.

Obama continues to support all of these programs, and has even called for substantially increasing military aid to Israel for an unprecedented ten years (Stephen Zunes, *Foreign Policy in Focus,* March 4). It appears, then, that Palestinians may be offered fried chicken, but nothing more. Israel's forced separation of Gaza from the West Bank since 1991, intensified with U.S. support after a free election in January 2006 came out "the wrong way," has also been studiously ignored in Obama's "new initiative," thus further undermining prospects for any viable Palestinian state.

Gaza's forced separation from Palestine, and its miserable condition, have been almost entirely consigned to oblivion, an atrocity to which we should not contribute by tacit consent. Israeli journalist Amira Hass, one of the leading specialists on Gaza, writes that, "The restrictions on Palestinian movement that Israel introduced in January 1991 reversed a process that had been initiated in June 1967.

"Back then, and for the first time since 1948, a large portion of the Palestinian people again lived in the open territory of a single country—to be sure, one that was occupied, but was nevertheless whole.... The total separation of the Gaza Strip from the West Bank is one of the greatest achievements of Israeli politics, whose overarching objective is to prevent a solution based on international decisions and understandings and instead dictate an arrangement based on Israel's military superiority.... Since January 1991, Israel has bureaucratically and logistically merely perfected the split and the separation: not only between Palestinians in the occupied territories and their brothers in Israel, but also between the Palestinian residents of Jerusalem and those in the rest of the territories and between Gazans and West Bankers/Jerusalemites. Jews live in this same piece of land within a superior and separate system of privileges, laws, services, infrastructure and freedom of movement."

The leading academic specialist on Gaza, Sara Roy, adds that, "Gaza is an example of a society that has been deliberately reduced to a state of abject destitution, its once productive population transformed into one of aid-dependent paupers.... Gaza's subjection began long before Israel's recent war against it. The Israeli occupation—now largely forgotten or denied by the international community—has devastated Gaza's economy and people, especially since 2006.... After Israel's December [2008] assault, Gaza's already compromised conditions have become virtually unlivable. Livelihoods, homes, and public infrastructure have been damaged or destroyed on a scale that even the Israel Defense Forces admitted was indefensible.

"In Gaza today, there is no private sector to speak of and no industry. 80 percent of Gaza's agricultural crops were destroyed and Israel continues to snipe at farmers attempting to plant and tend fields near the well-fenced and patrolled border. Most productive activity has been extinguished.... "Today, 96 percent of Gaza's population of 1.4 million is dependent on humanitarian aid for basic needs. According to the World Food Programme, the Gaza Strip requires a minimum of 400 trucks of food every day just to meet the basic nutritional needs of the population. Yet, despite a 22 March decision by the Israeli cabinet to lift all restrictions on food-stuffs entering Gaza, only 653 trucks of food and other supplies were allowed entry during the week of May 10, at best meeting 23 percent of required need. Israel now allows only 30 to 40 commercial items to enter Gaza compared to 4,000 approved products prior to June 2006" (*Harvard Crimson*, June 2, 2009).

Exterminate All The Brutes

It cannot be too often stressed that Israel had no credible pretext for its December attack on Gaza, with full U.S. support and illegal use of U.S. weapons. Near-universal opinion asserts the contrary, claiming that Israel was acting in self-defense. That is utterly unsustainable, in light of Israel's flat rejection of peaceful means that were readily available (see "Exterminate all the Brutes" at www.chomsky.info). That aside, Israel's siege of Gaza is itself an act of war, as Israel of all countries certainly recognizes, having repeatedly justified launching major wars on grounds of partial restrictions on its access to the outside world.

One crucial element of Israel's siege, little reported, is the naval blockade. Peter Beaumont reports from Gaza that, "On its coastal littoral, Gaza's limitations are marked by a different fence where the bars are Israeli gunboats with their huge wakes, scurrying beyond the Palestinian fishing boats and preventing them from going outside a zone imposed by the warships" (*Guardian*, May 27). According to reports from the scene, the naval siege has been tightened steadily since 2000. Fishing boats have been driven steadily out of Gaza's territorial waters and towards the shore by Israeli gunboats, often violently without warning and with many casualties. As a result of these naval actions, Gaza's fishing industry has virtually collapsed because of the contamination caused by Israel's regular attacks, including the destruction of power plants and sewage facilities.

These Israeli naval attacks began shortly after the discovery by the British Gas group of what appear to be quite sizeable natural gas fields in Gaza's territorial waters. Industry journals report that Israel is already appropriating these Gazan resources for its own use, part of its commitment to shift its economy to natural gas. The standard source, *Platt's Commodity News*, reports (February 3, 16) that, "Israel's finance ministry has given the Israel Electric Corp. approval to purchase larger quantities of natural gas from BG than originally agreed upon, according to Israeli government sources [which] said the state-owned utility would be able to negotiate for as much as 1.5 billion cubic meters of natural gas from the Marine field located off the Mediterranean coast of the Palestinian controlled Gaza Strip. Last year the Israeli government approved the purchase of 800 million cubic meters of gas from the field by the IEC.... Recently the Israeli government changed its policy and decided the state-owned utility could buy the entire quantity of gas from the Gaza Marine field. Previously the government had said the IEC could buy half the total amount and the remainder would be bought by private power producers."

The pillage of what could become a major source of income for Palestine is surely known to U.S. authorities. It is only reasonable to suppose that the intention to steal Palestine's limited resources is the motive for preventing Gaza fishing boats to enter Gaza's territorial waters. It would also not be a great surprise if we were to discover some day that the same intention was in the background of the criminal U.S.-Israeli attack on Gaza in December 2008.

The restrictions on movement used to destroy Gaza have long been in force in the West Bank as well, with grim effects on life and the economy. The World Bank has just reported that Israel has established "a complex closure regime that restricts Palestinian access to large areas of the West Bank.... The Palestinian economy has remained stagnant, largely because of the sharp downturn in Gaza and Israel's continued restrictions on Palestinian trade and movement in the West Bank." The World Bank "cited Israeli roadblocks and checkpoints hindering trade and travel, as well as restrictions on Palestinian building in the West Bank, where the Western-backed government of Palestinian President Mahmoud Abbas holds sway" (AP, Avi Issacharoff, *Ha'*

aretz, May 6). All of this constitutes what Israeli activist Jeff Halper calls a "matrix of control" to subdue the colonized population, in pursuit of Defense Minister Moshe Dayan's recommendation to his colleagues shortly after the 1967 conquests that we must tell the Palestinians in the territories that "we have no solution, you shall continue to live like dogs, and whoever wishes may leave, and we will see where this process leads" (Yossi Beilin, Mehiro *shel* Ihud).

Growth of Settlements

Turning to the second bone of contention, settlements, there is indeed a confrontation, but it may again be less dramatic than portrayed. Washington's position was presented most strongly in Hilary Clinton's much-quoted statement rejecting "natural growth exceptions" to the policy opposing new settlements. Netanyahu, along with President Peres and, in fact, virtually the whole Israeli political spectrum, insists on permitting "natural growth" within the areas that Israel intends to annex, complaining that the U.S. is backing down on Bush's authorization of such expansion within his "vision" of a Palestinian state.

Senior Netanyahu cabinet members have gone further. Minister Yisrael Katz announced that "the current Israeli government will not accept in any way the freezing of legal settlement activity in Judea and Samaria" (*Ha'aretz*, May 31). The term "legal" in U.S.-Israeli parlance means "illegal, but authorized by the government of Israel." In this usage, unauthorized outposts are termed "illegal," though apart from the dictates of the powerful, they are no more illegal than the settlements granted to Israel under Bush's "vision." The harsh Obama-Clinton formulation is not new. It repeats the wording of the 2003 Road Map, which stipulates that in Phase I, "Israel freezes all settlement activity (including natural growth of settlements)." All sides formally accept the Road Map—consistently overlooking the fact that Israel, with U.S. support, at once added 14 "reservations" that render it inoperable.

If Obama were serious about opposing settlement expansion, he could easily proceed with concrete measures, for example, by reducing U.S. aid by the amount devoted to this purpose. That would hardly be a radical or courageous move. The Bush I administration did so (reducing loan guarantees). But after the Oslo accord in 1993, President Clinton left calculations to the government of Israel.

Obama administration officials informed the press that the Bush I measures are "not under discussion," and that pressures will be "largely symbolic" (Helene Cooper, *NYT,* June 1). In short, Obama "understands."

The U.S. press reports that, "A partial freeze has been in place for several years, but settlers have found ways around the strictures...construction in the settlements has slowed but never stopped, continuing at an annual rate of about 1,500 to 2,000 units over the past three years. If building continues at the 2008 rate, the 46,500 units already approved will be completed in about 20 years.... If Israel built all the housing units already approved in the nation's overall master plan for settlements, it would almost double the number of settler homes in the West Bank" (Isabel Kirshner, *NYT,* June 2).

The probable source, Peace Now, which monitors settlement activities, estimates that the two largest settlements would double in size.

"Natural population growth" is largely a myth, Israel's leading diplomatic correspondent, Akiva Eldar, points out, citing demographic studies by Col (Ret.) Shaul Arieli, Deputy Military Secretary to Former Prime Minister and incumbent Defense Minister Ehud Barak. Settlement growth consists largely of Israeli immigrants in violation of the Geneva Conventions, assisted with generous subsidies. Much of it is in direct violation of formal government decisions, but carried out with the authorization of the government, specifically Barak, considered a dove in the Israeli spectrum (Eldar, *Ha'aretz*, June 2). Some deride the "long-dormant Palestinian fantasy," revived by Abbas, "that the United States will simply force Israel to make critical concessions, whether or not its democratic government agrees" (Jackson Diehl, *WP*, May 29).

He does not explain whether refusal to participate in Israel's illegal expansion—which, if serious, would "force Israel to make critical concessions"—would be improper interference in Israel's democracy.

Diehl also refers to a recent Olmert peace plan of unprecedented generosity offered to Abbas, which he turned down, though it yielded just about everything to which Palestinians might reasonably aspire. Others have also confidently referred to this mysterious plan and its rejection by Abbas. Efforts to unearth the plan have so far been unavailing. The only sources detected in an assiduous search by David Peterson are comments by Palestinians in the Arab media that appear to be part of internal conflict about power sharing, not the usual source for Western commentators. Eliot Abrams dates the plan to January 2009 (*WP*, April 8, citing unspecified press reports, while also falsifying earlier plans for which records exist—June 3 response to query about his sources).

If there were any truth to this tale, one can be confident that it would be trumpeted by Israeli propaganda and its enthusiasts here as a welcome demonstration that Palestinians simply will not accept peace, even the most moderate of them. It is highly dubious on other grounds. For one thing, Olmert was in no position to offer any credible proposal, having announced his resignation as he was facing indictment for serious corruption charges. The alleged plan is also hard to reconcile with the steady ongoing expansion of settlements under Olmert, vitiating even far less forthcoming offers. Returning to reality, all of these discussions about settlement expansion evade the most crucial issue about settlements —what Israel has already established in the West Bank.

The evasion tacitly concedes that the illegal settlement programs already in place are somehow acceptable (putting aside the Golan

Heights, annexed in violation of Security Council orders)—though the Bush "vision," apparently accepted by Obama, moves from tacit to explicit. What is in place already suffices to ensure that there can be no viable Palestinian self-determination. Hence, there is every indication that even on the unlikely assumption that "natural growth" will be ended, U.S.-Israeli rejectionism will persist, blocking the international consensus as before.It might be different if a legitimate "land swap" were under consideration, a solution approached at Taba and spelled out more fully in the Geneva Accord reached in informal high-level Israel-Palestine negotiations. The Accord was presented in October 2003, welcomed by much of the world, rejected by Israel, and ignored by the U.S.

> Turning to truth, there is a third side, with a decisive role throughout: the U.S. But that participant in the conflict is unmentioned. The omission is understood to be normal and appropriate, hence unmentioned.

There is a "land swap" under consideration, but a radically different one. The ultra-right Israeli leader Avigdor Lieberman, now foreign minister, proposed to reduce the non-Jewish population of Israel by transferring concentrations of Israeli Arabs (specifically, Wadi Ara in the Galilee) to a derisory "Palestinian state"—over the overwhelming opposition of the victims, to be sure. When first advanced, these ideas were denounced as virtually neo-Nazi, which is a little odd. They were first proposed by Democratic Socialist political philosopher Michael Walzer who wrote 30 years before Lieberman that those who are "marginal to the nation" (Palestinians) should be "helped to leave" in the interests of peace and justice. These ideas have now shifted to the political center in Israel, and are praised by *New York Times* Israel correspondent Ethan Bronner, who writes that the left, likes Lieberman's "willingness to create two states, one Jewish, one Palestinian, which would involve yielding areas that are now part of Israel" in a land swap (*NYT,* February 12)—a polite way of saying that Israeli citizens of the wrong ethnicity will be transferred by force from a rich first world country try to "fried chicken."

The Cairo Speech

Obama's June 4 Cairo address to the Muslim world kept pretty much to his well-honed "blank slate" style—saying very little of substance, but in a personable manner that allows listeners to write on the slate what they want to hear. CNN captured its spirit in headlining a report "Obama looks to reach the soul of the Muslim world." Obama had announced the goals of his address in an interview with *NYT* columnist Thomas Friedman (June 3): "'We have a joke around the White House,' the president said. 'We're just going to keep on telling the truth until it stops working—and nowhere is truth-telling more important than the Middle East'." The White House commitment is most welcome, but it is useful to see how it translates into practice.

Obama admonished his audience that it is easy to "point fingers.... But if we see this conflict only from one side or the other, then we will be blind to the truth: the only resolution is for the aspirations of both sides to be met through two states, where Israelis and Palestinians each live in peace and security."

Turning to truth, there is a third side, with a decisive role throughout: the U.S. But that participant in the conflict is unmentioned. The omission is understood to be normal and appropriate, hence unmentioned. Friedman's column is headlined "Obama speech aimed at both Arabs and Israelis." The front-page *Wall Street Journal* report on Obama's speech appears under the heading "Obama Chides Israel, Arabs In His Overture to Muslims."

Other reports are the same. The convention is understandable on the doctrinal principle that though the U.S. government sometimes makes "mistakes," its intentions are by definition benign. Washington has always sought desperately to be an honest broker, only yearning to advance peace and justice. The doctrine trumps truth, of which there is no hint in the speech or the mainstream coverage.

Obama once again echoed Bush's advocacy of two states, without saying what he means by the phrase "Palestinian state." His intentions are clarified not only by crucial omission, but also by his one explicit criticism of Israel: "The United States does not accept the legitimacy of continued Israeli settlements. This construction violates previous agreements and undermines efforts to achieve peace. It is time for these settlements to stop." That is, Israel should live up to Phase I of the 2003 Road Map, though the truth is that Obama has ruled out even steps of the Bush I variety to withdraw from participation in these crimes.

The operative words are "legitimacy" and "continued." By omission, Obama indicates that he accepts Bush's "vision." The vast existing settlement project and infrastructure is "legitimate," thus ensuring that the phrase "Palestinian state" means "fried chicken."

Even-handed, Obama also had an admonition for the Arab States: they "must recognize that the Arab Peace Initiative was an important beginning, but not the end of their responsibilities." Plainly, it cannot be a meaningful "beginning" if Obama continues to reject its core principles: implementation of the international consensus. But to do so is evidently not Washington's "responsibility" in Obama's vision, presumably because the U.S. has no responsibilities other than to persist in its traditional vocation of doing good.

On democracy, Obama said that "we would not presume to pick the outcome of a peaceful election"—as in January 2006, when Washington turned at once to severe punishment of the Palestinians because it did not like the outcome of the peaceful election. Obama politely refrained from comments about his host, President Mubarak, one of the most brutal dictators in the region, though elsewhere he has had some illuminating words about him. As he was about to board the plane to Saudi Arabia and Egypt, the two "moderate" Arab states, "Mr. Obama signaled that while he would mention American concerns about human rights in Egypt, he would not challenge Mr. Mubarak too sharply, calling him a 'force for stability and good' in the Middle East.... Mr. Obama said he did not regard Mr. Mubarak as an authoritarian leader. 'No, I tend not to use labels for folks,' Mr. Obama said. The president noted that there had been criticism 'of the manner in which politics operates in Egypt,' but he also said that Mr. Mubarak had been 'a stalwart ally, in many respects, to the United States'" (Jeff Zeleyna and Michael Slackman, *NYT*, June 4).

On Nuclear Weapons

Obama also had observations on nuclear weapons, a matter of no slight significance in the light of his focus on Iran. Obama repeated his hope for their general abolition and called on all signers of the Non-Proliferation Treaty to abide by the responsibilities it imposes. His comments pointedly excluded Israel, which is not a signer of the NPT, along with India and Pakistan, all of them supported by the U.S. in their development of nuclear weapons—Pakistan under Reagan, India under Bush II. India and Pakistan are now escalating their nuclear weapons programs to a level that is highly threatening (e.g., Jeffrey Smith and Joby Warrick, "Nuclear Aims By Pakistan, India Prompt U.S. Concern," *WP*, May 28, 2009). But our significant role in this confrontation confers no "responsibility."

Some who are placing their hopes in Obama have cited remarks of Assistant Secretary of State Rose Gottemoeller: "Universal adherence to the NPT itself—including by India, Israel, Pakistan and North Korea—also remains a fundamental objective of the United States." But the threat that her comment might mean something was quickly allayed by the report of a senior Israeli diplomat that Israel had received assurances that Obama "will not force Israel to state publicly whether it has nuclear weapons...[but will] stick to a decades-old U.S. policy of 'don't ask, don't tell'." As the Institute for Public Accuracy was quick to remind us, the Bush administration had adopted Gottemoeller's stand, calling for "universal adherence to the Non-Proliferation Treaty (Julian Borger, *Guardian*, May 6, Reuters, May 21).

It appears, then, that "universality" applies to Iran's alleged programs, but not to the actual ones of U.S. allies and clients—not to speak of Washington's own obligations under the NPT.

With regard to Iran's nuclear programs, Obama chose his words carefully. He said that "any nation—including Iran—should have the right to access peaceful nuclear power if it complies with its responsibilities under the nuclear Non-Proliferation Treaty." His words again reiterate the Bush administration's position: it too held that Iran could "access peaceful nuclear power." But the contentious issue has been whether Iran has the rights guaranteed to signers of the NPT under Article IV: "Nothing in this Treaty shall be interpreted as affecting the inalienable right of all the Parties to the Treaty to develop research, production, and use of nuclear energy for peaceful purposes without discrimination and in conformity with Articles I and II of this Treaty," which refer to nuclear weapons.

There is a considerable difference between research and production, as Article IV permits, and "access," which Bush and Obama are willing to permit, meaning access from the outside. That has been the heart of the dispute—and remains so. The Non-aligned Movement, most of the world's states—has forcefully affirmed Iran's position (which is also supported by the majority of Americans). The "international community"—a technical term referring to Washington and whoever happens to agree with it—opposes allowing Iran the rights guaranteed to NPT signers, Obama, by careful choice of misleading words, indicates his continued adherence to this stand.

There is a sensible approach to the threat of nuclear weapons in the region: to join in the overwhelming international support (including a large majority of Americans) for a nuclear-weapons-free zone, including Iran, Israel, and U.S. forces deployed there. Adequate verification is by no means impossible. That should mitigate, if not terminate, the regional nuclear weapons threat. But it is not on the agenda.

It is too easily forgotten that the U.S. is officially committed to establishing a NWFZ in the region, in accord with Security Council Resolution 687 in 1991. This Resolution assumes special significance for the U.S. and UK, because they appealed to it in their half-hearted attempt to provide at least some thin legal basis for their invasion of Iraq. The Resolution calls for elimination of Iraqi WMD and delivery systems, as a step towards "the goal of establishing in the Middle East a zone free from weapons of mass destruction and all missiles for their delivery and the objective of a global ban on chemical weapons" (Article 14). Since that includes Israel, it was never intended seriously by the U.S. and UK and it was quickly dispatched to the memory hole, along with other inconvenient truths that escape the commitment to "keep on telling the truth until it stops working."

It should perhaps be added that despite much fevered rhetoric, rational souls understand that the Iranian threat is not the threat of attack, which would be suicidal. Wayne White, former deputy director of the Near East and South Asia office of State Department intelligence (INR), quite plausibly estimates the likelihood that the Iranian leaders would carry out "some quixotic attack against Israel with a nuclear weapon," thus instantly destroying Iran and themselves, as "down there with that 1 percent possibility." Also timely is his confirmation, from direct knowledge as the INR Iraq intelligence analyst at the time, that Israel's 1981 attack on Iraq's nuclear reactor did not end Saddam's nuclear weapons program, but initiated it. No one wants Iran—or anyone—to develop nuclear weapons, but it should be recognized that the perceived threat is not that they will be used in a suicide mission, but rather the threat of deterrence of U.S.-Israeli actions to extend their domination of the region. If the concern were Iranian nuclear weapons, there would be ways to proceed.

Suspending Rationality

Obama's "new initiative" is spelled out more fully by John Kerry, the 2004 Democratic presidential candidate, then chair of the Senate Foreign Relations Committee, in an important speech at the Brookings Institute on March 9 (kerry.senate.gov/cfm/record). In interpreting Kerry's words, we have to suspend normal rationality, and agree that the actual facts of history are completely irrelevant. What is important is not the contrived picture of past and present, but the plans outlined.

Kerry urges that we acknowledge that our honorable efforts to bring about a political settlement have failed, primarily because of the unwillingness of the Arab states to make peace. Furthermore, all of our efforts "to give the Israelis a legitimate partner for peace" have foundered on Palestinian intransigence. Now, however, there is a welcome change. With the Arab Initiative of 2006, the Arab States have finally signaled their willingness to accept Israel's presence in the region. Even more promising is the "unprecedented willingness among moderate Arab nations to work with Israel" against our common enemy Iran. "Moderate" here is used in its technical meaning: "willing to conform to U.S. demands," irrespective of the nature of the regime. "This re-alignment can help to lay the groundwork for progress towards peace," Kerry said, as we "re-conceptualize" the problem, focusing on the Iranian threat.

Kerry goes on to explain that there is also at last some hope that a "legitimate partner" can be found for our peace-loving Israeli ally: Abbas and the Palestinian Authority. How then do we proceed to support Israel's new legitimate Palestinian partner? "Most importantly, this means strengthening General [Keith] Dayton's efforts to train Palestinian security forces that can keep order and fight terror.... Recent developments have been extremely encouraging. During the invasion of Gaza, Palestinian Security Forces largely succeeded in maintaining calm in the West Bank amidst widespread expectations of civil unrest. Obviously, more remains to be done, but we can help do it."

Routinely, Kerry describes the attack on Gaza as entirely right and just, by definition, since the U.S. crucially participated in it. It doesn't matter, then, that the pretext lacks any credibility, under principles that we all accept—with regard to others.

General Dayton's forces, armed and trained in Jordan with Israeli participation and supervision, are the soft side of population control. The tougher and more brutal forces are those trained by the CIA.

Preventive Security

Kerry is right that we can do more to ensure that West Bank Palestinians are so effectively controlled that they cannot even protest the slaughter in Gaza—let alone move towards meaningful self-determination. For this task, the U.S. can draw on a long history of colonial practice, developed in exquisite detail during the U.S. occupation of the Philippines after the murderous conquest a century ago, then widely applied elsewhere. This sophisticated refinement of traditional imperial practice has been highly successful in U.S. dependencies, while also providing means of population control at home. These matters are spelled out in groundbreaking work by historian Alfred McCoy (*Policing America's Empire*). Kerry should be familiar with these techniques from his service in South Vietnam.

Applying these measures to Palestine, collaborationist paramilitary forces can be employed to subdue the domestic population with the cooperation of privileged elites, granting the U.S. and Israel free rein to carry forward Bush's "vision" and Olmert's Convergence-plus. Gaza can, meanwhile, be kept under a strangling siege as a prison and occasional shooting gallery. Washington's new initiative for Middle East peace, so it is hoped, will integrate Israel among the "moderate" Arab states as a bulwark for U.S. domination of the vital energy-producing regions. It fits well into Obama's broader programs for Afghanistan and Pakistan where military operations are escalating and huge "embassies" are being constructed on the model of the city-within-a-city in Baghdad, clearly signaling Obama's intentions (Saeed Shah and Warren Strobel, *Mc-Clatchy Newspapers*, May 27).

The "re-conceptualization" is evidently satisfactory to U.S. high-tech industry, which continues to enhance its intimate relations with Israel. One striking illustration is a gigantic installation that Intel is constructing in Israel to implement a revolutionary reduction in size of chips, expecting to set a new industry standard and to supply much of the world with parts from its Kiryat Gat facility. Relations between the U.S. and Israeli military industry remain particularly close. Israel continues to provide the U.S. with a strategically located overseas military base for prepositioning weapons and other functions. Intelligence co-operation goes back half a century. These are among the unparalleled services that Israel provides for U.S. militarism and global dominance. They afford Israel a certain leeway to defy Washington's orders—though it is skating on thin ice if it tries to push its luck, as history has repeatedly shown. So far the jingoist extremism of the current government has been constrained by more sober elements: for example, the shelving of the proposals to require a loyalty oath and to prevent citizens from commemorating the Nakba—the disaster for Palestinians in 1948. But if Israel goes too far, there might indeed erupt a confrontation of the kind that many commenta- tors perceive today, so far, with little basis.

21.

Torture Has Been
Routine Practice

Torture is the least of the many crimes of aggression, terror,
subversion, and economic strangulation that have darkened U.S. history

The torture memos released by the White House in April elicited shock, indignation, and surprise. The shock and indignation are understandable—particularly the testimony in the Senate Armed Services Committee report on the Cheney-Rumsfeld desperation to find links between Iraq and al-Qaeda, links that were later concocted as justification for the invasion, facts irrelevant. Former Army psychiatrist Major Charles Burney testified that "a large part of the time we were focused on trying to establish a link between Al Qaeda and Iraq. The more frustrated people got in not being able to establish this link...there was more and more pressure to resort to measures that might produce more immediate results"—that is, torture. The McClatchy press reported that a former senior intelligence official familiar with the interrogation issue added that, "The Bush administration applied relentless pressure on interrogators to use harsh methods on detainees in part to find evidence of cooperation between al Qaida and the late Iraqi dictator Saddam Hussein's regime.... [Cheney and Rumsfeld] demanded that the interrogators find evidence of al Qaida-Iraq collaboration.... 'There was constant pressure on the intelligence agencies and the interrogators to do whatever it took to get that information out of the detainees, especially the few high-value ones we had, and when people kept coming up empty, they were told by Cheney's and Rumsfeld's people to push harder'." These were the most significant revelations, barely reported.

While such testimony about the viciousness and deceit of the Administration should indeed be shocking, the surprise at the general picture revealed is nonetheless surprising. A narrow reason is that even without inquiry, it was reasonable to suppose that Guantanamo was a torture chamber. Why else send prisoners where they would be beyond the reach of the law—incidentally, a place that Washington is using in violation of a treaty that was forced on Cuba at the point of a gun? Security reasons are alleged, but they are hard to take seriously. The same expectations held for secret prisons and rendition, and were fulfilled.

From Z Magazine, June 2009

A broader reason is that torture has been routine practice from the early days of the conquest of the national territory, and then beyond, as the imperial ventures of the "infant empire"—as George Washington called the new Republic—extended to the Philippines, Haiti, and elsewhere. Furthermore, torture is the least of the many crimes of aggression, terror, subversion, and economic strangulation that have darkened U.S. history, much as in the case of other great powers. Accordingly, it is surprising to see the reactions even by some of the most eloquent and forthright critics of Bush malfeasance—for example, that we used to be "a nation of moral ideals" and never before Bush "have our leaders so utterly betrayed everything our nation stands for" (Paul Krugman). To say the least, that common view reflects a rather slanted version of history.

Occasionally the conflict between "what we stand for" and "what we do" has been forthrightly addressed. One distinguished scholar who undertook the task is Hans Morgenthau, a founder of realist international relations theory. In a classic study written in the glow of Camelot, Morgenthau developed the standard view that the U.S. has a "transcendent purpose" of establishing peace and freedom at home and indeed everywhere, since "the arena within which the United States must defend and promote its purpose has become world-wide." But as a scrupulous scholar, he recognized that the historical record is radically inconsistent with the "transcendent purpose" of America.

We should not, however, be misled by that discrepancy, Morgenthau advises. In his words, we should not "confound the abuse of reality with reality itself." Reality is the unachieved "national purpose" revealed by "the evidence of history as our minds reflect it." What actually happened is merely the "abuse of reality." To confound abuse of reality with reality is akin to "the error of atheism, which denies the validity of religion on similar grounds." An apt comparison.

The release of the torture memos led others to recognize the problem. In the *New York Times*, columnist Roger Cohen reviewed a book by British journalist Geoffrey Hodgson, who concludes that the U.S. is "just one great, but imperfect, country among others." Cohen agrees that the evidence supports Hodgson's judgment, but regards it as fundamentally mistaken. The reason is Hodgson's failure to understand that "America was born as an idea, and so it has to carry that idea forward." The American idea is revealed by America's birth as a "city on a hill," an "inspirational notion" that resides "deep in the American psyche"; and by "the distinctive spirit of American individualism and enterprise" demonstrated in the Western expansion. Hodgson's error is that he is keeping to "the distortions of the American idea in recent decades," the "abuse of reality" in recent years.

Legacy

Let us turn to "reality itself" and the "idea" of America from its earliest days. The inspirational phrase "city on a hill" was coined by John Winthrop in 1630, borrowing from the Gospels, and outlining the glorious future of a new nation "ordained by God." One year earlier his Massachusetts Bay Colony established its Great Seal, which depicts an Indian with a scroll coming out of his mouth. On it are the words "Come over and help us." The British colonists were thus benevolent humanists, responding to the pleas of the "miserable" natives to be rescued from their bitter pagan fate.

The Great Seal is a graphic representation of "the idea of America," from its birth. It should be exhumed from the depths of the psyche and displayed on the walls of every classroom. It should certainly appear in the background of all of the Kim Il-Sung-style worship of the savage murderer and torturer Ronald Reagan, who blissfully described himself as the leader of a "shining city on the hill" while orchestrating ghastly crimes and leaving a hideous legacy.

This early proclamation of "humanitarian intervention," to use the currently fashionable phrase, turned out to be very much like its successors, facts that were not obscure to the agents. The first Secretary of War, General Henry Knox, described "the utter extirpation of all the Indians in most populous parts of the Union" by means "more destructive to the Indian natives than the conduct of the conquerors of Mexico and Peru." Long after his own significant contributions to the process were past, John Quincy Adams deplored the fate of "that hapless race of native Americans, which we are exterminating with such merciless and perfidious cruelty...among the heinous sins of this nation, for which I believe God will one day bring [it] to judgment." The merciless and perfidious cruelty continued until "the West was won." Instead of God's judgment, the heinous sins bring only praise for the fulfillment of the American "idea" (Reginald Horsman, *Expansion and American Indian Policy*, Michigan State, 1967; William Earl Weeks, John Quincy Adams and *American Global Empire*, Kentucky, 1992).

There was, to be sure, a more convenient and conventional version, expressed for example by Supreme Court Justice Joseph Story, who mused that "the wisdom of Providence" caused the natives to disappear like "the withered leaves of autumn" even though the colonists had "constantly respected" them (Nicholas Guyatt, *Providence and the Invention of the United States, 1607-1876*, Cambridge, 2007).

The conquest and settling of the West indeed showed individualism and enterprise. Settler-colonialist enterprises, the cruelest form of imperialism, commonly do. The outcome was hailed by the respected and influential Senator Henry Cabot Lodge in 1898. Calling for intervention in Cuba, Lodge lauded our record "of conquest, colonization, and territorial expansion unequalled by any people in the 19th century" and urged that it is "not to be curbed now," as the Cubans too are pleading with us to come over and help them (cited by Lars Schoultz, *That Infernal Little Cuban Republic*). Their plea was answered. The U.S. sent troops, thereby preventing Cuba's liberation from Spain and turning it into a virtual colony, as it remained until 1959. The "American idea" is illustrated further by a remarkable campaign, initiated virtually at once to restore Cuba to its proper place economic warfare with the clearly articulated aim of punishing the population. There are to be sure critics who hold that our efforts to bring democracy to Cuba have failed, so we should turn to other ways to "come over and help them." How do these critics know that the goal was to bring democracy? There is evidence: our leaders proclaim it. There is also counter-evidence, i.e. the declassified internal record, but that can be dismissed as just "the abuse of history."

American imperialism is often traced to the takeover of Cuba, Puerto Rico, and Hawaii in 1898. But that is to succumb to what historian of imperialism Bernard Porter calls "the salt water fallacy," the idea that conquest only becomes imperialism when it crosses salt water. Thus, if the Mississippi had resembled the Irish Sea, Western expansion would have been imperialism. From Washington to Lodge, those engaged in the enterprise had a clearer grasp.

After the success of "humanitarian intervention" in Cuba in 1898, the next step in the mission assigned by Providence was to confer "the blessings of liberty and civilization on all the rescued peoples" of the Philippines (in the words of the platform of Lodge's Republican Party)—at least those who survived the murderous onslaught and large-scale torture and other atrocities that accompanied it. These fortunate souls were left to the mercies of the U.S.-established Philippine constabulary within a newly devised model of colonial domination, relying on security forces trained and equipped for sophisticated modes of surveillance, intimidation, and violence (Alfred McCoy, *Policing America's Empire*, 2009). Similar models were adopted in many other areas where the U.S. imposed brutal National Guards and other client forces, with consequences that should be well-known.

In the past 60 years, victims worldwide have also endured the CIA's "torture paradigm," developed at a cost reaching $1 billion annually, according to historian Alfred McCoy, who shows that the methods surfaced with little change in Abu Ghraib. There is no hyperbole when Jennifer Harbury entitles her penetrating study of U.S. torture, *Truth, Torture, and the American Way*.

It is misleading, to say the least, when investigators of the Bush gang's descent into the sewer lament that, "in waging the war against terrorism, America had lost its way" (McCoy, *A Question of Torture*, 2006; also McCoy, "The U.S. Has a History of Using Torture," Jane Mayer, "The Battle for a Country's Soul," *New York Review of Books*, August 14, 2008).

Innovations & Paradigms

Bush-Cheney-Rumsfeld et al. did introduce important innovations. Ordinarily, torture is farmed out to subsidiaries, not carried out by Americans directly in their government-established torture chambers. Alain Nairn, who has conducted some of the most revealing and courageous investigations of torture, points out that "What the Obama [ban on torture] ostensibly knocks off is that small percentage of torture now done by Americans while retaining the overwhelming bulk of the system's torture, which is done by foreigners, under U.S. patronage. Obama could stop backing foreign forces that torture, but he has chosen not to do so." Obama did not shut down the practice of torture, Nairn observes, but "merely repositioned it," restoring it to the norm, a matter of indifference to the victims. Since Vietnam, "the U.S. has mainly seen its torture done for it by proxy—paying, arming, training, and guiding foreigners doing it, but usually being careful to keep Americans at least one discreet step removed." Obama's ban "doesn't even prohibit direct torture by Americans outside environments of 'armed conflict,' which is where much torture happens anyway....[H]is is a return to the status quo ante, the torture regime of Ford through Clinton, which, year by year, often produced more U.S.-backed strapped-down agony than was produced during the Bush/Cheney years" (*News and Comment*, January 24,

2009, www.allannairn.com). Sometimes engagement in torture is more indirect. In a 1980 study, Latin Americanist Lars Schoultz found that U.S. aid "has tended to flow disproportionately to Latin American governments which torture their citizens...to the hemisphere's relatively egregious violators of fundamental human rights."

That includes military aid, is independent of need, and runs through the Carter years. Broader studies by Edward Herman found the same correlation and also suggested an explanation. Not surprisingly, U.S. aid tends to correlate with a favorable climate for business operations and this is commonly improved by murder of labor and peasant organizers and human rights activists, and other such actions, yielding a secondary correlation between aid and egregious violation of human rights (Schoultz, *Comparative Politics*, January 1981; Herman, in Chomsky and Herman, *Political Economy of Human Rights I*, South End, 1979; Herman, *Real Terror Network*, 1982).

These studies precede the Reagan years, when the topic was not worth studying because the correlations were so clear. And the tendencies continued to the present. Small wonder that the president advises us to look forward, not backward—a convenient doctrine for those who hold the clubs. Those who are beaten by them tend to see the world differently, much to our annoyance.

An argument can be made that implementation of the CIA's "torture paradigm" does not violate the 1984 Torture Convention, at least as Washington interprets it. Alfred McCoy points out that the highly sophisticated CIA paradigm, based on the "KGB's most devastating torture technique," keeps primarily to mental torture, not crude physical torture, which is considered less effective in turning people into pliant vegetables. McCoy writes that the Reagan administration carefully revised the international Torture Convention "with four detailed diplomatic 'reservations' focused on just one word in the convention's 26 printed pages"—the word "mental." "[T]hese intricately-constructed diplomatic reservations re-defined torture, as interpreted by the United States, to exclude sensory deprivation and self-inflicted pain—the very techniques the CIA had refined at such great cost."

When Clinton sent the UN Convention to Congress for ratification in 1994, he included the Reagan reservations. The president and Congress, therefore, exempted the core of the CIA torture paradigm from the U.S. interpretation of the Torture Convention. Those reservations, McCoy observes, were "reproduced verbatim in domestic legislation enacted to give legal force to the UN Convention." That is the "political land mine" that "detonated with such phenomenal force" in the Abu Ghraib scandal and in the shameful Military Commissions Act passed with bipartisan support in 2006.

Accordingly, after the first exposure of Washington's latest resort to torture, constitutional law professor Sanford Levinson observed that it could perhaps be justified in terms of the "interrogator-friendly" definition of torture adopted by Reagan and Clinton in their revision of international human rights law (McCoy, "US has a history"; Levinson, "Torture in Iraq & the Rule of Law in America," Daedalus, Summer 2004).

Bush/Obama & The Courts

Bush went beyond his predecessors in authorizing prima facie violations of international law and several of his extremist innovations were struck down by the Courts. While Obama, like Bush, affirms our unwavering commitment to international law, he seems intent on substantially reinstating the extremist Bush measures. In the important case of *Boumediene v. Bush* in June 2008, the Supreme Court rejected as unconstitutional the Bush administration claim that prisoners in Guantanamo are not entitled to the right of habeas corpus.

Glenn Greenwald reviews the aftermath. Seeking to "preserve the power to abduct people from around the world" and imprison them without due process, the Bush administration decided to ship them to Bagram, treating "the *Boumediene* ruling, grounded in our most basic constitutional guarantees, as though it was some sort of a silly game—fly your abducted prisoners to Guantanamo and they have constitutional rights, but fly them instead to Bagram and you can disappear them forever with no judicial process." Obama adopted the Bush position, "filing a brief in federal court that, in two sentences, declared that it embraced the most extremist Bush theory on this issue," arguing that prisoners flown to Bagram from anywhere in the world —in the case in question, Yemenis and Tunisians captured in Thailand and the UAE"—can be imprisoned indefinitely with no rights of any kind—as long as they are kept in Bagram rather than Guantanamo."

In March, a Bush-appointed federal judge "rejected the Bush/Obama position and held that the rationale of *Boumediene* applies every bit as much to Bagram as it does to Guantanamo." The Obama administration announced that it would appeal the ruling, thus placing Obama's Department of Justice "squarely to the right of an extremely conservative, pro-executive-power, Bush 43-appointed judge on issues of executive power and due-process-less detentions," in radical violation of Obama's campaign promises and earlier stands.

The case of *Rasul v Rumsfeld* appears to be following a similar trajectory. The plaintiffs charged that Rumsfeld and other high officials were responsible for their torture in Guantanamo, where they were sent after they were captured by Uzbeki warlord Rashid Dostum. Dostum is a notorious thug who was then a leader of the Northern Alliance, the Afghan faction supported by Russia, Iran, India, Turkey, and the Central Asian states, joined by the U.S. as it attacked Afghanistan in October 2001. Dostum then turned them over to U.S. custody, allegedly for bounty money.

The plaintiffs claimed that they had traveled to Afghanistan to offer humanitarian relief. The Bush administration sought to have the case dismissed. Obama's Department of Justice filed a brief supporting the Bush position that government officials are not liable for torture and other violations of due process, because the Courts had not yet clearly established the rights that prisoners enjoy (Daphne Eviatar, "Obama Justice Department Urges Dismissal of Another Torture Case," *Washington Independent*, March 12, 2009).

It is also reported that Obama intends to revive military commissions, one of the more severe violations of the rule of law during the Bush years. There is a reason. "Officials who work on the Guantánamo issue say administration lawyers have become concerned that they would face significant obstacles to trying some terrorism suspects in federal courts. Judges might make it difficult to prosecute detainees who were subjected to brutal treatment or for prosecutors to use hearsay evidence gathered by intelligence agencies" (William Glaberson, "U.S. May Revive Guantanamo Military Courts," *New York Times,* May 1, 2009). A serious flaw in the criminal justice system, it appears.

There is much debate about whether torture has been effective in eliciting information—the assumption being, apparently, that if it is effective then it may be justified. By the same argument, when Nicaragua captured U.S. pilot Eugene Hasenfus in 1986 after shooting down his plane delivering aid to Reagan's contra forces, they should not have tried him, found him guilty, and then sent him back to the U.S., as they did. Rather, they should have applied the CIA torture paradigm to try to extract information about other terrorist atrocities being planned and implemented in Washington, no small matter for a tiny and poor country under terrorist attack by the global superpower. And Nicaragua should certainly have done the same if they had been able to capture the chief terrorism coordinator, John Negroponte, then ambassador in Honduras, later appointed counter-terrorism Czar, without eliciting a murmur. Cuba should have done the same if they had been able to lay hands on the Kennedy brothers. There is no need to bring up what victims should have done to Kissinger, Reagan, and other leading terrorist commanders, whose exploits leave al-Qaeda far in the distance, and who doubtless had ample information that could have prevented further "ticking bombs."

Such considerations, which abound, never seem to arise in public discussion. Accordingly, we know at once how to evaluate the pleas about valuable information.

Torturer's Cost-Benefit Analysis

There is, to be sure, a response: our terrorism, even if surely terrorism, is benign, deriving as it does from the city on the hill. Perhaps the most eloquent exposition of this thesis was presented by *New Republic* editor Michael Kinsley, a respected spokesperson of "the left." America's Watch (Human Rights Watch) had protested State Department confirmation of official orders to Washington's terrorist forces to attack "soft targets"—undefended civilian targets—and to avoid the Nicaraguan army, as they could do thanks to CIA control of Nicaraguan airspace and the sophisticated communications systems provided to the contras. In response, Kinsley explained that U.S. terrorist attacks on civilian targets are justified if they satisfy pragmatic criteria: a "sensible policy [should] meet the test of cost-benefit analysis," an analysis of "the amount of blood and misery that will be poured in, and the likelihood that democracy will emerge at the other end"—"democracy" as U.S. elites determine (*Wall Street Journal*, March 26, 1987).

His thoughts elicited no comment, to my knowledge, apparently deemed acceptable. It would seem to follow, then, that U.S. leaders and their agents are not culpable for conducting such sensible policies in good faith, even if their judgment might sometimes be flawed.

Perhaps culpability would be greater, by prevailing moral standards, if it were discovered that Bush administration torture cost American lives. That is, in fact, the conclusion drawn by U.S. Major Matthew Alexander [pseudonym], one of the most seasoned interrogators in Iraq, who elicited "the information that led to the U.S. military being able to locate Abu Musab al-Zarqawi, the head of al-Qa'ida in Iraq," correspondent Patrick Cockburn reports. Alexander expresses only contempt for the harsh interrogation methods: "The use of torture by the US," he believes, not only elicits no useful information, but "has proved so counter-productive that it may have led to the death of as many U.S. soldiers as civilians killed in 9/11." From hundreds of interrogations, Alexander discovered that foreign fighters came to Iraq in reaction to the abuses at Guantanamo and Abu Ghraib, and that they and domestic allies turned to suicide bombing and other terrorist acts for the same reason (Cockburn, "Torture? It probably killed more Americans than 9/11," *Independent*, April 6, 2009).

Another standard pretext for torture is the context of the "war on terror" that Bush declared after 9/11, a "crime against humanity" carried out with "wickedness and awesome cruelty," as Robert Fisk reported. That crime rendered traditional international law "quaint" and "obsolete," Bush was advised by his legal counsel Alberto Gonzales, later appointed attorney general. The doctrine has been widely reiterated in one or another form in commentary and analysis.

The 9/11 attack was doubtless unique, in many respects. One was where the guns were pointing. Typically it is in the opposite direction. In fact, that was the first attack of any consequence on the national territory since the British burned down Washington in 1814. Another unique feature was the scale of terror by a non-state actor. But horrifying as it was, it could have been worse. Suppose that the perpetrators had bombed the White House, killed the president, and established a vicious military dictatorship that killed 50,000-100,000 people and tortured 700,000, set up a huge international terror center that carried out assassinations, helped impose comparable military dictatorships else-

where, and implemented economic doctrines that destroyed the economy so radically that the state had to virtually take it over a few years later. That would have been a lot worse than 9/11.

And it happened, in what Latin Americans often call "the first 9/11," in 1973. The numbers have been changed to per capita equivalents, a realistic way of measuring crimes. Responsibility traces straight back to Washington. Accordingly, the—quite appropriate—analogy is out of consciousness, while the facts are consigned to the "abuse of reality" that the naïve call history.

It should also be recalled that Bush did not declare the "war on terror," he re-declared it. Twenty years earlier, the Reagan administration came into office declaring that a centerpiece of its foreign policy would be a war on terror, "the plague of the modern age" and "a return to barbarism in our time," to sample the fevered rhetoric of the day. That war on terror has also been deleted from historical consciousness because the outcome cannot readily be incorporated in the canon. Hundreds of thousands were slaughtered in the ruined countries of Central America and many more elsewhere—among them an estimated 1.5 million in the terrorist wars sponsored in neighboring countries by Reagan's favored ally apartheid South Africa, which had to defend itself from Nelson Mandela's African National Congress, one of the world's "more notorious terrorist groups," Washington determined in 1988. In fairness, it should be added that 20 years later Congress voted to remove the ANC from the list of terrorist organizations, so that Mandela is now at last able to enter the U.S. without obtaining a waiver from the government (Joseba Zulaika and William Douglass, *Terror and Taboo,* 1996; Jesse Holland, AP, May 9, 2009, *NYT*).

Exceptionalism & Amnesia

The reigning doctrine is sometimes called "American exceptionalism." It is nothing of the sort. It is probably close to universal among imperial powers. France was hailing its "civilizing mission" while the French Minister of War called for "exterminating the indigenous population" of Algeria. Britain's nobility was a "novelty in the world," John Stuart Mill declared, while urging that this angelic power delay no longer in completing its liberation of India. This classic essay on humanitarian intervention was written shortly after the public revelation of Britain's horrifying atrocities in suppressing the 1857 Indian rebellion. The conquest of the rest of India was in large part an effort to gain a monopoly of opium for Britain's huge narco-trafficking enterprise, by far the largest in world history, designed primarily to compel China to accept Britain's manufactured goods. Similarly, there is no reason to doubt the sincerity of Japanese militarists who were bringing an "earthly paradise" to China under benign Japanese tutelage, as they carried out the rape of Nanking. History is replete with similar "glorious" episodes. As long as such "exceptionalist" theses remain firmly implanted, the occasional revelations of the "abuse of history" can backfire, serving to efface terrible crimes. The My Lai massacre was a mere footnote to the vastly greater atrocities of the post-Tet pacification programs, ignored while indignation focused on this single crime. Watergate was doubtless criminal, but the furor over it displaced incomparably worse crimes at home and abroad—the FBI-organized assassination of black organizer Fred Hampton as part of the infamous COINTELPRO repression or the bombing of Cambodia, to mention two egregious examples. Torture is hideous enough, but the invasion of Iraq is a far worse crime. Quite commonly, selective atrocities have this function.

Historical amnesia is a dangerous phenomenon, not only because it undermines moral and intellectual integrity, but also because it establishes the groundwork for crimes that lie ahead.

22.

Obama on Israel-Palestine

Undermining a peaceful settlement with carefully framed deceit

Barack Obama is recognized to be a person of acute intelligence, a legal scholar, careful with his choice of words. He deserves to be taken seriously—both what he says and what he omits. Particularly significant was his first substantive statement on foreign affairs, on January 22 at the State Department, when introducing George Mitchell to serve as his special envoy for Middle East peace. Mitchell is to focus his attention on the Israel-Palestine "problem" in the wake of the recent U.S.-Israeli invasion of Gaza. During the murderous assault, Obama remained silent, apart from a few platitudes, because, he said, there is only one president—a fact that did not silence him on many other issues. His campaign did, however, repeat his statement that, "If missiles were falling where my two daughters sleep, I would do everything in order to stop that." He was referring to Israeli children, not the hundreds of Palestinian children being butchered by U.S. arms, about whom he could not speak because there was only one president.

On January 22, however, the one president was Barack Obama, so he could speak freely about these matters, avoiding, however, the attack on Gaza, which had, conveniently, been called off just before the inauguration. Obama's talk emphasized his commitment to a peaceful settlement. He left its contours vague, apart from one specific proposal: "The Arab peace initiative," Obama said, "contains constructive elements that could help advance these efforts. Now is the time for Arab states to act on the initiative's promise by supporting the Palestinian government under President Abbas and Prime Minister Fayyad, taking steps towards normalizing relations with Israel, and by standing up to extremism that threatens us all." Obama was not directly falsifying the Arab League proposal, but the carefully framed deceit was instructive. The Arab League peace proposal does indeed call for normalization of relations with Israel in the context—repeat, in the context—of a two-state settlement in terms of the longstanding international consensus, which the U.S. and Israel have blocked for over 30 years, in international isolation, and still do. The core of the Arab League proposal, as Obama and his Mideast advisers know very well, is its call for a peaceful political settlement in these terms, which are well-known, and recognized to be the only basis for the peaceful settlement to which Obama professes to be committed. The omission of that crucial fact can hardly be accidental and signals clearly that Obama envisions no departure from U.S. rejectionism. His call for the Arab states to act on a corollary to their proposal, while the U.S. ignores even the existence of its

From Z Magazine, March 2009

central content, which is the pre-condition for the corollary, surpasses cynicism.

The most significant acts to undermine a peaceful settlement are the daily U.S.-backed actions in the occupied territories, all recognized to be criminal: taking over valuable land and resources and constructing what the leading architect of the plan, Ariel Sharon, called "Bantustans" for Palestinians—an unfair comparison because the Bantustans were far more viable than the fragments left to Palestinians under Sharon's conception, now being realized. But the U.S. and Israel continue to oppose a political settlement in words, most recently in December 2008, when the U.S. and Israel (and a few Pacific islands) voted against a UN resolution supporting "the right of the Palestinian people to self-determination" (passed 173 to 5, U.S.-Israel opposed, with evasive pretexts).

Obama had not one word to say about the settlement and infrastructure developments in the West Bank and the complex measures to control Palestinian existence, designed to undermine the prospects for a peaceful two-state settlement. His silence is a grim refutation of his oratorical flourishes about how "I will sustain an active commitment to seek two states living side by side in peace and security."

Also unmentioned is Israel's use of U.S. arms in Gaza, in violation not only of international, but also U.S. law. Or Washington's shipment of new arms to Israel right at the peak of the U.S.-Israeli attack, surely not unknown to Obama's Middle East advisers. Obama was firm, however, that smuggling of arms to Gaza must be stopped. He endorses the agreement of Condoleezza Rice and Israeli foreign minister Tzipi Livni that the Egyptian-Gaza border must be closed—a remarkable exercise of imperial arrogance. The *Financial Times* observed, "As they stood in Washington congratulating each other, both officials seemed oblivious to the fact that they were making a deal about an illegal trade on someone else's border—Egypt in this case. The next day, an Egyptian official described the memorandum as 'fictional'." Egypt's objections were ignored.

Returning to Obama's reference to the "constructive" Arab League proposal, as the wording indicates, Obama persists in restricting support to the defeated party in the January 2006 Palestinian election, the only free election in the Arab world to which the U.S. and Israel reacted, instantly and overtly, by severely punishing Palestinians for opposing the will of the masters. A minor technicality is that Abbas's term ran out on January 9 and that Fayyad was appointed without confirmation by the Palestinian parliament (many of them kidnapped and in Israeli prisons). *Ha'aretz* describes Fayyad as "a strange bird in Palestinian politics. On the one hand, he is the Palestinian politician most esteemed by Israel and the West.

However, on the other hand, he has no electoral power whatsoever in Gaza or the West Bank." The report also notes Fayyad's "close relationship with the Israeli establishment," notably his friendship with Sharon's extremist adviser Dov Weisglass. Though lacking popular support, he is regarded as competent and honest, the latter attributes not the norm in the U.S.-backed political sectors. Obama's insistence that only Abbas and Fayyad exist conforms to the consistent Western contempt for democracy unless it is under control. Obama provided the usual reasons for ignoring the elected government led by Hamas. "To be a genuine party to peace," Obama declared, "the quartet [U.S., EU, Russia, UN] has made it clear that Hamas must meet clear conditions:

- recognize Israel's right to exist

- renounce violence

- abide by past agreements

Unmentioned, as usual, is the inconvenient fact that the U.S. and Israel firmly reject all three conditions. In international isolation, they bar a two-state settlement including a Palestinian state. They, of course, do not renounce violence and they reject the quartet's central proposal, the "road map." Israel formally accepted it, but with 14 reservations that effectively eliminate its contents (tacitly backed by the U.S.). It is the great merit of Jimmy Carter's *Palestine: Peace not Apartheid*, to have brought these facts to public attention for the first time—and in the mainstream, the only time. It follows, by elementary reasoning, that neither the U.S. nor Israel is a "genuine party to peace." But that cannot be. It is not even a phrase in the English language.

It is perhaps unfair to criticize Obama for this further exercise of cynicism because it is close to universal, unlike his scrupulous evisceration of the core component of the Arab League proposal, which is his own novel contribution.

Omitted are the inconvenient facts that the U.S.-Israel are not only dedicated to the destruction of any viable Palestinian state, but are steadily implementing those policies. Or that, unlike the two rejectionist states, Hamas has called for a two-state settlement in terms of the international consensus—publicly, repeatedly, explicitly.

Obama began his remarks by saying: "Let me be clear, America is committed to Israel's security. And we will always support Israel's right to defend itself against legitimate threats." There was nothing about the right of Palestinians to defend themselves against far more extreme threats, such as those occurring daily, with U.S. support, in the occupied territories. But that again is the norm. Also normal is the enunciation of the principle that Israel has the right to defend itself. That is correct, but vacuous: so does everyone. But in the context, the cliché is worse than vacuous. It is more cynical deceit. The issue is not whether Israel has the right to defend itself, like everyone else, but whether it has the right to do so by force. No one, including Obama, believes that states enjoy a general right to defend themselves by force. It is first necessary to demonstrate that there are no peaceful alternatives that can be tried. In this case, there surely are. A narrow alternative would be for Israel to abide by a ceasefire, for example, the ceasefire proposed by Hamas political leader Khaled Mishal a few days before Israel launched its attack on December 27. Mishal called for restoring the 2005 agreement. That agreement

called for an end to violence and uninterrupted opening of the borders, along with an Israeli guarantee that goods and people could move freely between the two parts of occupied Palestine, the West Bank, and the Gaza Strip. The agreement was rejected by the U.S. and Israel a few months later after the free election of January 2006 turned out "the wrong way."

The broader and more significant alternative would be for the U.S. and Israel to abandon their extreme rejectionism and join the rest of the world—including the Arab states and Hamas —in supporting a two-state settlement in accord with the international consensus. It should be noted that in the past 30 years there has been one departure from U.S.-Israeli rejectionism. The negotiations at Taba in January 2001, appeared to be close to a peaceful resolution when Israel prematurely called them off. It would not, then, be outlandish for Obama to agree to join the world, even within the framework of U.S. policy, if he were interested in doing so.

In short, Obama's forceful reiteration of Israel's right to defend itself is another exercise of cynical deceit—though not unique to him. The deceit is particularly striking in this case because the occasion was the appointment of Mitchell as special envoy. Mitchell's primary achievement was his leading role in the peaceful settlement in Northern Ireland. It called for an end to IRA terror and British violence. Implicit is the recognition that, while Britain had the right to defend itself from terror, it had no right to do so by force because there was a peaceful alternative: recognition of the legitimate grievances of the Irish Catholic community that were the roots of IRA terror. When Britain adopted that course, the terror ended. The implications for Mitchell's mission with regard to Israel-Palestine are so obvious that they need not be spelled out. Obama also praised Jordan for its "constructive role in training Palestinian security forces and nurturing its relations with Israel"—which contrasts strikingly with U.S.-Israeli refusal to deal with the freely elected government of Palestine, while savagely punishing Palestinians for electing it with pretexts which, as noted, do not withstand a moment's scrutiny. It is true that Jordan joined the U.S. in arming and training Palestinian security forces so that they could violently suppress any manifestation of support for the miserable victims of the U.S.-Israeli assault in Gaza, also arresting supporters of Hamas and the prominent journalist Khaled Amayreh, while organizing their own demonstrations in support of Abbas and Fatah, in which most participants "were civil servants and school children who were instructed by the PA to attend the rally," according to the *Jerusalem Post.* Our kind of democracy. Obama made one further substantive comment: "As part of a lasting cease-fire, Gaza's border crossings should be open to allow the flow of aid and commerce, with an appropriate monitoring regime...." He did not, of course, mention that U.S.-Israel had rejected much the same agreement after the January 2006 election and that Israel had never observed similar subsequent agreements on borders.

Also missing is any reaction to Israel's announcement that it rejected the ceasefire agreement. As reported at once in the press, "Israeli Cabinet Minister Binyamin Ben-Eliezer, who takes part in security deliberations, told Army Radio that Israel wouldn't let border crossings with Gaza reopen without a deal to free [Gilad] Schalit" (AP, January 22); "Israel to keep Gaza crossings closed.... An official said the government planned to use the issue to bargain for the release of Gilad Shalit, the Israeli soldier held by the Islamist group since 2006" (*Financial Times*, January 23); "Earlier this week, Israeli Foreign Minister Tzipi Livni said that progress on Corporal Shalit's release would be a precondition to opening border crossings that have been mostly closed since Hamas wrested control of Gaza from the West Bank- based Palestinian Authority in 2007" (*Christian Science Monitor*, January 23); "an Israeli official said there would be tough conditions for any lifting of the blockade, which he linked with the release of Gilad Shalit" (*FT*,

January 23), among many others. Shalit's capture is a prominent issue in the West, another indication of Hamas's criminality. Whatever one thinks about it, it is uncontroversial that the capture of a soldier of an attacking army is far less of a crime than kidnapping of civilians, exactly what Israeli forces did the day before the capture of Shalit, invading Gaza city and kidnapping two brothers, then spiriting them across the border where they disappeared into Israel's prison complex. Unlike the much lesser case of Shalit, that crime was virtually unreported and has been forgotten, along with Israel's regular practice for decades of kidnapping civilians in Lebanon and on the high seas and dispatching them to Israeli prisons, often held for many years as hostages. But the capture of Shalit bars a ceasefire. Obama's State Department talk about the Middle East continued with "the deteriorating situation in Afghanistan and Pakistan...the central front in our enduring struggle against terrorism and extremism."

A few hours later, U.S. planes attacked a remote village in Afghanistan, intending to kill a Taliban commander. "Village elders, though, told provincial officials there were no Taliban in the area, which they described as a hamlet populated mainly by shepherds. Women and children were among the 22 dead, they said, according to Hamididan Abdul Rahmzai, the head of the provincial council" (*LA Times*, January 24). Afghan president Karzai's first message to Obama after he was elected in November was a plea to end the bombing of Afghan civilians, reiterated a few hours before Obama was sworn in. This was considered as significant as Karzai's call for a timetable for departure of U.S. and other foreign forces. The rich and powerful have their "responsibilities." Among them, the *New York Times* reported, is to "provide security" in southern Afghanistan, where "the insurgency is homegrown and self-sustaining."

23.

Elections 2000 and 2008

Neither election took the concept of democracy seriously

The most striking fact about the November 2000 elections is that they were a statistical tie (for Congress as well, virtually). The most interesting question is what this shows, if anything, about the state of functioning democracy. For many commentators, the fact that the presidency "is hinging on a few hundred votes" reveals the extraordinary health and vigor of American democracy (former State Department spokesperson James Rubin). An alternative interpretation is that it confirms the conclusion that there was no election in any sense that takes the concept of democracy seriously.

Under what conditions would we expect 100 million votes to divide 50-50, with variations that fall well within expected margins of error of 1-2 percent? There is a very simple model that would yield such expectations—people were voting at random. If tens of millions of votes were cast for X vs. Y as president of Mars, such results would be expected. To the extent that the simplest model is valid, the elections did not take place.

Of course, more complex models can be constructed and we know that the simplest one is not strictly valid. Voting blocs can be identified and sometimes the reasons for choices can be discerned. It's understandable that financial services should overwhelmingly support Bush, whose announced plans included huge gifts of public resources to the industry and even more commitment than his opponent to the demolition of quasi-democratic institutions (Social Security in particular). And it is no surprise that affluent white voters favored Bush while union members, Latinos, and African-Americans opposed him ("supported Gore," in conventional terminology).

But blocs are not always easy to explain in terms of interest-based voting and it is well to remember that voting is often consciously against interest. For example, in 1984 Reagan ran as a "real conservative," winning what was called a "landslide victory" (with under 30 percent of the electoral vote) and a large majority of voters opposed his legislative program, and 4 percent of his supporters identified themselves as "real conservatives." Such outcomes are not too surprising when over 80 percent of the population feels that the government is "run for the benefit of the few and the special interests, not the people," up from about half

From Z Magazine, January 2001; February 2009

in earlier years. When similar numbers feel that the economic system is "inherently unfair" and working people have too little say, and that "there is too much power concentrated in the hands of large companies for the good of the nation." Under such circumstances, people may tend to vote (if at all) on grounds that are irrelevant to policy choices over which they feel they have little influence. Such tendencies are strengthened by intense media/advertising concentration on style, personality, and other irrelevancies (in the presidential debates. Will Bush remember where Canada is?; Will Gore remind people of some unpleasant know-it-all in 4th grade?).

Public opinion studies lend further credibility to the simplest model. Harvard's Vanishing Voter Project has been monitoring attitudes through the presidential campaign. Its director, Thomas Patterson, reports that "Americans' feeling of powerlessness has reached an alarming high," with 53 percent responding "only a little" or "none" to the question: "How much influence do you think people like you have on what government does?" The previous peak, 30 years ago, was 41 percent. During the campaign, over 60 percent of regular voters regarded politics in America as "generally pretty disgusting."

In each weekly survey, more people found the campaign boring than exciting, by a margin of 48 to 28 percent in the final week. Three-fourths of the population regarded the whole process as largely a game played by large contributors (overwhelmingly corporations), party leaders, and the PR industry, which crafted candidates to say "almost anything to get themselves elected," so that one could believe little that they said even when their stand on issues was intelligible.

On almost all issues, citizens could not identify the stands of the candidates—not because they are stupid or not trying. It is, then, not unreasonable to suppose that the simplest model is a pretty fair first approximation to the truth about the election and that the country is being driven even more than before towards the condition described by former President Alfonso

Lopez Michaelsen of Colombia, referring to his own country as a political system of power sharing by parties that are "two horses with the same owner." Furthermore, that seems to be general popular understanding.On the side, perhaps the similarities help us understand Clinton's great admiration and praise for Colombian democracy and for the grotesque social and economic system kept in place by violence.

The fact that after a decade in which Colombia was the leading recipient of U.S. arms and military training in the hemisphere—and the leading human rights violator, in conformity with a well-established correlation—it attained first place worldwide in 1999, with a huge further increase now in progress (Israel-Egypt are a separate category).

When an election is a largely meaningless statistical tie and a victor has to be selected somehow, the rational procedure would be some arbitrary choice, say, flipping a coin. But that is unacceptable. It is necessary to invest the process of selecting our leader with appropriate majesty, an effort conducted for five weeks of intense elite dedication to the task, with limited success, it appears.

The five weeks of passionate effort were not a complete waste. They did contribute to exposing racist bias in practices in Florida and elsewhere —which probably have a considerable element of class bias, concealed by the standard refusal in U.S. commentary to admit that class structure exists, and the race-class correlations.

There was also at least some slight attention to a numerically far more significant factor than the ugly harassment of black voters, electoral chicanery, and disenfranchisement through incarceration. The day after the election, Human Rights Watch issued a (barely-noted) study reporting that the "decisive" element in the Florida election was the exclusion of 31 percent of African American men, either in prison or among the more than 400,000 "ex-offenders" permanently disenfranchised. HRW estimates than "more than 200,000 potential black voters [were] excluded from the polls." Since they overwhelmingly vote Democratic, that "decisively" changed the outcome. The numbers overwhelm those debated in the intense scrutiny over marginal technical issues (dimpled chads, etc.). The same was true of other swing states. In seven states, HRW reported, "one in four black men is permanently barred" from voting; "almost every state in the U.S. denies prisoners the right to vote" and "fourteen states bar criminal offenders from voting even after they have finished their sentences," permanently disenfranchising "over one million ex-offenders." These are African American and Latino out of any relation to proportion of the population, or even to what is called "crime." "More than 13 percent of black men (some 1.4 million nationwide) are disenfranchised for many years, sometimes for life, a result of felony convictions, many for passing the same drugs that Al Gore smoked and George W. snorted in years gone by," University of New Mexico Law Professor Tim Canova writes.

The few reports in the mainstream U.S. press noted that the political implications are highly significant, drawing votes away from Democratic candidates. The numbers are large. In Alabama and Florida, over 6 percent of potential voters were excluded because of felony records; "for blacks in Alabama, the rate is 12.4 percent and in Florida 13.8 percent"; "In five other states—Iowa, Mississippi, New Mexico, Virginia and Wyoming—felony disenfranchisement laws affected one in four black men" (*NY Times*, November 3, citing human rights and academic studies).

The academic researchers, sociologists Jeff Manza (Northwestern), and Christopher Uggen (Minnesota), conclude that "were it not for disenfranchised felons, the Democrats would still have control of the U.S. Senate. If the Bush-Gore election turns out to be as close as the Kennedy-Nixon election, and Bush squeaks through, we may be able to attribute that to felon disenfranchisement."

Re-examining close Senate elections since 1978, they conclude further that "the felon vote could have reversed Republican victories in Virginia, Texas, Georgia, Kentucky, Florida, and Wyoming, and prevented the Republican takeover" (*Los Angeles Times*, September 8). Citing the same studies, the *Santa Fe New Mexican* (November 19) pointed out that 5.5 percent of potential voters in New Mexico—where the election was also a statistical tie—were disenfranchised by felony convictions.

"As many as 45 percent of black males in the state can't vote—the highest ratio in the country," though the total figures are not as dramatic as Florida. Figures were not available for Hispanics, who constitute 60 percent of the state's prisoners (and about 40 percent of the estimated population), but the conclusions are expected to be comparable. "Neither party seems interested in addressing the issue, Manza said. Republicans feel they have little to gain because these voters are thought to be overwhelmingly Democratic. And, he added, 'Democrats are sufficiently concerned about not appearing to be weak on crime that I'm sure they would not be jumping up and down on this'."

The last comment directs attention to a critically important matter, discussed prominently abroad (see Duncan Campbell, *Guardian*, November 14; Serge Halimi and Looc Wacquant, *Le Monde Diplomatique*, December 2000; also Earl Ofari Hutchinson, *Christian Science Monitor*, December 14). For the past eight years, Clinton and Gore disenfranchised a major voting bloc that would have easily swung the election to Gore. During their tenure in office, the prison population swelled from 1.4 to 2 million, removing an enormous number of potential Democratic voters from the lists, thanks to the harsh sentencing laws. Clinton-Gore were particularly devoted to draconian Reagan-Bush laws, Hutchinson points out.

The core of these practices is drug laws that have little to do with drugs but a lot to do with social control: removing superfluous people and frightening the rest. When the latest phase of the "war on drugs" was designed in the 1980s, it was recognized at once that "we are choosing to have an intense crime problem concentrated among minorities" (Daniel Patrick Moynihan, one of the few Senators who paid attention to social statistics). "The war's planners knew exactly what they were doing," criminologist Michael Tonry wrote, reviewing the racist and class-based procedures that run through the system from arrest to sentencing—and that continue a long and disgraceful tradition (see Randall Shelden, *Controlling the Dangerous Classes: A Critical Introduction to the History of Criminal Justice*).

Twenty years ago, the U.S. was similar to other industrial countries in rate of incarceration. By now, it is off the spectrum, the world's leader among countries that have meaningful statistics. The escalation was unrelated to crime rates, which were not unlike other industrial countries then and have remained stable or declined. But they are a natural component of the domestic programs instituted from the late Carter years, a variant of the "neoliberal reforms" that have had a devastating effect in much of the third world. These "reforms" have been accompanied by a notable deterioration in conventional measures of "economic health" worldwide, but have had a much more dramatic impact on standard social indicators: measures of "quality of life."

In the U.S., these tracked economic growth until the "reforms" were instituted, and have declined since, now to about the level of 40 years ago, in what the Fordham University research institute that has done the major studies of the topic calls a "social recession" (Marc and Marque Luisa Miringoff, *The Social Health of the Nation*; also see Paul Street, *Z Magazine*, November 2000). Economic rewards are highly concentrated, and much of the population becomes superfluous for profit and power.

Marginalization of the superfluous population takes many forms. Some of these were the topic of a recent *Business Week* cover story entitled "Why Service Stinks" (October 23). It reviewed refinements in implementing the 80-20 rule taught in business schools—20 percent of your customers provide 80 percent of the profits—and you may be better off without the rest. The "new consumer apartheid" relies on modern information technology (in large measure a gift from an unwitting public) to allow corporations to provide grand services to profitable customers, and to deliberately offer skimpy services to the rest, whose inquiries or complaints can be safely ignored. The experience is familiar and carries severe costs—how great when distributed over a large population, we don't know, because they are not included among the highly ideological measures of economic performance. Incarceration might be regarded as an extreme version, for the least worthy.

Incarceration has other functions. It is a form of interference in labor markets, removing working-age males, increasingly women as well, from the labor force. Calculating real unemployment when this labor force is included, the authors of an informative academic study find the U.S. to be well within the European range, contrary to conventional claims (Bruce Western and Katherine Beckett, *American Journal of Sociology,* January 1999; also *Prison Legal News,* October 2000). They conclude that what is at issue is not labor market interference, but the kind that is chosen: job training, unemployment insurance, and so on, on the social democratic model; or throwing superfluous people into jail.

In pursuing these policies, the U.S. has separated itself from other industrial countries. Europe abandoned voting restrictions for criminals decades ago.

Iin 1999, the Constitutional Court of South Africa gave inmates the right to vote, saying that the "vote of each and every citizen is a badge of dignity and personhood." Prior to the "neo-liberal reforms" and their "drug war" concomitant, the U.S. was heading in the same direction, the *National Law Journal* (October 30) comments: "The American Bar Association Standards on Civil Disabilities of a Convicted Person, approved in 1980, state flatly that '[persons] convicted of any offense should not be deprived of the right to vote' and that laws subjecting convicts to collateral civil disabilities 'should be repealed'." Without continuing, the Clinton-Gore programs of disenfranchising their own voters should be understood as a natural component of their overall socioeconomic conceptions. The elections themselves illustrate the related conception of the political system of two horses with the same corporate owner. None of this is new. There is no "golden age" that has been lost, and this is not the first period of concentrated attack on democracy and human rights. Insofar as the November 2000 elections are worth discussing, they should, I think, be seen primarily from these perspectives.

Elections 2008

The word that immediately rolled off of every tongue after the presidential election was "historic." And rightly so. A Black family in the White House is truly a momentous event. There were some surprises. One was that the election was not over after the Democratic convention. One might expect that the opposition party would have a landslide victory during a severe economic crisis, after eight years of disastrous policies on all fronts including the worst record on job growth of any post-war president and a rare decline in median wealth, with an incumbent so unpopular that his own party had to disavow him and a dramatic collapse in U.S. standing in world opinion. The Democrats did win, barely. If the financial crisis had been slightly delayed, they might not have.

A good question is why the margin of victory for the opposition party was so small, given the circumstances. One possibility is that neither party reflects public opinion at a time when 80 percent think the country is going in the wrong direction and that the government is run by "a few big interests looking out for themselves," not for the people. A stunning 94 percent object that government does not attend to public opinion. As many studies show, both parties are well to the right of the population on many major issues, domestic and international. It could be argued that no party speaking for the public would be viable in a society that is business-run to an un-

usual extent. Evidence for that description is substantial. At a very general level, evidence is provided by the predictive success of political economist Thomas Ferguson's "investment theory" of politics, which holds that policies tend to reflect the wishes of the powerful that invest every four years to control the state. More specific illustrations are numerous. To select one virtually at random, for 60 years the U.S. has failed to ratify the core principle of international labor law, which guarantees freedom of association. Legal analysts call it "the untouchable treaty in American politics," and observe that there has never even been any debate about the matter.

Many have noted Washington's dismissal of conventions of the International Labor Organization as contrasted with the intense dedication to enforcement of monopoly pricing rights for corporations ("intellectual property rights"). The two candidates in the Demo- cratic primary were a woman and an African American. That, too, was historic. It would have been unimaginable 40 years ago. The fact that the country has become civilized enough to accept this outcome is a considerable tribute to the activism of the 1960s and its aftermath, an observation with lessons for the future. In some ways, the election followed familiar patterns. The McCain campaign was honest enough to announce that the election wouldn't be about issues. Sarah Palin's hairdresser received twice the salary of McCain's foreign policy adviser, the *London Financial Times* (*FT*) reported, probably an accurate reflection of significance for the campaign. Obama's message of "hope" and "change" offered a virtual blank slate on which supporters could write their wishes. One could search websites for position papers, but correlation of these to policies was hardly spectacular and, in any event, what enters into voters' choices is what the campaign places front and center, as party managers know well.

The Obama campaign greatly impressed the public relations industry, which named Obama "Advertising Age's marketer of the year for 2008," easily beating out Apple. The industry's regular task is to create uninformed consumers who will make irrational choices, thus undermining market theories. It recognizes the benefits of undermining democracy in much the same way.

Brand Obama

The *FT*, the world's premier business daily, reports the enthusiasm of the PR industry over the marketing of "brand Obama." Particularly impressed are those who "helped pioneer the packaging of candidates as consumer brands 30 years ago," when they designed the Reagan campaign. Obama is likely to "have more influence on boardrooms than any president since Ronald Reagan, [who] redefined what it was to be a CEO" by teaching the lesson that, "You had to give them a vision."

Reagan's visionary performance led to "the 1980s and 1990s reign of the imperial CEO," an office that registered such towering successes as destroying the financial system and exporting much of the real economy while amassing huge personal fortunes, based largely on the ability to choose the boards that determine salary and bonuses, thanks to regulations established by the nanny state for the rich.

Obama had expressed his admiration for Reagan as a "transformative figure." He was not referring to the rivers of blood that Reagan spilled from Central America to southern Africa and beyond. Nor was he referring to Reagan's great effectiveness in helping transform Pakistan into a nuclear-armed state with powerful radical Islamic forces, with consequences that Obama regards as the major foreign challenge to his Administration. So, yes, Reagan was a transformative figure abroad. At home as well, though Obama was not referring to Reagan's crucial role in transforming the U.S. from the world's leading creditor to the world's leading debtor, or converting it from an industrial society rather resembling Europe to one in which real wages for the majority stagnate and social indicators decline while a few who are favored by government policy gain fabulous wealth, among other forms of social malaise.

Rather, Obama was referring to the imaginary figure constructed by a remarkable PR campaign, which anointed Reagan as the High Priest of free markets and small government, culminating in a reverential commemoration of the Great Man that was reminiscent of the veneration of Kim il-Sung, one of the more embarrassing moments of the modern history of Western political culture.

The imagery is untainted by Reagan's breaking modern records in government intervention in the economy, while also somewhat increasing the size of government. Just to mention a few highlights, he was the most protectionist president in post-war American history, virtually doubling protectionist barriers in order to try to save the U.S. economy from takeover by more efficient Japanese producers. He called on the Pentagon to devise programs to instruct backward American management in modern production techniques; he bailed out Continental Illinois Bank and others while setting the stage for the huge Savings & Loan bailout—his "star wars" fantasies were sold to the business world, plausibly, as a huge taxpayer-funded bonanza to high tech industry, and on and on.

The term "Reagan" here refers not to the pathetic creature in the White House who, among other notable performances, put on his cowboy boots and declared a national emergency because the Nicaraguan army was two days from Texas—rather, to those who formulated and executed the policies of his Administration. Reagan's "vision," like most heralded "visions," was entirely independent of his deeds. The vision that was constructed by the doctrinal institutions is indeed one of dedication to unfettered free markets and "democracy promotion." The creation of the "vision" was indeed a marketing triumph of which those who "helped pioneer the packaging of candidates as consumer brands 30 years ago" should be proud, as they celebrate their greatest triumph yet in 2008. The Center for Responsive Politics reports that once again elections were bought: "The best-funded candidates won 9 out of 10 contests and all but a few members of Congress will be returning to Washington." Before the conventions, the viable candidates with most funding from financial institutions were Obama and McCain, with 36 percent each. Preliminary results indicate that by the end, Obama's campaign contributions, by industry, were concentrated among law firms (including lobbyists) and financial institutions, with Obama favored by a considerable margin. The investment theory of politics suggests some conclusions about guiding policies of the new Administration.

The power of financial institutions reflects the increasing shift of the economy from production to finance since the liberalization of finance in the 1970s, a root cause of the current economic crisis: the financial collapse of 2008, ongoing recession in the real economy, and the miserable performance of the economy for the large majority, whose real wages stagnated for 30 years, while benefits and social indicators declined. The steward of this impressive record, Alan Greenspan, attributed his success to "growing worker insecurity," which led to "atypical restraint on compensation increases"—and corresponding increases into the pockets of those who matter. Greenspan's failure even to perceive the dramatic housing bubble, following the collapse of the earlier tech bubble that he oversaw, was the immediate cause of the current financial crisis, as he has ruefully conceded.

Reactions to the election from across the spectrum commonly adopted the "soaring rhetoric" of the Obama campaign. Veteran correspondent John Hughes wrote that, "America has just shown the world an extraordinary example of democracy at work," while to British historian-journalist Tristram Hunt, the election showed that America is a land "where miracles happen," such as "the glorious epic of Barack Obama" (leftist French journalist Jean Daniel). "In no other country in the world is such an election possible," said Catherine Durandin of the Institute for International and Strategic Rela-

tions in Paris. Many others were no less rapturous. The rhetoric has some justification if we keep to the West, but elsewhere matters are different. Consider the world's largest democracy, India. The chief minister of Uttar Pradesh, which is larger than all but a few countries of the world and is notorious for the horrifying treatment of women, is not only a woman, but a Dalit ("untouchable"), at the lowest rung of India's disgraceful caste system.

Turning to the Western hemisphere, consider its two poorest countries: Haiti and Bolivia. In Haiti's first democratic election in 1990, grassroots movements were organized in the slums and hills and, though without resources, elected their own candidate, the populist priest Jean-Bertrand Aristide. The results astonished observers who expected an easy victory for the candidate of the elite and the U.S., a former World Bank official.

True, this victory for democracy was soon overturned by a military coup, followed by years of terror and suffering to the present, with crucial participation of the two traditional torturers of Haiti, France and the U.S. (contrary to self-serving illusions). But the victory itself was a far more "extraordinary example of democracy at work" than the U.S. miracle of 2008.

The same is true of the 2005 election in Bolivia. The indigenous majority, the most oppressed population in the hemisphere (those who survived), elected a candidate from their own ranks, a poor peasant, Evo Morales. The electoral victory was not based on soaring rhetoric about hope and change or body language and fluttering of eyelashes, but on crucial issues, very well known to the voters, such as control over resources, cultural rights, and so on. Furthermore, the election went far beyond pushing a lever or even efforts to get out the vote. It was a long and intense popular struggle in the face of severe repression, which had won major victories, such as defeating the efforts to deprive poor people of water through privatization.

These popular movements did not simply take instructions from party leaders. Rather, they formulated the policies that their candidates were chosen to implement. That is quite different from the Western model of democracy, as we see in the reactions to Obama's victory. In the liberal *Boston Globe*, the headline of the lead story observed that Obama's "grass-roots strategy leaves few debts to interest groups": labor unions, women, minorities, or other "traditional Democratic constituencies."

That is only partially right because massive funding by concentrated sectors of capital was ignored. But leaving that detail aside, the report is correct in saying that Obama's hands are not tied because his only debt is to "a grass-roots army of millions"—who took instructions, but contributed essentially nothing to formulating his program. At the other end of the doctrinal spectrum, a headline in the *Wall Street Journal* reads "Grass-Roots Army Is Still at the Ready"— namely, ready to follow instructions to "push his agenda," whatever it may be.

Obama's organizers regard the network they constructed "as a mass movement with unprecedented potential to influence voters," the *Los Angeles Times* reported. The movement, organized around the "Obama brand" can pressure Congress to "hew to the Obama agenda." But they are not to develop ideas and programs and call on their representatives to implement them. These would be among the "old ways of doing politics" from which the new "idealists" are "breaking free." It is instructive to compare this picture to the workings of a functioning democracy such as Bolivia. The popular movements of the third world do not conform to the favored Western doctrine that the "function" of the "ignorant and meddlesome outsiders"—the population—is to be "spectators of action" but not "participants" (Walter Lippmann, articulating a standard progressive view). Perhaps there might even be some substance to fashionable slogans about "clash of civilizations."

In earlier periods of U.S. history, the public refused to keep to its assigned "function." Popular activism repeatedly brought about substantial gains in freedom and justice. The authentic hope of the Obama campaign is that the "grass-roots army" organized to take instructions from the leader might "break free" and return to "old ways of doing politics," by direct participation in action.

In Bolivia, as in Haiti, efforts to promote democracy, social justice, and cultural rights, and to bring about desperately needed structural and institutional changes are, naturally, bitterly opposed by the traditional rulers, the Europeanized, mostly white elite in the Eastern provinces, the site of most of the natural resources currently desired by the West. Also, naturally, their quasi-secessionist movement is supported by Washington, which once again scarcely conceals its reflexive distaste for democracy when outcomes do not conform to strategic and economic interests. The generalization is familiar to serious scholarship, but does not make its way to commentary about the revered "freedom agenda."

To punish Bolivians for showing "the world an extraordinary example of democracy at work," the Bush administration cancelled trade preferences, threatening tens of thousands of jobs on the pretext that Bolivia was not cooperating with U.S. counter-narcotic efforts. In the real world, the UN estimates that Bolivia's coca crop increased 5 percent in 2007, as compared with a 26 percent increase in Colombia, the terror state that is Washington's closest regional ally and the recipient of enormous military aid. AP reports that, "Cocaine seizures by Bolivian police working with DEA agents had increased dramatically during the Morales administration."

"Drug wars" have been used as a pretext for repression, violence, and state crimes, at home as well. After Morales's victory in a recall referendum in August 2008, with a sharp increase in support over his 2005 success, rightist opposition turned violent, leading to assassination of many peasants supporting the government. After the massacre, a summit meeting of UNASUR, the newly-formed Union of South American Republics, was convened in Santiago, Chile. The summit issued a strong statement of support for the elected Morales government, read by Chilean

President Michelle Bachelet. The statement declared "their full and firm support for the constitutional government of President Evo Morales, whose mandate was ratified by a big majority"—referring to his overwhelming victory in the referendum a month earlier. Morales thanked UNASUR for its support, observing that, "For the first time in South America's history, the countries of our region are deciding how to resolve our problems, without the presence of the United States."

Turning to the future, what can we realistically expect of an Obama administration? We have two sources of information: actions and rhetoric. The most important actions prior to taking office are selection of staff and advisers. The first selection was Joe Biden for vice president. Biden was one of the strongest supporters of the Iraq invasion among Senate Democrats, a long-time Washington insider, who consistently votes with his fellow Democrats—though not always, as when he brought cheer to financial institutions by supporting a measure to make it harder for individuals to erase debt by declaring bankruptcy.

The first post-election appointment was for the crucial position of chief of staff: Rahm Emanuel, one of the strongest supporters of the Iraq invasion among House Democrats and, like Biden, a long-term Washington insider. Emanuel is also one of the biggest recipients of Wall Street campaign contributions, the Center for Responsive Politics reports. He "was the top House recipient in the 2008 election cycle of contributions from hedge funds, private equity firms and the larger securities/investment industry." Since being elected to Congress in 2002, he "has received more money from individuals and PACs in the securities and investment business than any other industry"; these are also among Obama's top donors. Emanuel's task is to oversee Obama's approach to the worst financial crisis since the 1930s, for which his and Obama's funders share ample responsibility.

In an interview with an editor of the *Wall Street Journal*, Emanuel was asked what the Obama administration would do about "the Democratic congressional leadership, which is brimming with left-wing barons who have their own agenda," such as slashing defense spending (in accord with the will of the majority of the population) and "angling for steep energy taxes to combat global warming," not to speak of the outright lunatics in Congress who toy with slavery reparations and even sympathize with Europeans who want to indict Bush administration war criminals for war crimes. "Barack Obama can stand up to them," Emanuel assured the editor. The Administration will be "pragmatic," fending off left extremists.

Labor journalist and lawyer Steve Early writes that, "While running for office, Obama said he strongly backed the Employee Free Choice Act, a long-overdue labor law reform measure that should be part of his promised economic stimulus plan. However, when Obama recently introduced his top economic advisers and talked about steps to "jolt" the economy in January, the Act was not part of the package. More disturbing, his new chief of staff, Rahm Emanuel, declined to say whether the White House will support the Employee Free Choice Act.... [Workers] would be watching closely to see whether their plight merits the same helping hand so quickly extended to Wall Street." Obama's transition team is headed by John Podesta, Clinton's chief of staff.

The leading figures in his economic team are Robert Rubin and Lawrence Summers, both enthusiasts for the deregulation that was a major factor in the current financial crisis. As Treasury Secretary, Rubin worked hard to abolish the Glass-Steagall act, which had separated commercial banks from financial institutions that incur high risks. Economist Tim Canova comments that Rubin had "a personal interest in the demise of Glass-Steagall." Soon after leaving his position as Treasury Secretary, he became "chair of Citigroup, a financial-services conglomerate that was facing the possibility of having to sell off its insurance underwriting subsidiary...the Clinton administration never brought charges against him for his obvious violations of the Ethics in Government Act."

Not surprisingly, Citigroup was a leading beneficiary of the Paulson bailout. That breaks little new ground. Walter Wriston, the CEO of its predecessor Citicorp, followed World Bank/ IMF advice and lent so heavily to Latin America that when the debt crisis broke out in 1982, only a bailout (via the IMF) "saved Citicorp from a preemptive run on its interbank deposits, which could have been fatal," international economist David Felix wrote—adding that Wriston, like the Treasury Secretaries, were firm believers in pure laissez-faire: "for others, not themselves."

These are the normal workings of state capitalism, for other industries as well. In a detailed analysis of corporate reliance on state intervention, Winfried Ruigrok and Rob van Tulder (*The Logic of International Restructuring*) conclude that, "At least 20 companies in the 1993 Fortune 100 would not have survived at all as independent companies, if they had not been saved by their respective governments," and that many of the rest gained substantially by demanding that governments "socialise their losses."

Such government intervention, they observe, "has been the rule rather than the exception over the past two centuries." That is apart from the crucial state role, particularly in the post-World War II period, in socializing the costs and risks of research and development while privatizing profit. A feature of commentary on the 2008 financial industry bailout is that it was perceived as a radical departure from the norm, raising the threat of "socialism." That is far from true.

The bailout of Rubin's Citigroup was necessary, Paul Krugman wrote, but it was done in a manner that was "an outrage: a lousy deal for the taxpayers." That holds for the bailout generally. His fellow Nobel laureate Joseph Stiglitz observed, "As we pour money in, they can pour money right out" if we "don't have a veto." If the government—in a functioning democracy, the public—does not have a degree of control, the banks can pour the public funds into their own pockets for recapitalization or acquisitions or loans to government-guaranteed borrowers, thus undermining the alleged purpose of the bailout. That is what happened, though details are obscure because the recipients refuse to say what they are doing with the gift from taxpayers. Indeed they regard the question as outrageous, so the Associated Press discovered when it sought answers: "no bank provided even the most basic accounting for the federal money," most ignoring the request or saying, "We're choosing not to disclose that." Again, normal workings of state capitalism. The "ignorant and meddlesome outsiders" are to be satisfied with "necessary illusion" and "emotionally potent over-simplifications," as the disting- uished moralist Reinhold Niebuhr explained.

After leaving the government for Citigroup Rubin was replaced as Treasury Secretary by Summers, who presided over legislation barring federal regulation of derivatives, the "weapons of mass destruction" (Warren Buffett) that helped plunge financial markets to disaster. He ranks as "one of the main villains in the current economic crisis," according to Dean Baker, one of the few economists to have warned accurately of the impending crisis. Placing financial policy in the hands of Rubin and Summers is "a bit like turning to Osama Bin Laden for aid in the war on terrorism," Baker adds. Another achievement of Rubin and Summers (together with Alan Greenspan) was to prevent Brooksley Born, head of the Commodity Futures Trading Commission, from regulating credit default swaps. "The best example of politics thwarting effective regulation," Baker writes.

Obama's appointment for Treasury Secretary, Timothy Geithner, a close associate of Summers, elicited a favorable reaction from Wall Street, which may be "hoping that little will change with Geithner at Treasury," Tim Canova observes: "Supporters of President-elect Obama will be tempted to embrace the experience argument, and it is true that Geithner and Summers have lots of experience at crisis management and doling out bailout funds to their Wall Street clientele."

As the crisis began to hit, Geithner hinted that he would use the enormous leverage he had as president of the New York Fed to impose some controls on exotic financial instruments, but "there is no evidence," Canova writes, "that there has been much action, even though Geithner has used this time to negotiate multi-billion-dollar bailouts and deals associated with the collapse of Bear Stearns, Lehman Brothers, AIG, and now Citigroup." He adds that "the selection of Geithner and Summers to top administrative posts rewards past failure and protects special interests [and] also sends the wrong message to those who thought they were voting for change."

Not much help in "changing" the world of finance can be expected from the Democratic Congress either. Charles Schumer, who led the Democratic Senatorial Campaign Committee, broke records in obtaining contributions from Wall Street, helping the Democrats win Congress and increasing "the industry's clout in the capital," the *New York Times* reported. He also "helped save financial institutions billions of dollars in higher taxes or fees. He succeeded in limiting efforts to regulate credit-rating agencies, for example, sponsored legislation that cut fees paid by Wall Street firms to finance government oversight, pushed to allow banks to have lower capital reserves and called for the revision of regulations to make corporations' balance sheets more transparent." He also weakened efforts to regulate bank debt and supervise the credit-rating agencies, also agents of disaster. His personal reward was to collect more campaign contributions from the financial industry than anyone in Congress except for John Kerry. "He built his career in large part based on his ties to Wall Street [and] has given the Street what it wanted," said the director of a leading firm that advises investors on the regulatory system. The business press reviewed the records of Obama's Transition Economic Advisory Board, which met on November 7 to determine how to deal with the financial crisis. In *Bloomberg News*, Jonathan Weil concluded that, "Many of them should be getting subpoenas as material witnesses right about now, not places in Obama's inner circle."

About half "have held fiduciary positions at companies that, to one degree or another, either fried their financial statements, helped send the world into an economic tailspin, or both." Is it really plausible that "they won't mistake the nation's needs for their own corporate interests?" He also pointed out that chief of staff Emanuel "was a director at Freddie Mac in 2000 and 2001 while it was committing accounting fraud."

Dean Baker observes that, "Obama faced the same sort of problem as those hoping to de-Baathify Iraq following the overthrow of Saddam Hussein. It would have been almost impossible to establish a government without including members of the Baath party, since membership was a virtual requirement for holding a position of responsibility under Saddam Hussein. Similarly, it would have been almost impossible to get to the top echelons of power, or even the middle ranks, during the Clinton-Bush years without giving lip-service to the policies of one-sided financial deregulation and bubble-driven growth that were so fashionable at the time." And those leading Obama's economic team gave more than lip service. They were instrumental in designing the policies that have led to the present crisis. A headline in the *Financial Times* reads, "Applause as Obama picks all-star team."

No one is relevantly mentioned who is not on the right. Bush speechwriter David Frum said, "I cannot recall the last time Republicans felt so positive towards a Democratic presidential figure." Fellow speechwriter Michael Gerson wrote that, "Obama's appointments reveal not just moderation but maturity.... Whatever the caveats, Obama is doing something marvelously right"—where the term "right" should be understood in its dual meaning. Critical choices in foreign affairs followed much the same script, eliciting applause from Henry Kissinger, among others. Even superhawk Richard Perle felt "relieved.... Contrary to expectations, I don't think we would see a lot of change." Retiring senior Republican Senator John Warner, former chair of the Armed Services Committee, said, "the triumvirate of Gates, Clinton and Jones to lead Obama's national security team instills great confidence at home and abroad and further strengthens the growing respect for the president-elect's courage and ability to exercise sound judgment in selecting the best and the brightest to implement our nation's security policies."

Clinton and Gates need no comment. Security analyst Robert Dreyfuss describes former Marine commandant James Jones, Obama's new National Security Adviser, as "Obama's hawk," who "seems least compatible with Obama" among his hawkish team—though there is little reason beyond "hope" to justify the judgment about compatibility. Jones, Dreyfuss observes, "is a fierce advocate of NATO expansion," Clinton's policy that instantly reneged on firm promises to Gorbachev, guaranteeing confrontation with an encircled Russia. Jones urges that NATO should move to the South as well as the East, to expand U.S. control over Middle East energy supplies (in favored terminology, "safeguarding energy security").

He also advocates a "NATO response force," which will give the U.S.-run military alliance "much more flexible capability to do things rapidly at very long distances." Europe is reluctant, but will probably succumb as usual to pressure from a militaristic and expansionist Administration in Washington. The new Director of National Intelligence is Dennis Blair, former head of the U.S. Pacific Command. In that post he was a strong supporter of U.S. military ties with the murderous Suharto regime in Indonesia, sometimes skirting State Department and congressional objections. In early 1999, Indonesian violence began to increase again in East Timor, far surpassing anything in Kosovo prior to the NATO

> It would have been almost impossible to get to the top echelons of power, or even the middle ranks, during the Clinton-Bush years without giving lip-service to the policies of one-sided financial deregulation and bubble-driven growth that were so fashionable at the time." And those leading Obama's economic team gave more than lip service. They were instrumental in designing the policies that have led to the present crisis.

bombing—and of course the background of U.S. backed atrocities was far worse than anything in the Balkans. Blair was sent by the National Security Council to urge Indonesian general Wiranto to curb the violence. Instead, "Blair took a cordial approach," Alan Nairn reported. He told Wiranto that he "looks forward to the time Indonesia will resume its proper role as a leader in the region," according to U.S. officials who reviewed a cable written about the trip—which coincided with a particularly brutal slaughter in a church in Liquica, leaving dozens killed. Blair proposed new U.S. training programs for Indonesia, which were implemented, right through the last paroxysms of violence in September that practically destroyed what was left of the tortured country.

As his special assistant on the Middle East, Obama selected Dan Kertzer, Clinton-Bush Ambassador to Egypt and Israel. According to the well-informed Israeli diplomatic correspondent Akiva Eldar, Kertzer took part in writing Obama's speech to the Israeli lobbying organization AIPAC in June 2008. This remarkable text went well beyond Bush in its obsequiousness, even declaring that, "Jerusalem will remain the capital of Israel, and it must remain undivided," a position so extreme that his campaign had to explain that his words didn't mean what they said. Kretzer is close to Obama adviser Dennis Ross, whose position as a negotiator for the failed Camp David negotiation was that Israel has "needs"—including parts of the occupied territories—while Palestinians only have "wants," which therefore are less significant. His disgraceful book on the negotiations evades the major issue—the illegal Israeli settlements that expanded steadily under Clinton—and terminates conveniently just before its major thesis about Arafat's culpability completely collapsed at the Taba negotiations, in Clinton's last month in office. Like other Obama Middle East advisors, Ross has been closely associated with the Washington Institute for Near East Policy (WINEP), an offshoot of AIPAC and a barely disguised component of the Israeli lobby. Clinton's record of support for Israeli extremism is well-known.

Asked in a press conference about the recycling of familiar faces, Obama responded that "Americans would be rightly 'troubled' if he overlooked experience simply to create the perception of change." Explaining further, he said: "What we are going to do is combine experience with fresh thinking. But understand where the vision for change comes from first and foremost: It comes from me."

That should satisfy doubters impressed by the persuasive rhetoric about "change" and "hope." It is hoped, and indeed is highly likely, that Obama will reverse some of the more flagrant abuses of the Bush administration in dismantling the legal system. But it is not easy to be too confident. Obama's choice for Attorney General, Eric Holder, has a decent reputation in the legal profession.

However, he explained on CNN that we cannot adhere to the Geneva Conventions in interrogation of those accused of terrorism—which seems to mean that torture of suspects is legitimate, in gross violation of the foundations of international humanitarian law, by which the U.S. is theoretically bound.

The primary concern for the Administration will be to arrest the financial crisis and the simultaneous recession in the real economy. But there is also a monster in the closet: the notoriously inefficient privatized health-care system, which threatens to overwhelm the federal budget if current tendencies persist. A majority of the public has long favored a national health-care system, which should be far less expensive and more effective, comparative evidence indicates (along with many studies). As recently as 2004, any government intervention in the health-care system was described in the press as "politically impossible" and "lacking political support"— meaning: opposed by the insurance industry,

pharmaceutical corporations, and others who count. In 2008, however, first Edwards, then Obama and Clinton, advanced proposals that approached what the public have long preferred. These ideas now have "political support." What has changed? Not public opinion, which remains much as before. But by 2008, major sectors of power, primarily the manufacturing industry, had come to recognize that they were being severely damaged by the privatized health care system. Hence the public will is coming to have "political support." The shift tells us something about dysfunctional democracy, and the struggles that lie ahead.

The rich countries are devoting enormous resources to resolving the financial crisis that is harming their economies, adopting measures that they barred when similar crises struck the less fortunate—the financial crisis of 1997-98, for one; and today as well. But there is more to say. And it is said, even if it is scarcely heard. The financial crisis, severe as it is, pales alongside the global food crisis, which has added 120 million people to the rolls of malnourished, according to Oxfam, bringing the total to almost one billion, nearly one in seven people: "This is hunger on so vast a scale that it is difficult to understand how the world arrived at this point." The journal *New Nation*, in Bangladesh, observes aptly that, "It's very telling that trillions have already been spent to patch up leading world financial institutions, while out of the comparatively small sum of $12.3 billion pledged in Rome earlier this year, to offset the food crisis, only $1 billion has been delivered. The hope that at least extreme poverty can be eradicated by the end of 2015, as stipulated in the UN's Millennium Development Goals, seems as unrealistic as ever, not due to lack of resources but a lack of true concern for the world's poor. Whether the American, European or any other government infused bailout packages rectify the financial crisis or not, chances are that 16 October 2009 will bring similarly devastating news about the plight of the world's poor and which is likely to remain that: mere 'news' that requires little action, if any at all." Returning to the Obama programs, internationally, there is not much of substance on the largely blank slate. What there is gives little reason to expect much to change from Bush's second term, which stepped back from the radical ultranationalism and aggressive posture of the first term, also discarding some of the extreme hawks and opponents of democracy (in action, that is, not soothing words), like Rumsfeld and Wolfowitz. The immediate issues have to do mostly with the Middle East. On Israel-Palestine, rumors are circulating that Obama might depart from the U.S. rejectionism that has blocked a political settlement for over 30 years, with rare exceptions, notably for a few days in January 2001 before promising negotiations in Taba were called off prematurely by Israel. The record, however, provides no basis for taking the rumors seriously. I have reviewed Obama's formal positions as of early 2008 elsewhere (*Perilous Power*), and will put the matter aside here, except to note that they have become more ominous since. Particularly disturbing is his reaction to the vicious Israeli assault on Gaza, opening with Israel's violation of a ceasefire on November 4, as voters were going to the polls to elect Obama, then breaking out in full fury on December 27. To these crimes Obama's response has been silence—unlike, say, the terrorist attack in Mumbai, which he was quick to denounce, along with the "hateful ideology" that lies behind it. In the case of Gaza, his spokespersons hid behind the mantra that "there is one president at a time," and repeated his support for Israeli actions when he visited the Israeli town of Sderot in July: "If missiles were falling where my two daughters sleep, I would do everything in order to stop that." But he will do nothing, not even make a statement, when U.S. jets and helicopters with Israeli pilots are causing incomparably worse suffering to Palestinian children. After the November election, Israeli president Shimon Peres informed the press that on his July trip to Israel, Obama had told him that he was "very impressed" with the Arab League peace proposal that calls for full normalization of relations with Israel along with Israeli withdrawal from the occupied territories—basically, the long-standing international consensus that the U.S. and Israel have unilaterally blocked (and that Peres has never accepted—in fact, in his last days as prime minister in 1996 he held that a Palestinian state can never come into existence).

That might suggest a change of heart, except that the right-wing Israeli leader Binyamin Netanyahu said that on the same trip, Obama had told him that he was "very impressed" with Netanyahu's plan, which calls for indefinite Israeli control of the occupied territories. The paradox is plausibly resolved by Israeli political analyst Aluf Ben, who points out that Obama's "main goal was not to screw up or ire anyone. Presumably he was polite, and told his hosts their proposals were 'very interesting'—they leave satisfied and he hasn't promised a thing." Understandable, but it leaves us with nothing except his fervent professions of love for Israel and disregard for Palestinian concerns.

On Iraq, Obama has frequently been praised for his "principled opposition" to the war. In reality, as he has made clear, his opposition has been entirely unprincipled throughout. The war, he said, was a "strategic blunder." When Kremlin critics of their invasion of Afghanistan called it a strategic blunder, we did not say that they were taking a principled stand. After intensive debate, the government of Iraq agreed on a Status of Forces Agreement (SOFA) on the U.S. military presence in Iraq. The talks dragged on, the *Washington Post* reported, because Iraq had insisted on "some ma-

> I have reviewed Obama's formal positions as of early 2008 elsewhere (Perilous Power) and will put the matter aside here, except to note that they have become more ominous since. Particularly disturbing is his reaction to the vicious Israeli assault on Gaza, opening with Israel's violation of a ceasefire on November 4, as voters were going to the polls to elect Obama, then breaking out in full fury on December 27.

jor concessions, including the establishment of the 2011 withdrawal date instead of vaguer language favored by the Bush administration [and] also rejected long-term U.S. military bases on its soil." Iraqi leaders "consider the firm deadline for withdrawal to be a negotiating victory," Reuters reports: Washington "long opposed setting any timetable for its troops to withdraw, but relented in recent months," unable to overcome Iraqi resistance.

Throughout the negotiations, the press regularly dismissed the obstinate stance of the Maliki government as regrettable pandering to public opinion. U.S.-run polls continue to report that a large majority of Iraqis oppose any U.S. military presence, and believe that U.S. forces make the situation worse, including the "surge." That judgment is supported, among others, by Middle East specialist and security analyst Steven Simon, who writes in *Foreign Affairs* that the Petraeus counterinsurgency strategy is "stoking the three forces that have traditionally threatened the stability of Middle Eastern states: tribalism, warlordism, and sectarianism. States that have failed to control these forces have ultimately become ungovernable, and this is the fate for which the surge is preparing Iraq.

A strategy intended to reduce casualties in the short term will ineluctably weaken the prospects for Iraq's cohesion over the long run." It may lead to "a strong, centralized state ruled by a military junta that would resemble the Baathist regime Washington overthrew in 2003," or "something very much like the imperial protectorates in the Middle East of the first half of the 20th century" in which the "'club of patrons' in the capital would dole out goods to tribes through favored conduits." In the Petraeus system, "the U.S. military is performing the role of the patrons—creating an unhealthy dependency and driving a dangerous wedge between the tribes and the state," undermining prospects for a "stable, unitary Iraq." Iraqi opposition to the U.S. presence was underscored by reporting from across Iraq after parliamentary approval of the SOFA. The *International Herald Tribune,*

drawing from interviews by Iraqi journalists from around the country, reported opposition to the pact on grounds that the Iraqi government had been "bullied into a deal by an occupying force," that the U.S. would not live up to its terms, and that the central government gained too much power. Apart from one voice disturbed by the parliamentary brawl, there was no report of opposition on grounds that U.S. forces were needed to defend Iraqi interests.

The latest Iraqi success culminates a long process of resistance to demands of the U.S. invaders. Washington fought tooth and nail to prevent elections, but was finally forced to back down in the face of popular demands for democracy, symbolized by the Ayatollah Sistani. The Bush administration then managed to install their own choice as prime minister, and sought to control the government in various ways, meanwhile also building huge military bases around the country and an "embassy" that is a virtual city within Baghdad—all funded by congressional Democrats. If the invaders do live up to the SOFA that they have been compelled to accept, it would constitute a significant triumph of nonviolent resistance. Insurgents can be killed, but mass nonviolent resistance is harder to quell.

Many comparisons are being drawn between Vietnam and Iraq, most of them untenable. One, which is not being discussed, is of some interest. In both cases, Washington was faced with strong pressure from the invaded countries to withdraw. JFK discovered a few months before his assassination that the U.S. client regime was seeking a peaceful diplomatic settlement that would lead to U.S. withdrawal. To avert this threat, his Administration backed a military coup to install a more compliant regime in South Vietnam. As the internal and public record very clearly demonstrates, JFK did contemplate withdrawal (as was accurately reported at the time), but, crucially, only after U.S. victory was assured. The record also shows that he remained dedicated to this goal to the end. Efforts to evade the very clear and unambiguous facts are compelled to resort to alleged Machiavellian plots by the leader that have left no trace in the record, or to tidbits of evidence that reveal that the commentators accept Washington's right to impose the settlement of its choice. In the case of Iraq, in contrast, Washington has been unable to resort to such means to get rid of a government that is calling upon it to leave. There are many reasons for the differences. One is that the domestic population today is much less willing to tolerate U.S. aggression than it was in the early 1960s. A few years later strong opposition did develop, but only when the U.S. invasion far exceeded the scale of its aggression and crimes in Iraq. Within the political class and the media it is reflexively assumed that Washington has the right to demand terms for the SOFA in Iraq.

No such right was accorded to Russian invaders of Afghanistan or indeed to anyone except the U.S. and its clients. For others, we rightly adopt the principle that invaders have no rights, only responsibilities, including the responsibility to attend to the will of the victims and to pay massive reparations for their crimes. In this case, the crimes include strong support for Saddam Hussein through his worst atrocities on Reagan's watch, then on to Saddam's massacre of Shiites under the eyes of the U.S. military after the first Gulf War; the Clinton sanctions that were termed "genocidal" by the distinguished international diplomats who administered them and resigned in protest, and that also helped Saddam escape the fate of other gangsters whom the U.S. and Britain supported to the very end of their bloody rule; and the war and its hideous aftermath. No such thoughts can be voiced in polite society. The Iraqi government spokesperson said that the tentative SOFA "matches the vision of U.S. President-elect Barack Obama." Obama's vision was in fact left somewhat vague, but presumably he would go along in some fashion with the demands of the Iraqi government. If so, that would require modification of U.S. plans to ensure control over Iraq's enormous oil resources while reinforcing its dominance over the world's major energy producing region. Obama's announced "vision" was to shift forces from Iraq to

Afghanistan. That stand evoked a lesson from the editors of the *Washington Post*: "While the United States has an interest in preventing the resurgence of the Afghan Taliban, the country's strategic importance pales beside that of Iraq, which lies at the geopolitical center of the Middle East and contains some of the world's largest oil reserves." Increasingly, as Washington has been compelled to accede to Iraqi demands, tales about "democracy promotion" and other self-congratulatory fables have been shelved in favor of recognition of what had been obvious throughout to all but the most doctrinaire ideologists: that the U.S. would not have invaded if Iraq's exports were asparagus and tomatoes and the world's major energy resources were in the South Pacific.

The NATO command is also coming to recognize reality in public. In June 2007, NATO Secretary-General Jaap de Hoop Scheffer informed a meeting of NATO members that "NATO troops have to guard pipelines that transport oil and gas that is directed for the West," and more generally to protect sea routes used by tankers and other "crucial infrastructure" of the energy system.

That is the true meaning of the fabled "responsibility to protect." Presumably the task includes the projected $7.6-billion TAPI pipeline that would deliver natural gas from Turkmenistan to Pakistan and India, running through Afghan's Kandahar province, where Canadian troops are deployed. The goal is "to block a competing pipeline that would bring gas to Pakistan and India from Iran" and to "diminish Russia's dominance of Central Asian energy exports," the *Toronto Globe & Mail* reported, plausibly outlining some of the contours of the new "Great Game."

Obama strongly endorsed the then-secret Bush administration policy of attacking suspected al-Qaeda leaders in countries that Washington has not (yet) invaded, disclosed by the *New York Times* shortly after the election. The doctrine was illustrated again on October 26, when U.S. forces based in Iraq raided Syria, killing eight civilians, allegedly to capture an al-Qaeda leader. Washington did not notify Iraqi Prime Minister Maliki or President Talabani, both of whom have relatively amicable relations with Syria, which has accepted 1.5 million Iraqi refugees and is bitterly opposed to al-Qaeda. Syria protested, claiming, credibly, that if notified they would have eagerly apprehended this enemy. According to *Asia Times*, Iraqi leaders were furious, and hardened their stance in the SOFA negotiations, insisting on provisions to bar the use of Iraqi territory to attack neighbors. The Syria raid was harshly condemned in the Arab world. In pro-government newspapers, the Bush administration was denounced for lengthening its "loathsome legacy" (Lebanon), while Syria was urged to "march forward in your reconciliatory path" and America to "keep going backwards with your language of hatred, arrogance and the murder of innocents" (Kuwait). For the region generally, it was another illustration of what the government-controlled Saudi press condemned as "not diplomacy in search of peace, but madness in search of war."

Obama was silent. So were other Democrats. Political scientist Stephen Zunes contacted the offices of every Democrat on the House and Senate Foreign Relations Committees, but was unable to find any critical word on the U.S. raid on Syria from occupied Iraq. Presumably, Obama also accepts the more expansive Bush doctrine that the U.S. not only has the right to invade countries as it chooses (unless it is a "blunder," too costly to us), but to attack others that Washington claims are supporting resistance to its aggression. In particular, Obama has not criticized the raids by Predator drones that have killed many civilians in Pakistan.

These raids have consequences: people have the odd characteristic of objecting to slaughter of

> Obama strongly endorsed the then-secret Bush administration policy of attacking suspected al-Qaeda leaders in countries that Washington has not (yet) invaded, disclosed by the New York Times shortly after the election. The doctrine was illustrated again on October 26, when U.S. forces based in Iraq raided Syria, killing eight civilians, allegedly to capture an al-Qaeda leader.

family members and friends. There has been a vicious mini-war waged in the tribal area of Bajaur in Pakistan, adjacent to Afghanistan. The BBC describes widespread destruction from intense combat, reporting further that, "Many in Bajaur trace the roots of the uprising to a suspected U.S. missile strike on an Islamic seminary, or madrassa, in November 2006, which killed around 80 people." The attack on the school, killing 80-85 people, was reported in the mainstream Pakistani press by physicist and dissident activist Pervez Hoodbhoy, but ignored in the U.S. as insignificant. Events often look different at the other end of the club. Hoodbhoy observed that the usual outcome of such attacks "has been flattened houses, dead and maimed children, and a growing local population that seeks revenge against Pakistan and the U.S." Bajaur today may be an illustration of the familiar pattern.

On November 3, General Petraeus, the newly appointed head of the U.S. Central Command that covers the Middle East region, had his first meeting with Pakistani President Asif Ali Zardari, Army Chief General Ashfaq Parvez Kayani, and other high officials. Their primary concern was U.S. missile attacks on Pakistani territory, which had increased sharply in previous weeks. "Continuing drone attacks on our territory, which result in loss of precious lives and property, are counterproductive and difficult to explain by a democratically elected government," Zardari informed Petraeus. His government, he said, is "under pressure to react more aggressively" to the strikes. These could lead to "a backlash against the U.S.," which is already deeply unpopular in Pakistan. Petraeus said that he had heard the message, and "we would have to take [Pakistani opinions] on board" when attacking the country. A practical necessity, no doubt, when over 80 percent of the supplies for the U.S.-NATO war in Afghanistan pass through Pakistan.

Pakistan developed nuclear weapons, outside the Non-Proliferation Treaty (NPT), thanks in no small measure to Ronald Reagan, who pretended not to see what his ally was doing. This was one element of Reagan's "unstinting support" for the "ruthless and vindictive" dictator Zia ul-Haq, whose rule had "the most long-lasting and damaging effect on Pakistani society, one still prevalent today," the respected analyst Ahmed Rashid observes. With Reagan's firm backing, Zia moved to impose "an ideological Islamic state upon the population." These are the roots of many of "today's problems—the militancy of the religious parties, the mushrooming of madrassas and extremist groups, the spread of drug and Kalashnikov culture, and the increase in sectarian violence." Hoodbhoy comments accurately that, "Radical extremism is the illegitimate offspring of a union between the United States under Ronald Reagan, and Pakistan under General Zia-ul-Haq." CIA analyst Bruce Riedel, a specialist on the region, adds that, "All of the nightmares of the 21st century come together in Pakistan," including Lashkar-e-Taiba, which is blamed for the terrorist atrocities in Mumbai in November 2008.

The Reaganites also "built up the [Inter-Services Intelligence Directorate, ISI] into a formidable intelligence agency that ran the political process inside Pakistan while promoting Islamic insurgencies in Kashmir and Central Asia," Rashid continues. "This global jihad launched by Zia and Reagan was to sow the seeds of al Qaeda and turn Pakistan into the world center of jihadism for the next two decades." Meanwhile Reagan's immediate successors left Afghanistan in the hands of the most vicious jihadis, later abandoning it to warlord rule under Rumsfeld's direction. The fearsome ISI continues to play both sides of the street, supporting the resurgent Taliban and simultaneously acceding to some U.S. demands. The U.S. and Pakistan are reported to have reached "tacit agreement in September [2008] on a don't-ask-don't-tell policy that allows unmanned Predator aircraft to attack suspected terrorist targets" in Pakistan, according to unidentified senior officials in both countries. "The officials described the deal as one in which the U.S. government refuses to publicly acknowledge the attacks while Pakistan's government continues to complain noisily about the politically sensitive strikes."

Once again problems are caused by the "ignorant and meddlesome outsiders" who dislike being bombed by an increasingly hated enemy from the other side of the world.

The day before this report on the "tacit agreement" appeared, a suicide bombing in the conflicted tribal areas killed eight Pakistani soldiers, retaliation for an attack by a U.S. Predator drone that killed 20 people, including two Taliban leaders. The Pakistani parliament called for dialogue with the Taliban. Echoing the resolution, Pakistani Foreign Minister Shah Mehmood Qureshi said, "There is an increasing realization that the use of force alone cannot yield the desired results." Afghan President Hamid Karzai's first message to president-elect Obama was much like that delivered to General Petraeus by Pakistani leaders: "end U.S. airstrikes that risk civilian casualties."

His message was sent shortly after coalition troops bombed a wedding party in Kandahar province, reportedly killing 40 people. There is no indication that his opinion was "taken on board." Karzai has informed the Afghan public that, "He is powerless to halt U.S. airstrikes in his country and he would stop American warplanes if he could," the Voice of America reported. He informed a UN Security Council delegation visiting Kabul that he has demanded a timeline for withdrawal of foreign forces from his country. But this plea has also not been "taken on board" within the U.S. political and doctrinal systems. The British command has warned that there is no military solution to the conflict in Afghanistan and that there will have to be negotiations with the Taliban, risking a rift with the U.S., the FT reports. Correspondent Jason Burke, who has long experience in the region, reports that "the

Taliban have been engaged in secret talks about ending the conflict in Afghanistan in a wide-ranging 'peace process' sponsored by Saudi Arabia and supported by Britain."

Some Afghan peace activists have reservations about this approach, preferring a solution without foreign interference. A growing network of activists is calling for negotiations and reconciliation with the Taliban in a National Peace Jirga, a grand assembly of Afghans, formed in May 2008. At a meeting in support of the Jirga, 3,000 Afghan political figures and intellectuals, mainly Pashtuns, the largest ethnic group, criticized "the international military campaign against Islamic militants in Afghanistan and called for dialogue to end the fighting," AFP reported. The interim chair of the National Peace Jirga, Bakhtar Aminzai, "told the opening gathering that the current conflict could not be resolved by military means and that only talks could bring a solution. He called on the government to step up its negotiations with the Taliban and Hizb-i-Islami groups." The latter is the party of the extremist radical Islamist warlord Gulbuddin Hekmatyar, a Reagan favorite responsible for many terrible atrocities, now reported to provide core parliamentary support for the Karzai government.

Aminzai said further that "We need to pressure the Afghan government and the international community to find a solution without using guns." A spokesperson added, "We are against Western policy in Afghanistan. They should bury their guns in a grave and focus on diplomacy and economic development." A leader of Awakened Youth of Afghanistan, a prominent antiwar group, says that we must end "Afghanicide—the killing of Afghanistan." In a joint declaration with German peace organizations, the National Peace Jirga claimed to represent "a wide majority of Afghan people who are tired of war," calling for an end to escalation and initiation of a peace process.

The deputy director of the umbrella organization of NGOs in the country says that of roughly 1,400 registered NGOs, nearly 1,100 are purely Afghan operations: women's groups, youth groups, and others, many of them advocates of the Peace Jirga.

Though polling in war-torn Afghanistan is a difficult process, there are some suggestive results. A Canadian-run poll found that Afghans favor the presence of Canadian and other foreign troops, the result that made the headlines in Canada. Other poll findings suggest some qualifications. Only 20 percent "think the Taliban will prevail once foreign troops leave." Three-fourths support negotiations between the Karzai government and the Taliban, and more than half favor a coalition government. The great majority, therefore, strongly disagree with the U.S.-NATO focus on further militarization of the conflict, and appear to believe that peace is possible with a turn towards peaceful means. Though the question was not asked, it is reasonable to surmise that the foreign presence is favored for aid and reconstruction. A study of Taliban foot soldiers carried out by the *Toronto Globe & Mail*, though not a scientific survey as they point out, nevertheless yields considerable insight.

All were Afghan Pashtuns, from the Kandahar area. They described themselves as Mujahadeen, following the ancient tradition of driving out foreign invaders. Almost a third reported that at least one family member had died in aerial bombings in recent years. Many said that they were fighting to defend Afghan villagers from air strikes by foreign troops. Few claimed to be fighting a global Jihad, or had allegiance to Taliban leader Mullah Omar. Most saw themselves as fighting for principles—an Islamic government—not a leader. Again, the results suggest possibilities for a negotiated peaceful settlement without foreign interference. A valuable perspective on such prospects is provided by Sir Rodric Braithwaite, a specialist on Afghanistan who was UK ambassador to Moscow during the crucial 1988-92 period when the Russians withdrew (and the USSR collapsed), then becoming chair of the British Joint Intelligence Committee. On a recent visit, Braithwaite spoke to Afghan journalists, former Mujahideen,

214

professionals, people working for the U.S.-based "coalition"—in general, to "natural supporters for its claims to bring peace and reconstruction." In the *FT*, he reports that they were "contemptuous of President Hamid Karzai," regarding him as another one of the puppets installed by foreign force. Their favorite was "Mohammad Najibullah, the last communist president, who attempted to reconcile the nation within an Islamic state, and was butchered by the Taliban in 1996: DVDs of his speeches are being sold on the streets. Things were, they said, better under the Soviets. Kabul was secure, women were employed, the Soviets built factories, roads, schools and hospitals, Russian children played safely in the streets. The Russian soldiers fought bravely on the ground like real warriors, instead of killing women and children from the air. Even the Taliban were not so bad: they were good Muslims, kept order, and respected women in their own way. These myths may not reflect historical reality, but they do measure a deep disillusionment with the 'coalition' and its policies."

Specialists on the region urge that U.S. strategy should shift from more troops and attacks in Pakistan to a "diplomatic grand bargain—forging compromise with insurgents while addressing an array of regional rivalries and insecurities" (Barnett Rubin and Ahmed Rashid in *Foreign Affairs*, November-December 2008). They warn that the current military focus "and the attendant terrorism" might lead to the collapse of nuclear-armed Pakistan, with grim consequences. They urge the incoming U.S. administration "to put an end to the increasingly destructive dynamics of the Great Game in the region" through negotiations that recognize the interests of the concerned parties within Afghanistan as well as Pakistan and Iran, but also India, China, and Russia, who "have reservations about a NATO base within their spheres of influence" and concerns about the threats "posed by the United States and NATO" as well as by al-Qaeda and the Taliban. The immediate goal should be "Lowering the level of violence in the region and moving the global community toward genuine agreement on the long-term goals," thus allowing Afghans to confront their internal problems peacefully. The incoming U.S. president must put an end to "Washington's keenness for 'victory' as the solution to all problems, and the United States' reluctance to involve competitors, opponents, or enemies in diplomacy." It appears that there are feasible alternatives to escalation of the cycle of violence, but there has been little hint of it in the electoral campaign or political commentary. Afghanistan and Pakistan do not even appear among foreign policy issues on the Obama campaign's website.

Iran, in contrast, figures prominently—though not of course as compared with effusive support for Israel; Palestinians remain unmentioned, apart from a vague reference to a two-state settlement of some unspecified kind. For Iran, Obama supports tough direct diplomacy "without preconditions" in order "to pressure Iran directly to change their troubling behavior," namely pursuing a nuclear program and supporting terrorism (presumably referring to support for Hamas and Hezbollah). "If Iran continues its troubling behavior, we will step up our economic pressure and political isolation." And as Obama informed the AIPAC, "I will do everything in my power to prevent Iran from obtaining a nuclear weapon"—up to nuclear war, if he meant what he said.

Furthermore, Obama will strengthen the NPT "so that countries like North Korea and Iran that break the rules will automatically face strong international sanctions." There is no mention of the conclusion of U.S. intelligence with "high confidence" that Iran has not had a weapons program for five years, unlike U.S. allies Israel, Pakistan, and India, which maintain extensive nuclear weapons programs in violation of the NPT with direct U.S. support, all unmentioned here as well. The final mention of Iran is in the context of Obama's strong support for Israel's "right to self defense" and its "right to protect its citizens."

This commitment is demonstrated by Obama's co-sponsorship of "a Senate resolution against Iran and Syria's involvement in the war, and insisting that Israel should not be pressured into a ceasefire that did not deal with the threat of Hezbollah missiles." The reference is to Israel's U.S.-backed invasion of Lebanon in 2006, with pretexts that are hardly credible in light of Israel's regular practices. This invasion, Israel's fifth, killed over 1,000 Lebanese and once again destroyed much of southern Lebanon as well as parts of Beirut.

This is the sole mention of Lebanon among foreign policy issues on Obama's website. Evidently, Lebanon has no right of self defense. In fact who could possibly have a right of self defense against the U.S. or its clients?

Nor does Iran have such rights. Among specialists, even rational hawks, it is well understood that if Iran is pursuing a weapons program, it is for deterrence. In the conservative National Interest, former CIA weapons inspector David Kay speculates that Iran might be moving towards "nuclear weapons capability," with the "strategic goal" of countering a U.S. threat that "is real in Teheran's eyes," for good reasons that he reviews. He notes further that, "Perhaps the biggest agitator of all in this is the United States, with its abbreviated historical memory and diplomatic ADD." Wayne White, formerly deputy director for the Near East and South Asia in State Department intelligence, dismisses the possibility that Supreme Leader Khamenei and the clerical elite, who hold power in Iran, would throw away the "vast amounts of money" and "huge economic empires" they have created for themselves "in some quixotic attack against Israel with a nuclear weapon," if they had one. The probability of that is virtually undetectable, he points out.

White agrees that Iran might seek weapons capability (which is not the same as weapons) for deterrence. He goes on to suggest Iran might also recall that Saddam Hussein had no nuclear weapons program when Israel bombed its Osiraq reactor in 1981, but that the attack led him to initiate a program using nuclear materials it had on hand as a result of the bombing. At the

time, White was Iraq analyst for State Department intelligence, with access to a rich body of evidence. His testimony adds internal U.S. intelligence confirmation to the very credible evidence available at once, later strengthened by reports of Iraqi defectors, that the Israeli bombing did not terminate, but rather initiated, Saddam's pursuit of nuclear weapons. U.S. or Israeli bombing of Iranian facilities, White and other specialists observe, might have the same effect. Violence consistently elicits more violence in response.

These matters are well understood by informed hardliners. The leading neoconservative expert on Iran, Reuel Marc Gerecht, formerly in the CIA Middle East division, wrote in 2000 that: "Tehran certainly wants nuclear weapons; and its reasoning is not illogical. Iran was gassed into surrender in the first Persian Gulf War; Pakistan, Iran's ever more radicalized Sunni neighbor to the southeast, has nuclear weapons; Saddam Hussein, with his Scuds and his weapons-of-mass-destruction ambitions, is next door; Saudi Arabia, Iran's most ardent and reviled religious rival, has long-range missiles; Russia, historically one of Iran's most feared neighbors, is once again trying to reassert its dominion in the neighboring Caucasus; and Israel could, of course, blow the Islamic Republic to bits. Having been vanquished by a technologically superior Iraq at a cost of at least a half-million men, Iran knows very well the consequences of having insufficient deterrence. And the Iranians possess the essential factor to make deterrence work: sanity. Tehran or Isfahan in ashes would destroy the Persian soul, about which even the most hard-line cleric cares deeply. As long as the Iranians believe that either the U.S. or Israel or somebody else in the region might retaliate with nuclear weapons, they won't do something stupid." Gerecht also understands very well the real "security problem" posed by Iranian nuclear weapons, should it acquire them: "A nuclear-armed Islamic Republic would of course check, if not checkmate, the United States' maneuvering room in the Persian Gulf. We would no doubt think several times about responding to Iranian terrorism or military action if Tehran had the bomb and a missile to deliver it. During the lead-up to the second Gulf War, ruling clerical circles in Tehran and Qom were abuzz with the debate about nuclear weapons. The mullahs...agreed: if Saddam Hussein had had nuclear weapons, the Americans would not have challenged him. For the 'left' and the 'right,' this weaponry is the ultimate guarantee of Iran's defense, its revolution, and its independence as a regional great power."

With appropriate translations for the doctrinal term "Iranian terrorism," Gerecht's concerns capture realistically the threat posed by an Iran with a deterrent capacity (Iranian military action is quite a remote contingency).

While as usual ignored as irrelevant to policy formation, U.S. public opinion is close to that of serious analysts and also to world opinion. Large majorities oppose threats against Iran, thus rejecting the Bush-Obama position that the U.S. must be an outlaw state, violating the UN Charter, which bars the threat of force. The public also joins the majority of the world's states in endorsing Iran's right, as a signer of the NPT, to enrich uranium for nuclear energy (the position endorsed also by Cheney, Rumsfeld, Wolfowitz, Kissinger and others when Iran was ruled by the tyrant imposed by U.S.-UK subversion). Most important, the public favors establishment of a nuclear-weapons-free zone in the Middle East, which would mitigate and perhaps eliminate this highly threatening issue.

Such observations as these suggest an interesting thought experiment. What would be the content of the "Obama brand" if the public were to become "participants" rather than mere "spectators in action?" It is an experiment well worth undertaking, and there is good reason to suppose that the results might point the way to a saner and more decent world.

24.

Government Involvement with Science and Art

The role of science in the government

A s a graduate student at Penn State, I had made it almost a requirement to read at least three or four Noam Chomsky books a year. If you read enough Chomsky, you start wondering, "What is his outlook on my line of work?" Over the years I had been doing music interviews with bands, but I wanted to try a different sort of interview about the U.S government's involvement with science and the arts.

MIKSE: What is your perspective on science and its role in the development of progress?

CHOMSKY: It's right at the core. If you mean professional science, for a long time it didn't make much of a direct contribution in getting things done. The point at which true science began to really influence practice is pretty recent. Take MIT. When I got here almost 60 years ago, it was an engineering school. People learned how to make things—build a bridge, make an electrical circuit. It was mostly craft. You learned things the way a good carpenter learns things. There were science courses and math courses, but they were pretty much service courses, techniques for engineers. Within 20 years, if you wanted to build things or make things, you didn't go to MIT, you went to Northeastern or Wentworth Institute or some place like that. This has become a science university. The reason was because of the change that took place. Science had something to say to the practical arts and there was a huge explosion of technology: computers, software, IT, satellites, microelectronics. A lot of these massive changes came out of fundamental science. Furthermore, technology started to change much faster. If you wanted to train engineers of the future, there's not much point training them in the technology of today. It's going to be much different 20 years from now, so you study fundamental science. The same thing took place in medicine. Until, say, a century ago, there was a real question studied by the historians of medicine. If you went to a doctor, your chances of improvement would be no better than 50 percent because it's mostly intuition and craft. I remember doctors in my childhood who would do things such as leeches, which was supposed to bring out the blood. That changed a lot with the development of the first sulfur drugs, antibi-

Oliver Mikse interviews Chomsky. From
Z Magazine, May 2010

otics, and so on—and also advanced surgical techniques. But these were all consequences of the contributions of real science, such as biology, to the practice of medicine. It's not the first time. Like the early industrial revolution, the physical principals are not the most sophisticated ones.

By now, not only the world, but the survival of the species depends on sophisticated science. We're not going to get out of the environmental crisis unless there are significant scientific innovations, figuring out some way to harness solar power. That's not going to happen by itself. Unfortunately, a lot of science tradition throughout the years has been going into developing better means of destruction.

The early agricultural revolution 10,000 years ago was based on the science of the day; that is, figuring out how to grow crops more effectively. It was pretty sophisticated. One of the things that's been discovered that surprised contemporary scientists and anthropologists is that, quite commonly, when the West goes into some cultures like Liberia and proposes scientific agriculture, its yields decline. What's happened is that there's a tremendous amount of technical lore that isn't written down and is usually passed from mother to daughter. Agriculture was usually women's work, but very complex lore—you should plant this seed under this rock because the sun hits it at a certain hour and so on and so forth. That lore wasn't known by most men in the community, let alone anyone else. When scientific agriculture comes in, it destroys it and brings in Western concepts of agriculture—high use of fertilizer, other inputs, to deal with a decline in yields. So science isn't simply what we do in an MIT laboratory.

What is the general public's outlook on science and the arts? Is it even possible to measure?

You can take polls, but they give you strange results. The United States is a strange country. I don't think there's any other industrial country or part of the modern world where you get half the population thinking the world was created 10,000 years ago. That's a unique U.S. phenomenon. Listen to talk radio sometimes, which I do a lot when I'm driving. It's a segment of popular opinion. I happened to catch Rush Limbaugh interviewing Sarah Palin. For anybody who cares about possible survival, it's pretty frightening. It was all leading questions, "Sarah, what do you think of global warming?" "Oh, that's just made up by elitist liberals who are taking our jobs who don't care about us poor people. It's nothing like that. Look out the window, do you see any palm trees? Well, that takes care of global warming."

It's not just talk radio. You can read it in the front page of the *New York Times*. There was an article a couple of days ago asking if global warming is science or snake oil? They presented two views to balance it. One was the view of 99 percent of people who know anything about the topic. The other was the view of Senator James Inhofe who says it's all fake and a couple others, or maybe Rush Limbaugh. Those are the two views. You don't say that about the flat earth hypothesis or did the holocaust happen? You don't balance two views like that.

To get back to your question, if you look at popular attitudes, they're dangerous and they're affected very significantly by massive propaganda. If you want to get to the core of irrationality, the deepest level has to be market systems. In a market system—we have only a partial market system—but markets have inherent what they call "inefficiencies," really lethal inefficiencies. We're living through one right now: the financial crisis. It's an inherent part of markets that if you make a transaction, then you look out for yourself not other people. That's called in economics an externality. If you're, say, a Goldman Sachs executive and you make a loan or investment or something, if you're functioning "properly" you cover your own risk. But you don't cover what's called systemic risk—the risk to society and the system in general. When you look at most of the business world—particularly the energy corporations, but also the business world in general—for them the survival of the species is an externality. When you're making decisions you cannot take that into account. They're legally obligated not to take it into account. If you're a CEO of a corporation you are legally obligated to maximize profit and market share, not to pay attention to consequences.

If you did you'd be out of a job because someone else would come in who is interested in profit. That's inherent to markets. You can find ways to counter them with large-scale regulation and other stuff, but in a market system what you have is the business community committed to destroying everything they own and making it impossible for their grandchildren to survive. It's not that they're bad people. If you ask them, do they care about their grandchildren, they say sure, they'd do anything for them.

Meanwhile, in their institutions, they have to disregard it. So there's massive business propaganda trying to convince people that humans have no effect on global warming because that doesn't increase short-term profit. If they knock down energy legislation, they'll do better in the next quarter. Those are very profound irrationalities. One of the consequences is that there's a very destructive belief system.

In your book Failed States, *one of the points you bring up is how government policy is very frequently the opposite of what people want. Is it the same when it comes to science and the arts?*

The way public opinion is portrayed is incredibly misleading. For example, take welfare state policies, social policies, aid for the poor, Social Security. What you read in the headlines is that the public is against them. If you take a look at social attitudes, they're entirely different. Even among people who identify themselves in polls, there's still considerable majorities and support for education and health, the government, for the poor and so on. There are only two exceptions that are striking. One exception is blacks. People who call themselves conservative or "anti-government" think we're giving too much to blacks. Take a look at the black population: it's a deep depression for them right now. But

we're giving too much away to them. That's an example of old-fashioned American racism.

The other exception is welfare. People say they're opposed to welfare. That's a Reaganite contribution. If welfare means some rich black woman driving up in her limousine to get your hard-earned money at the welfare office, people say they're against it. On the other hand, if you ask the same people, "Are you in favor of more government aid to, say, women who have low incomes with children?" They say they're in favor of that, but they're not in favor of "welfare."

You get the same answer to foreign aid. A large majority say we give too much away to those "undeserving" people out there. Then when you ask the same people what they think foreign aid should be, it turns out it's far higher than what it actually is. You have to be really careful in studying what attitudes really are.

Another thing that's surprising is that a considerable majority thinks the U.S. shouldn't take the lead in international crises, it should rely on the United Nations. In fact, the majority of the population thinks we should give up the veto in the Security Council. Take Iran. I don't know what the attitudes are now because there's been a tremendous propaganda campaign over the last two years. But two years ago, a very large majority of the population thought Iran should have the right to enrich uranium as a signer of the non-proliferation treaty, but of course not have nuclear weapons. Over time this propaganda does change attitudes, though. If the polls were taken now, they'd say Iran is a major threat.

So, propaganda works. But still there's a substantial split between public attitudes and public policies. Same on health care. If you read the headlines, they tell you that the public is turning against Obama's health-care program, which is true. They say it's because we want to get the government off our backs. But you take a look at the polls that those headlines are based on and they show that you have people against it because it doesn't go far enough, that they gave everything away, like the Medicare buy-in, and so on.

A strong focus of the previous and current Administration is on safety of the public. As such, money is being cut from science and the National Institute of Health and shifted more towards militarization.

If I may interrupt, the safety of the public is a low priority for governments. In the Bush administration, for example, terror was quite a low priority and it's very clear. Take invading Iraq. The invasion of Iraq was undertaken with the assumption that it would increase terror and, in fact, it did, significantly. Their data showed that it went up a factor of seven the year after the invasion. Take after 9/11. If there had been any concern for reducing terror, there was a policy that could have been pursued. The jihadi movement is a big movement and it bitterly condemned al-Qaida. It condemned the 9/11 attacks as non-Islamic. There were also sharp condemnations from universities and radical clerics.

Suppose you were interested in reducing terror, what could have been done was to exploit the fact that the jihadi movement, let alone the general population, was appalled by this. You try to isolate al-Qaida and break them off from their constituencies and supporters. Instead, the government decided to do the opposite. It decided to weld the jihadi movement back together and create massive new recruiting for al-Qaida. That's what the invasions of Afghanistan and Iraq did.

Would it be more precise to say that funding has been shifted towards militarization?

Under the Bush administration, there were significant cuts. It was a very anti-science administration. But let's take Obama, who's supposed to be progressive. You read every day about the deficit. The headlines are concerned that the debt's been misplaced. In fact, if you want to reduce the deficit, most economists will tell you—even conservative economists—the way to do it is to spend more government money. With a bigger stimulus it will get people back to working. That will increase economic growth, it will increase taxes. It's pretty much the consensus among economists and it's pretty straightforward.

Let's take a look at the deficit. Where is it coming from? Almost half of next year's deficit is coming from the military budget. Obama has submitted the biggest military budget of any president since World War II. And it's close to half the deficit. Are they talking about reducing the military budget? No. What they're talking about is reducing Social Security, services for the population. If you're an executive in the business roundtable, or business lobbies, it's just what you want. Their power is extraordinary.

One of the issues that was discussed in the movie The Corporation *is that the genetic code is slowly being owned by corporations as they copyright different genes for profit. What do you think the ethical merits are of this?*

One of the main issues of the World Trade Organization was called "trade and services." What are services? "Services" are usually anything a person cares about, like education, health, environment. So what are trade and services? Well, to the WTO, et al., they mean that anything people care about is put into the hands of unaccountable private tyrannies. That's a tremendous attack on democracy. It means you can have formal democratic institutions, but there's nothing for them to do because everything is in the in the hands of private tyrannies—corporations.

Switching topics a little bit, Harold Varmus and other intellectuals have been appointed chairs of the Presidential Counsel of Advisors for Science and Technology for the Obama administration. What role does this counsel essentially play and have they influenced legislation in the past at all?

Take a look at modern science and technology, like computers, the Internet, satellites, lasers, buying things at Wal-Mart—which comes from trade which comes from containers. Anywhere you look, you'll find major contributions of the state sector to the advanced economy. That came from scientists in the early post-war period who persuaded the government to pour a lot of money into developing fundamental science.

You could argue that maybe it's right, maybe it's wrong, but what was interesting about it was that it was done in a way that demonstrated their fear and hatred of democracy. They didn't come to the public and say, "Look, you guys should pay more taxes so maybe your grandchildren will have a PC." What they said was, "The Russians are coming and we've got to defend ourselves so we need a huge military budget." You can see it at MIT. This is one of the main places where it happened. In the 1950s and 1960s, MIT was maybe 90 percent funded by the Pentagon. But it wasn't doing military work, it was developing the advanced economy of the future.

If you look at the years since, Pentagon funding has declined. It hasn't disappeared, but it's declined and funding from the National Institute of Health and health-related funding has gone up. Why? Because the cutting edge of the economy of the future is biology-based, not electronic based. So the public is being ripped off in a different fashion.

Take a walk around the area near MIT. What you see are startup firms in genetic engineering, bioengineering, biotechnology, and the big guys like Novartis who feed off the public trough. They want the public to pay the cost of research and development while they get the benefits. If you look back 50 years ago, what you found were small startup and electronic firms feeding off of funded technology.

That's the way the economy works, but it was initiated by far-sighted scientists and I suppose the advisors today are doing the same thing. They have an interest in science—a lot of them are real scientists and want serious scientific work going on—but they've got to have the same concerns as Obama. If the investment community doesn't like what you're doing, you're out of business because they're the guys who own and dictate policy, so you've got to have an eye on that.

Is that one of reasons why recently in England David Nutt, who was the government advisor on drugs and marijuana, was fired? Because he didn't agree with government policy?

It certainly looked like that. Actually, the marijuana case is very interesting. Why is marijuana criminalized? It's comparably less dangerous than alcohol and massively less dangerous than tobacco. If you look at deaths from substances, way out in the lead is tobacco with millions of deaths all over the place. Tobacco not only harms the user, it harms everyone else, so deaths from passive smoking and being around people who smoke are way higher than deaths from hard drugs.

The next most lethal substance is alcohol in terms of deaths, but also alcohol harms other people. Alcohol makes people violent. A lot of domestic abuses are from alcohol. Drunk driving kills people. So, alcohol is not only extremely harmful for the user, but for everyone else, too. But it's not criminalized. When you get down to marijuana, it's probably not good for you, but coffee is not good for you either.

I don't think there's been a single overdose of marijuana recorded in how many millions of users, but that's the one that's criminalized. The reasons for it go back to racism. Look at the history of marijuana criminalization. It started early in the last century—Mexicans were using it. Most prohibitions have been geared towards the "dangerous classes," poor working people and so on.

When prohibition ended, there was a big government bureaucracy left and they had to have something to do, so they started to call Senate hearings on marijuana. The American Medical Association testified and said there's nothing wrong with it, but they were disregarded. There were a few scare stories that it makes people insane and makes people criminals, so then comes the big marijuana scare.

In 1971—there have been studies of this—not only the government, but the whole elite sector from right to left had two big problems. One was that young people were getting out of control; they weren't disciplined. There were studies from the liberal sector saying we have to do something about these institutions responsible for the indoctrination of the young. They're not doing their job. Kids are thinking too much, they're too free, they're out of control, so there was a "law and order" campaign.

There was another problem. By around 1970, criticism of the Vietnam War was getting beyond legitimate bounds. For liberal educated America, you cannot say the United States did anything wrong. Maybe some individuals did, but they can't do anything wrong by definition. The U.S. can make mistakes, but they can't be criminals. That's a deep element of the intellectual culture across the spectrum.

In 1971, a lot of people were saying the war was criminal. A majority of the American population was saying the war was fundamentally wrong and immoral, not a mistake, and that's dangerous. So you have to do something about that. They had to turn us into the victims by concocting the myth of an addicted army.

> There were studies from the liberal sector saying we have to do something about these institutions responsible for the indoctrination of the young. They're not doing their job. Kids are thinking too much, they're too free, they're out of control, so there was a "law and order" campaign.

If you listened to Walter Cronkite, he would say that the "commies" are not only attacking our boys with rifles, they're attacking them with drugs. They're going to come back and start a criminal rampage in the country and they're going to destroy us. That was across the spectrum. Actually, there are studies and it turns out that drug addiction among soldiers was at the level of the youth culture—pretty much what you'd expect. There was addiction, it was alcohol, but that's not considered addiction.

So what you have is this mythology that was used by the law and order side as the reason the youth were going crazy, and they won't listen to us because they're all high on pot. So you declare a war on drugs. And it worked. By 1977, Jimmy Carter was able to give a press conference in which he was asked, "Do we owe anything to the Vietnamese?" He answered by saying no we don't because the destruction was mutual.

Around the same time the economy was being financialized. There was a reduction of productive industry, which means no jobs for working class people who happened to be black, so you have to do something with the superfluous population. What are you going to do with them? Toss them in jail. It was around that time—from Reagan until now—that the incarceration rate went from the norm for industrial countries to way beyond any country that has statistics. Look who's there. A very high percentage are blacks and now Hispanics who are there on drug charges. So it was a way to get rid of the superfluous population. It was a way of turning us into the good guys in Vietnam. It was a way of imposing law and order. And abroad it's just a cover for counterinsurgency. You want to, say, carry out chemical warfare in Colombia to clear the land for multinationals to drive the population away? You call it a drug war.

It's quite interesting because study after study shows that the drug war has no effect on drug use or even drug prices. The price of cocaine in New York stayed about the same, despite the huge amount of money that went into it.

Why do you think that in this modern time, people cling to the idea of intelligent design regardless of the evidence present for evolution?

It's partly that. But remember, it's mostly a U.S. phenomenon. In part, it's due to strains in the culture that go back to the early colonists. Remember this country was settled by religious fanatics. Take a look at the colonists who came over from England. There's a streak of providentialism, meaning carrying out God's will, hich is very strong in American culture, including the leading figures. There was an article last year in

Seed magazine called "The Essential Parallel between Science and Democracy" and it talks about U.S. policy favoring an alliance between science and business. Do you feel that an alliance like this is ideal if we are to expect the maximum benefits of the scientific community?

Let's take everything we talked about. Do you use a computer? That's science contributing to business. Is it a good thing to do? Maybe, but if you go back to the 1950s, suppose people were given a choice, an honest choice, "Look, do you want your grandchildren to have an iPod or do you want better health and education?" Maybe they would have said, "I want my grandson to have an iPod." But they weren't given that choice. These are real decisions that have to be made. Should we have solar energy? Yeah, I think we should. Should it be an honest choice among the population or should it be overwhelmed by business propaganda, which says it's all a liberal farce?

But there's no general comment to make about science and the public good. I mean it all depends on social and economic conditions, on power relations, on commitment to democracy.

At the time of this interview, Oliver Mikse was a graduate student at Penn State Hershey Medical Center and a freelance journalist for Punknews.org.

25.

Human Rights in the New Millennium

Poverty is the worst human rights crisis

Before trying to address the current state of human rights, it is worth considering what is admitted into that sacred canon. The question constantly arises, quite concretely. For example, on the International Day for the Eradication of Poverty in October, when Amnesty International declared that, "Poverty is the world's worst human rights crisis." Or two days before that, on World Food Day, when the UN food agency reported that the number of people going hungry rose to over 1 billion, while rich countries sharply cut back food aid because of the priority of bailing out banks, and Oxfam reported that 16,000 children are dying a day from hunger-related causes—that is twice Rwanda-level killing just among children—not for 100 days, but every day, and increasing. And the issues regularly arise even in the richest country in the world, where the question of whether health care is a human right is being hotly debated while some 45,000 people a year die from lack of insurance, unknown numbers from utterly inadequate insurance, in the only industrial society I know of where health care is rationed by wealth, not need.

In all these cases, the lives could be saved by a tiny fraction of the Gross Domestic Product (GDP) of the rich countries, so the question is whether they recognize the right to life as among human rights. There is a gold standard on human rights—the founding documents of the UN—the Charter, and the Universal Declaration of Human Rights (UD). The charter guarantees the right to be protected from what was declared at Nuremberg to be the "supreme international crime," differing from other war crimes in that it encompasses all the evil that follows: the crime of aggression, which is reasonably well-defined. In practice, the Charter has long ago been revoked. Article 2(4) is in the wastebasket. There are sophisticated arguments in the international law literature to show that it doesn't mean what it says, when we carry out aggression, that is; no such questions arise when Russia or Saddam Hussein do. The U.S. has been, in large measure, the global sovereign since World War II and remains so despite the increasing diversity of the global economy in past decades. Hence its practices are of great significance in considering the prospects for human rights. It is, for example, of great significance that the U.S. is self-exempted from international law—John F. Kennedy's armed attack against South Vietnam in 1962—to mention one case of no slight import that took place

From Z Magazine, June 2010

in the real world, but not in official history, opening the most severe crimes of aggression since World War II.

The Case of Nicaragua

Sometimes there have been candid explanations of the reasons for the U.S. exemption from international law. One instructive case was during the U.S. war against Nicaragua in the 1980s, which, incidentally, falls under "aggression" as defined at Nuremberg. As you know, Nicaragua brought a case against the U.S. to the International Court of Justice (ICJ). The case was presented by Abram Chayes, a distinguished Harvard University law professor and former legal adviser to the State Department. Most of his case was rejected by the Court on the grounds that, in accepting ICJ jurisdiction in 1946, the U.S. had entered a reservation excluding itself from prosecution under multilateral treaties, among them the UN and OAS Charters.

The Court therefore restricted its deliberations to customary international law and a bilateral U.S.-Nicaragua treaty. Even on these very narrow grounds, the Court charged Washington with "unlawful use of force"—in informal usage, international terrorism—and ordered it to terminate the crimes and pay substantial reparations, which would have gone far beyond paying off the huge debt that was strangling Nicaragua. The U.S. dismissed the judgment, then vetoed two Security Council resolutions supporting it and calling on states to observe international law. It was helped by Britain, which abstained.

Congress at once passed bipartisan legislation to escalate the war. The Court was dismissed as a "hostile forum" (*New York Times* editors), much as the U.S. and Israel now dismiss the UN generally as biased and hostile, because it does not always follow orders. The Court decision went further. It prohibited any form of intervention that interferes with the right of "choice of a political, economic, social and cultural system, and

the formulation of policy." The judgment applies to many other crimes, among them the U.S. assault against Cuba for 50 years, including extensive and acknowledged international terrorism and savage economic warfare.

U.S. rejection of the Court decision in the Nicaraguan case was explained by State Department legal advisor Abram Sofaer, now George Shultz Senior Fellow in Foreign Policy and National Security Affairs at the Hoover Institute, whose publications tell us that "Reagan's spirit seems to stride over the country, watching us like a warm and friendly ghost," the kind of words rarely heard outside of Pyongyang, and in this case Stanford University (though they are not alone in worship of the deity).

Sofaer explained that the majority of the world "often opposes the United States on important international questions," so that we must "reserve to ourselves the power to determine" which matters fall "essentially within the domestic jurisdiction of the United States, as determined by the United States"—in this case, international terrorism that practically destroyed the targeted country. Honest, and accurate. His explanation, and much else like it, merits more attention than it receives—that is, more than virtually zero.

There is not much point going on about the self-exemption of the powerful from international law, because it is too obvious to those who are willing to look. Let us turn then to the second of the founding UN documents, the UD. The rights I referred to earlier fall under socioeconomic rights, Article 25. But that Article too is in the wastebasket. One leading academic specialist on these matters, Philip Alston, writes that after a brief detour caused by popular pressure in the 1970s, U.S. human rights policy returned under Reagan to "the unqualified rejection of economic, social, and cultural 'rights' as rights" —that means unqualified rejection of two-thirds of the UD. It should be stressed that these provisions have exactly the same status as others. That has not been in question, at least in the international arena, since the UD was approved in 1948. It was emphasized again at the 2005 UN World Summit. Washington agreed, while rejecting the principle, under the usual veil of silence.

There have been some open expressions of utter contempt for the guarantees of socioeconomic rights. A case in point is Soviet UN Ambassador Andrei Vyshinsky, who dismissed them as just a "collection of pious phrases." He was joined by U.S. Ambassador Jeane Kirkpatrick, recently honored by Condoleezza Rice as one of the stellar figures of American diplomacy. For Kirkpatrick, the socioeconomic provisions of the UD are "a letter to Santa Claus.... Neither nature, experience, nor probability informs these lists of 'entitlements,' which are subject to no constraints except those of the mind and appetite of their authors."

The same stand was elaborated by Paula Dobriansky, Undersecretary of State for Global Affairs under Bush II, Assistant Secretary of State for Human Rights and Human Affairs in the Reagan and Bush I administrations. In the latter capacity, she took pains to dispel what she called "myths" about human rights, the most salient being the myth that so-called "'economic and social rights' constitute human rights." She denounced the efforts to obfuscate human rights discourse by introducing these spurious rights— which are entrenched in the UD, formulated at U.S. initiative, but rejected by Washington. Essentially the same view was expressed in 1990 by the U.S. Representative to the UN Commission on Human Rights, Ambassador Morris Abram, explaining Washington's solitary veto of the UN resolution on the Right to Development, which virtually repeated the socioeconomic provisions of the UD. These are not rights, Abram instructed the Commission. They yield conclusions that "seem preposterous." Such ideas are "little more than an empty vessel into which vague hopes and inchoate expectations can be poured," and even a "dangerous incitement." The fundamental error of the proposed "right to development" is that it takes Article 25 of the UD to mean what it clearly states, not as a mere "letter

to Santa Claus." U.S. practice conforms to these principles. The U.S. scarcely ever even ratifies enabling conventions that put some teeth into the letter to Santa Claus.

One example is the Convention on the Rights of the Child. It has been ratified by all countries other than the U.S. and Somalia—which has no functioning government. Or the International Covenant on Civil and Political Rights, "the leading treaty for the protection" of the subcategory of rights that the West claims to uphold, to quote Human Rights Watch and the American Civil Liberties Union, in a joint report on U.S. noncompliance with its provisions. The Covenant was ratified, after a long delay, but only with provisions to render it inapplicable to the U.S. Ratification was "an empty act for Americans," the report concludes.

Inapplicable to the U.S.

That is a considerable understatement. The few conventions that Washington ratifies are accompanied by reservations rendering them inapplicable to the U.S. That includes, among others, the Genocide Convention. A few years ago the U.S. appealed to that reservation in exempting itself from Yugoslavia's case against NATO. The Court agreed, correctly: the U.S. reserves the right to commit genocide, as was reported, but with no comment.

Another example is UN Convention Against Torture, the topic of considerable recent discussion. The rulings of Bush's Justice Department were bitterly condemned, with laments that under Bush "we have lost our way." But few asked what way we had lost. Torture has been routine practice from the early days of the conquest of the national territory, and then beyond, as imperial ventures extended to the Philippines, Haiti, and elsewhere. Of course torture was among the least of the many crimes that have darkened U.S. history, much as in the case of other great powers. Accordingly, it was surprising to see the reactions even by some of the most eloquent and forthright critics of Bush malfeasance: for example, that we used to be "a nation of moral ideals" and never before Bush "have our leaders so utterly betrayed everything our nation stands for" (Paul Krugman). To say the least, that common view reflects a rather slanted version of history.

Furthermore, it is far from clear that the Bush Justice Department violated U.S. law. That was pointed out by legal scholar Sanford Levinson, who observed that there is a legal basis for rulings authorizing torture. Washington did ratify the anti-torture Convention, but only after the Senate provided what Levinson calls a more "interrogator-friendly" definition of torture than in the Convention, a version used by the president's legal advisers in justifying the practices in Guantánamo, Iraq, Afghanistan, and who knows where else, not to speak of unknown numbers sent by "rendition" to countries where torture is virtually guaranteed—practices extended under Obama, along with other severe Bush administration violations of elementary human rights, like denial of habeas corpus.

In this case, the matter is still in the courts where Obama is appealing a decision by a hardline Bush appointee, who held that the Supreme Court ruling on Guantánamo applies also to the U.S. prison at Bagram Air Base in Afghanistan. Obama's Justice Department maintains that the U.S. government must be authorized to kidnap people anywhere in the world and send them into its secret prison systems without charges or rights, perhaps an indication of the prospects for human rights in the new millennium.

Fuller significant facts about torture are discussed by historian Alfred McCoy, the author of some of most important works on the history of torture. McCoy points out that the highly sophisticated CIA torture paradigm developed in the 1950s keeps primarily to mental torture, not crude physical torture, which is considered less effective in turning people into pliant vegetables. The CIA was basing itself on the "KGB's most devastating torture technique" and recent experimental work, McCoy writes. He reviews how the Reagan administration revised the UN Tor-

ture Convention "with four detailed diplomatic 'reservations' focused on just one word in the convention's 26-printed pages," the word "mental." These reservations re-defined torture to exclude the techniques refined by the CIA and applied worldwide. When Clinton sent the UN Convention to Congress for ratification in 1994, he included the Reagan reservations. The President and Congress therefore exempted the core of the CIA torture paradigm from the U.S. interpretation of the Torture Convention. Those reservations, McCoy observes, were "reproduced verbatim in domestic legislation enacted to give legal force to the UN Convention." That, he says, is the "political land mine" that "detonated with such phenomenal force" in the Abu Ghraib scandal and in the shameful Military Commissions Act that was passed with bipartisan support in 2006, and has been renewed by Obama, in slightly different form. So protection from torture goes the way of socioeconomic and cultural rights: it does not enter into the human rights canon.

There are other revealing examples. To select one instructive case, for 60 years the U.S. has failed to ratify the core principle of international labor law, which guarantees freedom of association. Legal analysts call it "the untouchable treaty in American politics," and observe that there has never even been any debate about the matter. This is particularly striking alongside of the intense dedication to enforcement of rights of corporations, as in safeguarding monopoly pricing rights of unprecedented scale, a core element of the highly protectionist World Trade Organization system.

Such contrasts lead to situations that are highly revealing about the prospects for human rights. Right now, the two American political parties are competing to see which can uphold more fervently its dedication to the sadistic doctrine that undocumented immigrants must be denied health care. Their stand is consistent with the legal principle, established by the Supreme Court, that these creatures are not "persons" under the law, hence are not entitled to the rights granted to persons. And at the very same moment, the Court is considering the question of whether corporations should be permitted to purchase elections openly instead of doing so only in more indirect ways, a complex constitutional matter because the courts have determined that unlike undocumented immigrants, corporations are real persons under the law, and in fact have rights far beyond those of persons of flesh and blood, including rights granted by the mislabeled "free trade agreements." These revealing coincidences elicit no comment. The law is indeed a solemn and majestic affair.

I do not want to suggest that nothing has improved with regard to concern for human rights. A significant HR culture has developed among the general population, and that has had consequences that governments and other power systems have been unable to ignore completely, a very important matter.

Humanitarian Intervention

Let's turn to the question of how official doctrines have evolved since the collapse of the USSR. Prior to that, there was a reflexive justification for any act of violence: forceful intervention, subversion, sabotage, terror, and other prima facie violations of international law and human rights—the Russians are coming, period. But with the fall of the Berlin wall that option was gone. The Bush I administration responded with a National Security Strategy and a military ("defense") budget, which announced that nothing was about to change. Therefore, a new pretext would be needed. As if by magic, one was provided by the intellectual community. The 1990s were declared to be the opening of a new era in the West, dedicated to the "emerging norm of humanitarian intervention." The new era was accompanied by a chorus of self-glorification, which may have no counterpart in intellectual history. It peaked as the U.S.-UK prepared to bomb Serbia, an attack featured in Western discourse as the jewel in the crown of

the "emerging norm," when the U.S. was at the "height of its glory," in a "noble phase" of its foreign policy with a "saintly glow," acting from "altruism alone" in leading the "enlightened states" on their missions of mercy, led by the "idealistic New World bent on ending inhumanity," opening a new page of history by acting on "principles and values" for the first time—to cite a few of the accolades by eminent Western intellectuals.

There were a few difficulties confronting the flattering self-image that was constructed with such enthusiasm. One problem was that the traditional victims of Western intervention vigorously objected. The meeting of the South Summit of 133 states, convened in April 2000, issued a declaration, surely with the bombing of Serbia in mind, rejecting "the so-called 'right' of humanitarian intervention, which has no legal basis in the United Nations Charter or in the general principles of international law." The wording reaffirms the UN Declaration on Friendly Relations of 1970.

The wording was repeated in later years, among other occasions at the Ministerial Meeting of the Non-aligned Movement in Malaysia in 2006, again representing the traditional victims in Asia, Africa, Latin America, and the Arab world. The same conclusion was drawn in 2004 by the high-level UN Panel on Threats, Challenges and Change, with prominent Western figures participating. The Panel adopted the view of the ICJ and the Non-aligned Movement, concluding that, "Article 51 [of the Charter] needs neither extension nor restriction of its long-understood scope." The Panel added that ,"For those impatient with such a response," which of course bars the jewel in the crown and many other current acts of Western violence, "the answer must be that, in a world full of perceived potential threats, the risk to the global order and the norm of nonintervention on which it continues to be based is simply too great for the legality of unilateral preventive action, as distinct from collectively endorsed action, to be accepted. Allowing one to so act is to allow all"—which is, of course, unthinkable. The same position was adopted by the UN World

Summit a year later, affirming the unchanging position of the Global South, the traditional victims.

Responsibility To Protect

Apparently, "humanitarian intervention" wouldn't do, though it lingers. Something else was needed and, lo and behold, a new doctrine emerged just in time: "Responsibility to Protect," familiarly known as R2P, now the topic of a substantial literature, many conferences, new organizations, and journals, and much praise. The praise is justified, at least in one respect. We may recall Gandhi's response to the question of what he thought about Western civilization. He's alleged to have said "it would be a good idea." The same holds of R2P. It would be a good idea.

On that much everyone should agree. But then the usual problems arise: just what is R2P and when does it apply? On the first question—what is R2P?—there are two versions. One is the position of the Global South formulated in the 2005 UN World Summit. A different position is in the founding document of R2P, the Report of the International Commission on Intervention and State Sovereignty on Responsibility to Protect, of which the leading figure and spokesperson is Australia's Gareth Evans.

It is important to distinguish these two radically different conceptions. The World Summit basically reiterated positions already adopted by the UN, at most focusing more sharply on certain components of them. The Summit reiterates the stand of the South and the High Level Panel that forceful action can only be carried out under Security Council authorization, though it allowed an exception for states of the African Union, granted a qualified right of intervention within the AU itself. If that exception were generalized, the consequences would be interesting. For example, Latin American countries would be authorized to carry out large scale terror in the U.S. to protect victims of U.S. violence in the hemi-

sphere—the conclusion that is immediate, but never drawn, oddly. We can therefore put the AU exception aside, though it is commonly adduced by proponents of R2P to show that it is not an instrument of imperialism, but rather is rooted in the South—as it is, in the World Summit version of R2P.

The crucial paragraphs of the Summit declaration, all agree, are 138 and 139. Their provisions had not been seriously contested and, in fact, had been affirmed and implemented, specifically with regard to apartheid South Africa. Furthermore, the Security Council had already determined that it can even use force under Chapter VII to end human rights abuses, civil war, and violations of civil liberties: Resolutions 925,929, 940, mid-1994. As analysts have rightly observed, "most states are signatories to conventions that legally oblige them to respect the human rights of their citizens," as resolved again by the Summit declaration. It is therefore not at all surprising that the General Assembly adopted the Summit declaration, while the sharp North-South split on "the so-called 'right' of humanitarian intervention" persisted without change. The second version of R2P, in the Evans Report, differs fundamentally from the Summit declaration. In its crucial paragraph, the Commission considers the situation in which "the Security Council rejects a proposal or fails to deal with it in a reasonable time." In that case, the Report authorizes "action within area of jurisdiction by regional or sub-regional organizations under Chapter VIII of the Charter, subject to their seeking subsequent authorization from the Security Council."

This paragraph is plainly intended to apply retrospectively to the bombing of Serbia, just what was forcefully rejected by the global South and the World Summit version of R2P. This provision of the Evans commission effectively authorizes the powerful to use force at will. The reason is clear: the powerful unilaterally determine their own "area of jurisdiction." The OAS and AU cannot do so, but NATO can, and does. NATO unilaterally determined that its "area of jurisdiction" includes the Balkans, but, interestingly, not NATO itself, where shocking crimes were committed against Kurds in southeastern Turkey through the 1990s, all off the agenda because of the decisive military support for them by the leader of the Free World, peaking in the very year when it was praised for the "noble phase" of its foreign policy with "a saintly glow"; and of course with the aid of other NATO powers. NATO later determined that its "area of jurisdiction" extends to Afghanistan. And well beyond. Secretary-General Jaap de Hoop Scheffer informed a NATO meeting in 2007 that "NATO troops have to guard pipelines that transport oil and gas that is directed for the West," and more generally have to protect sea routes used by tankers and other "crucial infrastructure" of the energy system. The expansive rights accorded by the Evans Commission are in practice restricted to NATO alone, radically violating the principles adopted by the World Summit. They open the door wide for resort to R2P as a weapon of imperial intervention at will.

Dangerous Incitements

How is R2P applied in practice? The answer will surprise no one who has the slightest familiarity with history or elementary understanding of the structure of power. Consider just a few examples. There is no thought of devoting pennies to protect the huge numbers dying from hunger and lack of health care or deprivation of other "rights" that are dismissed as "myths" and "dangerous incitement" by Washington. Protected populations are also barred from protection, among them the victims of the U.S.-Israeli attack in Gaza, who are protected persons under the Geneva conventions.

Those who are the direct responsibility of the Security Council also are unable to appeal to R2P. For example, Iraqis subjected to murderous sanctions under the saintly glow of Clinton's policies, and Blair's, sanctions that were condemned as genocidal by the administrators of the

UN programs, the respected international diplomats Denis Halliday and Hans von Sponeck, both of whom resigned in protest for that reason. Or the victims of the worst massacres of recent years in the Eastern Congo where only the ultra-cynical might suspect that the neglect has something to do with the fact that the worst offender is the U.S. ally, Rwanda, and that multinationals are making a mint from robbing the region's rich mineral resources with the crucial aid of the militias tearing the place to shreds.

There is also a lot to say about the jewel in the crown, Kosovo, but in England that (and the Balkans generally) is a matter of fanatic religious doctrine, much more extreme than evoked by Israel in the U.S., so one cannot talk about it without a lot of time and a full apparatus of footnotes and even that only evokes impressive tantrums.

R2P is rather like "democracy promotion." The leading scholar/advocate of this cause, neo-Reaganite Thomas Carothers, ruefully concludes from his careful inquiries that the U.S. promotes democracy if and only if that stance conforms to strategic and economic interests, a pattern that runs through all administrations. Leaders are "schizophrenic," he concludes with puzzlement. Critics sometimes speak of "double standards."

But there is no puzzle, just a single standard. The standard was described accurately enough by Adam Smith, speaking of England in his day, where the "merchants and manufacturers" were the "principal architects" of policy and made sure that their own interests "have been most peculiarly attended to," however "grievous" the effect on others, including the people of England, but much more so the victims of "the savage injustice of the Europeans," particularly the victims of England in India, his prime concern. Much has changed, but the principle remains.

There was great indignation last summer when General Assembly President Miguel D'Escoto called a session devoted to R2P. The *London Economist* warned of the danger that, "An angry, inconclusive General Assembly debate" might undermine this "idealistic effort to establish a new humanitarian principle," now "coming under attack at the United Nations"—an attack that the journal conjured up. As I mentioned, virtually no one opposes R2P in the form adopted at the World Summit, though there is very good reason to oppose the Evans Commission version and the selective application of the Summit declaration.

The *Economist* editors were encouraged, however, that the angry opponents they invented (of whom I was one, incidentally) would at least be countered by one panel member, "Gareth Evans, a former Australian foreign minister and roving global troubleshooter, [who] makes a passionate claim on behalf of a three-word expression, which (in large part, thanks to his efforts) now belongs to the language of diplomacy: the 'responsibility to protect'." Their ode to Evans is accompanied by a picture showing him with his hand on his face, grieving that his bold and passionate claim is coming under threat. The subtitle reads: "a lifelong passion to protect."

There is a different picture from about the same time. It shows Evans with his Indonesian counterpart, Ali Alatas, joyously celebrating the Treaty they had signed granting Australia the right to rob the oil resources of what the Treaty calls "the Indonesian Province of East Timor." The Treaty offered nothing to the remnants who survived the Western-backed onslaught on East Timor. It is, furthermore, "the only legal agreement anywhere in the world that effectively recognizes Indonesia's right to rule East Timor," the Australian press reported. The Evans-Alatas picture is familiar among those who happen to see a problem when their own countries provide the decisive support for aggression that led to one of the worst slaughters of the modern period, continuing right through the chorus of self-congratulation in 1999 at a level beyond Kosovo before the NATO bombing. And the past record far exceeded the atrocities of the Balkans. It is an uncomfortable topic, so the factual record is best avoided, or denied, as is regularly done, sometimes in remarkable ways.

The journal's choice of a photograph should come as no surprise. Twenty years earlier, when the basic facts of the near-genocidal slaughter carried out with U.S.-UK support were well-known, the editors described the great mass murderer and torturer Suharto as "at heart benign"—towards foreign investors, at least—while denouncing the "propagandists for the guerrillas" in East Timor and Irian Jaya with their "talk of the army's savagery and use of torture," including the Church in East Timor, thousands of refugees in Australia and Portugal, Western diplomats and journalists who had chosen to see, the most respected international human rights monitors, and a UN-backed truth commission, —all referred to as "propagandists," rather than champions of human rights—because they had the wrong story to tell.

And who could be a more noble and passionate supporter of R2P than the person who celebrated his achievement of granting Australia the rights to the sole resources of the territory brutalized with Australian support, while explaining that it matters little because "the world is a pretty unfair place, littered with examples of acquisition by force." True enough, a matter that appears to be of slight concern to the advocates of selective R2P and to the Western intellectuals who feign great indignation at the other fellow's crimes, while condoning or denying their own, updating a leading theme of the inglorious history of intellectuals from the earliest records.

What then are the hopes for human rights in the new millennium? The answer is the one that reverberates through history, including recent years. It is not a law of nature that we have to subordinate ourselves to the violence and deceit of the "principal architects" of policy and the doctrinal manipulation of the servants of power. As in the past, an aroused and organized public can carve out space for authentic concern for human rights more easily than ever because we can benefit from the legacy of past struggles and their achievements.

26.

The Unipolar Moment and the Obama Era

The principal architects of policy are now financial institutions and multinational corporations

In thinking about international affairs, it is useful to keep in mind several principles of considerable generality and import. The first is the maxim of Thucydides: the strong do as they wish and the weak suffer as they must. It has an important corollary: every powerful state relies on specialists in apologetics whose task is to show that what the strong do is noble and just and if the weak suffer, it is their fault. In the contemporary West, these specialists are called "intellectuals" and, with only marginal exceptions, they fulfill their assigned task with skill and self-righteousness, however outlandish the claims, a practice that traces back to the origins of recorded history.

A second leading theme was expressed by Adam Smith. He was referring to England, the greatest power of his day, but his observations generalize. Smith observed that "the principal architects" of policy in England are the "merchants and manufacturers" and they make sure that their own interests are well served by policy, no matter how "grievous" the effect on others, including the people of England, but most severely those who suffer "the savage injustice of the Europeans" elsewhere. Smith was one of those rare figures who departed from the normal practice of depicting England as an angelic power, unique in world history, selflessly dedicating itself to the welfare of the barbarians.

A telling illustration was John Stuart Mill, one of the most decent and intelligent of Western intellectuals. In a classic essay, he explained in these terms why England had to complete its conquest of India for the purest humanitarian ends. He wrote at the time of England's worst atrocities in India when the true end of further conquest was to enable England to gain a monopoly on opium and to establish the most extraordinary narco-trafficking enterprise in world history, in order to force China with gunboats and poison to accept British manufacturers, which China did not want. Mill's oration

From a talk given in Mexico City in September 2009 for the 25th Anniversary of La Journada, the independent newspaper. Published in Z Magazine, March 2010 is the cultural norm. Smith's maxim is the historical norm.

Today, the principal architects of policy are not "merchants and manufacturers," but rather financial institutions and multinational corporations. A sophisticated current version of Smith's maxim is the "investment theory of politics" developed by political economist Thomas Ferguson, which regards elections as occasions when groups of investors join together to control the state, by essentially buying elections. It is a very good predictor of policy over a long period, as he has shown.

For 2008, then, we should have anticipated that the interests of the financial industries would have priority for the Obama administration; as they were his major funders and much preferred Obama to McCain. So we find the main business magazine, *Business Week*, exulting that the insurance industries have won the struggle for health care and that the financial institutions that created the current crisis are emerging unscathed and even strengthened, after an enormous public bailout—setting the stage for the next crisis, the editors point out.

And, as they go on to discuss, other corporations have learned valuable lessons from these triumphs and are now organizing major campaigns to undermine any effort to enact even mild measures on energy and conservation, in full knowledge that success will deny their grandchildren any hope for a decent survival. It is not, of course, that they are bad or ignorant people. Rather, the decisions are institutional imperatives. Those who choose not to follow the rules are excluded, sometimes in remarkable ways.

Elections in the U.S. are extravaganzas that are largely run by the huge public relations industry, which developed a century ago in the freest countries in the world—Britain and the U.S.

But anyone who looks at a TV ad knows that business devotes huge resources to creating uninformed consumers who make irrational choices. The same devices that are used to undermine markets are adapted to undermining democracy, creating an uninformed electorate that will make irrational choices among a narrow set of options.

—where popular struggles had gained enough freedom so that the public could not easily be controlled by force. The architects of policy, therefore, recognized that it would be necessary to control attitudes and opinions. Control of elections is one element of the task. The U.S. is not a "guided democracy" like Iran, where candidates have to be approved by the ruling clerics. In free societies like the U.S., it is concentrations of private capital that approve candidates and, among those who pass through the filter, outcomes are almost always determined by campaign spending.

Architects of Policy

Political managers are well aware that on issues the public often disagrees sharply with the architects of policy. Accordingly, electoral campaigns avoid issues in favor of slogans, oratorical flourishes, personalities, and gossip. Every year, the advertising industry gives an award for the best marketing campaign of the year. In 2008, it was won by Obama, who beat out Apple computers. Executives were euphoric. They exulted openly that this was their greatest success since they began marketing candidates as they do toothpaste and life-style drugs, a technique that took off during the neoliberal period, first with Reagan.

In an economics course, one learns that markets are based on informed consumers making rational choices. But anyone who looks at a TV ad knows that business devotes huge resources to creating uninformed consumers who make irrational choices. The same devices that are used to undermine markets are adapted to undermining democracy, creating an uninformed electorate that will make irrational choices among a narrow set of options compatible with the interests of the two parties, which are best regarded as competing factions of the single business party. In both the business and political worlds, the architects of policy have regularly been hostile to markets and democracy, except for temporary advantage. Of course, rhetoric is different, but the facts are quite clear.

Adam Smith's maxim has some exceptions, which are instructive. One important contemporary illustration is Washington's policies towards Cuba since it gained independence 50 years ago. The U.S. is an unusually free society, so we have good access to internal records that reveal the thinking and plans of the architects of policy. Within months after Cuban independence, the Eisenhower administration formulated secret plans to overthrow the regime and initiated programs of terror and economic warfare, which were sharply escalated by Kennedy and continued in various forms until the present day. From the outset, the explicit intent was to punish the people of Cuba sufficiently so that they would overthrow the "criminal regime." Its crime was identified as "successful defiance" of U.S. policies dating back to the 1820s, when the Monroe Doctrine declared the U.S. intent to dominate the Western hemisphere, tolerating no interference from abroad or within.

While the bipartisan policies towards Cuba accord with the maxim of Thucydides, they conflict with Adam Smith's principle and hence give special insight into policy formation. For decades, the American population has favored normalization of relations with Cuba. Ignoring the will of the population is normal, but more interesting in this case is that powerful sectors of the business world also favor normalization—agribusiness, energy, and pharmaceutical corporations, and others who commonly set the basic framework of policy. Their interests in this case are overridden by a principle of international affairs that does not receive proper recognition in the scholarly literature of international relations, what we may call "the Mafia principle." The Godfather does not tolerate "successful defiance," even from a small storekeeper who fails to

pay protection money. It is too dangerous. It must, therefore, be stamped out, and brutally, so that others understand that disobedience is not an option. Successful defiance of the Master could be a "virus" that will "spread contagion," to borrow Kissinger's term when he was preparing the overthrow of the Allende government. That has been a leading doctrine of foreign policy for the U.S. during the period of its global dominance and, of course, has many predecessors. U.S. policy towards Iran since 1979 is another current illustration.

It took time to realize the objectives laid out in the Monroe Doctrine and they still face many impediments, but the goal is enduring and unchallenged. It took on even greater significance as the U.S. became the dominant global power after World War II, displacing its British rival. The reasoning has been lucidly explained. For example, when Washington was preparing to overthrow the Allende government in Chile, the National Security Council observed that, if the U.S. could not control Latin America, it could not expect "to achieve a successful order elsewhere in the world"—that is, to impose its rule effectively. Washington's "credibility" would be undermined, as Henry Kissinger put it. Others, too, might turn to "successful defiance" if the Chilean "virus" was not destroyed before it could "spread contagion." Therefore, parliamentary democracy in Chile must go—as happened on the first 9/11 in 1973, which is gone from history in the West, though in terms of consequences for Chile and beyond, it far outweighs the terrible crimes of 9/11.

While these three—the maxims of Thucydides and Smith and the Mafia principle—do not account for every foreign policy decision, they do cover quite a wide range, as does the corollary about the role of intellectuals. They are not the end of wisdom, but they are a good beginning.

With just that much background, let us turn to the "unipolar moment," which has been the topic of a great deal of scholarly and popular discussion since the collapse of the Soviet Union 20 years ago, leaving the U.S. as the sole global superpower instead of merely the primary superpower as before. We learn a lot about the nature of the Cold War and about events unfolding since, by looking at how Washington reacted to the disappearance of its global enemy, the "monolithic and ruthless conspiracy" to take over the world, as John F. Kennedy decribed it.

A few weeks after the fall of the Berlin wall, the U.S. invaded Panama. The purpose was to kidnap a minor thug who was brought to Florida and sentenced for crimes that he had committed, for the most part, while on the CIA payroll. He had switched from valued friend to evil demon by attempting some successful defiance, dragging his feet on supporting Reagan's terrorist wars in Nicaragua.

The invasion killed several thousand poor people in Panama, according to Panamanian sources, and reinstated the rule of U.S.-linked bankers and narcotraffickers. It was hardly more than a footnote to history, but it did break the pattern in some respects. One was that a new pretext was needed and it was quickly supplied—the threat of Hispanic narcotraffickers seeking to destroy the United States. The "drug war" had been declared by Richard Nixon, but took on a new and significant role during the unipolar moment.

The need for a new pretext also guided the official reaction in Washington to the collapse of the superpower enemy. Within months, the Bush Senior administration outlined Washington's new course. In brief, everything will stay much the same, but with new pretexts. We still need a huge military system, but for a new reason: the "technological sophistication" of third world powers. We have to maintain the "defense industrial base"—a euphemism for state-supported high-tech industry. We must maintain intervention forces directed at the Middle East energy-rich regions—where the significant threats to our interests "could not be laid at the Kremlin's door," contrary to decades of deceit. All of this was passed over quietly, barely even reported. But for those who hope to understand the world, it is quite instructive.

As a pretext for intervention, the "war on drugs" was useful, but much too narrow. A more sweeping pretext was needed. Intellectual elites quickly turned to the task and fulfilled their mission. They declared a "normative revolution" that granted the U.S. the right of "humanitarian intervention" as it chose, for the noblest of reasons, by definition. The traditional victims were unimpressed, to put it mildly. High-level conferences of the global South bitterly condemned what they called "the so-called 'right' of humanitarian intervention." A refinement was therefore necessary, so the concept of "responsibility to protect" was devised in its place. Those who pay attention to history will not be surprised to discover that the Western powers exercise their "responsibility to protect" in a highly selective manner, in strict adherence to the three maxims. The facts are disturbingly obvious and require agility on the part of the intellectual classes.

The Fate of NATO

Another question that came to the fore as the unipolar moment dawned was the fate of NATO. The traditional justification for NATO was defense against Russian aggression. With the USSR gone, the pretext evaporated. Naïve souls who have faith in prevailing doctrine would have expected NATO to disappear as well. Quite the contrary. NATO was quickly expanded. The details are revealing, both about the Cold War, about what has followed, and about how state policy is formed and implemented.

As the Soviet Union collapsed, Mikhail Gorbachev made an astonishing concession. He agreed to allow a unified Germany to join a hostile military alliance run by the global superpower, even though Germany alone had almost destroyed Russia twice in the 20th century. There was, however, a quid pro quo. The Bush administration promised Gorbachev that NATO would not extend to East Germany, certainly not farther East. They also assured Gorbachev that, "NATO would be transforming itself into a more political organization." Gorbachev also proposed a nuclear-free zone from the Arctic to the Black Sea, a step towards a "zone of peace" to remove any threat to Europe, East or West. That proposal was dismissed.

Clinton came into office shortly after and Washington's commitments quickly vanished. There is no need to comment on the promise that NATO would become a more political organization. Clinton expanded NATO to the East and Bush II went beyond. Obama apparently intends to carry the expansion forward. On the eve of Obama's first trip to Russia, his special assistant for National Security and Eurasian affairs informed the press that, "We're not going to reassure or give or trade anything with the Russians regarding NATO expansion or missile defense." He was referring to U.S. missile defense programs in Eastern Europe and NATO membership for Russia's neighbors, Ukraine and Georgia, both steps understood by Western analysts to be serious threats to Russian security, likely to inflame international tensions.

In mid-September, the Obama administration announced a readjustment of its anti-missile systems in Eastern Europe. That led to a great deal of commentary and debate, which, as in the past, skillfully evaded the central issue. The systems are advertised as defense against an Iranian attack. But that cannot be the motive. The chance of Iran launching a missile attack, nuclear or not, is about at the level of a large asteroid hitting the earth. The purpose of the U.S. interception systems, if they ever work, is to prevent any retaliation to a U.S. or Israeli attack on Iran—that is, to eliminate any Iranian deterrent. Anti-missile systems are a first-strike weapon and that is understood on all sides. But that seems to be one of those facts best left in the shadows. Returning to NATO, its declared jurisdiction is by now even more expansive than Russia's borders. Obama's National Security Adviser, Marine Commandant James Jones, urges that NATO move to the

> The systems are advertised as defense against an Iranian attack. But that cannot be the motive. The chance of Iran launching a missile attack, nuclear or not, is about at the level of a large asteroid hitting the earth.

South as well as the East, so as to reinforce U.S. control over Middle East energy supplies. General Jones also advocates a "NATO response force," which will give the U.S.-run military alliance "much more flexible capability to do things rapidly at very long distances," a goal the U.S. is working hard to achieve in Afghanistan.

NATO Secretary-General Jaap de Hoop Scheffer informed a NATO conference that, "NATO troops have to guard pipelines that transport oil and gas that is directed for the West" and more generally to protect sea routes used by tankers and other "crucial infrastructure" of the energy system. That decision spells out more explicitly the post-Cold War policies of reshaping NATO into a U.S.-run global intervention force, with special concern for control over energy. Presumably the task includes protection of the projected $7.6-billion pipeline that would deliver natural gas from Turkmenistan to Pakistan and India, running through Afghan's Kandahar province, where Canadian troops are deployed. The goal is "to block a competing pipeline that would bring gas to Pakistan and India from Iran" and to "diminish Russia's dominance of Central Asian energy exports," the Canadian press reported, outlining some of the contours of the new "Great Game," in which the U.S.-run international intervention force is to be a major player.

From the earliest post-World War II days, it was understood that Western Europe might choose to follow an independent course, perhaps the Gaullist vision of a Europe from the Atlantic to the Urals. In this case the problem is not a "virus" that might "spread contagion," but a pandemic that might bring down the whole system of global control. NATO was partially intended to counter this serious threat. Current NATO expansion and the ambitious goals of the new NATO, carry these objectives further. So matters have proceeded through the unipolar moment, adhering well to the standard principles of international affairs. More specifically, the policies conform closely to doctrines of world order that were formulated by high-level U.S. planners during World War II.

The Grand Area

From 1939, they recognized that whatever the outcome of the war, the U.S. would become a global power, displacing Britain. Accordingly, they developed plans for the U.S. to exercise control over a substantial portion of the globe. This "Grand Area," as they called it, was to comprise at least the Western hemisphere, the former British empire, the Far East, and Western Asia's energy resources. In this Grand Area the U.S. would hold "unquestioned power" with "military and economic supremacy" and would act to ensure the "limitation of any exercise of sovereignty" by states that might interfere with its global designs. At first, planners thought that Germany might prevail in Europe, but as Russia began to grind down the Wehrmacht, the vision became more expansive and the Grand Area was to incorporate as much of Eurasia as possible, at least Western Europe, the economic heartland of Eurasia.

Detailed and rational plans were developed for global organization, with each region assigned what was called its "function." The South in general was assigned a service role to provide resources, cheap labor, markets, investment opportunities, and other services, such as export of pollution and waste. At the time, the U.S. was not much interested in Africa, so it was handed over to Europe to "exploit" for its reconstruction from wartime destruction.

One might imagine different relations between Europe and Africa in the light of history, but these were not considered. In contrast, Middle East oil reserves were understood to be "a stupendous source of strategic power" and "one of the greatest material prizes in world history," the most "strategically important area in the world," in Eisenhower's words. Control of Middle East oil would provide the United States with "substantial control of the world," influential planners recognized.

Those who regard historical continuities as significant might recall that Truman's planners were echoing the doctrines of Jacksonian Democrats at the time of the annexation of Texas and conquest of half of Mexico a century earlier. These predecessors anticipated that the conquests would provide the U.S. with a virtual monopoly over cotton, the fuel of the early industrial revolution: "That monopoly, now secured, places all other nations at our feet," President Tyler declared. That way the U.S. might overcome the British deterrent, the great problem of the day, and gain unprecedented international influence. Similar conceptions guided Washington in its oil politics.

Accordingly, Eisenhower's National Security Council explained, the U.S. must support harsh and brutal regimes and block democracy and development, even though this elicits a "campaign of hatred against us," as President Eisenhower observed—50 years before George W. Bush plaintively asked, "Why do they hate us," deciding that it must be because they hate our freedom.

The Threat of Democracy

With regard to Latin America, post-World War II planners concluded that the primary threat to U.S. interests is posed by "radical and nationalistic regimes [that] appeal to the masses of the population" and seek to satisfy the "popular demand for immediate improvement in the low living standards of the masses" and development for domestic needs. These tendencies conflict with the demand for "a political and economic climate conducive to private investment," with adequate repatriation of profits and "protection of our raw materials." A large part of subsequent history flows from these unchallenged conceptions. In the special case of Mexico, a Latin America Strategy Development

Workshop at the Pentagon in 1990 found that U.S.-Mexico relations were "extraordinarily positive," untroubled by stolen elections, state violence, torture, scandalous treatment of workers and peasants, and other minor details. Participants in the Workshop did, however, see one cloud on the horizon—the threat of "a 'democracy opening' in Mexico," which, they feared, might bring "into office a government more interested in challenging the U.S. on economic and nationalist grounds." The "cure" that was recommended was a U.S.-Mexican treaty that would "lock Mexico in" to the neoliberal reforms of the 1980s and would "tie the hands of the current and future governments" of Mexico with regard to economic policy, NAFTA, duly imposed by executive power, in opposition to the public will.

As NAFTA went into effect in 1994, President Clinton also instituted Operation Gatekeeper, which militarized the Mexican border. As he explained, "We will not surrender our borders to those who wish to exploit our history of compassion and justice." He had nothing to say about the compassion and justice that inspired the establishment of those borders and did not explain how the High Priest of neoliberal globalization dealt with the observation of Adam Smith that "free circulation of labor" is a foundation stone of free trade.

The timing of Operation Gatekeeper was surely not accidental. It was anticipated by rational analysts that opening Mexico to a flood of highly-subsidized U.S. agribusiness exports would sooner or later undermine Mexican farming and that Mexican businesses would not be able to withstand competition from huge state-supported corporations that must be allowed to operate freely in Mexico under the treaty. One likely consequence would be flight to the United States, joined by those fleeing the countries of Central America, ravaged by Reaganite terror. Militarization of the border was a natural remedy. Popular attitudes towards those fleeing their countries—called "illegal aliens"—are complex. They perform valuable services as super-cheap and easily exploitable labor. In the U.S., agribusi-

ness, construction, and other industries rely substantially on them and they contribute to the wealth of the communities where they reside. On the other hand, they awaken traditional anti-immigrant sentiment, a striking and persistent feature of this immigrant society, with a history of shameful treatment of immigrants.

The Kennedy brothers have been much-lauded as American heroes. In the late 19th century, they would have had to walk past restaurants in Boston with signs saying "No dogs or Irish." Now Asian entrepreneurs are sparking innovation in the high tech sector. A century ago, racist Asian exclusion acts would have barred them from the country as threats to the purity of American society. But whatever the history and the economic realities may be, immigrants have been perceived by poor and working people as a threat to their jobs, livelihood, and lifestyles. It is important to bear in mind that the people protesting angrily today have real grievances. They are victims of the financialization of the economy and the neoliberal globalization programs that are designed to transfer production abroad and to set working people in competition with each other worldwide, thus lowering wages and benefits, while protecting educated professionals from market forces and enriching owners and managers—the Smith maxim again. The effects have been severe since the Reagan years, and often manifest themselves in extremely ugly ways that are featured right now on the front pages. The two political parties are competing to see which can proclaim more fervently its dedication to the sadistic doctrine that "illegal aliens" must be denied health care.

Their stand is consistent with the legal principle, established by the Supreme Court, that these creatures are not "persons" under the law, hence are not entitled to the rights granted to persons. At the very same moment, the Court is considering the question of whether corporations should be permitted to purchase elections openly instead of doing so only in more indirect ways—a complex constitutional matter because the courts have determined that, unlike undocumented immigrants, corporations are real persons under the law and, in fact have rights far beyond those of persons of flesh and blood, including rights granted by the mislabeled "free trade agreements." These revealing coincidences elicit no comment. The law is indeed a solemn and majestic affair.

The spectrum of planning is narrow, but it does allow some variation. The Bush II administration went far to the extreme of aggressive militarism and arrogant contempt, even for allies. It was condemned for these practices, even within the mainstream. Bush's second term was more moderate. Some of the most extreme figures were expelled—Rumsfeld, Wolfowitz, Douglas Feith, and others. Cheney could not be removed because he was the Administration. Policy began to return more towards the norm. As Obama came into office, Condoleezza Rice predicted that he would follow the policies of Bush's second term and that is pretty much what happened, apart from a different rhetorical style, which seems to have charmed much of the world, perhaps out of relief that Bush was gone.

One basic difference between Bush and Obama was expressed very well by a senior adviser of the Kennedy administration at the height of the Cuban missile crisis. Kennedy planners were making decisions that literally threatened Britain with obliteration, but were not informing the British. At that point the advisor defined the "special relationship" with Britain: Britain, he said, is "our lieutenant—the fashionable word is 'partner'." Britain naturally prefers the fashionable word. Bush and his cohorts addressed the world as "our lieutenants."

Thus, in announcing the invasion of Iraq, they informed the UN that it could follow U.S. orders or be "irrelevant." Such brazen arrogance naturally aroused hostility. Obama adopts a different course. He politely greets the leaders and people of the world as "partners" and only in private continues to treat them as "lieutenants." Foreign leaders much prefer this stance and the public, too, is sometimes mesmerized by it. But it is wise to attend to deeds, not rhetoric and demeanor.

Arena of Force

The current world system remains unipolar in one dimension: the arena of force. The U.S. spends almost as much as the rest of the world combined on military force and is far more advanced in the technology of destruction. It is also alone in having hundreds of military bases all over the world and in occupying two countries in the crucial energy-producing regions. Here, it is also establishing huge mega-embassies, each a city-within-a-city, a clear indication of future intentions. In Baghdad, the costs of the mega-embassy are projected to rise from $1.5 billion this year to $1.8 billion annually in the coming years. The costs for their counterparts in Pakistan and Afghanistan are unknown, as is the fate of the enormous military bases that the U.S. has established in Iraq.

The global basing system is now being extended to Latin America. The U.S. has been expelled from its bases in South America, most recently from the Manta base in Ecuador, but has recently arranged to use seven new military bases in Colombia and it, presumably, intends to maintain the Palmerola base in Honduras, which played a central role in Reagan's terrorist wars. The U.S. Fourth Fleet, which was disbanded in 1950, was reactivated in 2008, shortly after Colombia's invasion of Ecuador. Its responsibility covers the Caribbean, Central and South America, and the surrounding waters. The Navy defines its "various operations" to "include counter-illicit trafficking, Theater Security Cooperation, military-to-military interaction and bilateral and multinational training." The reactivation of the Fleet elicited protest and concern from the governments of Brazil, Venezuela, and others.

South American concerns have also been aroused by an April 2009 document of the U.S. Air Mobility Command, which proposes that the Palanquero base in Colombia could become a "cooperative security location" from which "mobility operations could be executed." The report noted that from Palanquero, "Nearly half the continent can be covered by a C-17 (military transport) without refueling." This could form part of "a global en route strategy," which "helps achieve the regional engagement strategy and assists with the mobility routing to Africa." For the present, "the strategy to place [the base] at Palanquero should be sufficient for air mobility reach on the South American continent," the document concludes, but it goes on to explore options for extending the system to Africa with additional bases, all of which are to form part of the system of global surveillance, control, and intervention.

These plans form part of a more general policy of militarization of Latin America. Training of Latin American officers has sharply increased in the past decade, well beyond Cold War levels. Police are being trained in light infantry tactics. Their mission is to combat "youth gangs" and "radical populism"—the latter a term that should be understood all too well in Latin America.

The pretext is the "war on drugs," but it is hard to take that seriously, even if we accept the extraordinary assumption that the U.S. has the right to conduct this "war" in foreign lands. The reasons are well known and were spelled out once again in February 2009 by the Latin American Commission on Drugs and Democracy led by former Latin American presidents Cardoso, Zedillo, and Gavíria. Their report concluded that the drug war had been a complete failure and urged a drastic change of policy, away from forceful measures at home and abroad and towards much less costly and more effective measures. Studies run by the U.S. government and others have shown that by far the most cost-effective way to control use of drugs is prevention, treatment, and education.

They have shown further that the least effective and most costly methods are out-of-country operations, such as fumigation and interdiction. The fact that the least effective and most costly methods are consistently chosen over much superior ones is enough to tell us that the goals of the "war on drugs" are not the announced ones. To determine the actual goals, we can adopt the legal principle that predictable consequences provide evidence of intent. And the consequences are not obscure. The programs underlie counterinsurgency abroad and a form of "limpieza social" (social cleansing) at home, dispatching huge numbers of superfluous people, mostly black males, to penitentiaries, a neoliberal phenomenon that has led to by far the highest incarceration rate in the world since the programs took off 30 years ago.

The reasons for Nixon's large-scale revival of the "war on drugs" were not at all obscure. Nixon and the right, joined by elite sectors quite generally, faced two crucial problems in the early 1970s. One was the rising opposition to the Vietnam War, which was beginning to cross a boundary that must be zealously guarded. Some were even charging Washington with crimes, not merely errors committed in an excess of benevolence and naiveté, as liberal commentators declared, obeying the well-established corollary to the maxim of Thucydides. A related problem was activism, particularly among young people, which was bringing about an "excess of democracy," liberal intellectuals warned, while calling for restoration of obedience and passivity and, in Nixonian hands, much harsher measures.

The drug war was a perfect remedy. With the enthusiastic participation of the media, a myth was concocted of an "addicted army" that would bring down domestic society as the shattered troops returned home, all part of an insidious communist plot. "The Communists [in Vietnam] are battling American troops not only with firepower but with drugs," the respected liberal media leader Walter Cronkite proclaimed, while his colleagues lamented that the "worst horror to have emerged from the war" is the plague of addiction of American troops (Stewart Alsop). Others chimed in as well, with impressive conformity. The plague was a complete myth, as historian Jeremy Kuzmarov has shown—though there was indeed extremely serious alcohol and even worse tobacco addiction. But the myth served its dual purposes. The U.S., thus, became the victim of the Vietnamese, not the perpetrator of crimes against them. The sacred image of the "city on the hill" was preserved. And the basis was laid for a "law and order" campaign at home to discipline those who were straying beyond the bounds of subordination to power and doctrine. Successes were substantial.

Arousing no criticism or comment, President Carter could explain that we owe the Vietnamese no debt because "the destruction was mutual." For Reagan the war was a "noble cause." President Bush senior was able to go on, with no visible objection, to inform the Vietnamese that we can never forgive their crimes against us, but out of compassion we will agree to let them join the world we rule if they show good faith in dealing with the only moral issue remaining from the noble cause, dedicating themselves to finding the bones of American flyers shot down while bombing Vietnam.

But though the successes have indeed been substantial, they were far from complete. Activism not only continued but expanded, with significant civilizing effects on the general society.

Though the world is unipolar in the military dimension, that has not been true for sometime in the economic dimension. By the early 1970s, the world was becoming economically "tripolar," with comparable centers in North America, Europe, and northeast Asia.

By now the global economy has become even more diverse, particularly with the rapid growth of Asian economies that defied the rules of the neoliberal "Washington Consensus."

Latin America, too, is beginning to free itself from this yoke. U.S. efforts to militarize Latin America are a response to these developments, particularly in South America, which, for the first time since the European conquests, is beginning to address fundamental problems that have plagued the continent. There are the beginnings of moves towards integration of countries that have mostly been oriented towards the West, not each other, and also to diversify economic and other international relations. Still more significant are the problems of internal integration. There are, at last, some serious efforts to address the Latin American pathology of rule by narrow wealthy sectors in the midst of a sea of misery, with the wealthy free from responsibility except to enrich themselves—quite unlike East Asia. One measure is capital flight. In Latin America, it approximates the crushing debt. In East Asia, it has been tightly controlled. In South Korea, for example, during the period of its rapid growth, capital export could bring the death penalty.

These developments in Latin America, sometimes led by impressive mass popular movements, are of great significance. Not surprisingly, they elicit bitter reactions among traditional elites, backed by the hemispheric superpower. The barriers are formidable, but if they can be overcome, the results may significantly change the course of Latin American history, with no small impact beyond.

27.

The U.S. in Mexico & Elsewhere

Plan Merida, preemptive counter-insurgency effort?

RICARDO LEZAMA: On December 1, 2011, the U.S. approved the sale of bunker busters to the UAE that will probably be used against Iran. Then Ehud Barack reiterated Israel's goal of striking Iran's nuclear facilities.

NOAM CHOMSKY: It's intended as a threat, of course. These bunker busters, also called deep penetration bombs, are the biggest weapons in the U.S. arsenal short of atomic bombs. They were planned during the Bush administration, but they kind of languished. When Obama came in, one of his first moves was to accelerate production of them and they're now being delivered far ahead of schedule. They're intended just for Iran. Nobody has suggested another purpose.

They were first put on Diego Garcia—the island in the Indian Ocean that the U.S. uses. The British kicked the population out. It's now used as one of the main U.S. military bases for attacking/policing Central Asia and threatening Iran.

There are reports of Israeli Special Forces inside Iran.. How close are we to a proxy war with Iran?

It is an open question. As far as I can tell the Israeli military and intelligence are opposed to it. No moral objection, they think it too dangerous for Israel. In the United States the same appears to be true. However, the political leadership in Israel is unpredictable. A couple of days ago an important Israeli opinion poll was released. It showed, quite interestingly, that the majority of the Israeli public is in favor of a nuclear weapons free zone in the Middle East, which would include Iran and Israel. This would make the Israeli military arsenal subject to inspection by the international agency and surveillance. They've [the Israeli Military] never been willing to do that and still aren't now. It's just the public that wants it. The U.S. and Israel have blocked moves like this so far.

A few days ago there was an air strike against Pakistani soldiers. Has the political leadership in the U.S. considered the potential loss of a nuclear

Ricardo Lezama interviews Chomsky.
Published in Z Magazine, February 2012

weapon, its going rogue and falling to the hands of someone, maybe their old allies?

Well, if they haven't considered it, they are really out of their minds because even the U.S. ambassador warned them about it. We know from Wikileaks that there is a serious danger if the U.S. continues its provocative activities toward Pakistan. There is an increasing chance that nuclear weapons, or some components of them, might leak to Jihadi groups. They're a small minority in Pakistan and they've probably interlaced themselves into management of the complex nuclear weapons system. That's a real danger. The same is true of the assassination of Bin Laden. It clearly increased that danger. By now the Pakistani public, an overwhelming majority, are furious at the United States. What happens to Pakistan is far more significant globally than anything that might happen in Afghanistan.

A lot of the information we know about special operations mentality comes from ex-special operations soldiers. One of them is Stan Goff. I was wondering if you had heard of him?

There is a good deal of information coming out about these operations. The U.S. now has them, apparently, in dozens of countries. It has expanded very rapidly under Obama. There's pretty good work on this by a number of people. One of the best is Nick Turse. He's done a lot of work on this and he is very reliable. It's highly likely that some of these so-called accidents in Iran have to do with either Israeli or U.S. special operations.

Originally my intent was to talk about Mexico so I'll just jump right to it. The RAND corporation has called supply-side interdiction the most inefficient approach to the drug war. Do you think that the U.S. Plan Merida, which is supposed to be about drugs,, is preemptive counterinsurgency?

The so-called drug war has been going on for a long time, but the contemporary version started under Nixon. It had, essentially, no effect on the price and availability of drugs. Furthermore, as you mentioned, even government studies show that if you really want to deal with drugs, the proper way to do it is prevention and treatment not coercive police action, border controls, or out of country operations. However, if you look at the policies, they are almost exactly the opposite of what the studies say is going to work. Prevention and treatment is very little funded, but it's the most cost effective. Out-of-country operations are the least effective and the most costly, but those are being pursued. The same is true of border control and police operations.

There really are only two possible conclusions. Either they're crazy, which we can eliminate, or they have other things in mind. If you want to make a judgment about intention, one of the first things you look at are likely consequences. If certain acts have likely consequences and are pursued over and over, you can plausibly surmise that those are the intentions. In this case, there are very definite consequences. We see them right in front of us.

Within the United States, the consequence of the drug war is a very high level of imprisonment of poor people. Race and class are pretty closely correlated in the United States so it means a very high percentage of blacks and, to a lesser extent, Hispanics, are flooding the jails. That's the domestic consequence. The consequence outside of the country—Colombia or Mexico—is counter-insurgency. So there is a plausible conclusion, which is to get rid of people who are superfluous in a financialized productive economy and to promote counterinsurgency elsewhere.

The drug barons that survive in Mexico do so with U.S. support. There is a case reported by the LA Times of a man caught and promised immunity by American intelligence. That didn't pan out. So now his defense is trying to figure out if they can have access to classified documents that could prove he was cooperating with the DEA and the FBI. Could it be that engaging in this drug war is an attempt to add value to the drug economy?

I heard one good Mexican economist explain this. Of course, it's hard to get precise figures because it's clandestine, but his estimate was that about a third of the Mexican economy depends on narco-trafficking. There was a study published about a year ago in *La Jornada*. A couple of universities did a study on Mexican businesses and narco-trafficking and some huge number—I think maybe 80 percent—were involved somehow in the narco-trafficking business. Maybe those numbers are a little off, but I don't see there is much doubt that it's a core part of the Mexican economy. After NAFTA the Mexican economy consists largely of narcotrafficking, remittances from abroad, and oil.

They say that the number one export is people.

People means remittance is coming back. And that was a pretty predictable consequence of NAFTA. It's no coincidence that in the year NAFTA was passed, 1994, Clinton began militarizing the border. It had been a pretty open border. In 2009, the RAND Corporation also published some commentary regarding Mexico's threat to the U.S. It named drug trafficking as one of the threats to regional stability, but then it also ambiguously defined an even bigger threat: left-wing nationalism seeking to retake old Mexican territory.

You know the chance that any Mexican movement, whether it is nationalist or anything else, might threaten to take over the parts of Mexico that the U.S. is occupying—the U.S. is sitting on half of Mexico—but the chances that anything like that would happen are miniscule. Just take a look at a comparison of military force. I don't think that's a serious issue. Nationalism is a threat, but not because it's going to conquer the United States. Nationalism in the international affairs literature is often referred to as a virus that can spread contagion. So if one region moves towards successful independent nationalism, that's a virus. Others might catch the disease and try to do it themselves. Pretty soon you have a spread of independent national-nationalist societies that are separating themselves from U.S. domination. In fact, that's a major theme of the post-war period—preventing viruses all over the place.

The U.S. base that's going to be established in Australia, what do you think of it?

Remember the U.S. already has dozens of U.S. bases in Australia. A new one is in Darwin in the north. Obama said he would send 2,500 Marines there. That's obviously intended as a threat to China and it's not the only one. Right now there is a major confrontation in South Korea. There is an island, Jeju, which is known as the world island of peace where the U.S. and the South Korean government are planning to destroy a large part of the coast line to establish a major naval base a couple of hundred miles from China. So there are a lot of provocative actions like that going on. And they're not denying there is a lot of danger in it.

At the time of this interview, Ricardo Lezama was a student at the University of California-Davis, studying psychology and linguistics.

28.

Israel, Palestine, and Campus Activism

All Muslims are subjected to Islamaphobia that is endemic to the U.S.

LEZAMA: What kind of repression do Palestinian Americans face in the U.S.?

CHOMSKY: In America, for one thing, all Muslims are subjected to a kind of Islamaphobia that is endemic to the United States and ranges from being detained in the airport, being followed by the FBI, problems at colleges and elsewhere. Palestinians, of course, are a part of that and there has been more in the past than today for Palestinian scholars in universities. For example, there have been efforts to defame them as anti-Israeli terrorists. However, it is the kind of repression that is familiar to ethnic groups out of favor with the U.S. government. I have plenty of Palestinian friends who make out fine. It is not off the charts. But if you're a Mexican American in Arizona and you get pulled over, the police can claim you're doing anything, basically.

In March 2012, the Israeli Air Force bombed the Gaza strip. I thought this was a particularly harsh period for Palestinians. I was hoping you could give us a brief overview of what happened?

Go back to June 2008 when a ceasefire was reached between Israel and Hamas, the dominant force in the Gaza strip. Right after the ceasefire there were no missiles at all fired by Hamas at Israel. Their missiles don't amount to much. They are kind of homemade missiles. The missile launches from Hamas stopped altogether during that period, even though Israel didn't observe the ceasefire. Part of the ceasefire was that Israel was supposed to stop the siege. Still, no Hamas missiles. You can read that on the official Israeli government website. In November 2008, the day of the presidential election, Israeli military forces invaded Gaza and killed half a dozen Hamas militants. That was followed by a missile exchange for a couple of weeks in both directions. Like always, all the casualties were Palestinian, but there were some Hamas missiles, followed by a much heavier, far bloodier, response from

Ricardo Lezama interviews Chomsky.
Published in Z Magazine, November 2012

246

Israel. This leads us to mid-December 2008. At that point, Hamas offered to renew the ceasefire. Israel considered the offer, rejected it, and decided instead to invade and attack Gaza. That is Operation Cast Lead, which started on December 27, 2008. It was brutal and murderous.

There is a very good account of Operation Cast Lead by independent participants. For example, there were a couple of Norwegian doctors working at the Gaza hospital through the attack. They just called it infanticide. The IDF killed a lot of children, were attacking ambulances, committing all kinds of atrocities. [These doctors] wrote a very graphic and dramatic account of what the invasion was like. The Israeli military must have killed 1,500 people.

There was a UN Security Council effort to call a ceasefire early in January, but the U.S. blocked it. It was very carefully planned. It ended right before Obama's inauguration. The point of that was to protect Obama from having to say anything critical about it. He was asked about it before he was elected and said, "I can't comment on that, I am not president." It started a few days before the election and ended before the inauguration.

When he was asked about it after the election, Obama took the position that we should move forwards. There was no punishment for those involved and it was a really criminal assault on a completely defenseless population. There was no pretext for it. They claim it was to protect the population from Hamas missiles, but an easy way to do that would have been to renew the ceasefire.

Israel is talking a lot about attacking Iran.

My suspicion is that they are trying to create the circumstances under which the U.S. will attack Iran—they don't want to do it themselves. I would not be surprised if they staged some kind of an incident in the Persian Gulf, which would not be hard. You and I can do it. The Persian Gulf is lined with U.S. Naval missiles, aircraft carriers, destroyers, and so on. Any small inci-

dent, a skiff, or, a boat bumping into an aircraft carrier could lead to a vicious response.

Actually, we should bear in mind that the United States is already at war with Iran by Pentagon standards. The assassinations—which is terrorism—the cyberwar, the economic warfare, are all considered by the United States as acts of war if they are done to us, but not if we do it to them. So, by our standards, we are already attacking Iran. The question is how much further we will take it.

An important aspect of this is never discussed in the United States. There is a pretty straightforward solution—a diplomatic solution namely, move towards establishing a nuclear weapons-free zone in the region. That is strongly supported by virtually the entire world. The U.S. has been blocking the solution for years. However, support for it is so strong that Obama was forced to agree to it in principle, but stated that Israel has to be excluded. Well, that is a joke. Israel has hundreds of nuclear weapons, carries out aggression, is a violent state, refuses to allow inspections, and so on.

To say that Israel has to be exempted kills the prospect of a nuclear weapons-free zone in the Middle East. This situation is coming to a head in December. There is to be an international conference on a nuclear weapons free-zone in the Middle East. Israel just announced that it is refusing to participate.

Will the U.S. participate?

So far, there is nothing official. If anybody believes Iran is a threat, which I think is pretty much fabricated, this is the way to do it: impose a nuclear weapons-free-zone. Of course, that would mean Israel has to join the Non-Proliferation Treaty. The U.S. has to stop protecting the Israeli development of nuclear weapons. That is what is required to end whatever you think the threat of Iran is. As usual, the media is suppressing this information. I don't think they even reported the fact that Israel announced its withdrawal. It was announced on the Israeli press.

Assuming that the U.S. does not go into all out war —ground troops, airstrikes, and so on—which is what the Israeli's want.

I don't think they expect ground troops, they expect, or want, a major missile and aerial assault. Israel could do it, too. Israel has submarines, which they received from Germany, which can carry nuclear-tipped missiles. I'm pretty sure they are deployed in the Gulf.

Why don't they do it themselves?

They are afraid it would be too costly. For one thing, the world would be furious. Even in Europe, Israel is regarded as the most dangerous state in the world and it is becoming a pariah state. Of course, in the third world, in the Arab and Muslim world it is feared and hated. They would rather have the United States do it.

There will be consequences for the Palestinians.

The Palestinians are in a dire state now. There is a political settlement, which is agreed on by the entire world, the UN Security Council, the International Court of Justice, World Court, by everyone, namely, a two state solution. A straightforward solution.

What about the idea that Gaza and the West Bank should be contiguous?

That's required. The Oslo agreement stipulates explicitly that the West Bank and Gaza strip are a single territory. Ever since they signed the Oslo agreement, the United States and Israel have been dedicated to undermining it. The U.S. can violate law freely but it is never reported. Everybody else is too weak to do anything about it. The U.S. is just a rogue state.

What should people in the U.S. do in response?

They should be breaking through the media and general doctrinal barriers to come to know what is going on. They should be helping people learn about this. I don't have any secret sources of information. Everything I have said is public knowledge, but it is not known by anyone.

I think that has been done on college campuses in California and elsewhere. But then the administrators begin charging for use of these spaces. They essentially price out minority organizations. Actually, it has changed a lot in the past four or five years. Just to illustrate, at UCLA back in 1985, I was invited to give philosophy lectures. I said sure, but the next day I got a call from campus police asking if they could have uniformed police accompany me everywhere I went. I said no. The next day I saw police following me everywhere I went. They are not hard to detect in a philosophy seminar.

I could not walk from the faculty club to other parts of campus. The reason is that they had just picked up a lot of death threats. They don't want someone killed on campus. I gave the talk at Royce Hall, the big campus hall, but it was like airport security—one entry, everybody's bag had to be checked. The next day there was a huge attack in the *Daily Bruin*.

First of all, it was a huge attack on me, but also on the professor who invited me. In fact, there was an effort to take away the tenure of the professor who invited me. That was in 1985. I was back in UCLA maybe a year ago. There was a huge mob, very supportive, hard to get a critical word of what I was saying. That is a huge change. It changed because of student activism. It's the kind of thing you asked about, "What should people do?"

If you get negative responses at a campus, do you get the same sort of thing happening in libraries?

It's the same thing. I can give the talk in public meetings, libraries etc. The general atmosphere has changed enormously. Even in my own university, MIT, if I was giving a talk on Israel-Palestine. Until maybe ten years ago, I had to have police protection. Now, it is unheard of. There is just a big change. The same is true in the town where I live. The propaganda is not as effective as it used to be. That is exactly why the IDF group (Stand With Us) has to go around campuses trying to counter the support for Palestine. It is trying to reverse the change in attitudes.

What do you think of the Caravan for Peace?

I think it's important. I met Sicilia a couple months ago. He's an impressive guy. Everything depends on how many people the message reaches. You can't count on the media, but others can. In fact, all through Latin America, there is a major effort to decriminalize marijuana, maybe more, but, at least, marijuana. In Uruguay, they are instituting state production of marijuana. In most of the hemisphere, there is a strong effort to decriminalize it. In the Cartagena meetings—the hemispheric meetings held a cou-

ple of months ago—the United States and Canada were totally isolated on that issue. Everyone wanted to move in that direction. In fact, my guess is that if there are ever hemispheric meetings, the U.S. will not attend. The U.S. has lost Latin America on a lot of issues. The reason is pretty obvious: they are the victims. The U.S. is responsible for both the demand and the supply—the supply of arms since the arms are coming in from the U.S. What is tearing Mexico to shreds are the arms coming in from Texas and Arizona. They are getting it at both ends. They are the ones getting massacred and smashed up. All through the hemisphere—Colombia, Guatemala, Honduras, and Mexico, of course, where it is a disaster. Naturally, they want to get out of it and the U.S. won't do it. The Caravan could be a way of educating Americans about it.

At the time of this interview, Ricardo Lezama was a student at the University of California-Davis, studying psychology and lingustics.

29.

Imminent Crises

"Appreciable risk of ultimate doom"

There are actually three crises that I think are worth telling about, at very high priority. One is the Rapture, if you like. It has to do with the threat of nuclear war, which is very high—unimaginably high—certainly unacceptably so. And that assumption is very widely accepted among strategic analysts and others. In the U.S. strategic community, the official strategic analysts in the government regard the prospect of a dirty bomb as completely inevitable in the U.S. and the possibility of a real nuclear weapon as very high, which would mean apocalypse.

There was an article a couple of months ago by Robert McNamara called "Apocalypse Soon" in which he joined the general consensus among analysts that on the current course of policy—mostly U.S. policy which is driving it—a nuclear war is inevitable. McNamara and the former defense secretary William Perry, Graham Allison, an American political scientist and professor at the John F. Kennedy School of Government at Harvard, and many others give a subjective estimate that the probability of a nuclear terror attack within the next decade is 50 percent or higher. Subjective estimates don't mean much, but it shows you what people are thinking—even in mainstream journals like the American Academy of Arts and Sciences, which is not given to hyperbole. Two leading strategic analysts a couple of months ago argued in some detail that the current policies of the Bush administration carry what they call "an appreciable risk of ultimate doom."

So that's one major crisis and how imminent it is anyone knows. It could be tomorrow. Everything's in place for it. The second one is familiar and I won't say that much about it—that's the threat of environmental catastrophe, which is not imminent in the sense that it's going to happen soon, but the decision as to whether to ensure that it does happen is soon. In fact, it might be right now.

So, for example, a couple of days ago a group of leading scientists from the National Academies of a number of counties and the National Academy of Sciences in the U.S., addressed a petition to the leaders of G8—the 8 industrial countries who were meeting in Scotland in a few months—urging them to take immediate steps to avert a threat, the details of which are unknown, but it could be catastrophic and it could be unavoidable if it's allowed to drag on too long. Again, the U.S. is alone in refusing to take any steps. That's the second imminent crisis.

Transcribed from a talk at Z Media Institute, 2005.
Published in Z Magazine, January 2013.

The third one that I have in mind is actually connected with those two. When I say the U.S. is refusing to take any steps, that's only true if you assume that the U.S. is not a functioning democracy. When you read a report in the press, saying the U.S. refused almost alone to sign the Kyoto Protocol, that's only if you exclude the population of the U.S. because an overwhelming majority of the U.S. population is in favor of signing the Protocol and, in fact, are so strongly in favor that a majority of Bush voters assumed that he was in favor, too, because it's such an obvious thing to do.

So U.S. policies are carrying an appreciable risk of ultimate doom and will continue to do so if the U.S. doesn't function as a working democracy, which is the third crisis—namely, democracy deficit—which means a country that has formal democratic institutions, but they don't function. It's extreme in the U.S. and when there's a democracy deficit in the most powerful nation in the world, and that nation has the capacity to pursue—and is pursuing—policies which carry an appreciable risk of ultimate doom and maybe apocalypse soon, and maybe irreversible environmental catastrophe, then the democracy deficit is a very serious problem and, therefore, the third imminent crisis.

Apocalypse Soon, Ultimate Doom

The first crisis, and surely the most serious, really is imminent and once it happens the result is total nuclear war. Actually, we've come extremely close in the past. You may remember that we are coming up to the 50th anniversary of what should be a famous manifesto by Bertrand Russell and Albert Einstein—July 1955—in which they pleaded with the people of the world to put aside other concerns, to think of themselves as members of the human species, and ask themselves whether they want the species to survive. They point out, sensibly, that we have a stark, dreadful, drastic choice: either doom the species to extinction or end war. That was the choice in 1955 and it's an even more urgent choice today. Of course, the choice to end war hasn't happened. And it's something of a miracle that "ultimate doom" hasn't happened already. It certainly has come very close. By all common agreement, the closest it came was in 1962 at the time of the Cuban Missile Crisis when we were within a hair of terminal nuclear war. It was known already by the participants in the crisis on all sides that the threat of nuclear war was very serious, but how serious it was finally became clear in October 2002 at the 40th anniversary retrospective meeting in Havana of American, Russian, and Cuban participants in the crisis, which Arthur Schlesinger, President Kennedy's advisor, described as the most dangerous moment in history. But they learned it was much worse than they thought. At the most dangerous moment in the crisis, Kennedy put a quarantine around Cuba. Russian ships were approaching the quarantine zone and there were submarines with them. What was unknown at the time was that those submarines had torpedoes with nuclear warheads. When they came under attack by American destroyers, the Russian submarine commanders thought there was a nuclear war going on and ordered the torpedoes fired.

Russian command orders are that three commanders have to authorize firing of the weapons. Two agreed, a third refused to agree and countermanded the order, and that's why we're still here. One word stopped the firing of the first nuclear weapons since Nagasaki, with almost unimaginable consequences.

That information was exposed in 2002 and it was quite intriguing to see the reaction. You have to have had a microscope to see it because there was barely any coverage in the press, either here or in England. I didn't check other countries, but it was probably less. That was particularly striking because that moment—October 2002—was being described by very serious analysts—the head of the Stimson Center, for example—as the most dangerous moment since the Cuban Missile Crisis.

The missile crisis was, in part, a reaction to a major international terrorist campaign that President Kennedy had organized. His brother, Robert, was the head of it and his highest priority was to bring the "terrors of the earth" to Cuba—a phrase from Schlesinger who, in his biography of Robert Kennedy, describes the latter's near fanaticism in pursuing this terror campaign. That was certainly part of the background to the crisis, which came within a word of nuclear war and, subsequently, the threat of international terrorism in October 2002. Clearly, the Russell/Einstein warning was more stark and dreadful than what they indicated in 1955.

There have been many other times in the past 50 years when survival hung by a thread, when nuclear missiles came very close to being fired. The NATO policy—meaning U.S. policy—is for missiles with nuclear warheads to be on automated response, a hair trigger alert. That means if the computer systems determine there is an attack on the U.S. or any NATO country, they have to provide the computer analysis of whether it's happening. If there is a warning —and there have been many warnings—human analysis has 3 minutes to determine whether it's real and then it gives the president 30 seconds to make a decision, so it's been reported. In 1986, Gorbachev had called for the total abolition of nuclear weapons. That ran into an impasse because of Reagan's space militarization program—what's called Star Wars. By 1994, the Russians reversed their no first strike policy and reverted to the NATO program of first strike/automated response and so on.

The reason for that is not too well known, but it should be. It had to do with the negotiations at the end of the Cold War. The U.S. wanted a unified Germany to be incorporated within NATO, which was a serious danger to the Soviet Union—now Russia. Nonetheless, Gorbachev agreed to that on the condition—which was given by George Bush I—that NATO would not expand eastward. Clinton reversed that guarantee and NATO expanded eastward, a terrible danger to the Soviet Union. In response, the Russians dropped their call for a ban on nuclear weapons and reverted to the NATO doctrine of first strike and their missiles remain on hair trigger alert. The Russian systems are nowhere near as good as the American ones and, since the 1990s when the Russian economy totally collapsed and probably lost about 50 percent of its capacity, there was a huge demographic disaster. Millions of people died. Their computer systems are undoubtedly far more deteriorated, which means the threat of accidental war again rises.

Increasing The Danger

Further, U.S. policies are increasing the danger, very consciously. By now the U.S. spends approximately as much on the military as the rest of the world—estimated at 47 percent of total world spending (Swedish Research Institute estimate). It was understood that what's called "the transformation of the military" was going to lead almost inevitably to a response by potential adversaries and it did. The Russians sharply increased military spending after the Bush administration came in and in response to the U.S. tripling of its military spending, the Russians held their first war games in decades at which they displayed new, more sophisticated offensive missiles aimed at the U.S., all on alert, making the thread on which survival hangs even thinner. These are some of the reasons for the concerns of mainstream strategic analysts about ultimate doom and the possibility being increased. The U.S. is so far ahead of them in weaponry that the Russians are compelled to shift missiles constantly across their huge territory to counter U.S. threats.

That adds to another risk, namely the risk that they'll be stolen. The U.S. is well aware that Chechen rebels have been casing Russian railroad stations, certainly with the intention of stealing missiles. If one missile is stolen with some launch device, that means the end of some American city. If several are stolen, it could mean whole nations are destroyed. There's nothing secret about this—you can read it not only in the technical literature, but in the *Washington Post*, places like that. It's understood that the increase in military spending is having precisely this result. But it's just not a significant problem. It's not that the Administration wants ultimate doom, it's just that it's not a high priority. There are much higher priorities than whether the species survives.

One much higher priority is to stuff more money into the pockets of their rich friends and dominate the world in the short term. The thinking is standard and it drives policy, and it will continue to, as long as the democratic deficit reigns and as long as policy is out of control of public opinion. The same is true of a potential environmental catastrophe.

There have been attempts over the last 50 years to strengthen the thin thread on which our survival rests. The most important was the Non-Proliferation Treaty (NPT) of 1968, which went into effect in 1970. This May [2005] was the regular five-year review of the NPT by participating states, which was almost everyone. It met in New York and ended up a total fiasco. Nothing happened. It had been predicted by high level analysts that if this review failed, it might be the end of the treaty. There was barely any reporting of it. And the reporting I saw kept to the U.S. agenda, which was to focus on one part of the treaty. There are two crucial articles in the treaty. One is article six, which obligates the nuclear states to take good faith measures to eliminate nuclear weapons. It's a core part of the treaty. Of course, the U.S. refuses to allow this to be discussed, but the Bush administration was the first to have formally stated that it no longer accepts Article Six and that maintaining nuclear weapons is part of the U.S. arsenal. So the U.S. has officially said—no Article Six.

Furthermore, the U.S. is proceeding to violate it by planning to develop new nuclear weapons. Okay, that's one issue that was crucially part of the NPT review. You'll have to search pretty hard to find that one. There's also a unanimous World Court decision which obligates the nu-

clear powers to pursue this commitment under Article Six, which is connected to a series of other commitments. One is that the nuclear states sign the Comprehensive Test Ban Treaty. In 1999, the Republican Congress blocked it and the Bush administration took it off the agenda. So that's gone. Another condition was the Anti-Ballistic Missile Treaty, which the Bush administration rescinded.

There were a couple of others, but the most important one of all is FMCT or Fis-Ban—the treaty banning production of fissile materials —nuclear grade materials, such as highly enriched uranium. So the FMCT is absolutely crucial because it's well understood that if fissile materials continue to be produced, then a nuclear war is inevitable.

The Fissile Treaty had been under review for a long time. In November, it came up for a vote at the UN and the vote was 147-1 with 2 abstentions. One abstention was Israel—reflexive because of its ties to the U.S.—so that vote is insignificant. The second one is more interesting. It was Britain. In the latest issue of Britain's *Journal of the Royal Institute of International Affairs*, Britain is described as the spear-carrier for Pax Americana—and not with great pride. So the spear-carrier abstained and the British Ambassador explained why at the UN meetings. He said that the British government supported the fissile materials ban, but it couldn't accept this version of it because this version was too divisive, namely 147-1. That tells you something about the ranking of human survival among the priorities of the leadership of the world's most powerful state and its spear-carrier.

Let me turn to Article 4, which has to do with non-nuclear states. Article Six has to do with nuclear states. Article 4 grants the non-nuclear states the right to develop peaceful uses of nuclear energy. That's the one the U.S. wanted to focus on. That's why the NPT broke down because the U.S. insisted on focusing on Article 4, not on the total package. What does this have to do with? Well, it has to do with whether Iran should be permitted to pursue its legal right, under the treaty, to develop nuclear energy. The U.S. position is that Iran can only be doing this if they want nuclear weapons because there's no reason for an oil rich state like Iran to develop nuclear energy unless they're planning to develop nuclear weapons.

It's a little difficult for the U.S. to take that position, but, thanks to the loyalty of the media, they didn't have much trouble with it. One of the problems is that when Iran was being ruled by a U.S. client, namely the Shah, who was put in power by the U.S. and its spear-carrier back in 1953—overthrowing parliamentary democracy —the U.S. was in favor of Iran's developing nuclear energy on the grounds that they needed it because their oil was going to run out. U.S. universities—my own for example—were involved with deals with the Shah to train nuclear engineers, surely with the approval of the U.S. government. In fact, Henry Kissinger, then secretary of state, specifically asserted that Iran— then an ally—must proceed to develop nuclear energy.

However, there was a point to that. The fact of the matter is that, if you develop the capacity to enrich uranium for peaceful uses, it's not a long step to go on from there to nuclear weapons. So Article 4 is a real gap in the NPT. Something should be done to close that gap. That much is correct.

There are proposals for how to do that. The most important one—and the only one that makes any sense—is from the head of the International Atomic Energy Commission, Mohamed El Baradei, who proposed in an article in the *Economist*, and elsewhere, that production of fissile materials be under international control. That proposal is known and it's described in the strategic analysis literature as not pragmatic. That's a polite way of saying: the U.S. won't accept any international control of the production of fissile materials. And, since the U.S. will not accept international controls of any kind or international law or international obligations and treaties, this method of controlling the production of fissile materials—the sensible way of overcoming the gap in Article 4—that's ruled out

because it's not "pragmatic." Again, that's as long as the democratic deficit persists.

I'm pretty sure if it came up in a poll and people were asked: should we accept international guarantees and controls, I'm willing to bet, people would say yes, judging by other similar results. But it doesn't come up. These issues, of course, never come up because it's not for the general public to decide. But there's nothing very profound about it: if fissile materials are produced and there's no controls, they'll sooner or later turn into bombs, which means apocalypse soon, ultimate doom, either by failure of computer systems or by stealing missiles with nuclear warheads, or just making bombs.

Well, U.S analysts have proposed alternatives, which they say are more "pragmatic" than this one; that is, the nuclear powers, which means the U.S., provide a guarantee to every country that the U.S. will produce fissile materials and a guarantee that it will provide them for peaceful uses. So other countries should have trust in the U.S.—this is their pragmatic alternative. It's inconceivable that any country is going to trust the U.S., given its record.

And so the threat hangs very thin. The NPT broke down and nobody has any hope for the next one, which means that the critical issues that determine survival of the species—what Russell and Einstein were talking about—those issues for the moment are moot. There's no cut off treaty because it was blocked by that "divisive" 147-1 vote and the whole package of treaties that are part of the compact for the nuclear states are gone because they've all been rescinded and the Bush administration has already said it doesn't accept Article 6 and is going ahead to develop new nuclear weapons. That's where that one stands.

Again, this is a question on which the public ought to have a voice, but can't unless the issue is at least made public—which it isn't. Is Iran actually developing nuclear weapons? I don't know, but my guess, for what it's worth, is that, for once, U.S. claims are correct. In fact, I think that's widely accepted. One of Israel's leading military historians wrote an article concluding that, while he couldn't be certain that Iran was developing nuclear weapons, if they weren't, they were crazy because, of course, they ought to be developing nuclear weapons. They're completely surrounded by nuclear armed states. They're under serious threat by the world's superpower.

The U.S. has just taught a lesson to every country in the world. That if you want to protect yourself from invasion by the U.S., you'd better have a deterrent otherwise the U.S. will invade you. That's what the Iraq war was about. Iraq could be attacked because it was known to be defenseless. It was understood that Iraq was hanging together with scotch tape—there's no military, it's the weakest state in the region—so it's safe to attack it.

That's just telling the world that if you don't want to be invaded, then have a deterrent. There's only two deterrents around. Nobody can spend 47 percent of world military expenditures to match the U.S., so the only deterrents around are either nuclear weapons or terrorism.

A Terrorist Haven

In advance of the Iraq war, it was pointed out very widely in the international affairs literature—and even by intelligence agencies, including U.S. intelligence agencies, that the invasion of Iraq was likely to increase nuclear proliferation and increase the threat of terror. The Bush administration certainly was aware of that. Their own national intelligence estimate said that right before the war. But they went ahead and their predictions were verified, not surprisingly.

The very likely (we don't know) Iranian moves to develop at least the potential for nuclear weapons, meaning getting close enough so they can have a deterrent if they need it, is one example—same with North Korea, same with others. And the increase in terror is already verified. In fact, it was observed by intelligence agencies and independent analysts even during the war and by the end, it was completely verified

that, yes, it increased the threat of terror exactly as expected. The highest national intelligence estimate, in December 2004, concluded that the effect of the war, as anticipated, was to increase the threat of terror.

Remember that Iraq, whatever you think about it, was not involved in terror before the war nor did it had weapons of mass destruction (WMDs). But after the war, it became what's called a terrorist haven by intelligence analysts. In the words of the intelligence estimates, the Iraq war created a new category of professional terrorists—armed and trained. They'll be spreading around the world to carry out terrorist attacks and, obviously, increasing the threat of terror. Actually, it goes well beyond that.

Remember when the invasion took place, Bush, Blair, Powell, Rice, and the rest of them kept insisting that there was what they all called a single question: Will Iraq stop its production of WMDs? That was the single question on which the U.S. Congress agreed to authorize force and on which the war was allegedly started.

That single question was soon answered. And something interesting happened right afterwards. The answer to that single question that's usually given is not quite accurate. The answer is, usually, that they didn't have any WMDs and probably hadn't any for ten years or more. But they did have WMDs at some point—namely the ones provided to them by the U.S., Britain, and others during the 1980s, for their friend Saddam Hussein. The Reagan and Thatcher administrations provided their friend Saddam with substantial aid, including dual-use technology, which could be used to produce WMDs. This continued to the day of the invasion of Kuwait.

At that time, some of these weapons were still there. They had been under UN control after 1991 and UN inspectors were dismantling them, but there were still some there. What happened to them? Rumsfeld and Wolfowitz forgot to tell their troops that they should guard the sites. The only sites that were still being guarded were the oil ministry and the security ministry. That's why some of the most important treasures of civilization were looted and destroyed—the worst destruction since the Mongol invasion. The sites where the WMDs were kept were also massively looted, according to UN satellite inspections. They found 109 sites that were completely looted, including high precision equipment which could be used to develop nuclear weapons, missiles, bio-toxins, and so on. Where they've gone, nobody has a clue—presumably in the hands of terrorists. If there was anything remotely like a free press in the U.S. or England or France or Germany or anywhere, the headlines would be reading that, "The U.S. and Britain invaded to destroy WMDs that weren't there and the effect of their invasion was to provide WMDs—that they had given Saddam Hussein—to terrorists who they had organized and trained in Afghanistan as part of state policy." That's the headline. That's exactly what happened.

This is all quite apart from what happened to Iraq—an estimated 100,000 civilians dead by 2004, virtual doubling of malnutrition among young children, now down to the level of Burundi, below Uganda and Haiti, meaning permanent brain damage, hundreds of thousands of wasted children, This is in a country that had already been devastated by U.S./British sanctions, which killed nobody knows how many hundreds of thousands of people and probably kept Saddam in power. Why was it worthwhile? There's what's called a conspiracy theory, which is usually used to mean an obvious truth that no one's allowed to talk about. The conspiracy theory here is that the fact the U.S and Britain invaded Iraq had something to do with its having oil there. In fact, it has everything to do with it. Iraq is estimated to have the second largest oil reserves in the world.

The oil is unusually rich because it's largely untapped and it's extremely cheap because it's near the surface, which means huge profits for any corporations that get the rights to drill there, which will be the U.S. and Britain, it is hoped, thanks to the invasion.

But much more important than that is strategic power. Zbigniew Brzezinski, one of the more astute of the planning community, pointed out in a recent article, quite accurately, that one positive effect of the invasion of Iraq (he was not in favor of it), other than control of Mideast oil, is that it gives the United States what he called "critical leverage" over its rivals—namely European and Asian economies. That is what most of the conflicts in the Middle East have been about for 50 years—and no doubt critical leverage was crucial. That Europe and Japan might pursue an independent course has been a core concern of U.S. policy planning since the Second World War.

Critical Leverage

In the last 30 years or so, the world economy has become what's called tripolar—3 roughly comparable economic centers: North America, run by the U.S., Europe, and a northeast Asian complex (loosely linked to India) including: Japan, South Korea, China, and the SE Asian complex, which is now the most dynamic economy in the world, controlling maybe half of the world's foreign exchange. It's willingness to buy U.S. Treasury Bonds is keeping the U.S. afloat. So the world is tripolar, except the U.S. dominates as a military force. In every other dimension, it's just one of three and not necessarily the strongest.

If the U.S. can hold on to and maintain control of Iraq, that will be crucial. In fact, it's astonishing that it's had so much trouble. I assumed, along with many others, that this would be the easiest military occupation in history. The country was barely surviving—no military, no resistance, no outside support for resistance—and the invaders were able to put to an end two brutal regimes—Saddam's and the sanctions regime.

Actually, if they had put an end to the sanctions regime, the Iraqi people would have probably put an end to Saddam's regime. One of the major effects of the sanctions was to devastate civilian society, strengthen the dictator, and force people to rely on him for survival. If that hadn't been the case, there's a strong likelihood that Saddam would have been sent the same way as a whole string of other monsters the U.S. and Britain supported right to the end—Ceausescu in Romania, Marcos in the Philippines, Suharto in Indonesia, Duvalier in Haiti. The fact of the matter is that the U.S. and Britain supported them right to the end when they were ultimately overthrown from within.

Anyway, it's happened, there's an utter catastrophe. It's not very clear what they can do about it. Even worse, from the U.S. point of view, the U.S. was compelled to accept elections in Iraq, so the new party line became that the U.S. is promoting democracy. You can take a look at the mainstream press. It was reporting quite openly that the U.S. was trying in every possible way to block elections. These were elections, by the way, forced by massive non-violent resistance, which the U.S. tried to take credit for, while attempting to subvert the outcome.

Brazen Liars

With all the fancy talk about democracy promotion, can the U.S. permit a sovereign, more or less democratic Iraq? Can it? The foreign minister of Iran recently said that Iran is strongly in favor of sovereignty in Iraq. Did anybody take him seriously? No, because you never take statements by political leaders seriously. There's a simple reason: they're totally predictable, therefore, they carry no information whatsoever so you disregard them. They're predictable because everyone's always following noble objectives. Try to find an exception—Hitler, Stalin, Saddam, the Japanese fascists—they're just overflowing with love for everyone. See if you can find any case when they weren't supporting freedom, justice, every wonderful thing you can think of. For that reason, nobody pays much attention to the pronouncement of leaders. The only place where they do is maybe North Korea where, if the dear leader says something, I suppose the people believe it. The other example is

the U.S. and the West. Western intellectuals have to believe it when the dear leader says something. Remember the single question about the invasion of Iraq: Is Saddam going to stop producing WMDs? When that frittered out a few months later, the party line changed to what the liberal press called Bush's messianic vision to bring democracy and freedom to Iraq, the Middle East, and the universe.

I actually did a study of this and I couldn't find any deviation. This was instantly accepted by everyone. Yes, it was the messianic vision. In fact, there is one particle of evidence for it: the dear leader said so. Try to find some other evidence for it. Actually, there's massive evidence against it. Take a look at the timing. When did this become the messianic vision? A soon as the single question was answered. So Bush, Blair, and the rest are saying, we are among the most brazen liars in history. We drove you to war because we claimed we wanted the answer to the single question, but we weren't telling you that our real reason was the messianic vision. In other words, we are brazen liars, but you've got to believe us now. And everyone believes it. It becomes what the *Washington Post* calls maybe the most noble war in history run by idealist-in-chief Paul Wolfowitz, who's got a passion for democracy—and on and on.

So, can the U.S. accept the sovereignty of Iraq? Well, what would the policies be of a sovereign, democratic Iraq? It's not hard to imagine. It would have a Shiite majority. One of its first policies would be to improve relations with Shiite Iran. They don't particularly love Iran, but they'd rather have a friendly neighbor than a hostile one. They'd probably try to continue the process of integrating Iraq into the general Muslim region.

There's another problem lurking in the background. Saudi Arabia next door happens to have a Shiite population right on the border. Furthermore, that Shiite population happens to be sitting on most of the oil. They'd been oppressed for years and the turmoil of the war had led to pressures for a degree of autonomy. A sovereign independent Iraq would only increase that. So here you have the specter of a Shiite alliance, independent of the U.S., controlling most of the world's oil. The U.S. is going to accept that? Furthermore, Iraq is likely to move to regain its natural position in the Arab World as a leading state, if not the leading state—highly educated population, huge resources, etc. That's a position that goes back to biblical times, under various names, which means they'll re-arm and they'll have to confront the regional enemy, Israel, which means they'll probably have to develop WMDs, if only for deterrence.

So here's what we're looking at—a Shiite alliance controlling most of the world's oil, re-arming, maybe developing, WMDs, independent of the U.S. Is it imaginable that the U.S. is going to accept this?

And there's more. In fact, the best witnesses for the defense of the messianic vision should be advocates for democracy promotion. The leading one by far is Thomas Carothers, the head of the Carnegie Endowment Program on law and democracy, who published a book in which he reviews democracy promotion after the Cold War. He's a strong advocate of democracy promotion. He calls himself a neo-Reaganite. He was in the state department under Reagan as part of the democracy promotion project. What he concludes in his very book—which is really quite scholarly—is that there's a strong line of continuity in the U.S. with regard to democracy promotion. He says every Administration is schizophrenic. Why? They promote democracy only in cases that support U.S. strategies and economic objectives. If they don't support U.S. objectives, the U.S. doesn't support democracy. In fact, it often overthrows it.

To finish the story, Carothers also happened to write a book about democracy promotion in the 1980s. Again, he's writing partly from an insider's perspective. He thinks the Reagan programs are very sincere. He greatly admires them, participated in them, but he says they were a failure—as he points out, a systematic failure. In the regions where the U.S. had limited power, mainly the Southern Cone of the Western Hemisphere, there was real progress toward democracy which the U.S. tried to block. In the regions where U.S. power was greatest, there was no progress toward democracy—a kind of accidental correlation.

Carothers says the reason is that the U.S. would permit only top down forms of democracy with traditional elites in power, elites that have been allied with the U.S. in very undemocratic societies. So there was no progress.

What we have, on the one hand, is a mountain of reasons for not taking the rhetoric about Bush's messianic vision seriously, and only one reason for taking it seriously, namely, it was declared by the dear leader after the single question got the wrong answer.

One final word about the third problem, which is, in a way, the core of the democracy deficit. There is a huge gap between public opinion and public policy. Right before the November elections, there were major studies of public opinion carried out by some of the most prestigious institutions that monitor it. The studies received virtually no reporting—two or three newspapers. What they found was that on foreign and domestic policy, the bi-partisan media consensus is way to the right of the general population on issue after issue. It's one of the reasons why the elections had to carefully avoid issues and keep to imagery to delude the public. And it continues. When the Federal Budget came out, again major studies of public opinion on what the budget ought to be were almost exactly the opposite of what the budget was.

The studies show that the public is overwhelmingly in favor of cutting the military spending, of increasing social spending—health, education—more funding for renewable energy, more funding for the UN, which the public, unlike the political parties, very strongly supports—so strongly that a majority of the public, amazingly, even thinks the U.S. should give up the veto and follow majority opinion at the UN.

In general, there's just an enormous gulf between opinion and public policy which is in many ways a very optimistic conclusion—very optimistic. What it means is there are tremendous opportunities for educating people enough so they understand their own opinions are not idiosyncratic—that they are public opinion—and on to organizing and activism. We've got every imaginable opportunity to do something to put an end quickly to crises which really are extremely severe and, in some cases, imminent.

30.

The Most Dangerous Belief

Designing the meaning of your life

MORRIS/HOLDER: The main body of the following questions were posed by younger folks. The age range is roughly 12 through 20. Most of the young people with whom we spoke included in their questions: "What is the meaning of life?"

CHOMSKY: The meaning of life is what you make of it. Life does not have any meaning apart from that, for a human, a dog, a bacterium, or anything else. It is up to you what the meaning of your life is. So, it is partially under your control.

If someone were to say, "Life is just a bowl of cherries?"

If that is the way you want to look at life, fine. If you decide your life is maximization of goods, then that is the meaning of life. We can have sympathy for you, but that is what it is. If you decide that your life is friendship, love, mutual aid, mutual support, a community of people who try to increase their own and other people's happiness and welfare, then that is the meaning of life. But there is no external force that decides.

Of the 30 or 40 young people to whom we posed the question, "If you could ask a question of someone who is considered one of the smartest people in the world, what would you ask?" Most of them asked that question—what do you think is driving the need to answer that question about the meaning of life?

Transcribed from a talk at Z Media Institute, 2005. Published in Z Magazine, January 2013.

It is probably the sense of either unwillingness or inability to take your life in your own hands. If you see yourself as a creature of external forces, buffeted by a market, government, parental authority, whatever it may be, then you search for something elsewhere that will tell you what the meaning of your life is. If you have developed (it is a value judgment) what I think of as a healthy respect for yourself and others, you will design the meaning of your life. Of course, you can't do it completely. You may want to be a world champion high jumper, let us say, and you may not be able to achieve that, but you can shape your life to a substantial extent and that way give it meaning, in fact, discover the meaning as you proceed—you don't know in advance. It is after you develop relationships that you discover their value.

Do you think the key would be in the relationship itself? For example, in some collective meaning?

Unless you are a hermit. If a person decides I'm going to be a hermit, I'll get myself a piece of land in Montana, I'll farm it, I'll live by myself, I won't pay any attention to other human beings, I'll have no form of communication with others, okay, that is the meaning of your life. I know people who have become hermits. I met one climbing a mountain once. The guy was living in a mountain hut and he just wanted to be alone. That is a choice you can have. For most people, life means warm, supportive social relationships. But you don't know it in advance.

Take, say, marriage. Suppose you get married when you are 20. You don't really know what the meaning of that relationship is. You may be discovering it 60 years later. As relationships mature, circumstances change, you have children—which adds a new dimension of meaning to your life that you can't imagine, or maybe it becomes sour. But these are things that develop through life and at each stage. If you do have the sense of self-respect and autonomy and concern for others you can, within the limits that external factors provide, determine and discover the meaning of your life. Discovery is a big part of it.

This is a question from a 12-year-old. "What do you think happens when people die?"

I believe the body deteriorates and that is the end of the person.

And from the same questioner: "If one is not a believer in religion, is it worth challenging others beliefs in things like reincarnation and an afterlife?"

I don't think there is any simple answer to that. You have to ask yourself whether the religious beliefs that you don't accept have a significance in other people's lives that would reduce the value of their lives if those beliefs were taken away from them. If that is the case, then it would be supreme arrogance to challenge their beliefs.

If, on the other hand, you think the beliefs are basically a burden, that they would be freer, more creative, more independent individuals without those irrational beliefs ("irrational" in that they are not based on evidence and argument), well, then, it makes sense to discuss the beliefs with them. It is not just religious beliefs, but any other beliefs as well.

These beliefs are a mitigating factor to life's pitfalls?

For many people, their religious beliefs are like a foundation for their survival and existence. I know people like that. So, a poor immigrant woman who has lived here (I'm thinking of somebody) for 50 years and worked her way up to the point where she had children, managed to get them to school—she lived a very hard life in the ghettoes, her husband had all kinds of problems and ended up in the army—but she created a kind of life for herself and she is an Evangelical Christian. A large part of her life is the community of believers that she is part of. So, for example, they have prayer sessions in the evenings where they visit people who are ill or have prayers for others they know who are ill or maybe disturbed, etc. And that enriches their lives and may even enrich the lives of the people they are praying with.

Why should anyone try to take that away by telling them there isn't going to be any Second Coming?

Or, suppose a mother would love to believe that her dying child is not gone forever, but that she will see him again in heaven. Do you have to give her lectures in epistemology?

There are plenty of people we call "religious," who belong to religious communities, but don't have these beliefs. If you go to a New England church in some middle class, professional, academic community, the people might not have any more beliefs than I do, but being part of that community is important for them, meeting on Sunday morning, going through the rituals. There are families who are held together by ceremonies—you come for this ceremony, for that ceremony, your life is built around it. You don't have to have any particular beliefs for that to function.

That is even true of ultra-orthodox people. I can think of my grandfather, for example, who was an ultra-orthodox Jew. If I had asked him whether he believed in God, I don't think he would have known what I was talking about. Religion was your life, the practices you carried out, your associations, where you spent your time, etc. You did say prayers which had words like "I believe," but it did not matter much whether you questioned them or didn't question them; they were just among the other practices.

The rituals served as a...

...as a structure of life. It is not for me. I don't want it, but if other people want it, is it my job to try to take it away from them? If it has harmful consequences for the person or for others, like if under the banner of religious belief you launch a crusade, let us say, well that is a different matter. But that is true of any belief, secular beliefs too. Actually, one of the most dangerous religious beliefs, maybe the most dangerous belief, is the secular faith in the sanctity and power of the state. We see that all the time.

Take what is called "American exceptionalism," the notion that we are unique in history; there is the fundamental benevolence of our leaders; they may make mistakes, but always with good intentions. That is one of the most dangerous beliefs. It is a religious belief and has no foundation in fact, and it is one of the most dangerous that exists. In fact, secular religions have been extremely dangerous. Nazism, for example, was a secular religion.

Would you place market fundamentalism in that category?

Yes, it is. The belief in markets is a religious belief. Rationally, we know of all kinds of fundamental, what are called, "inefficiencies" in markets. But the belief that they can solve everything and that everything can have a value determined by the market, I think you can regard that as a religious belief. The other day I happened to be reading a careful, interesting account of the state of British higher education. The government is a kind of market-oriented government and they came out with an official paper, a "White Paper" saying that it is not the responsibility of the state to support any institution that can't survive in the market. So, if Oxford is teaching philosophy, the arts, Greek history, medieval history, and so on, and they can't sell it on the market, why should they be supported? Because life consists only of what you can sell in the market and get back, nothing else. That is a real pathology.

The author of the article says, plausibly, that the government is trying to turn first rate universities into third rate commercial enterprises and also cheapen existence, weakens the society, turns it into some kind of a pathological creature, and people may adapt to it and decide, "that is the way I want to live" but then it is a sad society. It is just like societies of religious fundamentalists where people are really committed to the fundamentalist beliefs, to their own detriment and the harm of others. It can happen and, in fact, is happening.

Given the pathological nature of markets, why the continued perpetuation and belief? It is getting to the point where it might destroy the human future.

First of all, the beliefs are nuanced. The advocates of markets typically don't want them for themselves, they want them for others. Let's say you are the CEO of J.P. Morgan Chase and you may advocate markets, for others, but you don't want them for yourself. You want the government insurance policy that enables you to survive. And, as soon as you get in trouble, you run, cap in hand, to the taxpayer and say "save me." In fact, the bailouts are the least of it. There is a recent IMF study that tries to estimate where the profits of the big banks come from, and they conclude that they come almost entirely from the government insurance policy, not the bailouts, but the access to cheap credit, the higher credit-ratings because the agencies know you are going to be saved, and the chance to take risky and highly profitable transactions because you are not in danger if it breaks down. And, of course, what is called "systemic risk," the impact on others, isn't part of a market interaction, which is—suppose you sell me a car. In a market structure you are supposed to ask what is the best deal for you and I am supposed to ask what is the best deal for me. We are not supposed to ask what is the best deal for him [someone outside the immediate transaction], but there is an effect on him: there is another car on the road; there is more pollution; there are more traffic accidents, and that multiplies over the society. It can end up being a huge cost. Those are called externalities.

If the externalities are internalized, that is, if we had to pay for those consequences, probably only the super rich could ever drive a car. And there is no way to estimate those consequences. It would be an impossible calculation. How do you figure out what the cost is of the fact that five years from now he will have an accident, or get lung cancer or something? There is no possible way to do it.

There are what people call "libertarian economists" (a strange notion) who think you can calculate all of these things and life could be run by some sort of huge computer that makes every action you carry out a market transaction. Gary Becker, of the University of Chicago, a Nobel Laureate, received a Nobel Prize for things like this. Marriage, he argued, is an economic transaction. You measure the quality of the person, the possible gain you will get from being with that person, the loss that will come along because of conflicts and somehow out of that, you decide to get married. It is pathological. There are economists of that nature who argue against the existence of roads because why should I pay for a road in the other part of town that I am never going to use.

That undercuts my liberty, my freedom. So, if you believe in freedom you are against that. Well then, how do you get roads? If I want to drive from my house to MIT, I build a road. Then comes the question: "How do I keep other people from using it?" Easy, I hire an army. Suppose they hire a bigger army. I hire a still bigger army. That way we are all free. If some fiction writer imagined a concept of hell, it would be a market society.

There are actually people who think like this?

This is in the literature. In fact, it is believed abstractly because when push comes to shove, the advocates want markets for others. The whole history of imperialism is like that. So, for example, Britain advocated markets not for itself, but for its colonies. That way, what are called "liberal rules" were imposed on India and it de-industrialized, it collapsed, it became a poor impoverished society. England didn't follow them.

A striking example is the United States. When the United States became independent, it got advice from the leading economist of the day, Adam Smith, on what kind of policies it should follow. And the advice was not unlike what the economists on the World Bank give to poor countries today. Adam Smith's advice to the colonies was that they should do what they are good at and pursue what was later called their "comparative advantage." So, they were good at producing agricultural products, catching fish, exporting furs, and so on, so they should do those things. And they shouldn't manufacture anything because manufactured goods were done much better in England, which was true because it was more advanced.

So, import British manufactured goods, export raw materials. And, crucially, Smith urged, don't make an attempt to monopolize some of the valuable resources that you have. The most valuable resource of that period was cotton. It was kind of like oil in the 20th century, it fueled the early industrial revolution with textiles. So that is "sound economics," then and now. Countries like, say, Egypt and India had to follow "sound economics" because Britain imposed it on them.

The United States was free of that, so it did exactly the opposite. It raised tariffs and became the leader in protectionism, practically until the Second World War, to keep out superior British goods. It developed a textile industry, then a steel industry, then everything that follows from it like railroads, cars, and so on, keeping out superior British products. And it did not concentrate on exporting primary products, but built an industrial society. And it made a major effort to monopolize its resources. Cotton again was crucial and that required slaves, so slavery was a major factor in the economy.

In fact, slavery was one of the main reasons for the revolution. By the 1770s, Britain was beginning to pass laws that outlawed slavery. One famous decision by Lord Mansfield declared slavery to be so odious that it could not be tolerated in the British Isles. They tolerated it in their colonies, but that is another story. Pretty soon they went beyond that.

This was a slave-owning society, the leaders were mostly slaveowners and they saw the writing on the wall. They knew that if the colonies stayed within English jurisdiction and under British law, pretty soon slavery might be outlawed. It was probably a major factor in the revolution. And, incidentally, we have not escaped that legacy to this day. The Civil War is still being fought in the United States. Just take a look at the red and blue states in the elections—that is the Civil War. There are a lot of consequences to this. The legacy of slavery is far from gone. There was a very conscious effort to gain a monopoly of cotton. The Jacksonian presidents, in the 1840s —Tyler, Polk, and so on—talked about the importance of gaining a monopoly on cotton to bring England to our feet. England was the powerful state at the time, the United States was restricted in its expansion so it couldn't conquer Cuba or Canada because Britain was too strong. But, if we could just monopolize cotton, we could bring them to our feet. That was a large part of the motive for the conquest of about half of Mexico—to try to monopolize cotton. It is kind of striking that what the U.S. actually did was what Saddam Hussein was accused of doing.

When Iraq invaded Kuwait, the propaganda was "he is trying to monopolize the energy of the world and bring us to his feet," which was, of course, a total fantasy. But in the case of the United States, it was not a fantasy. They didn't manage to totally monopolize cotton, but did a good bit of it.

Anyhow, to go back to the original story, the U.S., like the CEO of J.P. Morgan Chase, didn't want to have the burden of "sound economics" for ourselves. It is much too harmful. But we'll impose it on others. Then we have a theory which says that is a good thing. If you are beating someone over the head, it is nice to develop a theory which says "I'm right and just and highly moral." If a patriarchal father decides he wants to beat his children it is always for their own good. And the same is true at almost any level. We invade and destroy Iraq for the benefit of the Iraqis. In the case of the market, it is buttressed by a kind of theory. There are theories, which under certain abstract conditions would lead to improvement in the overall welfare as measured by the number of commodities. If you follow these principles, Adam Smith was right. If the American colonies had just exported primary resources and imported British goods, then by some measure everyone would be, on average, better off but we would be India and they would be Britain.

A question from a 12-year-old: Why is there so much inequality. Is it possible to create a society free of inequality?

There has always been inequality. It is not a necessity. The contemporary inequality in the United States is crafted. If you go back to the 1950s and 1960s, not that far back, it was a much more equal society. It was highly unequal, but nothing like now. These were the periods of the greatest growth in American history, probably world history, very rapid growth, but it was egalitarian. The lowest quintile gained about as much as the upper quintile, of course, proportionally, so the rich got richer, but it was relatively distributed. In the 1970s that began to change as a result of specific policies.

Actually, there is a nice study of it by the Economic Policy Institute called "Failure by Design" and it was about how the design is crucial. There were always alternatives. Policies were designed in the late 1970s, accelerated by Reagan and Thatcher, and it became the kind of neoliberal world order designed in such a way as to create a society oriented towards market principles rather than mutual aid and solidarity—so bank bailouts began under Reagan, the economy became much more financialized, and they didn't do what banks did in the past.

A bank used to be a place where you put your extra cash and they would lend it to somebody who wants to buy a car or whatever it may be. Starting in the 1970s, banks became involved in complex and risky investments. All kinds of exotic devices developed. The very rapid flow of speculative capital radically increased. There was an acceleration of shifting production to places where workers could be more easily exploited, where there weren't environmental conditions—northern Mexico, southeastern China, etc.

Those processes did start to concentrate wealth. When you concentrate wealth you concentrate political power. We may pretend to be a democracy, but we are really a plutocracy. The more wealth you have the more political power you have. But as you concentrate wealth, you concentrate political power and that political power leads to legislation which concentrates wealth further. You have a vicious cycle going on and you end up with the situation we have now, the most extreme inequality in our history. In the 1950s and 1960s, there was substantial growth, but it was distributed. In the 1980s and 1990s and the last decade there is growth, but it goes almost entirely into the pockets of a tiny fraction of the population, a fraction of 1 percent gets a huge amount. All of that escalates and you end up with the kind of inequality we have.

There is no reason really why there should be any inequalities. Actually, Adam Smith argued that under conditions of perfect liberty there would be perfect equality. It is not a great argument, but he regarded that as a desideratum, a good thing (it is one of the reasons for the economic arrangements he was discussing). Well, that is probably not right, but you could move towards some form of equality.

The question then is, What do you mean by equality? For example, suppose I need a wheelchair and you are healthy. Should we have equal access to wheelchairs? A moral person wouldn't say that. But that is inequality. And that generalizes very broadly. People have different needs, different goals. Suppose I have two kids and one of them wants to become a concert pianist devoting his entire life to it and it means everything to him, and the other doesn't care that much, he has other interests.

I might, reasonably and morally, decide to expend more resources for the concert pianist—special training, camps, schools and so on—because it just means more to his life. Well, that is a form of inequality. Is it necessarily bad? I don't think so. People have different wishes, different needs, different ways of fulfilling themselves, and they should have the opportunity to do so.

If you had a society where everyone was guaranteed a shot at pursuing their goals, so long as it is not harmful to society,, but other things that have a positive goal, wouldn't that be the society we are trying to achieve?

Yes, it should. If a society has no surplus at all, like everybody has to slave to eat, then the question doesn't arise. If the society has some surplus, some capacity to allow people to cultivate other concerns, needs, interests, sure they should all have the opportunity to do so. And these will differ very much. For example, if one person decides (I am thinking of someone) I want to live the life of a third world woman and work for a relief organization in a poor country, fine, that is an opportunity. And that is the way this person happens to fulfill herself. Somebody else won't be satisfied with life unless they are a concert pianist, maybe living in poverty, they don't really care they just want to be a concert pianist. Okay, that should be an opportunity that can be fulfilled. If somebody wants to be a research scientist, a heart doctor, a carpenter who builds really good houses, fine. There are all kinds of ways in which human beings can find satisfaction in life, exercise their creative capacities, develop themselves, and so on.

It just occurred to me that what I proposed might be considered by some folks a form of libertarianism, which has many dark aspects.

It depends what you mean. "Libertarianism" is a very strange word. In the United States it means something quite different from the tradition. In the United States, libertarian means you are free to act as you choose. Traditional libertarianism is opposed to domination, hierarchy, and authority. American libertarianism is not concerned with these at all. In fact, its policies, whether the advocates recognize it or not, are designed to create a very extreme form of authority and domination in the hands of unaccountable institutions, private capital.

Suppose I am out of work and you need people to work in your factory and you are willing to offer me ten cents a day and if I don't have that, I'll starve. Okay, we could make a free contract in which we both benefit, in which I get 10 cents a day and you get my labor, which is worth maybe $100 a day and you enrich yourself and I barely survive. That is called a "free contract." People enter into it out of their own choice, they aren't coerced. Well, that is American libertarianism and its consequences are, first of all, destructive, but it will also lead quickly to extreme forms of domination and control in unaccountable hands. American libertarianism is opposed to the state because that interferes with liberty. But traditional libertarianism is opposed to any infringement on liberty—state, private, or whatever it may be.

The tale about roads I mentioned earlier comes from an American libertarian economist. It is pathological in my view and quite opposed to the conceptions of liberty and freedom that were developed during the Enlightenment, which were opposed to domination, not to the state as such. There are certain circumstances, like our societies, where the state is the only protector against predatory private power—like laws for health and safety in the workplace. An employer who is guided by the principal of "maximize my own wealth and power" has no reason to institute safety rules. If they do, it is out of their own good will, but that is out of the market system. If the rules are going to be enforced it is going to have to be by community decision. Incidentally, all of this interrelates with market ideology.

You learn in school, or wherever you study, that markets increase opportunities and choices—you've got all these commodities out there and you can pick them. It is true to a limited extent, but as markets also restrict opportunities.

For example, I am sitting here and I have to get home tonight. The market does offer choices, a Ford or a Toyota. But suppose I want to go by subway—the market doesn't offer that choice because that is a collective activity. So, markets restrict your choices to individual actions, separate from other people, and, typically, in conflict with other people. It even harms the individual by restricting choices that are better for them that they would prefer, but it also leads to a kind of pathological social order in which people are trying to beat each other down and raise themselves.

The pathological social order leads into the next question posed by older high school students. "If capitalism is the root cause of so many of the problems in the world—climate change, exploitation of working people, growing inequality, military aggression—should schools be teaching people to overthrow capitalism and, if so, what kind of learning/teaching might that entail?"

I am sort of sympathetic to that view, but I would put it a little differently. Rather than teach children to overthrow capitalism, I think a decent educational program could point out just what the questioners say. Let's take climate change, for example, which is going to wipe us out. It is an almost predictable consequence of capitalist structures, market structures that don't take into account externalities. That should be taught and children should come to understand it and then they should be in a position to decide whether they want to overthrow the system or not. But that is a little different than teaching them to overthrow the system. That is indoctrination. And the same on other issues.

Children should be encouraged to explore, create, work out answers that make sense to them, and I think the answers, in this case, would be like the questioners. But that is for the individual inquiring person to discover.

Do you think young people need guidelines for what is a call for revolutionary transformations?

Nothing is ever done that is completely self-discovered. There are always guidelines. For example, if you decide to raise this question, "Will capitalism destroy the environment?" that is already imposing some structure on the inquiry. So, yes, there ought to be structured inquiry. First of all, the guidelines should not be rigid. If a child or adult decides to question the guidelines, that is possible too. There is always going to be some set of presuppositions, some framework, but the ideal would be to try to encourage independence of thought and education, collective education, individual education within those

guidelines, while leaving open the possibility of challenging it.

Actually, that is the way science is taught at advanced levels. You are not taught: "Do anything." You are taught basic physics, you are expected to think it through, determine for yourself whether it makes sense, maybe challenge it, and challenges are not ruled out by any means. In fact, that is how progress is made.

Victor Jara, the Chilean singer—we recently commemorated his murder by Pinochet's henchmen—in talking about music, said that in the United States there is protest music, but in Latin America there are revolutionary songs. And that gets to a question, "Do you think popular music can be a tool in revolutionary change?"

Sure. It was in Latin America. But you can't just say "Let's have revolutionary songs." You have to have revolutionary social movements. They will create revolutionary songs, art, theater, and so on. It comes from the movements themselves. What he is talking about is revolutionary movements in Latin America which created the culture of revolution. It is not mechanical, there can be influences the other way, but I think that is the dominant force.

From a high school student: Do you think comedy and humor can be useful in politicizing people?

Sure, it's done all the time. Way back in history, the court jester was the one person who was given some latitude to satirize and criticize—and it probably opened minds to an extent. It certainly does now, all the time. Questioning authority is often done effectively through ridicule, mockery, lampooning, satire, that is a very effective device, and a perfectly legitimate one.

How would criticizing, lampooning, etc., move a person from being a liberal to a radical?

Take Mark Twain, one of the great satirists. He once said, "We should thank God for the three precious gifts that he [sic] gave us: freedom of speech, freedom of conscience, and the sense not to exercise either of them." As soon as you think what that means, it inspires you to do something. That is what good satire is.

We were talking before the interview about what we call "Chomsky zingers"—sarcastic barbs. Do you consciously bring humor or satire into your public presentations?

Sometimes. For example, I gave a talk the other day in which I was asking about whether capitalism and democracy are compatible—an old question. I wanted to talk about something a little different, whether democracy and existing capitalist democracy are compatible. So, really existing capitalist democracy, for short is "RECD," which can be pronounced "wrecked." For the rest of the time I talked about it just as "wrecked." That was conscious.

From a group of high school students: Is there a method of thinking or understanding that would be useful to young people in helping make better sense of the world?

I am asked a lot of questions like that and I haven't the slightest idea. As far as I know it is just simple honest virtues, qualities we all have if we decide to exercise them. It is like Mark Twain's quip. We have the capacities, we have the qualities, we have the opportunities, and we decide to exercise them or not. You can work hard, you can have an open mind, you can have a critical intelligence, we all have it if we want to exercise it. You can question authority and demand that it legitimate itself or you can accept passively what comes along and repeat it. Those are choices. We all have the capacity to exercise them. It is up to us whether we do or not.

How important is collective work?

Enormously important. Just walk down the halls of this department or the research institution, where you see people working together. Sometimes somebody will be working alone, but the way you create your own ideas is by trying them out and interacting with others who respond, qualify, change, and challenge you to think it through. That is what a good classroom situation ought to be like. I'll give an example again. One of the best math courses I ever took as a student was a graduate course in advanced algebra. The professor was a very good mathematician. In a standard class he would come into the classroom, erase the blackboard, write something down, stare at it, then turn to the class and ask, "Do you think that's a theorem?" Then the rest of the class was our effort to discover whether it was a theorem or not. People would have ideas about how you might try to prove it, somebody else had another idea. The professor kind of guided it, so if it went off track he would suggest something else, but you really discovered what it is like to prove something. He could have written down the proof and we all would have copied it and just repeated it on the test, but this was a totally different experience. If you learn how to discover and create, that is what good teaching ought to be, from kindergarten on up.

That segues into a question about the expression "education reform." A student asks, "Our schooling is mostly about testing and preparation for tests. It is rather boring. What can we do as young people to fight back and create a more meaningful education system?"

The idea of teaching to tests is a technique for creating people to serve in the Marine Corps or the equivalent form of conformity-to-orders in general society. It is not the way to create or allow the self-creation, of creative individuals living in a functioning democratic society. If you go back to the 18th century Enlightenment, these topics were discussed in a modern form for the first time. There were alternative models created of what education should be like. There was imagery used for them that was telling. One image was thinking of teaching as pouring a liquid into

268

a vessel and then the vessel regurgitates it. That is teaching to the test. We all know that is a pretty leaky vessel and you don't learn anything. You can take a course and study and memorize and pass the test and a week later you don't remember what the course was about. The other model, which is the recommended one, is thinking of education as laying out a string along which the student pursues or follows it in his or her own way, maybe modifying the string. So, meaning some kind of structure, but then you investigate and you learn how to inquire and create. That is a big difference.

Take, say, science education where this is explored a lot now. You can teach the answers, like "here's the periodic table, memorize it" or "here's the enzymes that do so and so" or "here's the structure of DNA, memorize it and repeat it." Or, you can have people discover it in a challenging way. There is a good program right here at MIT on developing creative educational programs. The person who directs it gave a couple of examples the other day.

One of them was having a class consider the question, "How can a mosquito fly in the rain?" It turns out to be a very difficult question. The force of a raindrop on a mosquito should crush it. If we were impacted with a force like that, relative to our size, we'd be flat as a pancake. So, how does the mosquito stay up? Then comes the question, "How does the mosquito fly altogether?" which is quite a challenging question. When you try to work through that question you learn physics, biology, aerodynamics, and you have to discover them, you don't just learn them, you discover them; you have to figure them out.

There are ways of designing programs like that which have been done at the kindergarten level up to the graduate student level. That is real education. Teaching to tests, just like the questioner said, deadens the mind, turns people into passive automata. You're told what to do, you do it, and you forget it because it went into your ear and out your hand and never stayed in your brain. It is a very destructive form of education as far as the value of an individual life is concerned

—or the society. Society will be harmed by that. That is why education at a research institution like MIT is always on the second model. Not a lot of attention is paid to tests except for evaluation of what's gone wrong, has the material been mastered, and so on.

One of the reforms they are imposing across the country is the linking of student test scores to teacher evaluations.

It is a way of demeaning teachers and undermining their self-confidence, turning them into people whose activity is basically of limited value so there is no respect for them. One thing that has been discovered, and is sort of obvious when you think about it, is that when teachers are respected and their own creativity and abilities are respected, you get a much better educational outcome. You can see that yourself. If you are given a position as teacher where you are a janitor and here is what you do and you do it and that is the end, you are not going to do a creative job of teaching.

Teaching is a difficult task and children are different. You have to respond to them differently, just like raising children is a difficult task and a creative task. There is no formula you can impose on every single one. You have to invent it as you go along. But that means you have self-respect and you have community respect and you are not demeaned and you are not forced to face evaluation, which already is demeaning, but especially by a measure like this.

Take that mosquito experiment. It might be that in a short-term test, children, or high school students, in this case, who went through that particular segment of the educational system, might not do as well on an exam the next day as somebody who just memorized it because they are learning something that the teaching-to-the-test kids did not learn, how to discover, learning the joy of discovery, the fun of doing it, the importance of doing it, the ability to do it next time for the next problem. If you just study for the test you may be able to regurgitate what you heard, but you don't know how to go onto the next problem or see any reason to. In fact, you end up seeing no point to education at all.

Why humiliate a population of people who are playing a crucial role in the lives of young people? It seems a grotesque form of humiliation.

It is purposeful. It is very effective. It is part of the whole effort, whether it is explicitly conscious or just a reflection of broader attitudes (you could argue), but there is a major effort to destroy the public school system and to destroy the concept of a public institution that guarantees a decent education to every child. Rather, the cost of education should be transferred to the person who is supposed to benefit from it. It is like raising tuition in college. It is not that it is a common good that should be cultivated for everyone as a social responsibility, but rather the individual has to pay for what they get and if they can't pay for it, they shouldn't have it. It is part of the general effort to impose a kind of business model on the whole society.

Well, how do you destroy an educational system, public education? If you want to privatize something, whatever it is, the railroads, the post office, the schools ensure that it is not going to work, maybe defunding it, or humiliating the participants so they can't do a good job. And pretty soon it won't be working and parents won't like it because the children aren't learning anything, so they will be willing to send their kids to private schools, or charter schools which are kind of fake private schools. And pretty soon you have dismantled the public system.

Why dismantle the public system? I think there are deep reasons for that. It is similar to eliminating Social Security and mass transportation. All of these things are based on a principle that you care about other people. Take public education. At my age, I don't have kids in school. I don't have grandchildren in school. So, why should I pay taxes so that somebody could go to school? Okay, if you are an American libertarian, the answer should be "you shouldn't, it is an imposition on my freedom if I am taxed so the kid across the street can go to school. So, let's get rid of it and privatize it so the kid's parents have to pay and if they can't pay, too bad for the kid, and so on." It is the same with Social Security. Take some disabled widow across town who does not have food to eat. "Why do I have to pay taxes for it? I'm not responsible for it. Maybe she married the wrong guy or they lost their money somehow. Whatever it may be, it is her problem, so why me?" So, let's get rid of Social Security, let's get rid of public schools, let's get rid of mass transportation and let everyone sit in traffic jams, all in the pursuit of liberty. There won't be any imposition on my individual right to do what I want. Maybe a libertarian could say, Okay, I can decide I want to be a nice guy, I'll give to charity so the kid can go to school.

An alternative is that it is understood as a community responsibility that people have rights. That is the way humans have lived for 95 percent of their history. Market economies were imposed by force along with the inhuman ideology that lies behind them. Ultimately, when people are involved in them, they accommodate to them and they change and you become the kind of pathological individual who can read Ayn Rand and not be disgusted. But that is a sad outcome for society. And I think humiliating teachers is just one part of this.

Under what moral authority does the U.S. operate when carrying out international aggression. For example, illegal aggression and occupation against the people of Iraq that has killed, by some estimates, one million people?

The answer to that was given in an interesting way by Secretary of State Kerry in a different situation, but using the same principle. Recently, U.S. Special Forces invaded Libya, kidnapped a man, Abu Anas al-Liby, in the streets of Tripoli, the capital of Libya, took him away, put him on a Navy ship in the Mediterranean for a couple of weeks of interrogation without trial and then sent him back to the country. Kerry happened to be in Indonesia. At a press conference he was asked, "Was this legal? Is it legal to invade another country, kidnap somebody, and take them away?" And he answered, straight out, "Yes, it is legal; it is in accord with our laws." Which is correct. U.S. law, even Supreme Court rulings, give the U.S. government the right to invade some other country, kidnap somebody, and take them away.

Laws and moral principles have validity if they are generalizable, otherwise not. So, an obvious question, which was not asked by the press when they reported it, should have been, "Does Cuba have the right to invade Florida, kidnap Luis Posada Carriles, a major terrorist responsible for all kinds of terrorist acts against Cuba, kidnap him and take him off to the Caribbean, interrogate him for a couple of weeks on a ship and then send him off to a Cuban prison? Do they have the right?" Well, we know the answer to that. But we, the U.S., have the right and nobody questions it. And that is the answer to your question. We have the right because we say "we own the world."

We weren't aware that U.S. law supersedes international law.

Oh, it does. Here it does. Not by law, but by practice—in fact, even in principle. Back in 1946, the World Court was established, part of the UN system. It was mostly a U.S. initiative. The World Court, the way it functions, is it can act in a case if the countries involved accept its jurisdiction, and not if they don't. If a country does not accept the Court's jurisdiction, the Court can't do anything. When the court was established, the U.S. added a condition. It said, we accept the jurisdiction of the Court except if it involves an international treaty—we cannot be charged under any international treaty. That means the UN Charter, the foundation of modern international law, the Organization of American States, their Charter, (which bans any intervention under any circumstances into another state in the hemisphere. Of course, we don't live up to that). We cannot

be charged with those things. And that continued. Take the Genocide Convention. The U.S. finally signed it after about 40 years, but with the condition that it was inapplicable to us. And that was upheld by the courts in a case that was brought by Yugoslavia. And, in general, the U.S. is immune to law. It is pretty well known.

The main establishment journal, Foreign Affairs, the journal of the Council on Foreign Relations, has an article on the United States and international treaties and conventions and it points out what everyone ought to know, that the U.S. does not accept them. It doesn't sign them, rarely signs them. So, like the Convention on the Rights of the Child, there are only two countries that haven't signed it, Somalia, which doesn't have a government, and the United States which is immune to international law.

The article in Foreign Affairs criticizes it on pragmatic grounds. It says that because the United States has isolated itself in the world and refuses to accept international laws and conventions and treaties, the rest of the world doesn't just stop. It is going on, creating a network of laws and conventions that govern international society, but that exclude the United States. So, they say, leaders of other countries don't even wait to hear what the United States has to say because the U.S. isn't going to sign it anyway. We are excluding ourselves from international society, which will indeed sooner or later be harmful, it already is.

During this latest farce in Washington, which astonished the world, there was a Chinese commentator who said, "If the United States can't learn to behave as a responsible member of the international community, then the world will have to be de-Americanized." So, kick 'em out and we'll go on without them. That is where U.S. policy is leading.

One of the major events in the United States in the post-Second World War era, late 1940s, was that China became independent. It separated itself from the U.S.-dominated world system. Notice how that is described in the United States, universally, as "the loss of China." And it had a big impact on American society. It is the basis of McCarthyism. Who was responsible for the loss of China? The State Department was decimated by the elimination of the Asia experts because they were responsible for the loss of China. And it goes on for years and into the present. It is a big issue. The tacit assumption is "we own the world" and if somebody becomes independent, we've lost it. What is striking is that this is never questioned. It is never even noticed—like Kerry's comment. It is legal because our law says it is fine.

From high school students: do you see a difference between knowledge and wisdom? It is often said that wisdom comes with age. Have you noticed a growth in wisdom as time has passed?

I think children, even young children, can have very wise comments and insights. There is certainly a difference between knowledge and wisdom. For example, you have knowledge if you can repeat facts and they are accurate, but wisdom means understanding, perception, and ability to apply your knowledge in new situations and so on. That is very different. Theoretically it is supposed to come with age, but I think the evidence is not so clear.

Other Z Books

37.7 Seconds
Z Reader on Patriarchy

We Own The World
Z Reader on Empire

Global Weirding
Z Reader on the Environment

Fanfare for the Future: Volume 1, Occupy Theory
by Michael Albert and Mandisi Majavu

Fanfare for the Future: Volume 2, Occupy Vision
by Michael Albert and Mark Evans

Fanfare for the Future: Volume 3, Occupy Strategy
by Michael Albert, Jessica Azulay, and David Marty

Forthcoming:
The Chomskly Sessions

Z Books

18 Millfield Street Woods Hole, MA 02543;508-548-9063
www.zcommunications.org